How Am I
to Be Heard?

Gender & American Culture

Edited by Margaret Rose Gladney

How Am

The University of North Carolina Press ❧ *Chapel Hill & London*

o Be Heard?

Letters of Lillian Smith

Manufactured in the
United States of America

Portions of this material were published previously in *Southern Changes,* a publication of the Southern Regional Council, and are as follows: "A Letter from Lillian Smith to Eleanor Roosevelt" (December 1987): 32–33; "A Letter from Lillian Smith to Glenn Rainey" (January–February 1988): 11–12; "A Letter from Lillian Smith to Board of Directors of the Committee for Georgia" (March–April 1988): 11–12; "A Letter from Lillian Smith to Editor of the *Atlanta Constitution*" (May–June 1988): 16–17; "A Letter from Lillian Smith to Carson McCullers" (July–August 1988): 17–19; "A Letter from Lillian Smith to Helen Lockwood" (September–October 1988): 22–23. Reprinted with permission of the publisher.

Library of Congress
Cataloging-in-Publication Data
Smith, Lillian Eugenia, 1897–1966.
How am I to be heard? : letters of Lillian Smith / edited by Margaret Rose Gladney.
    p. cm.— (Gender & American culture)
    Includes bibliographical references and index.
    ISBN 0-8078-2095-4 (hard : alk. paper)
    1. Smith, Lillian Eugenia, 1897–1966—Correspondence. 2. Women authors, American—20th century—Correspondence. I. Gladney, Margaret Rose. II. Title. III. Series.
PS3537.M653Z48 1993
813'.52—dc20 93-20225
[B]   CIP

The publication of this book has been aided by the generous support of the University of Alabama.

97 96 95 94 93   5 4 3 2 1

To all the women who have touched my life

and especially to Marcia and Chrissy Winter,

whose love and support have made all the difference

Contents

❧ Acknowledgments

In the fifteen years since I made my first trip to Clayton, Georgia, to interview Paula Snelling and Esther Smith about Lillian Smith and Laurel Falls Camp, I have received support and encouragement from numerous friends and colleagues, all of whom have helped to make this project one of the most meaningful learning experiences of my life. I want to express my deep appreciation to all the Smith family members—especially Esther Smith, Frank Smith, and Laurie Peeler—and to my other Clayton friends—Lou Howerton, Betty Murray, Susan Rogers, and Catherine Sale—for welcoming me into their homes, housing and feeding me, and sharing invaluable personal memories of Lillian Smith.

At the University of Alabama I have enjoyed an exceptionally supportive working environment. To my colleagues in American Studies—Lynne Adrian, Reid Badger, Ralph Bogardus, Jim Salem, and Margaret Vines—I am grateful for helping me every step of the way. Likewise, I thank my colleagues in Women's Studies—Rhoda Johnson, Elizabeth Meese, Alice Parker, and Carol Pierman—for friendship and helpful critiques of the manuscript. For major assistance with transcribing Smith's letters to computer discs, I wish to thank Yesho Atil, Judith L.

Bobroff, and Janie R. Ford. For equally valuable research assistance I thank Carol Coglan, John Howard, Nancy May, Mia Miller, Richard VerWiebe, and Marcia Wade, and for emergency technical assistance, Joe Moudry.

For helpful conversations and/or appraisals of my work at critical phases of this project I wish to thank Judy Belyeu, Joan E. Biren, Kimberly Brody, Gay Burke, Marta Field, Grace Gilchrist, Bruce Hagemann, Julia Hartman, Fred Hobson, Sherry Magill, Joan Mallonee, Mary and David Mathews, Suzanne Whitlock Morse, Nell Painter, Minnie Bruce Pratt, Adrienne Rich, Marsha Stock, Allen Tullos, and Candace Waid. I remain especially grateful to Lillian Smith scholars Patricia Brewer, Roseanne Camacho, Michelle Cliff, John Egerton, Lillian Jones, Anne Loveland, Kathleen Miller, Jo Ann Robinson, and Joan Titus, whose friendly support and willingness to share their research greatly enhanced this project.

For financial support of research related to this publication, I would like to express my appreciation to the University of Alabama Presidential Venture Fund, the University of Alabama Research Grants Committee, and the National Endowment for the Humanities. Additional support for secretarial assistance was provided by the Office of the Dean of the College of Arts and Sciences at the University of Alabama.

For archival information and research I am indebted to the staffs of each archive cited in this text. However, I owe a special thanks to Carmen Russell for extra help with the Lillian Smith Papers at the University of Florida and to Larry Gulley and the staff of the Hargrett Rare Books and Manuscript Library at the University of Georgia, without whose tireless efforts this book would not have been completed. For invaluable assistance in identifying the photograph of Sarah Spencer Washington's party for Lillian Smith, I am grateful to A'Lelia Bundles of Alexandria, Virginia, and Marie E. Boyd of the Atlantic City Free Public Library.

I would like to thank Iris Tillman Hill for her early interest in publishing my work on Lillian Smith and for recommending this project to Kate Torrey at the University of North Carolina Press. I am indeed fortunate to have had Kate as my editor and especially appreciate her steadfast belief in and enthusiasm for this project. Thanks also to Stevie Champion for her thoughtful and considerate copyediting and to Sandra Eisdorfer for her cheerful guidance through the stages of manuscript preparation and production.

Finally, I wish to acknowledge three especially significant sources of influence on this work: my parents, James and Margaret Gladney, who fostered an appreciation for the art of letter writing by writing letters to their children; the late Estelle Cone, who in response to a letter I had written her in 1967 or 1968 said to me, "You must write"; and Gail Baker, who twenty years ago, as instructor in the University of New Mexico's first women in literature class, said to me, "You are from the South; you must read Lillian Smith."

🦎 Preface

The story of Lillian Smith—novelist, essayist, and outspoken liberal activist—is that of a woman working to reconstruct the world, to create not just a place for herself in the world, but a world where she could find meaning and be heard. Smith's letters reveal her efforts to remake her world and the realities of that world. She used letters to influence others' thoughts and to mold their actions. She built, sustained, and occasionally ended relationships through her letters. Furthermore, her correspondence provides a context for a deeper understanding of her published work and presents additional historical evidence both to confirm and to challenge the official reading of her time.

Lillian Smith was born into an upper-class white family in the Deep South in 1897; she died in 1966. Throughout her life she came into conflict with her culture and its assumptions about race, class, gender, and sexuality. Because issues surrounding race so dominated life in the American South from the turn of the century through the civil rights era, it was almost impossible for Smith to address questions of gender, sexuality, or class without first dealing with race. An intellectual keenly interested in the political and literary ferment that began in the South in the 1920s, Smith entered the public arena as a writer in opposition to the Agrarians with the production of a small literary magazine, *Pseudopodia* (later changed to *North Georgia Review* and finally to *South Today*), which she coedited with Paula Snelling from 1936 to 1945. With the publication of her novel, *Strange Fruit*, in February 1944, she suddenly found herself the famous and then infamous author of a "big" best-seller. Selling at the astonishing rate of 25,000 to 30,000 copies a week even before it was banned in Boston, the novel sold a million copies in hard cover and over three million during her lifetime, was translated into fifteen languages, and was made into a Broadway play.

Through *South Today*, *Strange Fruit*, and her autobiographical critique of southern culture, *Killers of the Dream* (1949), Smith established herself as the most liberal and outspoken of white southern writers on issues of social, and especially racial, injustice. Yet Smith recognized that her society's concepts of race invariably intersected with those of gender, sexuality, and class. And although she rarely addressed class apart from race, issues of gender and sexuality emerge as a persistent subtheme in both her published and unpublished work. Her writing boldly explored the interrelatedness of her culture's attitudes toward race and sexuality and the ways in which the South's economic, political, and religious institutions perpetuated a de-humanizing existence for all its people—white and black, male and female, rich and poor. Through her writing and public speaking, she anticipated and actively supported the civil rights movement of the 1950s and 1960s. Before her death in 1966 she published seven books; since then two additional volumes of her collected work have appeared: *From the Mountain* (1972), which included articles from her magazine, and *The Winner Names the Age* (1978), a collection of her speeches and essays.

For her courageous and consistent fight against racial segregation Smith received national and international acclaim during her lifetime and inter-mittent acknowledgment after her death. Scholars of social change in the twentieth-century American South will find in Smith's correspondence valuable evidence for exploring the relationships between intellectual and political and literary history. Her letters also provide significant insight into the ongoing literary debate concerning the relationship between art and politics. She refused to separate the seemingly conflicting roles of artist and activist, and her letters reveal how and at what cost she related the two.

Neither biographers, historians, nor literary critics, however, have se-riously examined the full burden of her struggle as a woman living and writing in the Deep South in the five decades between the two feminist movements of the twentieth century. Previous assessments have failed to recognize the tensions and frustrations in Smith's life as, at least in part, a product of her search for affirmation and validation from the very forces she rebelled against—the patriarchal structure that perpetuates a racist and sexist society. Smith knew that her sex made an important difference in her experience, perception, and treatment as a writer, but throughout her life she wanted to be treated as though her sex did not matter. We now recognize that that illusion of "objective" approval was itself a product of the social construction of gender. If Smith's life is to be re-created so that its richness and complexity may be fully appreciated, historians and literary critics must push the boundaries of masculinist reasoning even further than she could. It is the purpose of this collection of her letters to construct a portrait of Lillian Smith that recognizes and challenges the attitudes toward gender and sexuality that have shaped and defined her life as a woman, her choices of self-definition, and her critical reception as a writer.

It is no accident that these letters are available for publication. Possessing a strong and well-founded sense of her own importance as a writer and historical figure, Smith wanted her life and work to be remembered. She arranged for her papers to be preserved, wrote extensive autobiographical notes for herself and potential biographers, and at least for the last decade of her life kept carbons of her correspondence. The voice in these letters, however, is often a public voice, for many of her personal papers have been destroyed.

In late November 1955, while Smith was completing a month as writer-in-residence at Vassar College, two young boys burglarized her home near Clayton, Georgia. The fire resulting from their mischievous activities consumed her bedroom and study and destroyed almost all of her personal belongings, unpublished manuscripts, and thousands of letters, including family memorabilia such as some twenty years of correspondence from Lillian to her older sister Bertha.[1] As a result of the fire, very few letters exist from Smith's childhood and young adult years. Most of the letters dated prior to 1955 and published here have been retrieved from the files of her correspondents.

Fortunately, just months before the fire Smith had deposited papers and correspondence relating to her literary magazine in the University of Florida library. Because of her political activism, a small but significant number of Smith's letters have been preserved in the files of such organizations as the Julius Rosenwald Fund, the National Association for the Advancement of Colored People, the Southern Conference for Human Welfare, the Congress of Racial Equality, and the Southern Regional Council, and in the papers of other notable individuals such as Eleanor Roosevelt, Martin Luther King, Jr., and psychologist Lawrence Kubie. Other primary collections of her correspondence include the files of her editors at Harcourt Brace Jovanovich, Inc., and W. W. Norton and Company.

The majority of her extant letters, however, are dated after the 1955 fire and are available today, in carbon copies, at the University of Georgia. Understandably, the bulk and content of these letters reflect an intentional reclaiming and rewriting of her own history. The devastating loss from the fire combined with Smith's thirteen-year battle with cancer to increase her desire to set the record straight about her life, her beliefs, and the meaning and importance of her work and to influence if not control how the world would measure her contributions to it.

Though we do not know the full extent of what was lost in the fire, it seems evident that before 1955 Lillian Smith and Paula Snelling intentionally destroyed most of their correspondence with each other, at least in part because they feared disclosure of the intimate sexual nature of their relationship. The absence of those personal letters clearly contributes to, but does not excuse, biographers' and critics' tendency to ignore or minimize the role of gender and sexual orientation in their reading of Smith. To create a full portrait of Smith, one that acknowledges the importance of gender and sexuality, it is merely necessary to bring into central focus her relationship for over forty years with Paula Snelling and the place and work that brought them together—Laurel Falls Camp.

Long before the publication of *South Today* or *Strange Fruit*, Lillian Smith was known to hundreds of young white women and their families throughout the South as "Miss Lil," director of Laurel Falls Camp, a highly popular, educationally innovative summer camp for girls in the mountains of northern Georgia. It was through her work with the camp that Smith first began systematically to examine and then confront her society's concepts of race and gender. Through the camp, she also came close to creating the world she wanted to live in, a world where every child could experience esteem, where individual creativity could be encouraged by a supportive community, where old ideas were questioned and new ones explored, and where differences could be appreciated. Not surprisingly, it was a world composed almost entirely of women, and Lillian Smith was in charge.

The camp was a kind of laboratory in which Smith developed and practiced many of her ideas about human development and social change; but it was also that all-important "safe space" where she herself could experience the supportive community of other intelligent, creative women and the place where she and Paula Snelling could make a life together. Through her relationship with Snelling, Smith found the primary rein-forcement for her own creative strength. Sara Evans and Harry Boyte have suggested that without the communal free spaces of black churches and union halls, the major movements for democratic social change in our country would not have taken place.[2] Something similar must be true in the lives of individuals who live "against the grain," especially those who, like Lillian Smith, prefigure larger movements for social change.

My interest in Smith's letters grew out of an oral history project, begun in 1978, in which I interviewed over fifty women throughout the South, in-cluding Paula Snelling and various members of Smith's family, who had been campers or counselors at Laurel Falls Camp. I was interested in Smith's work as a southern woman with other southern women, and I soon realized that the camp also played a central role in her development as a writer. While working in the Smith papers at the University of Florida and the University of Georgia, I found the quality and quantity of her corre-spondence most impressive. Having published three articles on her work with the camp and her portrayal of southern women, I saw in the collected letters a form of self-portrait of the author that vividly displays the variety and interrelatedness of her interests and talents, as well as her fundamental struggle as a woman writer.

Accordingly, in 1983 I obtained permission from the executors of Lillian Smith's estate to edit for publication a collection of her letters and began the selection process from within the major collections and, eventually, from twenty-five additional collections. From approximately 1,500 letters I have chosen 145 that, separately and collectively, best reveal the quality of Smith's writing and the richness and complexity of her intellect and her life.

Wherever possible I have preserved whole letters, but I have also edited many of them to eliminate unnecessarily redundant passages. Because of Smith's frequent use of ellipses, I have used bracketed ellipses—[. . .]—to indicate my editorial deletions. All closings have been deleted. With minor exceptions, such as the italicizing of book and magazine titles (which Smith frequently ignored) and the correction of obvious typographical errors (like "offical," "unconscous," "cant" for "can't," and the placement of periods outside quotation marks), the original spelling and punctuation have been preserved. The majority of her letters were written from her home near Clayton, Georgia; full headings, containing the place as well as the date, are given only for those written elsewhere. Dates that stand alone were in the original document. Dates or portions of dates that are enclosed in square brackets were determined by internal evidence or postmarks and should be considered approximate. Abbreviated credit lines immediately following each letter indicate the original form of the letter (handwritten, typed, or printed) and its bibliographic source.

In keeping with the multifaceted nature of her life, I have organized the letters chronologically, rather than thematically or topically. Introductory comments for each chapter and, where needed, each letter provide historical context and highlight recurring or dominant themes within that period of her life. Chapter 1 presents biographical data to help readers appreciate the importance of gender and sexuality in Smith's life and work. Each of the subsequent six chapters represents a significant phase in her life as a writer.

❦ Abbreviations

Each letter in this volume is followed immediately by an abbreviated two-part credit line that indicates the nature of the document from which the published version was derived and that document's location. (See the Bibliography for additional information on private and archival sources.) The abbreviation in lower-case letters indicates the following:

als	autographed letter signed
alu	autographed letter unsigned
fdr	first draft
p	printed version of letter
tlc	typed letter carbon
tls	typed letter signed
tlu	typed letter unsigned

The abbreviation in capital letters or name indicates the following:

AU	Atlanta University
BU	Boston University
CU	Columbia University
Daniel	Frank Daniel Collection
EU	Emory University
HBJ	Harcourt Brace Jovanovich Publishers

HP	Hyde Park
HU	Harvard University
Kubie	Lawrence Kubie Papers
LC	Library of Congress
LS	Lillian Smith Collection
NAACP	Records of the National Association for the Advancement of Colored People
Rainey	Glenn Rainey Collection
RFP	Rosenwald Fund Papers
SCHW	Southern Conference Human Welfare Papers
SHSW	State Historical Society of Wisconsin
SRC	Southern Regional Council Archives
TU	Tuskegee University
UF	University of Florida
UGA	University of Georgia, Lillian Smith Collection #1283
UGA 1283A	University of Georgia, Lillian Smith Collection #1283A
UGA 2126	University of Georgia, Lillian Smith Collection #2126
UGA 2337	University of Georgia, Lillian Smith Collection #2337
UT	University of Texas
YU	Yale University

How Am I

to Be Heard?

CHAPTER  ONE

Becoming a Writer

Born December 12, 1897, in the small town of Jasper, Florida, Lillian Smith was the eighth of ten children of Annie Hester Simpson and Calvin Warren Smith. Her mother's family had owned a rice plantation on the Satilla River near St. Mary's, Georgia, whereas her father's relations were less affluent farmers from Ware County, Georgia. By the time Lillian was born, however, her father embodied the American Dream of achieving self-fulfillment and financial success through hard work and positive thinking. He operated a turpentine and naval stores business in Jasper, bought and leased additional timberland in Mississippi and Florida, and owned part interest in the Jasper Electric Light and Waterworks Company. Always a religious and civic leader, he also served his community as chair of the board of education, as chair of the board of stewards of the Methodist church, and as an itinerant lay preacher. Thus, during Lillian Smith's childhood her family had enjoyed a position of social prominence and relative financial security, which enabled the five older children (Austin, Bertha, Joe, DeWitt, and

Annie Laurie) to pursue careers in engineering, music, the ministry, and education.[1]

In 1911 the Smiths' third son, DeWitt, contracted typhoid fever and died while attending Meridian College in Mississippi. Still mourning his son's death, Lillian's father took a trip to the mountains in the North Georgia mountains in the summer of 1912. While vacationing in Clayton he bought land on Old Screamer Mountain, which he deeded to his wife. There he built a summer home and in subsequent years added several cottages to house other family members and friends.[2] When the outbreak of World War I and a temporary ban on shipping triggered a financial collapse for his business in wholesale lumber and turpentine mills, only the North Georgia property was saved. In the summer of 1915, immediately after Lillian finished high school, the Smiths moved permanently to their summer home.

Although the Smiths liked the mountains and the mountain people, the move was quite a cultural shock for the family. In sharp contrast to the prosperity of Jasper, Lillian remembered Clayton in 1915 as a muddy little mountain village with very poor schools and no paved roads, a place where on Saturdays the country people often walked into the stores barefooted. Small farms, tourists, and moonshine formed the basis of the economy. Subsequently, life for the four younger Smiths—Frank, Lillian, Esther, and Wallace—revolved around helping their aging parents struggle to make a living. For Lillian especially, the often conflicting desires to help her parents and to pursue her own personal and professional interests dominated her late teenage and young adult years.

Immediately after moving to Clayton, Lillian attended a normal school summer session to earn certification and took her first job as principal in a two-teacher mountain school in Dillard, Georgia. Understandably, at age seventeen she felt anxious and unfit as a teacher and was generally depressed and homesick for her friends in Jasper. By the summer of 1916 her father had connected the cottages adjacent to their home with a covered walk, and, using the family's kitchen and dining room, the Smiths opened Laurel Falls Hotel to summer guests. Their mother cooked; Lillian and Esther waited tables and helped clean cabins. In her autobiographical notes Smith recalled: "They were hard summers physically; they kept Esther and me from having the fun of natural girlhood. I was so tired after working that I crawled up on my cot and read myself into oblivion."[3]

The previous fall, 1915, Lillian had enrolled in Piedmont College, a small liberal arts school at Demorest, Georgia. However, despite the offer of a full scholarship to return the following year, she decided to spend the winter of 1916–17 helping her parents manage a hotel that they had leased in Daytona Beach, Florida. There she also played piano with a symphony orchestra and fell in love with a violinist, a man twice her age. It was, she later wrote, her "first and most intense love affair . . . personal, intimate, but a real turn in my growth as a girl, a woman."[4] When she learned that he was married, she ended the relationship; but she followed his advice to continue her study of music at the Peabody Conservatory in Baltimore.

After her first year in Baltimore (1917–18), Smith spent another winter in Clayton: she decided to support the war effort by signing up with the Student Nursing Corps. When the war ended before she was called to duty, she returned to teaching and took a job as principal of a two-teacher school in Tiger, Georgia. During the week she roomed in the home of one of the families whose children she taught and ate their customary diet of hoecake, turnip greens, and fat pork. Each Friday she walked the three and one-half miles across the hills to her parents' home and her mother's cooking. In the fall of 1919 she returned to Peabody, where she continued her studies for three years.

There are no letters from that period, but Smith described some of her experiences later in her autobiographical notes. She remembered that her first year back at Peabody (1919–20) was an especially hard one financially because in the interim she had lost her jobs as an accompanist, and it took time to get them back. There were days when she ate only Hershey bars and drank coffee; she had to walk twenty-four blocks from the conservatory to work because she did not have a nickel for trolley fare. That year she roomed in the home of a retired English teacher, Josephine Gees, from one of Baltimore's socially prominent families. Smith made her landlady promise not to write her mother about her financial difficulties, and she did not let Gees know that she taught music in a rough part of the city down near the waterfront. Her part-time jobs included addressing envelopes for the Democratic party and playing piano for YWCA gym classes and recreation departments of American Can Company and Bethlehem Steel Works at Sparrows Point. She also taught a Sunday school class for an Episcopal mission in the slums. As she learned about urban poverty, immigrant laborers, and factories, she also dated Johns Hopkins medical students and described herself as "bohemian, arty art, reaching out for everything avant garde and liberal."[5]

Clearly, the years in Baltimore provided many opportunities for expanding her social consciousness. Smith's description of herself as avant-garde and bohemian marks her as one of the new generation of women in the

1920s who projected in their clothing and behavior an image of sexual assertiveness, openly rejecting conventional social mores. Not surprisingly, she was the first to shock Clayton with her bobbed hair and knee-length skirts when she returned in the summers to help with the family business.

In 1920 her father and brother Frank had converted the cottages of Laurel Falls Hotel into Laurel Falls Camp, the first private camp for girls in Georgia. The elder Smith's warm, energetic personality and natural fondness for children and his son's youthful good looks made for a very successful recruitment team, and Lillian Smith forty years later described the initial camp program as something of a "Kennedy-like energetic houseparty."[6] The campers learned to ride horseback, swim, play tennis, go on overnight camping trips, and sing songs around a camp fire. For counselors Calvin Smith selected socially respected women who were usually teachers or prominent community leaders and who were able to bring with them a group of girls from their respective communities. To supplement the camp income, however, the Smiths also leased a summer hotel, the Bynum House in Clayton, and put Lillian in charge of meals and guests there. Consequently, she had very little to do with the camp initially and generally felt bored with its operation.

During the summers of 1921 and 1922, however, Smith joined the Laurel Falls Camp staff as music counselor. In her notes she wrote that she and her sister Esther did interesting work with music and drama at the camp, but issues of gender and sexuality dominated her comments about those two summers: "I began to question a lot of things: the need of so many counselors to have satellites and crushes, the over-emotionalized atmosphere created by two or three very boyish and one or two masculine counselors." Smith reflected that her four years at the Baltimore YWCA had made her knowledgeable about "such attachments" and that she herself had been "moderately involved," but she had also been aware of the dangers of older women who "were unscrupulous in playing with the kids' emotions." Her notes concluded: "All this disturbed me but I knew no way to talk about it with my father."[7] Smith's definition of emotional health reflects her strong interest in Freudian psychology, but her sensitiveness to exploitation of the younger women by older women may also have been related to her involvement with older men during her early twenties.

By the spring of 1922 Smith had decided to give up her study of music in Baltimore and accept an invitation to teach music at a Methodist girls' school in Huchow (now Wu-hsing), China. The decision marked a turning point in her life. Although from early adolescence she had felt passionately committed to a career in music, by age twenty-four she had decided that she lacked both the desire and the skill to perform in public. "Actually," she wrote, "my talent for piano was small. What my teachers in my hometown and at Peabody Conservatory mistook for talent was my creativity. Empathy, sensitiveness, imagination, a sense of form, a phenomenal memory, and the power to reveal my deepest feelings—all this they mistook for pianistic talent." Yet her decision to go to China was also influenced by her dissatisfaction with her second love affair with an older man:

[The year-and-a-half affair] had turned into something of more sex than love, of shadowy excitement not based on a sharing of real interests. I loved a man without admiring his mind or respecting his hopes and ideals, or feeling the least interest in his small ambitions. I was a romantic, sensuous young girl of 23, but I had a cool canniness in the corner of me somewhere, and I knew nothing good and lasting could grow from what we were offering each other.[8]

In describing what was missing Smith also revealed what she considered important for a lasting intimate relationship: excitement based on shared interests as well as sexual attraction; admiration and respect for her partner's intellect, hopes, and ideals. There is no evidence that she ever found those qualities in a liaison with a man; however, those are the very characteristics she mentioned when describing her relationship with Paula Snelling.

Lillian Smith's father had hired Paula Snelling to work in the athletic department of Laurel Falls Camp in 1921. A native of Pinehurst, Georgia, Snelling had helped pay her way through Wesleyan College in Macon, Georgia, by teaching swimming, and she was known for her expertise in tennis and horseback riding; but when she first heard about Laurel Falls Camp she was teaching high school math in Athens, Georgia. Although both she and Lillian Smith were on the camp staff in the summers of 1921 and 1922, they did not know each other very well until they met again on the train to Clayton in July 1925. Smith was returning from three years in China, and Snelling had just completed a year at Columbia University, where she had earned a master's degree in psychology with a minor in English literature.[9]

Smith had reluctantly returned from China to assume the directorship of Laurel Falls Camp because her parents were in ill health and she felt obligated to help them. She accepted the new role, according to her memoirs, "much as a young musician might accept conscription in his country's army," but found little of interest in the camp and much there that troubled her.[10] She was disturbed to find a rather authoritarian atmosphere with an excessive emphasis on competition in camp activities. Her autobiographical notes record her continued concern about how to control erotic relationships between some of the counselors and campers:

> I realized then, without much of a psychological vocabulary that some women are dangerous creatures; and I faced the fact that my responsibility was to protect the girls in their emotional growth from the exploitation of such women. That it was much the same as a similar seduction or exploitation made by men. In fact, I have always treated homosexual affairs just as I do heterosexual affairs. There can't be a double standard: if we don't let the male life guard cuddle up with a fourteen-year-old kid on a camping trip we don't let a grown woman do it. This came as a shocking surprise to the two or three really confirmed homosexual women in my camp. They were shocked at me and my language[,] not at themselves.[11]

Many of the older counselors resented the new director because of her youth, and Smith remembered feeling "unable to defy counselors who had been with [her] father and who were far older and more experienced in the fields of sports and camping."[12] At the end of the 1925 camp season, she decided to fire all but four of the twenty-eight staff members. Paula Snelling was one of the four whom she retained. In the summer of 1926 Snelling was put in charge of athletics and in 1928, when Smith bought the camp from her father, she named Snelling assistant director.[13]

Although Smith had given up the idea of becoming a concert pianist when she left Peabody and went to China, she had not lost all hope of a career in music. When she returned from China, she initially planned to take a position teaching music in a college near Clayton to support herself during the fall and winter while working on plans for directing the camp the following summer. However, family responsibilities again took precedent; she turned down the teaching position for the fall of 1925 when her newly widowed brother Austin, then city manager of Fort Pierce, Florida, asked her to live with him and care for his two and one-half-year-old daughter. After an older sister-in-law assumed responsibilities for the child, Lillian remained in Florida to work as her brother's private secretary and assistant purchasing agent for the city of Fort Pierce. While learning of the inner workings of city government, she also wrote Laurel Falls Camp promotional materials and recruited staff and campers for the next summer. She found expression for her musical talents as organist for the Methodist church and in work with a community organization that sponsored local concerts. Of this period she wrote in her autobiographical notes: "By this time, my life actually did not seem my own; I was just carrying out other people's directives."[14]

After two years her brother Austin remarried and Smith, free of family responsibilities in Florida, decided to enroll for a semester in Columbia University's Teachers' College. There, in the fall term of 1927, she took courses in psychology, history, and education to help her develop the camp. To use her credits from Peabody, she also took a course in public school music in which she taught students at a ghetto school in Harlem.

Smith's notes about her semester in New York refer briefly to a friendship with another woman, a Laurel Falls Camp counselor named Katherine, who also had enrolled in classes for the semester at Teachers' College. The two shared an efficiency apartment and, after the term ended, drove Katherine's jalopy back to Georgia, arriving in Clayton "with twenty cents in [their] two purses." They spent the spring in the Smiths' old summer home, Woodland Lodge, which Frank Smith and his wife Maud managed as a summer hotel. It is not clear whether their relationship was sexual, but their friendship ended after that spring. Smith's analysis of that breakup offers additional insight into her expectations for personal relationships. In notes for a biographer she wrote:

> [Katherine] had grown too tied to me, wanted too much to live my life; she had her own training and talents and I felt it was terribly unwise; and the friendship instead of solidifying into a real bond was becoming more spuriously tempestuous and riddled with vague jealousy and envy [. . .]. Well, it was sad and awful; but I saw that somehow this bond built only on common interests at camp had to be broken. It ended later and drably when I had hoped somehow it could end decently and honorably and that we could, even so, be friends of a sort.[15]

By the spring of 1928, after three years of groping and struggling with the camp, Lillian Smith at age thirty was beginning to feel more confident about her abilities as director. Furthermore, her father's health had deteriorated to the point that she and her brother Frank had to assume their parents' financial responsibilities. Consequently, she decided to buy Laurel Falls Camp from the family, reasoning that "it was better to do it all, manage the money, too, than do the work and let my father and brother handle the money."[16] Her decision to buy the camp marked a significant step for her, beyond the role of dutiful daughter and into the position of independent businesswoman. On June 1, 1928, she signed the papers. After ten days of heavy rain, on June 11 the leaky dam broke—destroying the lake used for camp swimming and canoeing and flooding the highway and neighboring farmlands. It was her first major crisis as camp owner, and her description of her response to it reveals both her deep admiration and respect for her father and her image of herself as one who, like her father, could face ordeal quietly:

> I was quiet and easy through it all; I helped that night wherever I could; I said nothing about my misfortune. I was very pleased when my father took me for a little walk (his way, when he wanted to talk) and told me I was a very brave girl and full of iron; he was proud of me, he said, he felt I could take a hard blow well; that he had never been quite sure until now; but now, he was. I was so touched, so pleased; his praise meant a very great deal to me. I was actually scared half sick, I was trembling inside my soul at the future, I didn't know how on earth I'd handle this disaster; but his praise steadied me. And indeed, he helped me handle it well.[17]

Lillian Smith's father was her first and most enduring role model. When he died of cancer in April 1930, she was left with a great sense of emotional loss as well as heavy financial responsibilities. Yet his death also gave her a certain emotional and psychic freedom; after his death she began to solidify her relationship with Paula Snelling, and she began to write.

As a child Smith had demonstrated an interest in creative writing before she decided to devote herself to the study of piano. Interestingly, her work with Laurel Falls Camp, which initially had seemed only an obstacle to her music career, proved instrumental in redirecting her creative energies to that earlier childhood ambition. Writing promotional materials, pamphlets, and the "Laurel Leaves" newsletters she sent several times a year to potential campers, parents, and counselors helped her recognize and develop her writing skills. "The kids and the camp freed me, and I seemed to write easily and well about them," she recalled in her notes.[18] Another part of what "freed" her was the fact that the camp itself was largely a female world. As owner and director, Smith was in charge of that world—as she could be nowhere else—and she drew a great deal of sustenance from it. Through her work with the young women of Laurel Falls Camp she found emotional access to her own childhood and awareness of the socialization process so crucial to an understanding of herself as a white southern female and to her strength as a writer. Furthermore, through the camp Smith developed friendships with women who would provide primary emotional, psychological, and at times financial support throughout her life.

Central to that female support network and to her development as a writer was her relationship with Paula Snelling. Both women were intellectuals, and their relationship grew beyond their work at camp because of their mutual interests in psychology and literature, in people and ideas. After Smith's father died, her mother spent several winters with her sister in Miami. On those occasions, Smith shared an apartment with Snelling, who was then teaching high school math in Macon, Georgia. Of Snelling's influence in their early years together, Smith wrote: "She was intensely interested in books and poetry. We read together, we discussed literature a great deal, and it was through those discussions that I began to turn my creativity toward writing instead of music [. . .]. [I] began writing little clumsy things in 1930. [. . .] Without her encouragement I doubt I would have had the courage to go through those first four or five years of groping."[19]

The order and choice of subjects for Smith's earliest writings seem especially significant. Her first story was set in the Ivy Hill community, the black neighborhood of Clayton that bordered her camp property; but her feelings were not then deeply involved in that place, and she did not complete it. Realizing that she had to feel deeply in order to write, Smith turned to her memories of China and to her own personal experiences and those of people she had known well. Between 1932 and 1934 she wrote a novel called at first "Walls" and then "The Waters Flow On," which she described over thirty years later in notes for her friend Margaret Long:

A love letter to China it was in a deep sense but about six lonely white women (missionaries all from the arid South, U.S.A., who thought they had something to give China simply because they were Western and white. Well, they did, in a way; but not in the way a few of them believed). All this had fascinated me in China [. . .] but had continued to haunt me. I remembered the shadowy relationships, intense, passionate, but unnamed between some of these women and some of the Chinese girls. I wrote about this, I wrote about the old China being torn in two, about the new shaky China beginning to emerge; all the story set in an inland Chinese city where only 24 white people lived with 250,000 Chinese. It was soft, warm, passionate, vivid, naked, honest, lyrical and it scared the publishers to death. No one would dare publish this book. I laid it aside knowing I might never write so personal, so terribly honest a book again.[20]

Despite Smith's disclaimer, her choice of form and content clearly prefigured her later analyses of the American South. From her first serious writing Smith refused to accept the separation of personal and political spheres. Choosing to address issues of power at the heart of Western imperialism and racism, she explored the most intimate and sometimes taboo personal relationships and the ways those same-sex and/or interracial relationships both reflected and challenged the dynamics of power in the larger social order.

The "shadowy," "intense, passionate, but unnamed" relationships between women appear in significant though peripheral roles in her published fiction. In both *Strange Fruit* (1944) and *One Hour* (1959) Smith's treatment of lesbian and gay male relationships is part of a larger attack on society's generally rigid and repressive attitudes toward sexuality. In both novels her message is clear: society's ideas about sexual normalcy can be as destructive to the human psyche as the deeds of a lynch mob.

Having written about the abuse of power, hypocrisy, and cultural blindness exhibited by white American southerners (and other Westerners) in the remote world of China, Smith turned her critical vision more directly to her own backyard. In 1934 and 1935 she wrote three novellas: one was called "Every Branch in Me"; another, "Julia"; but the title of the third is unknown. Exploring the destructive emptiness of the southern lady ideal, "Julia" became the novel Smith continued to revise throughout her life. According to Snelling, had she completed it, "Julia" would have been Smith's most profound commentary on the subject of gender.[21] References to "Julia" throughout her letters provide further evidence that the subject of gender was never far from Smith's thinking.

While experimenting with the novella form, Smith wrote a second full-length novel, "Tom Harris and Family," which she described as chronological and rambling and in general not as good as the novellas. Partly because Smith felt that the characters or incidents, however fictionalized, too closely resembled those of living people, none of these was submitted to publishers. Only the "Julia" manuscript survived the fire of 1955.

It is significant that Smith began writing after her father's death; for, as the titles and brief descriptions of her early fiction indicate, she was quite consciously exploring her relationship to her family and the dynamics of power within her family as well as within the society in which she lived. At the same time, she was reading the works of Freud, Rank, Ferenczi, and Karl Menninger; and she found in psychoanalysis a means of dealing with her conflicting feelings about herself and her relationship to her family. In her biographical notes she recalled:

[P]sychoanalysis helped me come to grips with many of my false guilt feelings, and with my Puritanic upbringing; it also helped me loosen this awesome bond to my family which made me feel I must always be the "Martha" [dutiful, responsible daughter] in every situation, although I longed to get away from family, I was easily irritated by Mother and the "family as a whole" overwhelmed me. I felt differently from most of them [. . .]. I did not agree with the old ideas, I was part idealist, part iconoclast, part rebel. I was inclined to be leftist.[22]

As she struggled to find psychic clarity and to create a space for herself, Smith also found in psychoanalysis the theoretical basis for her work, both as director of Laurel Falls Camp and as a writer. Yet, as is often the case, she was limited as well as liberated by her choice of theories; for Freudian psychoanalysis did not allow for the possibility of mature or healthy homoerotic relationships. And, although she questioned some of Freud's ideas, she never did acknowledge fully the nature and significance of her relationship with Paula Snelling.

While sharing an apartment with Snelling in Macon, Smith became an active member of the city's liberal intellectual community. By the spring of 1935 she had been elected to the rather prestigious role of president of the Macon Writers Club when, once again, family responsibilities intervened to change her life. That spring, while vacationing in Orlando, Florida, her mother suffered a severe heart attack. When she was able to move her, Smith left the apartment in Macon and returned to Screamer Mountain. There she renovated Bide A Wee, her mother's cottage near Woodland Lodge, and assumed the responsibilities of caring for her mother until she died in 1938.

Looking back on the year 1935, Smith understandably called it a "mean" year but also "a transition year when we [she and Snelling] were breaking away from the past, or from much in our lives."[23] The breaking away was further precipitated that summer when, in a freak accident with one of the camp horses, Paula Snelling was knocked unconscious and nearly dragged to death, her throat split within a hair's breadth of the jugular vein, her face covered with hoofprints, and her ribs and teeth broken.[24] While recuperating, Snelling took a year's leave from teaching and stayed on the mountain with Smith and her mother. Although Snelling healed physically within a few months, her emotional and psychic recovery proved more difficult. Smith continued to work on her novellas, but both women felt the emotional stress of the daily care of an invalid and the confinement of the small mountain cottage. What seemed the "final blow" came during the Christmas holidays, when they learned that one of their favorite campers, age nineteen, had shot and killed herself.

In the face of accumulated grief and shock, and fearing that she and Snelling were in danger of losing themselves, Smith responded in a way that would become almost habitual in her later life—by creating a new project. In January 1936 she suggested that they start a literary magazine. Their "diversion" quickly became a major focus in their lives, individually and together. Snelling remained on the mountain with Smith and never returned to her teaching position in Macon; for, as she later recalled, "Who would give up something as interesting as the magazine to teach high school geometry? [. . .] When we started the magazine, I felt now this is something I can really grow with and express myself through."[25]

Despite constant financial struggles, the next ten years during which Smith and Snelling coedited the magazine and ran the camp were probably the most enjoyable in their lives. The magazine provided each a forum for her particular skills and interests: Smith, in fiction and editorial commentary; Snelling, in book reviews and longer critical essays.

To enliven their social life and in lieu of monetary payment for contributions to the magazine, the editors established a tradition of inviting contributors to spend a few days as their guests at the camp. Their guest lists expanded through the years to include a variety of people—editors, journalists, educators, political activists—mostly southerners, whom Smith and Snelling thought would be interesting to know and whom they viewed as being involved in "changing the South." They had their first biracial dinner party with guests from Atlanta in the fall of 1936. Sometimes the gatherings consisted of students from nearby universities or colleges invited to the camp for a weekend. At other times guests came for four or five days. Always the occasions were designed to encourage stimulating conversation and the exchange of provocative ideas. Such house parties were not merely social functions; they were also, in the tradition of intellectual salons, important political activities.[26] As with Laurel Falls Camp, through the magazine Smith was able to create on her mountain, at least periodically, another aspect of the South she wanted to live in: a place where intellectuals and artists could gather to exchange ideas, to examine their society, and perhaps to find ways to influence the development and direction of its future.

About the same time she began the magazine, Smith also began writing *Strange Fruit*. As she juggled her roles as editor, camp director, and novelist, she also looked for other ways to support her writing. Rosenwald fellowships for travel and study throughout the South provided some financial support in 1940 and 1941; but until the publication of Smith's best-seller, running the camp was necessary to finance the two women's writing careers.

Even before the publication of her novel, however, the magazine's increasingly bold stands against racial segregation in 1942 and 1943 inevitably pushed Smith more and more into the public arena. Then, less than a month after it was published in the spring of 1944, the fame of being a best-selling author was heightened when *Strange Fruit* was banned in Boston. The notoriety surrounding the novel's banning and the subsequent production of the Broadway play brought additional demands on her as a public speaker and writer. Initially, Smith tried to hold onto her communal resources and maintain the camp and the magazine as though she were not a national celebrity, but the demands of success were too great.

With a circulation of 10,000 the magazine had grown too big to be handled as a "kitchen table" operation. Smith wanted Snelling to take over as full-time editor, but Snelling lacked the self-confidence to do so. "I could never have come up with the ideas for the magazine or written the bulk of what was published in it—as Lil did," she said.[27] Consequently, they discontinued the publication of *South Today* in 1946.

It was not so easy, however, to decide to close the camp. With money from the publication of *Strange Fruit* Smith paid the mortgage on the camp, renovated facilities, bought new equipment for the theater and craft shop, and proved that she could have the largest and best camp ever despite the publication of her controversial best-seller. A fire in the camp kitchen in November 1944 meant major rebuilding and necessary cuts in enrollment for the 1945 season, but Smith was able to operate a smaller camp and to experiment with a more flexible and innovative curriculum because at last her creative institution did not have to make a profit. Yet the success of the camp still depended on good public relations; and although Smith had maintained good relationships with her camp patrons despite the publicity surrounding *Strange Fruit*, she correctly anticipated a harsher reaction to her nonfiction book, *Killers of the Dream* (1949). Furthermore, the strain of two years of celebrity status and the failure of the Broadway production of

Strange Fruit took their toll on Smith's physical health. Early in 1949 she knew that she could not meet the publication deadline for *Killers* and also open the camp. At age fifty-one, Smith closed the camp to devote her full energies to writing.

Ironically, however, Smith's freedom to write came at the expense of psychic and emotional security. In abandoning the roles of magazine editor and camp director for the role of writer, Smith lost the security of an acceptable gender role for her time and place. As camp director and magazine editor, she had felt constantly torn between her desires to write her novel, produce and promote the magazine, and create a successful camp; but she also had played a socially appropriate role for an unmarried intellectual woman. Furthermore, her personal relationship with Snelling had been protected because it could be viewed as a friendly business partnership. However, with neither the camp nor the magazine officially to employ Snelling, Smith found it difficult to justify their living arrangements and to maintain their relationship as one of equals. Although Smith valued her partner's emotional and intellectual support, after closing the camp she grew increasingly frustrated that Snelling did not have her own work. In the early 1950s the two women collaborated on plans for an anthology about research relating to mental, emotional, and physical disabilities; but much of Smith's part of the project evolved into her second book of autobiographical essays, *The Journey* (1954), and the anthology was never completed. Thereafter, Snelling was primarily employed as secretary, bookkeeper, and most respected critical audience for Smith.

After Smith discovered that she had cancer and underwent a radical mastectomy in 1953, she depended even more on Snelling's assistance in tending to the details of daily life. Yet the imbalance in their kinds of work remained a source of tension between them until 1961 when, feeling the increased pressure from Smith's hospital and medical bills, Snelling took a position as librarian at nearby Tallulah Falls School. To the end, however, Smith feared that her own success as a writer had stifled Snelling's creativity. Snelling maintained that she had never felt the desire or need to communicate with the world, to try to make herself understood as Smith did.[28]

Smith's shift from part-time to full-time writer affected not only her relationship with Snelling, but also her perception of herself, specifically her awareness of herself as woman. As camp director and coeditor of *South Today*, Smith had enjoyed a certain autonomy and respect, had operated from a position of strength and influence, at least in the world of politically progressive intellectuals and social elites of the New Deal South. Furthermore, although her increasingly strong stand against racial segregation had brought threats from reactionary political elements, the magazine itself posed no threat to the predominantly male world of journalism, and its editors had experienced no personal attacks in their roles as journalists and summer camp administrators. On the contrary, they received a great deal of acclaim in both capacities. As director of a girls' camp, Smith was free to observe, reflect upon, and even try to subvert the socialization of southern females. As magazine editor, she was in a position to encourage other women writers and even to discuss the limitations of traditional gender roles in an occasional essay or editorial. Yet, though the sudden fame of *Strange Fruit* brought temporary financial freedom and greatly expanded Smith's arena of influence as a social critic, it did not bring her widespread literary acclaim. When she gave up her role as part-time journalist to write full-time, she placed herself in a more vulnerable position financially; and she found it extremely difficult to make a living as a woman writing as she did in *Killers of the Dream*: confessionally and autobiographically, from the perspective of women and children, about racial and sexual fears in American culture. Although the popularity of *Strange Fruit* had gotten Smith a six-week tour of India in 1946 as part of the British government's effort to gain American support for India's famine victims, and the prodemocracy strains of *The Journey* helped secure the U.S. State Department's support for her second visit to India in 1956, neither her style nor her subject matter was acceptable to the literary establishment, the New Critics, or the general public in Cold War America.

Consequently, the struggle to be heard and recognized as a serious writer dominates Smith's correspondence in the 1950s and 1960s. Perhaps because she received so little literary recognition, she commented a great deal in her letters about herself as writer, about her own creative process, and about the literary, historical, and financial worth of her work.

Not surprisingly, her letters from the last decade of her life also refer more frequently to the problems of being a woman and reveal a heightened awareness of gender issues. "I am sorry that I am a woman (as far as my writing career is concerned)," she wrote her editor William Jovanovich, "but it just can't be helped."[29] Sympathizing with and encouraging her journalist friend Margaret Long, she commented: "A woman works ten times harder to be heard, remember, than does a man. This is too bad; it is just part of the female predicament."[30] Recurring references to the unfinished "Julia" provide further indications of her prevailing interest in the subjects of gender and sexuality.

Through Smith's letters emerges a self-portrait of a passionate intellectual whose prominence as a writer and commentator about race overshadowed her critique of gender roles and attitudes toward sexuality in Western culture. The time and place in which Smith wrote influenced not only her choice of subject but also the theoretical framework through which she analyzed that subject. However small, there existed both audience and intellectual support for her analysis of racial segregation in the 1940s, 1950s, and 1960s. By contrast, there did not exist during Smith's lifetime a comparable theoretical framework for exploring and analyzing the social construction of gender. Unable to escape the prevailing heterosexism of her culture, Smith wrote metaphorically of blocked relationships and thwarted expressions of sexuality while her own life remained a struggle to gain acceptance and approval from the men in power. Yet, even in the heart of that struggle, she insisted: "I know my worth."[31] From the strength of such self-affirmation comes the context through which Lillian Smith may now be heard.

CHAPTER TWO

Making a Space,

1917 – 1942

Lillian Smith's correspondence began at an early age with letters to older brothers and sisters who had left home to attend college. At least one of those siblings, her oldest sister Bertha (called Bird or Birdie by family members), saved her letters from the young Lillie (Smith's childhood name). After Bertha married Eugene E. Barnett in 1910 and moved to China to work with the YMCA, correspondence between the two sisters continued. Unfortunately, Bertha had returned those childhood letters to Lillian shortly before the 1955 fire that destroyed Smith's papers and personal belongings.

Despite that loss of family correspondence, five letters to Smith's parents survived in her father's camp papers, two of which have been selected as representative. Written between 1917 and 1928, they reflect a strong sense of responsibility for her parents' emotional and physical well-being. The majority of other letters in this chapter date from 1936, when Lillian Smith and Paula Snelling began *Pseudopodia*. These letters and the others from the late 1930s and early 1940s reflect the parallel and related development of Laurel Falls Camp and the magazine. Through these two endeavors Smith came closest to creating the world in which she wanted to live and, in the process, found her public voice.

The following letter to her father, written shortly after Smith enrolled in the Peabody Conservatory in Baltimore, reflects a concern for financial matters which necessarily accompanied Smith's other feelings for her parents. Although written to reassure and cheer her father, her admonition to him may be a message to herself as well, reflecting her conflicting feelings about leaving her parents and pursuing her own career.

[Baltimore, Md.]
Undated [Fall 1917]

Dearest Dad:

Your fears weren't realized and I did get my gymnasium position. I begin regular work tomorrow and think I shall enjoy it very very much. I like my boarding place very much. It is only 2 blocks from the Y.W.C.A. and only one block from Peabody Conservatory. I pay $24.00 a month but my laundry is included in that—also all medicine and doctors' bills. One thing that I shall have to pay extra for is my piano which will cost me $3.50 per month. The house is very nice and home like—also the meals are very good and wholesome.

I went to hear Sousa's Marine Band which consists of 300 pieces. It is simply magnificent! I surely did enjoy it all. One day last week, Casper and I went over to Gettysburg to see Coleman out at the U.S. cantonment.* It was very interesting. We ate in the Officers' Mess with a room full of officers and after dinner we went all over the famous old battle ground and it was so very interesting. I am enjoying my work up here very much. I only hope I shall be able to take in the big Symphony concerts. The season ticket for the winter is $7.00 for students studying in Peabody. There are so many many opportunities for hearing really good things. The very best singers

---

*Coleman Brown and Casper Peeler had been close friends of DeWitt Smith at Meridian College and had visited the Smiths in Florida. At the time of this letter Casper was a student at the University of Maryland Medical School in Baltimore; he later married LS's older sister, Annie Laurie.[1]

and players will all be here. Yesterday, Casper and I went through the Market. It is certainly unique. You would surely enjoy it. Every thing under this old sun from dried "chitlings" to chocolate bonbons—one can find there.

I would love to see you tonight. I am afraid that you are going to get awfully lonely up there. If you do—just pack up and go to Florida. By the way, don't forget you owe yourself a pair of shoes and a suit. Please don't cheat yourself, Dad, because it is just as much a sin to cheat yourself as it is to cheat anyone else. Lots and lots of love to my dear old Dad.

als, UGA

 After four years at the Peabody Conservatory, Smith accepted a three-year teaching position beginning in the fall of 1922 as director of music at Virginia School, a Methodist boarding school for girls in Huchow, Chekiang Province, China. In Huchow she was one of ten or twelve Westerners—American and English—in a city of 250,000 located in a remote area of eastern China. There were no roads or trains; all travel was by canals. In her autobiographical notes she recalled being "fascinated by the beauty, the exotic way of life, the fabulous architecture, the walls, the curving bridges, the craftsmanship of the peasants, [. . .] despite the dreadful disease and dirt and poverty and ignorance."[2]

Politically, she was living in the aftermath of China's 1911 revolution, which led to the founding of the Republic of China. Although the 1911 revolution had been initiated by Sun Yat-sen's Nationalist or Kuomintang party, with widely supported objectives of national independence, democratic government, and social justice, Sun did not achieve power in the end. Instead, the monarchy, bureaucracy, and Confucian ethos that had unified China for two thousand years were replaced by a military regime and years of great political instability. In the rural provinces, such as Chekiang, local gentry, warlords, and their mercenary troops warred against each other.[3] Smith remembered seeing bandits everywhere on a vacation trip up the Yangtze River in the summer of 1923 and expected the boat to be stopped and taken over at any time.[4]

The following letter to her father is especially revealing. Her commentary on the effects of war on the Chinese people, specifically the lowest class of unskilled laborers, the coolies, moves from horror at the "wanton cruelty" of the soldiers to condemnation of the Christians—those with whom she worked and by implication her own family members—who seemed willing to tolerate or acquiesce to such blatant injustice. Her declaration of pacifism and determination to suffer imprisonment rather than aid in any future war, and her plea for her brothers to do likewise, mark a shift from early 1918, when she had felt compelled to "do something for the war effort."[5]

By the spring of 1925 Smith was making plans to return to the United States to relieve her father of the burden of managing Laurel Falls Camp. The "new camp" refers to additional cabins built on the ridge of Screamer Mountain across the highway from the old camp. For at least one summer there were two camps, but by 1925 all camp activities were on the ridge and the Smiths' family home had become a summer inn called Woodland Lodge. Smith's letters indicate that she was even then planning ways to change the camp curriculum. She also may have been looking for ways to stretch the boundaries that camp imposed on her, although she did not express such sentiments in letters to her father.

Virginia School, Huchow, Chekiang Province, China
Monday Night, February 23rd [1925]

Dearest Dad:

According to the latest reports, the war is over—at least for a little while in this part of the country—Last week we heard such exciting rumors—that fighting had begun at Changshing, twenty miles from here. In fact that report was also in the Shanghai papers. It was contradicted here in Huchow the next morning. We have about ninety boarding pupils here too, which adds to the intensity of the excitement! Today thousands of soldiers are passing by the south gate of the city. Twenty thousand, we hear, are outside. The city is "buying them off" to keep them out of the city for fear of looting. The city has sent out food and supplies to the soldiers. The city is full of them also. This afternoon during school I heard a rumble as of wheels and a dull tramp tramp of feet going by our wall. Looking out my window I saw many soldiers passing with quite a lot of cannons or small machine guns. I couldn't see which they were.

The most terrible part of the whole war situation has been the poor old coolies. [. . .] We hear perfectly atrocious tales of the cruelty of the soldiers to them. It sounds like some of the German atrocity stories we heard during the war in Europe. The coolies were caught on the street and taken away with only the clothes that they had on their backs. The weather has been bitterly cold since then. Sick coolies who were of no use to the soldiers, returning to Huchow have told us that they were given no covering of any kind at night. Of course they had no beds. Slept anywhere they could find a little straw to crawl into. Often times, so we hear, they were given only a piece of bread for a day's food and absolutely no "tsai." "Tsai" are the greens, fish, meat combinations which they eat on their rice. And were beaten cruelly if they protested the least bit. The soldiers often would give a coolie an exceedingly heavy load to carry. The poor old thing would take off his long garment if he were fortunate enough to possess one, and place it on top of the load in order that he might be more free to move about. The soldiers oftentimes grabbed the garment and threw it away in a canal or over into a rice field where the coolie couldn't go to get it. Sheer wanton cruelty. No reason for it at all. One poor old coolie, really an old man, was kicked down a steep hill by a soldier because of some slight act that didn't please the soldier. When they found him at the bottom of the hill—there he lay with his neck broken. Our gardener we are afraid is dead. Many of the coolies have been sent back to the city, now that the soldiers are leaving Changshing, but we haven't yet been able to find our man among them. Most of them are sick and emaciated—many wounded. They say that many of the coolies have died. All of it makes one wonder how Christians can sit by and say: "Of course war is wrong—but"[.] There is no "but" to it. Personally I'll go to prison before I'll help in any way fighting in another war. And I hope my brothers will do likewise. The people of China are a peaceful people. They hate this fighting. They suffer terribly from it—and yet they are utterly helpless. They can do nothing. The whole country is in the hands of about six or eight generals each with his army devouring whom he dares devour.

You all are getting busy with camp affairs now. Is the new catalog out? I'm anxious to see one. I don't know just what I think about the idea of putting all girls over at the new camp. The plan has its distinct advantages but I also think there are some questionable ones.

[. . .]

I do not like the plan of having the first anxious mothers so near the camp and there so much of the time. I loathe the idea of anything bordering on "hotel keeping" again—and all the worries that that means: I do think it good as a money making scheme and we need money of course. As a temporary proposition it isn't bad. As a permanent one I have my doubts.

How about the gym? How will you arrange about that? Who are the teachers for the summer? Just *what* are you all planning for me to do?

What I want to do is this: go on all overnight hiking trips. Get to know the counsellors as I would be able to under those circumstances. See how our overnight camps are situated. Study the problems of camping—the food, the sleeping quarters, the leadership of the counsellors—the part that the girls have in "making camp." Incidentally teach the girls camp songs—have songs around the camp fire at nights and get to know the girls individually. I believe the most important phase of our summer camp is the hiking and overnight camping trips. I would like to study it thoroughly and work it out better than it has been worked out. Of course I would be in camp over Sunday and at many other times. I believe I would be in camp enough to "get on" to things there. I believe camp singing is best done in the actual trips themselves. I think it is necessary to have an accompanist at camp for the dancing and for any special music that is needed there.

If you think it best that I work right in the camp all the time—of course I shall be willing to do so—but I think the work I want to do is exceedingly important.

[...]

als, UGA 1283A

Despite assuming her father's debts and the added burden of a depressed economy, Smith by the early 1930s was well on her way to remaking Laurel Falls Camp and revising her own attitudes concerning its significance and potential value in her life. The following letter to counselors reflects the development of her educational philosophy, especially her growing interest in modern psychology and mental health.

TO COUNSELORS

May 20, 1932

Dear Counselors:

The responsibility which is ours this summer frightens me.

Parents this year are sending their daughters to us instead of the cheaper camps because, they say, we are giving girls something that is of permanent value.

Do we?

They say that we do not neglect even one child—that every child is given our sympathetic care and interest.

Is that true?

They say also that our girls are very happy; that they have the leadership of fine young women; that they have the affection of our counsellors without having the emotional crushes found in some camps where counsellors are not scrupulous in their relations with young girls.

They are saying so many things that you and I *want* to be true. But are they always true?

Let's come to camp this summer determined to give each child, no matter how much of a problem or how unattractive she may be, the best that we have in us.

Let's make camp a gay, happy place of silly fun—but underneath let's never forget our responsibility for every little or big girl who is with us.

You need to know more. How many of you are reading modern psychology, child study, cases in mental hygiene? Are you depending on me for such knowledge? Do you really think that I can furnish all that is necessary in expert knowledge of children? I have read many such books, but even if I had read everything written on the subject, it would not be enough. You and I must have a common background of knowledge—a common purpose.

Camp—a good camp—has progressed far from the old idea of a summer of sports. Unless we produce behavior changes in our children, we have *done nothing*; unless we take the most scrupulous care of our children's health and safety, we are failing the trust which parents have in us.

Come to camp with ideas, with determination to make your group happy, with a resolve to make of your relationship with them something fine and splendid.

And *read*!

tlc, UGA

 Smith's public writing career began in 1936, when she and Paula Snelling decided to coedit a literary magazine. According to Snelling, they started the project "with three ideas in mind: to find the creative forces at work in the South; to tell 'the honest truth' about everything (impossible of course); to write as beautifully as we could."[6]

To finance the venture, the two women sent announcements of the forthcoming *Pseudopodia* to about thirty friends. Two dozen subscriptions provided the seed money for the first issue, which appeared in the spring of 1936.

Despite the rather timid spirit reflected in the choice of title, the magazine's "birth announcement" clearly expressed the essential boldness of the undertaking in the editors' commitment to "difference" and to individuality of viewpoint, and a very specific opposition to the Vanderbilt Agrarian school of literary criticism—a stance Smith maintained throughout her writing career.

In the first issue the editors explained their choice of title. *Pseudopodia* referred to the zoological term *pseudopod*, which they defined as "a temporary and tender projection of the nucleus or inner-self, upon the success of whose gropings the nucleus is entirely dependent for its progress and sustenance." They had chosen the name partly for fun, they said, but also because they wished to encourage those whose writings had met with rebuffs. The magazine would concern itself with the South: with whatever seemed to them "artistic, vital, and significant," not to perpetuate "that sterile fetishism of the Old South" but to "expose rather than gloss over vapidness, dishonesty, cruelty, stupidity."[7]

Initially Snelling was editor, Smith associate editor. Smith hoped that taking responsibility for the magazine would help Snelling regain some of the self-confidence she had lost as a result of her nearly fatal accident with a camp horse. Furthermore, Smith already had her own writing projects as well as the camp to direct. From the beginning, however, Smith assumed major responsibility for the magazine, and after the first year her name appeared above Snelling's on the editorial page.

Undated [1936]

This is to announce the conception of another "Little Magazine" with literary yearnings. It will be christened PSEUDO-PODIA since it will feed largely upon those tentative feelers which you put out with the dream of getting them into the big magazines and which you either never quite have the courage to submit there or which are returned with what even in your more detached moments you suspect are unmerited rejection slips.

There are no restrictions as to the material and pattern of the clothes the infant shall wear. She will however be diminutive so only small garments can be made to fit at first.

We have strong predilections towards individuality of viewpoint and distinctiveness of style. We have so often been outraged by the axiom: "Different, therefore wrong" that we are almost tempted to set up as a working postulate: "Different, therefore right." Which does not mean that we are seeking the bizarre. If we should turn down your first attempt please don't take it to heart. One reason we are starting this magazine is that we want to be at the trigger end of a rejection slip for a change.

The birth is scheduled for April 1936, to be followed by quarterly celebrations of that event. Annual subscription $1.00 (One Dollar); individual copies twenty-five cents. Incoming dollars will be labeled and hoarded carefully and returned to the sender, in case—

Unsolicited manuscripts will not be returned unless accompanied by correctly stamped and addressed envelopes. They should be typewritten and double spaced.

The writer of each manuscript accepted for publication will receive no money yet, but a variation of the classic laurel wreath—an invitation to Laurel Falls (our mountain home) for a bacchanalian feast. The intoxicating beverage will be talk of art and literature. Those who can't imbibe steadily will find tennis, swimming, mountain-climbing and sleep easily available. The invitation is for a few days in June each year, for all contributors of the preceding twelve months. There will be two small prizes of five dollars each given yearly, one for the "best" poem, one for the "best" prose item submitted.

The embryonic PSEUDO-PODIA awaits a parental "shower" of manuscripts and subscriptions. Its hope for escaping infant damnation is a combination of faith and words—from you as well as from us.

tlu, Rainey/EU

 One of the initial sponsors of the magazine was Glenn Rainey, an English professor at Georgia Tech, whom Snelling and Smith first met when he spoke at the Macon Public Library. He remained a close friend and was a frequent contributor to the magazine throughout its existence.

The following letter to Rainey reflects the significant progress as well as a few of the problems Smith experienced in her first six months as coeditor of the magazine. According to Paula Snelling, the first issue of *Pseudopodia* had been mailed to "the initial 27 subscribers plus a few others whose names they had suggested plus whatever liberal publications we knew about and found addresses for." It was a pleasant surprise, however, that favorable notices appeared almost immediately in liberal papers and magazines, each bringing a few new subscribers and warm personal letters from some of the more established editors and literary figures.[8] Despite the detailed explanation of the meaning of *Pseudopodia* in the first issue, the editors received enough critical and humorous comments about it (including at least one letter addressed to "Pseudophobia") that they were soon looking for a new title. On the other hand, the favorable responses encouraged Smith briefly to consider shifting from a quarterly to a monthly publication.

In the second issue, however, Smith reported that her plan to review manuscripts of distinction had brought praise from editors, but not a single manuscript. As the dearth of fiction submissions continued to be a problem, the most significant fiction pieces published in the magazine were excerpts from Smith's own work in progress, including portions of a novel called "Maxwell, Georgia," which evolved into *Strange Fruit*, and portions of her China novel. However, as this letter also indicates, *Pseudopodia* was modestly successful in its efforts to nourish the literary pseudopod.

Another significant example of the magazine's early success is the fall 1936 publication of a chapter of W. J. Cash's *The Mind of the South*. Smith's requested review of *The Mind of the South* for that issue did not materialize because the book's publication date was postponed. A chapter from the book became the lead article for the fall 1936 issue, five years prior to its publication by Knopf, and Cash joined the growing number of new friends Smith and Snelling made through their work with the magazine.

October 4, 1936

Dear Glenn:

We are busy now with our plans for the next two or three issues of Pseudie [. . .]. First, we hope to find a more suitable name by spring. Second, we should like to have ten issues a year changing it to a monthly (saving for the summer months) if we can increase our circulation enough to warrant the additional expense. We shall continue it as a small pamphlet of sixteen pages until we do build a real circulation.

In this next issue which will be called our Fall issue we would like a lead article on *The Mind of the South*, W. J. Cash's new book to be published soon by A. Knopf. We have asked Mr. Knopf for a copy and if he is as cordial to us as the other publishers have been we shall probably get it free. If not, Pseudie will buy it and send it to you. We should hear very soon. We are delaying the next issue in order to have this lead article in it and have been waiting for Knopf to release the book. (I see I forgot in the first sentence to tell you that we want you to write this lead article and hope you will consent to do so). W. J. Cash, as you doubtless know is a liberal, thinks the Agrarians funny and has probably written an interesting book. If you will do this we know it will be an honor to Pseudie to publish it and we hope Ga. Tech hasn't piled so much work on you that you will not want to assume more.

Bernard DeVoto wrote that he liked John Allen's* article and asked more about him. He has given Paula a little reviewing to do for the *Sat-*

*Professor of journalism at Mercer College and editorial writer for the *Columbus Enquirer-Sun*.

urday Review of Literature—so if you are interested in attracting the attention of magazine editors perhaps Pseudie will not be a bad avenue of approach.

We would like to add to our more or less permanent features a brief, succinct little essay (how about that for redundancy?) based on three or four short stories in current magazines, or articles written either by southerners or about the south. Occasionally we would like one using several articles on economics, or international affairs (for while we want to be sectional we don't want to be provincial, God helping us). We would want this in the form of a critical essay, using these articles (or stories) as a sort of point of departure. Haven't you, after reading some particularly smug or ignorant or prejudiced, or brilliant article, wanted to sit down immediately and write an answer to it? That is the kind of thing we want, an emotional reaction but based on sound observation or thought. Ordinarily 300 to 600 words will be the amount of space we would like to give to it. Having a rapid fire reaction, a good mind, a sense of humor and some good barbed wit at your command, we at once think of you as a likely writer of some of these miniature essays. Would you like to try one? We'd be very interested to see it. We hope to convince ten or fifteen magazines that it will be to their interests to send us their magazines free for this purpose. The book publishers have been very responsive, all but one of them having sent every book we have requested of them.

We need to interest writers in contributing to our magazine. Can you offer any suggestions as to how to go about this? Gradually, but slowly, we are increasing the number of those who seem genuinely interested in the magazine and I am today writing Grant Knight of Uv. of Kentucky, Edd Parks of Uv. of Ga. and one or two more suggesting to them our needs and asking them to contribute if they will. But stories . . . Glenn, we simply have not got hold of any that please us. I am sending out a letter to the English Department of twenty southern colleges and universities and a few northern ones asking for names of talented young writers, undergrads or alumni . . . but what will be the outcome of this inquiry I don't know. It is too bad that Paula and I are not more gregarious human beings with numerous acquaintances who can write. We know few. Who are there in Atlanta who can write stories?

Do you know anybody who would be interested in (and could do) a series of brief articles on the order of Julian Meade's *I Live in Virginia?* using our dear old Georgia for his material? There are possibilities there and I wish we could find some one who would like to try some. We shall be grateful for any suggestions.

[P.S.] Your suggestion, Deeper South was good. Would just The Deep South be better? A writer in Hollywood wrote offering a $5.00 cash prize for the best name submitted by our readers for our little magazine.

We've had a nice column about Pseudie in the Charlotte *Observer*.

tls, Rainey/EU.

Upon receiving a copy of the *North Georgia Review* (*NGR*), Lewis Gannett, editor of the New York *Herald Tribune*, wrote the editors: "A lot of little magazines come to my desk and most are stale before they are born. You've got me interested. Here's my dollar. —And who are you, anyway?"[9] The tone of Smith's response reflects the tensions underlying her position as a woman and a writer. How is she to define herself so that she will be taken seriously? While claiming her regional identity, she pokes fun at the solidity of her southernness. She laughs at the juggling act she performs as camp director, magazine editor, and novelist and seems almost coy as she tries to sound neither too serious nor too eager to meet this powerful and influential man of the literary establishment. Hers is an old and potentially dangerous strategy: She must seem not to take herself seriously precisely so that he will. The opening line echoes a phrase used in a promotional letter to readers (perhaps enclosed in the copy of the magazine sent to Gannett), describing the magazine as "a two-year-old colt which though as yet lacking in size and looks, has high-stepping legs and ears cocked towards the race track."[10]

January 26, 1938

Dear Mr. Gannett:

It is nice of you to be interested in our high-stepping legs and cocked ears. And much easier to thank you for that generous dollar than to tell you who we are. But I shall try.

Georgians, both of us. Miss Snelling has spent only one year of her life out of Georgia and that was in New York where we provincials sooner or later go. My record isn't so good. I spent four in Baltimore in school, three in China.

For a living I direct Laurel Falls Camp for girls and Miss Snelling helps me. For amusement we have the little paper. I am running around with my tongue out most of the time hunting up another little camper to pay for another issue of the little magazine. And all the time when my tongue isn't out, I'm holding my breath for fear these southern parents will find out about the magazine and take their children out of my camp. So life even high up on this old mountain is not without its complexities.

Also I write novels. Wrote one about China that must surely hold the world's record on being nearly accepted by no less than ten or more publishers—if telegrams and long letters from publishers are symptomatic of hands edging close to the dotted line. It was not accepted. But since China is once more the heart of the news I am sending it out again. Maybe, just maybe this time, somebody will make a slip and sign. Am now writing a novel about Maxwell Georgia which concerns a love affair between a white boy and Negro girl, a revival, a lynching, and one or two other sweet motifs like that. But you who must spend so much of your time assisting at the borning of little novels surely do not want to hear about literary embryos and still-births.

We leave next week for a month in New York. Perhaps somehow, somewhere, we shall run into you. It will be pleasant if it happens.

tls, HU

In her autobiographical notes Smith wrote extensively about her ambivalent relationship with her mother. The following letter to Glenn Rainey written shortly after her mother's death confirms Smith's later recollections of anguish and disappointment at her own inability to have the relationship she wanted with her mother.

October 10, 1938

Dear Glenn:

Your friendship has meant much to me for a long time and your recent expressions have been singularly comforting to me because of the depth of your understanding—which seems always to fill in most reassuringly those hiatuses always there gaping at us human beings behind our words. [. . .]

I am left stunned by Mother's death. Not so much her absence which has in it a large element of relief both psychic and physical, but by the manner of her going and by her pitiable helplessness in the face of that final disintegration. I am oppressed by the hideous thought that our lack of faith in her simple theology shook her own at the last—that she did not have the comfort of those around her who could share with her her own trust and buttress her assurance in that future world which all her life she talked so wistfully of entering. It was the childhood world of her father, or so it seemed to me, that she wanted again, but she thought it was heaven and it was a heaven which became illusive and unreal to her placed against our silence. Although during her final swift and painful week in bed she said nothing, sometimes her eyes seemed to say heartbreaking things, and this I don't think I can ever forget. My relationship with my mother was never a comforting one for either of us and this too seems harder to bear just now than ever before. For although there was no congeniality of thought, no sharing of any deeply felt experience, it was a relationship of strange intimacy, of numberless efforts on my part to bridge the gap, only to fail, of millions of little acts which bound together two essentially alien human beings in a bond that is finally broken only with pain and difficulty.

My spirit is humbled as I face the failure of that relationship. It seems to me that I am intelligent enough and understanding enough and kind enough to have been able to work things out so that she and I could have had more pleasure together. But I failed completely and am cursed with that habit of mind that won't let me gloss it over or forget it.

Well—I'm getting to work. The family have all gone. Es left yesterday, looking so bewildered and drooped and lost (for she and Mother meant so much to each other and gave each other a great deal of happiness). Paula is back again, thank God. I did not ask her to come, knowing that her own Mother needed her. But her Mother's shoulder is healing nicely [. . .] and Paula came in unannounced the night before Mother died. She is a blessed person. So certain to understand and so helpful and so ready with me to seize on those moments when one can laugh and treat lightly what conventionally is never treated lightly—only thus making it possible to bear those pains which conventionally one is not supposed to have.

[. . .]

The trip is still being talked about. I have made inquiries as to sailing dates to see if I could possibly work in now as long a trip as three months before camp work begins to exert its pressure. We both want to get away. I think the novel would go better if I could tear out a few recent pages of memories and begin on a fresh sheet. And I think the ocean and new faces and new sounds would do this for me. Sometimes at night I still hear Mother calling me for something and I find Bide a Wee, as little as it is, very big with old haunting Smith memories.

[. . .]

Thomas Wolfe's death was to me almost in the nature of a personal loss. I had a special tenderness for that great little-boy violent and sensitive nature of his.

We'll send the magazine. The fall issue must come out—just now that "must" seems impossible to both of us but we are going to work today on it regardless of our reluctance and our mental emptiness.

tls, Rainey/EU

 In the winter of 1938–39 Smith and Snelling took a British freighter to Brazil. After spending a month in Belem, they traveled by Brazilian freighter down the coast as far as Rio before returning by Norwegian freighter to the United States. While in Belem Smith worked some on *Strange Fruit*, but primarily she mourned her mother's death and "pondered" her relationship to her family.[11] Undoubtedly, she and Snelling also spent some time considering future plans for their magazine; for, although the death of her mother left Smith physically freer than she had been since her return from China, she was still struggling to pay the camp mortgage while supporting herself, Snelling, and the magazine solely from the camp's meager profits. In Belem, therefore, they also decided to apply to the Rosenwald Fund for a fellowship for travel and study of the South.

Founded in 1928, the Julius Rosenwald Fund had focused primarily on developing black education until 1937, when a fellowship program open to southern whites as well as to blacks was established to broaden the fund's efforts to improve race relations. With the established record and clearly related interests and focus of the *North Georgia Review*, Smith and Snelling received joint Rosenwald fellowships in 1939 and again in 1940, a great boon to the magazine's development and to Smith's writing career. Their following Statement of Plan of Work from the application files of the Julius Rosenwald Fund papers was probably written in December 1938.

STATEMENT OF PLAN OF WORK

We, as co-editors of *The North Georgia Review*, are making joint application for a Rosenwald Fellowship. The funds, if obtained, will be used to further prepare ourselves as editors of this quarterly of literary and critical opinion. In part, the Fellowship will be used for specific study and research in southern literature and sociology; in part for further general study of world literature, social science, history, philosophy, art, ethnology, psychiatry, that we may have more complete bases of comparison and increased orientation for our specific field. Some of this study would be done in the New York libraries, some at the University of North Carolina. We are making joint application for one 1500.00 fellowship because each of us has obligations which will make it possible to devote only six months exclusively to the project, and as our researches are for a common purpose and take us to different cities we will divide the funds as the need rises rather than ask for separate fellowships of 750.00 each. Additional expenses incurred, we will be able to cover from private funds.

We are making application for the Fellowship on the merits of the potentialities of the little magazine. It is quite obviously and admittedly small, infrequent in appearance, and not widely known. But during the three years of its unaided existence it has won respectful reading and critical acclaim far beyond that which little magazines customarily receive. Copies of the *Review*, together with some of the comments which have been made about it, are being submitted to you under separate cover. It is our hope that the magazine will grow in content, circulation, influence as the editors grow in comprehension of the South's inherent problems and of their relationship to world movements. We plan to make the magazine a monthly as soon as it is practical to do so. We, and many of our readers, feel that one of the virtues of the *Review* is its sympathetic, respectful but critical appraisal of books by Negroes and of subjects involving racial relationships. Part of our study will be directed toward increasing our knowledge of this field.

The editors of the *Review* also have in mind, and are at work on a book of criticism of southern literature, which should be ready for publication within two or three years['] time. Much of the study done in connection with the magazine will also serve as preparation for the book.

Miss Smith is now near the end of the first draft of a novel, which Simon and Schuster expects to publish, dealing with two southern families, one white one black.

In short, the applicants for the Fellowship have definitely under way three major projects sufficiently allied that study and research made in connection with one serve as aid in the others. While the application is specifically made to further prepare the editors of the *North Georgia Review* for their task, it may be of interest to the Committee to know that other plans are under way which also should contribute toward the South's incipient willingness to move out from under the shade of dead magnolias.

tlu, RFP

Edwin R. Embree, president of the Julius Rosenwald Fund, wrote Smith on June 21, 1939, asking if she would be interested in writing "a novel on farm life in the South, especially on the struggle of the tenant farmer" [RFP]. The following response provides evidence of early concepts of *Strange Fruit*, including a clear description of her commitment to psychological and especially psychoanalytical theory as a lens through which to view and critique social, cultural, and economic issues.

July 7, 1939

Dear Mr. Embree:

This long delay in replying to your letter must be blamed on my role of camp director. With these little girls and their emotional problems clamoring at you, it is difficult (at least for me) to shift from the role of 'mama' to editor.

Your suggestion about the novel of course interests me. I am at the present time working on a group of four novels concerned with a town called Maxwell, Georgia. While focussing on the psychological aspects of my characters—rather than on their sociological milieu—I find it impossible to tear a character out of his environment. And so there is much concerning the agrarian and marketing problems of the inhabitants of this small town. But my stress is on the complexities of their relationships with their families and each other, on their religious dilemmas, on their racial relationships, etc.etc. The book I am now working directly on is concerned with a white family and a Negro family and their somewhat complex and subtle relationships with each other. I am using college bred Negroes in this story because I find myself none too interested in carrying on the old tradition of quaint Negroes. I also find myself intensely interested [in] the family relationships of Negroes and am emphasizing their emotional tie-ups with each other in this book.

I agree with you that a first class novel could do much to dramatize the problems of the southern farmer, and the interrelationships of southern business men, farmers, bankers, tenants, with each other. I hope my own books will play some small role in this direction. I suspect however that with my books this may be a secondary effort, as I tend always to think first of interpreting characters in terms of their many and complex relationships with their family, as these affect and are affected by their economic problems, their religious beliefs, their sexual and racial ideas.

[. . .]

In the first week of September, the exact dates not yet decided upon, we are having a group of southerners up with us at our camp for a few days. Mr. [Howard] Odum hopes to come, Mr. Rupert Vance is coming, W. T. Couch, Clarence Nixon, Lucy Randolph Mason, Arthur Raper, and a number of others. Of course it would make us very happy if you could join this group and spend a few days with us in good talk and relaxation. Our camp happens to be peculiarly fitted as a place for such a meeting and Miss

Snelling and I shall try, if you come, to give you some rest as well as an opportunity for an exchange of ideas with these men and women, many of whom must be good friends of yours.*

[. . .]

tls, RFP

Almost twenty-five years later, in notes for her biographers, Smith described in detail that memorable house party:

It was in late August, 1939; they were here that Sunday afternoon when Great Britain declared war against Germany. We sat in the library, most of us on the floor listening to the radio, staring at each other. We had just had a tough pacifist-war argument; some thinking we must get in, others saying we must stay out, war never solves anything etc. etc. Suddenly, over radio— someone with ESP must have turned it on—a voice told us THE WAR was on. And we knew, everyone of us sitting there that sooner or later we'd (USA) get in it. We were all very sad. We passed drinks around but even drinks were only sipped at, now and then. We were all depressed, and scared, too; we had so hoped Hitler would somehow give in, I guess; and even then we did not know the dread lengths he had gone to in Germany, Poland, Austria in persecuting the Jews. We did not know about concentration camps at that time—although we were beginning to hear rumors.

Now back to the gay part of the party. They (the men and the one wife) began coming in Friday shortly after noon. Camp had just closed (a few days earlier). It had been a big drum year at camp; that is, the kids had made about 40 drums and we had been drumming all kinds of primitive rhythms all summer long. Also, it was the year we had created our first ballet (growing plays) called Behind the Drums. About race. The only play that was about race but our first one was; it was definitely on our minds those days. And the drums had been used a great deal in the ballet. [. . .] So, Friday afternoon (or maybe Saturday afternoon, after some had been here overnight and had got the spirit of the place) we were high up on the ridge at its little peak (not the Mountain) beating the drums. Everybody was drumming. The men, some of them stodgy old professors

*In addition to those named in the letter, the invitation list included Clark Foreman, Mark Ethridge, John Temple Graves, Tarleton Collier, George Reynolds, R. B. Eleazer, Walter Paschal, W. W. Alexander, W. C. Henson, R. L. Foreman, Frank Graham, J. S. Pope, and Glenn Rainey.

at home, were sitting on the ground or kneeling drumming away with a glass of bourbon or scotch nearby. I remember one visitor (Trot Foreman, a business man from Atlanta) walking up those winding steps with his big suitcase in his hand. I waved him on, he came up to the top of the steps where we were, laid his suitcase down, shook hands with me, I offered him a glass of scotch and a drum, he took both, nodded at the others—without knowing who most of them were—and began to drum for all he was worth. It was fantastic—and fantastic fun. Somebody'd begin to make up a primitive song, or what we thought was one and sing it while the others drummed away. As it grew dark, I reverted once more to hostess, showed the new guests their cabins (they were scattered all through the camp) and told them when supper would be served.

Most of them I had never seen before; although all of them we had been corresponding with via *North Georgia Review* etc. Everyone we had selected turned out to be both a gentleman and a lot of fun and interesting. It was a lovely party: the talk was often brilliant, often controversial and hot, often amusing; everybody had this in common: a deep concern for a new and different South. Otherwise, we had socialists, one fellow traveler (if not communist—I think he was always fellow traveler) good old democrats, New dealers, professors who did not think politically but did think socially, a few people who thought in literary terms, only. We had wonderful food. Nobody drank too much; nobody got obscene or nasty in his talk, nobody was sexy: you see, their brains were electrified by all that was being said; everything we did was interesting; you didn't need sex—although all the men I remember had plenty of potency. . . . People were witty and civilized, honest and agonized,—and entertaining. They were put by me in the children's cabins—and I think the cabin cots, and open windows and rough, crude buildings got them in a out-of-door woodsy mood. Anyway, there was simplicity with sophistication, hilarity with good manners, and it was fun.[12]

TO GEORGE REYNOLDS, DIRECTOR OF FELLOWSHIPS,
JULIUS ROSENWALD FUND

February 14, 1940

My dear Mr. Reynolds:

Miss Snelling and I wish to make formal application for a renewal of the joint fellowship which we received in 1939 covering a period of six months. We are asking for the renewal for a similar period of time. As you perhaps remember, with the duties and obligations of our camp work and the magazine we are not able to put more than six months of concentrated effort on our special study and writing out of each year.

You perhaps remember that I hoped to give up my camp work in order to devote my full time to the work in which I find myself especially interested, but when the time came for me to make a decision, I simply could not do it. If I give up the camp then there is no possible way (that I can see now) of financing the magazine. And too, I am still carrying heavy family responsibilities which require far more money than I could make now in freelance writing or even with the aid of a Rosenwald fellowship.

You raised the question once or twice, half jokingly it is true, as to whether we really "needed" a fellowship. Without it, Miss Snelling would have to take up again her teaching of mathematics. She has no income except what I pay her as assistant director of the camp for the two months of the summer. The profit from my camp (and it is small) is going these years almost in its entirety to the paying off of the old mortgage on the camp bequeathed to me by a visionary father, to paying the deficit incurred by the magazine, and to my support for six months of the year. Without the fellowship I should simply have to find a part-time job and quit writing—which after all might not seriously affect the future welfare of the South.

We again make joint application because our collaboration in both writing and research is so extensive that it would be almost impossible to break our projects up into individual projects.

We don't know that we have made such brilliant accomplishments—I still hope you will be proud of me as one of the Rosenwald fellows when my book is published, but you may instead hang your head in shame—but we are sending in a report of our activities anyway and trust you will think we've at least made a decent record.

TRAVEL through portions of the South (South Carolina, North Carolina, Mississippi, Alabama) familiarizing ourselves with the states and sub-regions which we know least about.

1. Attended meetings: Southern Tenant Farmers Union in Blytheville, Ark.; 3 locals of mine and steel workers unions in the Birmingham vicinity; revival services in Mississippi; panel discussions, lectures at Chapel Hill, auditors at some of Dr. Odum's seminar groups; interracial conferences; meetings of Georgia Academy of Social Science;

meetings of the Ga. Division of the Southern Conference for Human Welfare.

2. Visited institutions: Mental hospitals in Arkansas, Mississippi, South Carolina; Juvenile courts in Atlanta; federal prison in Atlanta; spent one month at Chapel Hill; 2 days at Tuskegee Institute; one day and night at Talladega College; one day and night at University of Miss.; one day and night at Paine College; a few hours at St. Helena Island. Visited a few Negro and white public schools.

3. Visited various government (and other) projects and experiments: TVA; FSA cooperatives and resettlement projects in Arkansas, Alabama; Delta Cooperative Farm.

4. Talked in each community to as wide a variety of Negro and white people as possible: outstanding liberals, educators, artists, tourists camp operators, bell boys, psychiatrists, social workers, book dealers, ministers, lawyers, secretary of Negro Youth Congress—and drank an occasional egg nog with a remnant of old southern aristocracy, enjoying both.

5. Visited a number of craft centers, and experimental schools.

WRITING . . . . .

Jordan Is So Chilly, a novel, by Lillian Smith. It is now completed save for parts of five chapters. Simon and Schuster still interested in it. Novel deals with a Negro and a white family (both middle class) in a small south Georgia town. It is primarily a novel of character and personal relationships set in family context and in larger context of southern agriculture community.

Drums, a play, by Lillian Smith. A kind of rhythm-montage in song, speech and dance, showing the Negro's 300 years in America. Presented first by a group of 90 white children and adults as a creative project in racial and human understanding, at Laurel Falls Camp. Now being rehearsed for presentation by the drama department of Atlanta University. Partial recordings have been made of the play, and have been received enthusiastically by various groups, including the Ga. Div. of the Southern Conference for Human Welfare. The Negroes who have heard it have been usually deeply moved by it—Mr. Reid and Dr. Clement of Atlanta University said some very kind things about it. Before it can become of professional value as a play, the music for it must be worked out and orchestrated by some capable composer. It still in the opinion of its author has many amateurish qualities about it.

Sigmund Freud: A Critical Estimate, by Paula Snelling. Miss Snelling has been working on this study for some time, and before she received the fellowship award, for it has entailed much and wide reading and study. It is an attempt to present Freud's hypotheses, experiments, conclusions in a brief, comprehensible, readable but not too dilute form, for the intelligently interested layman; and to appraise Freud's contributions to civilizations. The essay will appear in two installments in the forthcoming issues of the *Review*. *Miscellaneous Writing*. The essays, articles, reviews, sketches, we have done during the year have appeared in *The North Georgia Review*. We feel that as long as we continue with the magazine we want our best writing to be in it. [. . .]

PLANS FOR CONTINUATION OF WORK, [. . .].

In our application last year we mentioned briefly a projected book on southern literature. It was our purpose at that time to appraise critically the past century of literature in the South. But as we have proceeded further with this study we have become convinced that we should shift focus and content to include a wider, fuller portrait of the South, letting its literature find its rightful place among the other varied and significant aspects for this book, now tentatively titled *Southbound*, we need much more reading and study.

A brief statement of the book's purpose and contents follows:*

THE KIND OF BOOK: There are few spots on the globe as interesting as the South; and perhaps none so rich in startlingly poignant paradoxes . . . Jefferson and Jim Crow . . . madonna and mulatto . . . church-steeple and noose . . . The last decade and a half has seen the first wide-spread attempts, even by historians and sociologists, to disentangle myth from actuality. No one has yet probed deeply enough into the mechanisms by which one has fed upon and been fed by the other. Most of the studies made have been channeled narrowly by specialists for special readers. The time has come, we think, when a synthesis should be attempted, written to appeal to the growing group, in the South and outside its boundaries, who would like to see the region in perspective. [. . .] It will not neglect those surface causes and effects which have been deciphered and stated by students from various fields; but it will also seek the source, direction, and power of those undertows which, for better or worse, determine a people's fate. Throughout the

---

*The proposed book on southern literature and culture was never completed; however, as outlined here it clearly contains the seeds of major themes Smith later developed in *Killers of the Dream*.

book, the Negro will be treated (as will the white man) as much without bias as the authors are capable. The Negro's viewpoint, hardships, contributions, accommodation-traits (so shockingly neglected by historians and literary men alike) will receive as much study and analysis as will be given to the white.

THE BOOK'S APPROACH:

The book's approach to the southern scene will be through its literature. For, we believe, literature not only mirrors (with clearness, or distortion) a region's surface life but serves as symbol and symptom of the dilemmas and ambivalence of its culture and of its human relationships; hence often holds within its content the means and mechanisms for understanding and interpreting those very elements of which it seems a mere reflection.

But contemporary southern literature itself cannot be understood and appraised out of its societal-racial-psychological context. Nor can it be used adequately as a tool for further understanding of the environment out of which it grew, without tracing back to their roots the dilemmas and triumphs of which it is an inherent part. Hence the necessity for a continuous process of relating, contrasting, interpreting its rationalizations and its dreams against the background of its environment.

So while we shall begin with southern literature, and return to it again and again and again throughout the study, while our focus will be turned on it more frequently than upon the environment out of which it springs, yet we must describe and explain that environment, and we hope to do this by drawing upon the vast amount of material which the social scientists have during the past few years with such scrupulous care and skill collected for the use of whoever needs it. We consider some of the writings of this group to belong to the body of southern literature itself; some of it seems rather a fund of facts from which one may draw one's own generalizations. With this new knowledge at their disposal (and implemented by the sharpened perceptions which psychoanalysis can give) critics should find a survey and analysis of literature in the southern scene richly rewarding. [. . .]

Part I. will deal with the present day South. Will picture (we trust in an emotionally fused, imaginative, vivid style) the various sub-regions, the many minor cultures, will show the region bound together by its peculiar economics and social problems, by its need for and acceptance of the Southern Myth. Will show the region's conflicts, ambivalence, its religious, race, sex attitudes, and its literature as an outgrowth of these factors and also a determining force in these very factors.

Part 2 will go back 100 years or more, gather up the economic, cultural, political, psychological strands that tie the South into its present hard knot; will study the genesis and growth of certain ideas which have created and perpetuated the southern myth and the resultant muddling of southern minds. Part 3 will appraise the ways out that are being tried here and there in the contemporary South (by literary men, social scientists and philosophers, politicians) with suggestions as to other levels at which the problem may be simultaneously attacked.

[. . .]

TOPICAL OUTLINE OF SUBJECTS TO BE STUDIED DURING PERIOD OF FELLOWSHIP RENEWAL. (The book itself will not be split into these sub-divisions. These are merely for purposes of systematic study.)

(1) *For general background* [. . .]: more reading along the lines of psychoanalysis, anthropology, the myth, history (especially a study of feudalism in England, and British feudalism as now to be seen in its colonies; and a study of certain eras in Chinese history from which there may come some illuminating analogies).

(2) *For specialized background regarding the South*: Agriculture as an exploitative industry (cotton, rice, sugar cane, tobacco, lumber). The credit octopus with its tentacles embedded in planter, merchant, sharecropper, and banker. Influence of the frontier, with its philosophy of waste, on natural resources of land and people; its peculiar effect on southern humor and wit, its encouragement of 'laziness' and violence, its over-evaluation of the 'low brow' and ignorance.

Rise of the Southern Myth. Formulation of ideas and rationalizations about the Negro, slavery, aristocracy, 'culture,' po' whites[,] concealment of the middle class of both races.

Guilt and God. Growth of evangelism—its role both a cause and effect of southern attitudes rising out of the economic and cultural set-up. Correlative growth of violence. States Rights, as philosophy and fetish. Its political and psychological effects.

The 'damyankee' in the South: as abolitionist, as protagonist of a competing economic system, as missionary-to-Negro, as reformer, as carpetbagger, as exploiter of southern resources, as holder of the money bag, and as the currently exploited tourist.

The factory in the South. Southern exploitation of southern resources.

Appalachia. The mountaineer and other isolated groups who have remained outside the main southern current yet have had marked influence on the southern mind and manner.

Ambivalence of sex mores . . . southern chivalry . . . white man's and black man's relation with Negro women and with white women. Growth of the sex myth.

The abortive agricultural revolt. Populism and its leaders. Demagogues in the South.

The Negro family and the white family. The role of the Negro mother in both Negro and white homes.

"Keeping the Negro in his place"—Jim Crow—poll tax—primaries—segregated schools. The segregated college. The Negro college graduate's adjustment to the South.

The Civil War and the war neurosis. Study of the shell-shocked southern gentleman—the rise of the vigorous female of Reconstruction and later days. Prototypes (to some extent surely) of the white ne'er-do-well of the "good families" of southern towns and his often militantly efficient sister. Influence of white church colleges on the attitudes of southerners.

The Negro (and white) in Reconstruction. Study of the origin of many defense mechanisms with which we now grapple.

Southern personality types—white and black. Stereotypes in real life as well as in fiction.

[. . .]

tls, RFP

 As editor of the magazine and a Rosenwald Fellow, Smith found increased opportunities for public action and political involvement. The following letter to Glenn Rainey indicates her response as a delegate to the second meeting of the Southern Conference for Human Welfare (SCHW), held in Chattanooga in April 1940.

Organized in 1938 as a coalition of southern liberals representing farmers, labor, politicians, educators, youth, journalists, and other professionals, the SCHW advocated wide-ranging reforms from improved labor conditions and expansion of Farm Security Administration programs to uniform federal and state voter registration procedures and federal aid to education. Today it is remembered primarily for its work to abolish the poll tax. Smith served as a member of its executive committee from 1942 to 1945. Her remarks to Rainey give some indication of why Smith has been described as the conference's "most important gadfly."[13] She consistently pushed for the organization to be more inclusive in its membership and more democratic in its practices.

Thursday
Undated [May 1940]

Dear Glenn:

[. . .]

I was very disappointed in that Chattanooga Conference. I shall not go into the reasons for my opinion just now but as I am commenting on it at some length in Dope With Lime* in Spring issue I want to check my impressions with those of other people. I am rather certain that Miss Mason and Miss Wilkins† considered it a good conference. From the point of view of 40 people it must have seemed a good conference. From the point of view of more than 700 others I rather doubt it—its failure, as I see it, being that there was no opportunity for the mass of those attending to participate in the conference. 700 of us meekly sat though 46 speeches, listening with what amounted to an absurd conscientiousness to every one of them, but the work, the discussions, the "real business" of the conference was attended to outside by these 40 who really managed everything. Dr. Graham mentioned to me last week over at Chapel Hill that he thought the Conference was splendid "everything went off without a ripple, didn't it Miss Smith?" "Yes," I agreed with him that it went off without a ripple. But is that quality of smoothness the criterion by which we are to judge the results of a conference on southern problems? It was far more like a Chautauqua than a conference.

[. . .]

tls, Rainey/EU

 Walter White, executive secretary of the National Association for the Advancement of Colored People (NAACP) and an early supporter of the magazine, wrote Smith on May 17, 1940, asking for details of an unpublicized

---

*LS's column in the *North Georgia Review*. "Dope With Lime" referred to the practice of drinking Coca-Cola with lime to cut the sweetness. Her column often contained a sprinkling of acid in a running commentary on southern life and letters.
†Lucy Randolph Mason, public relations director for the CIO (Congress of Industrial Organizations) in Atlanta, and Josephine Wilkins of the Georgia League of Women Voters.[14]

lynching referred to in a press story that quoted the *North Georgia Review* (LC). Evidently, the press story had cited the *NGR*'s reference to an unpublished lynching to dispute another news release issued by Jessie Daniel Ames and the Association of Southern Women for the Prevention of Lynching (ASWPL). As director of women's work for the Commission on Interracial Cooperation (forerunner of the Southern Regional Council), Ames organized the ASWPL in 1930. According to Jacquelyn Dowd Hall's excellent study of Ames and the ASWPL, *Revolt Against Chivalry*, "In May 1940 Ames released to the press a statement that, for the first time in her career, the South could boast of a 'lynchless year.'"[15]

TO WALTER WHITE

May 31, 1940

My dear Mr. White:

It is always pleasant to hear from you.

I am afraid that the *North Georgia Review* got more publicity than it either deserved or wanted (for it seems best to us still to avoid the sensational when we can, that is if we wish really to make an impress on the South) about my comment in *Dope With Lime*. This comment was in the mimeographed sheet which we send out occasionally between issues of the magazine. And while it certainly looked as if I was replying to Mrs. Ames it happened that our sheet was released before Mrs. Ames' news-release to Associated Press.

I commented in my picture of contemporary Georgia on various things[,] then I ended with my paragraph about "And we let a Negro be killed so quietly in Georgia a few weeks ago that no one's sensitive feelings were bruised in the least. . . ." I did not intend to be scooping a news-story nor to be taking issue with the ASWPL but intended it as a comment on what I believed to be authentic happenings.

Briefly this is the story I was commenting on: This spring I was down in Middle Georgia and happened to come into a town just two or three days after this Negro was killed. A cotton broker who is a good friend of mine told me about it with no idea that I would use the story, and forgetting for the time being that I edited a magazine. So I feel that I cannot use his name, as it would injure him greatly as well as be a breach of confidence. It seems that this Negro and his white boss got into some kind of argument out on the farm which resulted in the white man being killed by the Negro—with his hoe, I believe. Instead of the Negro being arrested and put in safe-keeping, he was left free and word was sent to the white boss's brother (I do not know by whom) who with one or two of his friends (so the story was told to me) went to the farm and shot the Negro down. Nothing was done to him in any way. Every one knew he did it but the cotton-broker who told me took it rather for granted that since the Negro had killed the white man, the white man's brother had a 'right' to shoot the Negro down. No one during the conversation suggested the Negro's right as an American citizen to a trial. I did not, for I wanted to get the full story and knew they would hush up if I seemed to be critical. That is the story. It isn't very sensational. And I did not mean to be telling it as a news-story. But to me it is just as much a lynching as if a mob had gone and done violence to the Negro.

Of course before this can go into the records the facts would have to be checked. If I had reported it as a news-story I would have checked my informant's story detail by detail before telling it. But I commented without giving name, date or place, and felt that since I believe the story to be certainly in its essence absolutely authentic, I had the right to make this comment.

If you (and the N.A.A.C.P.) or the Interracial Commission wish to investigate it and I can be of any help to you in this investigation I shall be glad to do so, and know I can put you in touch with people who can give you the facts on it—though I cannot give you the name of the man who told me. He is a prominent, respected citizen of the county however and knew, I feel absolutely certain, of what he spoke.

There is much we both want to talk to you about. I am about to finish up my novel on the white and the Negro families and I shall of course want you to approve of it. I hope you will.

tls, NAACP

Responding to her letter of May 31, 1940, Walter White asked Smith on June 5 to give him, confidentially, additional information about the lynching so that he could arrange for an investigation. He assured her: "The very last thing on earth I would want to do would be to cause any embarrassment or difficulty for you and Miss Snelling or to impede in any fashion the grand job you are doing there" (NAACP/LC, excerpted by permission of Jane White Viazzi).

Smith's reply not only provides the requested details concerning the previously unpublished lynching; it also reveals some of the constraints under which she worked, as well as her perception of a few of the differences between her family and Paula Snelling's. Smith wrote a similar letter on the same date to Ralph Davis of Tuskegee Institute with the following additional disclaimer:

I fully realize that from your point of view and from that of human decency all of this indecision and fear and circuitousness must seem foolish and almost silly, but even though my sympathies are completely with the Negro race and I ardently support justice, I cannot injure people who are family connections and who themselves had absolutely nothing to do with the killing, but were merely my informants. This is one of the old dilemmas which every sensitive and decent person has to deal with down here in the South. [UF]

July 13, 1940

Dear Mr. White:

I am going to give you the information as well as I can about the killing. I shall have to tell you frankly that the reason I have been so extremely hesitant about it is that my informant was Miss Snelling's brother-in-law. The Snellings, while as kind and good natured as the average white southerner, accept the prevailing customs and mores without giving them much criticism. Paula Snelling is quite different from the rest of her family and it has been even hard for them to accept fully her connection with the magazine although they have been very pleasant about it and at times very helpful to us. You can see, being the sensitive person that you are, how embarrassing it is for me to do anything that might give her family any kind of publicity or discomfort. It is because I do have confidence in your discretion and integrity that I am telling you this. If it concerned my family I would not hesitate for we are very different from each other and very independent of each other. I would let the blows fall where they happened to fall, knowing that most of them would be in sympathy with me and those who were not would accept it fairly well.

Now for the data that I can give you. It isn't very exact. The killing took place around April 16. It was told to me on the 17th. It happened either on the 16th or the 15th of April. Jim Whitehead, who lives in Pinehurst, Georgia but has his cotton business in Vienna, Georgia, gave me the information. The killing occurred in Dooly County or in Crisp County, the largest town being Cordele. I have not been able to find out in which of the two counties it occurred. At the time Mr. Whitehead told me of the incident he mentioned the name of the Negro who was killed and the white man who did the killing. But the names escaped my mind and since then I have not been able to secure them without causing a lot of trouble and suspicion. But I believe I can get them for you within the next week or two by using a somewhat circuitous method.

Other people in Pinehurst who might be able to give you information are the Methodist minister, whose name I do not know, Mr. A. M. Wilson, and Miss Julia Lewis, all residents of the town.

In Vienna I would suggest that Miss Emily Woodward be interviewed if she is in town, and also some of the Rountree family. If investigation would be carried to Cordele, a few miles south of Vienna, I have heard that the editor of the Cordele paper is very liberal. You might also talk with some of the Harris family. They are quite prominent in Cordele and some years ago I had one of their daughters in my camp. I shall send you the names of the two people involved as soon as I can get that information.

[...]

tls, NAACP

Despite the often conflicting demands Smith faced as camp director, magazine editor, and novelist, her correspondence indicates a great deal of creative interaction between these seemingly different interests in her life. The following letter to Glenn Rainey demonstrates more explicitly how current political events, specifically the anticipation of war, affected the creative activities of the camp and Smith's perspective on her work as writer as well as camp director. Characteristically, her analysis of war corresponded to her critique of other forms of human segregation, and she focused her attention on the underlying values and attitudes reflected in its presence.

September 19, 1940

[...]

We had a good summer, smooth as far as the mechanics of camp were concerned. Less encouraging to me as I watched War creep into our midst and twist feeling and thought. Our girls talked more about God, about hell, about believing every word of the Bible than in all my camp experience I have heard before. They were less tolerant of the Negro this summer (some holding bravely to their decency but others wavering) more inclined to defend the South . . . America . . . to hate Hitler and Germans . . . Even so, we had good talks, good evenings together . . . until I wrote a little play called 1940, A Play for a Young Girl. They wrote that play, not I,—I only put it down on paper. It came out of evenings when together we did not discuss war and peace, regimentation and death, but acted it out in singing and dance and impromptu chanting. Gathered together as we have done before in the library we spent several evenings doing this . . . first playing on the drums then beginning to talk about today, this year, what it meant to us, — election year — child refugees — Finland — propaganda — regimentation—then suddenly some one would get up and chant their feelings or dance them out. [. . .] And then one night, some girl spoke of conscription, of regimented youth camps, and to my astonishment their feelings of fear and panic poured out. Then I wrote the play. We were to give it—the girls were thrilled—we went to its first reading and rough "walking through" of the scenes. And suddenly my counselors turned against me. The play was unpatriotic they told me. Furthermore, it was not the kind of thing young girls should hear about. A first-year callow young counselor told me that "it wasn't good for children to hear about such things . . . they were too young." In all of my experience I have never felt so much resentment against me, such a refusal to work with me on a project. I bowed my head to the storm and stopped work on the play. Not because I was afraid to give that play but because I was afraid of seeing all the other values of summer destroyed by dissension and suspicion. But I gathered my children up one night and we went to the library and Esther read it to them. In all her life she must not have read so beautifully and so movingly. The children were deeply touched and profoundly impressed. A few counselors had straggled in—I had invited none of them—and some told me afterward that they regretted that we had given up the idea of producing the play . . . But that was Esther's magic, and they did not really believe what they said.

Well . . . I confess that I was awed by the incident. It has always been so simple and easy to hold the group in the "hollow of one's hand," so to speak, to win them over to almost any kind of project. But War's beat me. I had no more influence during that brief dissension when my loyal staff turned into a war mob than if I had been the cook.

But . . . I quickly got our minds on fun again—on the banquet and the barbecue and the children's surprise for the counselors—and so the summer ended in peace. I suppose you'd call it my appeasement policy. The children went home saying it was their happiest and best summer; the counselors went home saying the same. And believing it. But the director saw them all off feeling sadder than ever in her life she had felt about a summer.

[. . .]

[. . .] It is not the physical part of war that sickens me as it is what is happening to our minds and feelings.

tls, Rainey/EU

The following letter to Rainey is noteworthy for its depiction of Smith and Snelling's cooperative work on the magazine and for indications of early responses to *Strange Fruit* in manuscript form. In light of its later reception, it seems ironic that it was initially rejected as "not sensational enough" for Simon and Schuster.

Sunday night [February? 1941]

Dear Glenn:

It was good to hear your voice and to feel the old brain clicking away so clearly tonight. Paula and I both enjoyed it. I do want to ask you if you said you did approve of the lend-lease bill. I most strongly oppose it for it hands over too much power to Roosevelt and in my opinion no man has enough judgment, brains, experience and emotional stability to make the vast decisions that he will certainly be free to make—and will make—if these powers are turned over to him. I simply do not trust him that much. Or any one individual no matter how honest he is and scrupulous. Our unconscious motivations are too dangerous to be entrusted with such power.

[. . .]

I've done an article on internationalism which I hope you'll like. Paula and I are doing a series of five and this is the first. They are coming out under our names—both our names—but I'm afraid Paula will be ashamed to sign this one as she was unable to help much with it and it shows the lack of her 'imprint.' (She helped a great deal in ideas and thought. And her precision.) She seems physically well now but has little psychic energy—not enough to do creative work. It is very distressing to her and I've found it difficult to keep her encouraged. When she attempted to write and found that she couldn't, she became very anxious and distressed and depressed. She is feeling better now but she still cannot make herself write. But it is natural for her to feel this way and there is no cause for alarm. After all, she had a serious operation and was in fear about its being malignant for two weeks, just long enough for her—and me too—to live in a nice hell.* She just hasn't recovered yet from it all. Nor have I! Only I seem to be going nicely in high these days. I aim to get back on the novel just as soon as the magazine gets off to the printer's. I've made a little head-start on camp— enough to ease up on it for the next few weeks (with an hour or two a day spent on it) and I hope to get the novel in shape. Mr. Howe and I did not quite agree about it. He said that he thought it was a truer, more balanced interpretation of the South than either Faulkner or Caldwell—that it had 'authority' etc. but—. His 'but' being that it was not quite sensational

*The surgery was a hysterectomy.

enough to suit Simon & Schuster. He was so charming and sweet to me and really complimentary that I could not in my heart get either angry or hurt. But I felt kicked plumb to death in the middle—it coming so soon after Paula's operation. He insisted however on my not taking his word for it but telephoned the best agents in New York and made an appointment for me to talk to them. They are Steinbeck's agents. Well, God bless them, they are as enthusiastic about the book as Mr. Howe was not. They think it might be 'big stuff' and that kind of thing and they are anxious for me to finish it up. They said that it had more thesis-power than Richard Wright's (he is a favorite of theirs) and *said* that the last half of the book was as moving as anything they had read in a long long time. Well . . . of course it made me feel better. It naturally would. They may be as wrong in their way as I am almost certain Howe is in his. Howe had told me last spring that he did not like Freud or psychoanalytic psychology, so I knew right then that my chances were thin. But he continued to like everything in the *NGR* and would often write me about my articles and stories so I still had hope.

I did not mean to write like this. But one more thing. Dr. Karl Menninger, (author of *Human Mind, Man Against Himself*—and my favorite psychiatrist) is coming to visit me for a few days on March 2. That afternoon (Sunday) I am planning to ask my friends who I think he would enjoy the most up for the late afternoon and supper. I am counting heavily on you and Dorothy being with me. [. . .]

tls, Rainey/EU

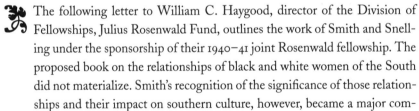 The following letter to William C. Haygood, director of the Division of Fellowships, Julius Rosenwald Fund, outlines the work of Smith and Snelling under the sponsorship of their 1940–41 joint Rosenwald fellowship. The proposed book on the relationships of black and white women of the South did not materialize. Smith's recognition of the significance of those relationships and their impact on southern culture, however, became a major component of her analysis of the interrelatedness of societal concepts of race and gender, informing *Strange Fruit* and more explicitly developed in *Killers of the Dream*.

The book by and about women for which Smith and Snelling were writing an article was to have been published by the Woman's Press in celebration of "Woman's Coming of Age" in the United States between 1840 and 1940, the theme of the Women's Centennial Congress held in New York City in November 1940. Other correspondence indicates that the collection of essays was not completed in time for publication and that Smith and Snelling's article was probably the essay published in the Winter 1941 issue of the *North Georgia Review* as "Man Born of Woman."[16]

Despite Smith's tendency to downplay the significance of her accomplishments in this report, as editor of the *North Georgia Review* she was already in demand as a speaker and receiving regional attention for her outspoken views on racial relationships.

August 15, 1941

Dear Mr. Haygood:

I wish we had some magnificent reports to give you of our activities. Quite the contrary. We are still in the midst of those activities that have to be labelled 'work in progress.' I think we have made some progress on the research for the book on Negro and White Women of the South—which Miss Snelling and I are doing together. That is not the title but the theme of the book. We are primarily interested in the psychological interactions of white and Negro women who have for three hundred years lived in such remote intimacy with each other. We think their relationships and the relationships they have had with the men of the white race especially have had a tremendous effect upon the culture and literature of the South. [. . .]

The magazine—another of our projects—is still extant. We plan to give it more of a push this fall.

My novel *Jordan is so Chilly* is now completed and is in the hands of Miss McIntosh, my agent. She is Steinbeck's agent and handles a great many of the well known writers' productions. She seems enthusiastic about the novel, thinks it has best-seller possibilities (although I myself fear that this war will not make people eager to read of their own problems). However six or seven publishers have asked to see it and perhaps something will come of it. I believe you know a little about it. It is concerned with a Negro family and a white family whose lives have become intertwined. It deals with educated Negroes and while concerned with social and economic implications focuses on the psychology of sex and religion. Miss McIntosh has been kind enough to say that it reminds her in style and mood of both Willa Cather and Julia Peterkin although perhaps I am more 'radical' and outspoken concerning taboos than either of those estimable ladies. We shall see how it comes out.

Our other project—the camp—has a way of using up much of our time but I sometimes think perhaps our work with girls who will some day be the women leaders of the South may be of some definite value. We have this year, as usual, worked on many genuinely interesting projects with them in racial relationships, and there is always up here much discussion of the South and its problems.

Other than those not very big accomplishments we have little to say that is impressive. I have made a number of talks on the South to such groups as the Y.M.C.A. student conferences, the wives of the Emory University faculty etc. etc. and have a number of invitations to speak next fall to the young people at various colleges and universities. As for honors: the biggest honor I have received was an anonymous letter threatening my life after a talk on the South which I made to the students at Blue Ridge.

Miss Snelling will have ready in a year or two a book of essays that should be of credit to her. I think her work while small in quantity is of a quality which may cause the South some day to be proud of her. She of course works with me in many ways on those projects which are my own rather than a part of our collaboration.

Miss Snelling and I have been invited to write articles for a number of magazines. [. . .] We did together an article for a book by women about women that was to come out last spring. There has been some difficulty with publishers, I am vague about details, and I do not know whether it will or will not be published. The other contributors were such women as Pearl Buck, Virginia Woolf, Dr. Karen Horney, and so on. I believe we were the only southern women invited to contribute to it. But the honor will be somewhat nebulous if the book never reaches publication.

Perhaps in a few months we shall have something to report that will seem more notable. Much of our work I fear is rather quiet and without fireworks.

[. . .]

tls, RFP

The following letter to M. O. Bousfield, director of Negro health for the Julius Rosenwald Fund, demonstrates additional ways Smith and Snelling used their contacts with the Rosenwald Fund to develop their magazine as an educational tool for changing southern society. A similar letter to Fred G. Wale, the fund's director for rural education, asked for data on rural southern schools [RFP]. The editors' answers to the questions asked in the DO YOU KNOW YOUR SOUTH? contest were published in the Winter 1941 issue of the *North Georgia Review*.

October 9, 1941

Dear Dr. Bousfield:

I shall be very grateful to you if you can, without its being too much bother for you, help me out on several questions concerning hospitals for Negroes in the South.

How many hospitals are there in the South for Negroes with Negro doctors on the staff and with Negro nurses? The only two I know are the Veterans Hospital at Tuskegee and the Goodrich-Flint in New Orleans. I've heard there is one in Durham, N. C. and I have an impression that there is one connected with the Meharry Medical College in Nashville. I shall feel indebted to you for any information you will give me about this matter.

Could you also tell me if there are Negro psychiatrists practicing in any of the southern (or northern) state mental hospitals? Have we in the South any private mental hospital for Negroes? Is there in the South any Negro unit of a state hospital system which could be described as 'adequate' in regard to staff, occupational therapy equipment, facilities for play and sports, theatre etc. etc. There is a travelling mental hygiene clinic system in South Carolina as of course you know. Do you happen to know whether Negroes are free to come to this clinic?

Miss Snelling and I are getting out a little pamphlet answering those questions we sent out last year titled DO YOU KNOW YOUR SOUTH? We have received so many requests for 'answers' that we've decided not only would it be a sporting thing to do, but perhaps a valuable project also. Hence we are neck deep in our own questions and learning more and more about this old South of ours. We are burdening our friends and acquaintances and many others on whom we have not the slightest claim I fear, with our questions. If you are too busy with your own projects to take time out for ours, don't feel badly about it. If you can take a little time out to answer our questions we both shall be very grateful.

tls, RFP

This letter to Glenn Rainey echoes Smith's published concerns about the nation's entry into World War II: how to maintain and expand the democratic process on the home front, fighting demagoguery and totalitarianism in Georgia and the South as well as abroad.[17] Significantly, she concluded that doing her part to win the war would mean doing her work as a writer. Publishing her ideas about democracy in her magazine, specifically calling for an end to racial segregation in all aspects of American life, would make her a highly controversial figure in Georgia even before the publication of *Strange Fruit*.

December 13, 1941

Dear Glenn:

[. . .]

The war. I am having to fight a profound depression. All I shall say now is that I have not changed my mind at all. The problem now with me is how we who feel as we do feel can best meet this situation, how we can do it creatively and not too fanatically but without one bit of compromise. I don't know yet. We have a statement in the magazine which we did while proof-reading it. I hope you will approve of our statement. I hope also that the full force of the espionage act of 1917 will not be functioning to the extent that they will ban our magazine. That act is a terrible thing. It has now gone into effect again. (So a newspaper article said which may be simply rumor.) I hope and feel many things which I shall not write about now.

[. . .]

The magazine, a veritable book, is at the printers and should soon be out. I hope it is all right. It is difficult to crystalize one's thoughts these days, to integrate one's emotions. It isn't with me a matter of courage. It is a matter of wisdom or lack of it. What is the right thing to do, the deeply right thing. . . . . .

We have worked hard this autumn and I think perhaps accomplished more than we usually do. The Rosenwald book (not the woman book which requires a tremendous amount of research and thought) is coming pretty well now. We are tentatively calling it SOUTH: Test Case for American Democracy. There are three parts to the book: the first covering the present South as much as a novelist would see it as is possible; the second is an analysis of southern feelings and attitudes; the third is called Expression in the South and covers the contemporary fiction, poetry, essay, sociological studies, newspaper columns, speeches, the Negro choirs (which seem an integral part of southern "expression" to me), and the Negro dance, with a little bit on southern painters and sculptors, and last but not least the conferences.

You may have heard that I cold-bloodedly turned down my first offer from Crowell. I know I sound fool-hardy but I did it with encouragement from my agent to do so. For although they offered a fine and generous contract we both felt that they fundamentally misinterpreted the book and hence I would have many arguments with them on revisions etc. Harcourt Brace asked to see it while we were still dealing with Crowell so we sent it over to them. Mr. Crowell at first got a little mad with the agent but must have cooled off for I had a very cordial little note from him the other day asking me to have lunch with him while in New York and stating that he was still immensely interested in my book. So that is that. I plan to spend two or three weeks of intensive work on the novel polishing it and filling in a few gaps for I sent it off last spring with some bad spots still left in it— knowing I'd have no chance to work on them for a good while. What the war will do I now do not know. But if I get my work done that will be my part.

tls, Rainey/EU

Commenting upon her recent trip to New York in a January 12 letter to the Raineys, Smith wrote that she had been encouraged by conversations with those she called liberals in New York and had decided to speak and act even more boldly than she had in the past about the need to grant full citizenship to Negroes (Rainey/EU). The following letter to Walter White provides a specific example of her increased outspokenness on race, while also recording her continuing efforts to find a publisher for her novel. Her willingness to speak publicly for an end to racial discrimination as part of rather than a threat to the "war effort" clearly separated Smith from other white southern liberals, especially other writers and journalists, in the early 1940s.[18] Yet her conviction that she was not alone among white southerners in her attitudes about racial democracy became a major premise in her approach to social change throughout her life.

Upon receiving the following letter, White sent a copy to Eleanor Roosevelt with a note describing Smith and Snelling as "two of the best informed persons I know regarding conditions and attitudes in the south" and urging that the proposal be placed in the hands of the president.[19]

February 14, 1942

Dear Walter:

[. . .]

Since you so generously suggested helping with the book I do want to tell you a little about it. Lambert Davis of Harcourt Brace read it, was very enthusiastic and after three or four hours of discussing it, he said that he would send me a contract in a few days. He took the matter up with my agent, Miss Mavis McIntosh, and the thing seemed settled. I came home, feeling naturally good about it. But when Lambert discussed it with the other two big boys on the firm before making me an advance they put thumbs down. "Afraid it would not sell" they said. I had the feeling that it was my complete frankness about the racial ambivalence of the South. I do not know. Anyway, Lambert felt that he had to call it off. He said they would let him offer me a contract but that they would not promote the book beyond the minimum. Davis is a decent person and seems to like the book, so he refused under those circumstances to go ahead with it, believing the book would be "buried." But he is still interested and is coming by next week or the week after to read my revisions up here at Clayton, hoping he can still persuade the firm into more enthusiasm.

He feels that the book has a real chance of being a "big book" and says he does not want to see the thing buried in somebody's list. He believes there are publishers who will see it as a thing to be promoted and promoted now when race is a real challenge to our country.

I am thinking about your Doubleday Doran friend. Would they like to see the thing? Would they be afraid of my race frankness? Surely they wouldn't, but it is a question. Not all the prejudice in the country is south of Washington as of course you know.

I shall be very grateful if you can find time to do something about it. I hope to have it revised to the place where I am willing for publishers to read it—by March 1st. I'll send it back to McIntosh and Otis, my agents then. In the meantime, if Doubleday wanted to discuss the book with Mavis McIntosh, they could, for she can give them a pretty good idea of what the book is about. My theme is basically concerned with the effect upon not only lives but minds and emotions which the concept of race in the South has. It is an indictment of the church in the South and I imagine the thesis is fairly apparent that the author doesn't think it is possible for a white person to be a Christian in the South; and hard for Negroes to be. The book however centers around character, and especially is concerned with the family relationships of two families, the white Deens, the colored Andersons.

Don't burden your mind with all of this if you are too pressed right now. I know you are always busy and I hate to ask such a favor of you, but I have grown afraid that the very racial prejudices of publishers are going to keep the book down. One publisher said that it was all right for negroes to write about these matters—but white people?

Walter—

After writing you this letter, I want to add this note—concerning a matter far more important than my personal worries about my novel!

It is so apparent that the world's stage is set for a magnificent act on the part of the Anglo-Saxons! If the British people would today give *India* her freedom, if Mr. Roosevelt by proclamation justified by war would give the Negro in America his full status of citizenship, it would cause a mighty exaltation to sweep over the face of the earth. Mr. Roosevelt is afraid. He has no reason to be. Beneath the South's terrible dullness and prejudice is a deep sense of guilt. I believe white southerners would draw in a deep breath and thank God for what he had done. I believe this. And I know my South. The stage is set. People are sending their sons to die for something that in their hearts they know does not exist. It isn't a light thing to give your son to death. I believe there is an inertia, a profound lack of identification of the American people with the war aims—as those aims really stand today—that is similar, shockingly, disturbingly similar to the feeling among the people of France before its fall. Have you read Pierre van Paassen's account of the mood of the French people? If Mr. Roosevelt is a great statesman, a great leader instead of merely a clever politician, he should be led to see this. I believe Henry Wallace can see this. I believe there are men and women North, South, East, West who will see this thing. This is the time. The South would "take" it today when in peace time they would not. Southerners deep in their hearts are cowards to public opinion. They play to a stage. They are the world's greatest actors. They would play up to this thing to the extent that race riots would be avoided. I do not believe southern people would dare have race riots over such an issue, although they are having race riots, as we both know, around the camps.

We are going to do what we can. How futile we feel as individuals! But the point is, we are not alone. There are thousands of people in America today whispering this, some saying it loud. We are going to send out an editorial to 5000 southerners, newspapers, government leaders. That is such a little thing! But if somehow we who believe this thing could unite. This is something worth fighting for. The war isn't.

[. . .] I hope I don't sound too melodramatic.

tls, NAACP/LC

🦋 With the expiration of their Rosenwald fellowships in 1941, Smith and Snelling were again searching for financial support for the magazine. Edwin

R. Embree, president of the Rosenwald Fund, maintained that part of the strength of the magazine lay in its ability to sustain itself "in a reasonably native fashion" rather than by money from a Yankee organization that, he feared, "might destroy at least part of its character and influence."[20] Indirectly, however, the Rosenwald Fund continued to support the magazine by employing Snelling and Smith, in 1942, 1943, and 1944, to travel throughout the South in search of potential fellowship recipients from among the region's college students.

Her travel work for the Rosenwald Fund provided further ammunition for Smith's increasingly active verbal war against racial discrimination in the South. Accordingly, she did not limit the publication of her findings to reports to her employers at the fund, or even to her editorial columns. Taking advantage of their mutual connection with the Rosenwald Fund, Smith sought the support and influence of Eleanor Roosevelt. The ideas and questions raised in the following letter reflect a class bias similar to that evident in Smith's vision of Laurel Falls Camp and the magazine as instruments of social change. Like W. E. B. DuBois's appeal to the "talented tenth," Smith directed her appeals to her society's educated leadership and to those in positions of recognized influence and power.

April 7, 1942

My dear Mrs. Roosevelt:

Paula Snelling and I have this past week completed a trip through the South during which we have interviewed for the Rosenwald Fund the young Negro and white college seniors who have applied for Rosenwald scholarship-aid grants.

We have found these interviews profoundly stirring and want in some way, to share our findings with you. Some of our talks with the young Negroes were very disturbing, some most heartening, nearly all sincere and realistic. We found in the young whites—though there were exceptions—a shocking ignorance of their South, a concern primarily with their personal affairs, a restlessness about the future, little awareness of the international picture and our place in it. We found few educated whites who had ever met an educated Negro; few young Negroes who had met a racially unprejudiced white. We interviewed only the 'cream' of the senior classes in 22 colleges.

Throughout the South, as we expected, we found many liberals giving up their liberalism 'for the duration.' Especially did this seem to be true of those who are labelled "friends of the Negro." The Negroes feel this too and are depressed and disheartened by the knowledge that many of their white friends disappear when crises arise.

Down in the Delta we found reaction rising like a great wave. Cotton is 26 cents in the Delta now and the general attitude among the planters is that neither Mr. Roosevelt nor God Himself is going to keep them from making some money while the making is good. There is a childish desperation in their attitude that would be awfully funny were they not so powerful. (Among my various activities is that of being a director of a summer camp for little rich girls. Some of these planters send their children to me in spite of my 'liberalism.' But this spring I find them on the defensive, very antagonistic to all liberal movements, growing suspicious of what I am teaching their children in my camp; so suspicious and antagonistic that I dared not tell them that I was on Rosenwald Fund business for their hospitality would not have been equal to such a strain being put upon it!)

There is something heartbreakingly valiant about the young of the Negro race, so eager to prove to white America their willingness to die for a country which has given them only the scraps from the white folks' democracy. There is resentment also; a quiet, strong resentment, running like a deep stream through their minds and hearts; something I think few white Americans are aware of, or want to face.

I shall be in Washington Friday, April 10th, at the Hay Adams House. I shall call Miss Thompson Friday morning and shall be honored to talk with you if you wish me to do so. I know you are a very busy person and I do not want to burden you further by a talk with me unless you think it will be useful to you to have in more detail this recent skimming of southern opinion.*

Should you let me talk with you I would like to discuss with you also the possibilities for making this new venture of the Rosenwald Fund a more creative and vital youth project. Some of us think—and Dr. Embree shares this opinion—that the project should be more than a mere selection of young whites and blacks for graduate study. Could they feel themselves a part of some big and creative effort, something that had to do directly with their South, that had adventure in it, it would become a significant experience for them, rather than merely one more year of university study. They need somehow to be brought together, to have actual experience with each

---

*Eleanor Roosevelt's response indicated that she was unable to meet with Smith on the requested date because she was then attending a Rosenwald Fund meeting.[21]

other, though heaven only knows how we can work it out in a South where such an idea can be mentioned now only in whispers. But how can the South ever work out its bi-racial problems when its intelligent and educated young whites and Negroes have never met an educated member of the other race?

I believe Miss Lucy Mason recently wrote you about Paula Snelling and me and our magazine *The North Georgia Review* which has now changed its name to *South Today*. I merely mention this kindness to us so that it will help you identify us.

There are many of us who are deeply grateful to you for your unwavering stand for the democratic decencies.

tls, HP

TO WALTER WHITE

June 2, 1942

Dear Walter:

I thought you might be interested in the fact that our printers have refused to print the magazine this time because of my editorial THERE ARE SOME THINGS WHITE FOLKS CAN'T SAY.* He has really been long-suffering I suppose, and we should not have been surprised that we have at last stumped our toe on his racial prejudice. He returned the copy (I had asked for some reprints and had sent it on ahead of the rest of the material) and said that he would not print it as he felt that it would stir up racial trouble in the South.

I enclosed a copy of the editorial that roused his protective instincts. I admit that it is pretty raw. I hope not too raw to be good strategy. It may be. If you think so, I wish you'd tell me. It spilled out of my indignation which had accumulated during a seven weeks' trip through the South.

Don't give the incident publicity please, as we think it perhaps wiser to say little about our struggles and defeats. The white liberals who accept us now might not if word got around that we were so "dangerous" that a printer had refused to print us! Lord—Lord—how funny it all would be if it weren't so tragic. The way so many white liberals are drawing in their democracy "for the duration" has sickened me. Men who spoke out "bravely" two years ago now evade race, as if it were a rattler . . .

*Published as "Portrait of the Deep South Speaking to Negroes on Morale," *North Georgia Review*, Spring 1942, 34–37.

Dr. Ira Reid and Mrs. [Jessie Daniel] Ames both are helping us find new printers. The magazine will be out soon.

[. . .]

TO EDWIN R. EMBREE

July 28, 1942

Dear Dr. Embree:

[. . .] Georgia is seething with race feeling. The papers in Macon are giving a fine build-up to race trouble. It has seemed to me that Gene Talmadge is deliberately building up this race trouble in order to arouse the voters to the "menace" in time for them to vote for him in September. One of his henchmen has a daughter in my camp. He was here not long ago and talked quite frankly with me about the race trouble. He seemed quite pleased about it, really, as if everything were going according to Gene's wishes. [. . .] I found my talk with him very interesting as it did not seem to occur to him that I was not a Talmadge woman, and I gathered some odds and ends of information which seemed fairly important to an understanding of the situation down here.

Ira Reid was here not long ago, feeling a profound discouragement. Mrs. Wormley, a Rosenwald fellow, also dropped in a week or two ago. I find that the campers and counselors accept my Negro friends very casually. We are playing with the idea of having Sterling Brown here for tea with the campers and counselors. We plan definitely to have him for lunch with us. I feel that the time is coming for definite and decent action as well as talk. While it may have been good strategy in the past to play safe, I am beginning to feel that a few decent southerners must break the spell which binds us all down here, by acting decently as well as talking decently. [. . .]

I am trying to feel my way through these nasty customs of ours, appraising each step I take as to its effect upon both whites and Negroes. Sometimes it is very difficult to know whether one is doing the "right" thing; the fool-hardy act or the wise act. But . . . I'm glad I'm living at this time . . . I cannot imagine any period in all man's history that could have been half as interesting.

[. . .]

CHAPTER THREE

Dropping Bombs on

Georgia's Peace,

1 9 4 3 — 1 9 4 6

Lillian Smith's letters from the years surrounding the publication of *Strange Fruit* and its production as a Broadway play
establish patterns of style and content repeated in correspondence throughout her life. Stylistically, they range from a few
personal letters to family and friends, some of her most informative and entertaining "Laurel Leaves," and comments to her
editor about her intent and others' responses to her novel, to
formal treatises written as a public figure speaking for or against
a political cause. Whether written as public statements or as
more personal conversations, Smith's letters from 1943 through
1946 outline the core of her discourse concerning segregation as

a symbol of cultural disease and the role of the artist in society, two integrally related themes dominating Smith's writing career.

Although Smith bemoaned her best-seller status and described fame as something to be mourned rather than wished for one's friends, the increasing notoriety of the magazine and novel forced her to clarify certain questions of process, of means and ends, in ways that ultimately enhanced her contribution as a writer. Her letter to Richard Wright addressed the heart of the problem for writers whose sensibilities and ideas grew out of the social activist ethos of the 1930s but who recognized the danger of one's work being used as a tool of any narrowly defined political ideology or organization. Smith rejected the basic premises of both the Agrarians, who in establishing the "new criticism" insisted upon a separation of art from recognizable social or political issues, and the communists, who she felt were too frequently willing to separate means and ends. Instead, she advocated a third position in which social and cultural issues are considered necessarily valid subjects for art, but the choice of which issue as well as the approach or method for addressing a given subject is determined by the individual artist. In her struggle with questions of priorities and how best to use her skills as a writer, Smith concluded, as she wrote in her letter of resignation from the board of the Southern Conference for Human Welfare: "My talent is that of clarifying issues; is that of telling the stark truth as I see it, with as much compassion as I am capable of."[1]

Letters from 1943 through 1946 reveal not only the increasing frequency and boldness of her stand for "racial democracy" but also the ways ideas and tactics she developed as camp director informed her work as social critic and popular author. Her letter to Guy Johnson declining an invitation to join the newly formed Southern Regional Council addressed the limits of purely political and economic analyses of southern social problems by suggesting that the key to understanding racial segregation might best be found in examining the psychological needs of children. Her advice to the Georgia Committee (a state branch of the Southern Conference for Human Welfare) referred to the effects of racist rhetoric on the psychological growth of children, and her criticism of the SCHW echoed her discussion with campers about the importance of "spinning bridges" to other people and to the future. Similarly, her emphasis on the importance of the camp's atmosphere of "silliness" and "whacky fun" correlated with her expressed desire for adults of different races to be able to relax and have fun together. She invited upper-class black and white women to the camp for a house party to relax and play, as well as talk seriously, together. The spirit of play became both a means and an end, and the two were not separated in Smith's political strategies. When she learned that *Strange Fruit* would be a best-seller, she invited her Clayton neighbors for tea and cakes, thereby diffusing potential hostility or dissension and building, once again, a spirit of community.

Just as Victorian ladies before her had adapted the role of hostess—one of their few legitimate avenues of influence—to achieve their own political ends, so Smith's choice of political tactics reflected her awareness of her class privilege. As she wrote Eleanor Roosevelt, December 14, 1943:

> I have been trying for six or seven years to prove to white southern women of my social class that we can speak out plainly about racial democracy, that we can take a public stand against discrimination and even against segregation without losing too much prestige and without suffering martyrdom. It seems very important to me for a southern woman to demonstrate this successfully. Because I am known for my work with children of wealthy southern families, I have had a fortunate position in the South, and I have made the most of it. [HP]

Likewise, as she dealt with threats and overt attempts to censor first the magazine and then her novel, Smith relied on the social and political contacts afforded her as a respected upper-class white lady. Her concern for the effect of publicity about her work on her family members, however, reflects not only her awareness of the power of class privilege but also an underlying fear of losing the corresponding protection supposedly afforded the lady whose reputation (defined as heterosexuality, class and racial solidarity) remained unquestioned.

Despite such fears, Smith continued to challenge the limits of her privilege even as her words challenged the liberal political and social leaders of her day to look beyond the war's end or the outcome of a given election to envision a world she could discuss with Laurel Falls campers. In that world southern white children were interested in the children of India and China as well as the children of a black woman lynched in Georgia.

TO WALTER WHITE

Sunday, January 17, 1943

Dear Mr. White:

I am enclosing copy of a letter I recently wrote Mr. Lewis of *PM*.* Thought you might be interested.

PM was a leftist-progressive newspaper published in Brooklyn, N.Y., from 1940 to 1948. Ralph Ingersoll was editor and Max Lerner, its best-known columnist.[2]

I have wanted to write you for many weeks, especially since Ralph Mc-Gill's below-the-belt swipe at you.* I thought it was a dirty piece of business. Ralph has a great way of hedging on all things that may offend his big-business buddies, then speaking out "most courageously" when the issue is something that will not offend them. I did not see that editorial until my brother called my attention to it several weeks later. Had I seen it at the time I certainly would have written a letter to the *Constitution* in your defense. I still intend to pay tribute to you in the next issue of *South Today*. I also have written Ralph McGill. But that is not enough. I consider you not only a great and unselfish leader of your people but an American for us all to be proud of and also one of my personal friends. I don't let folks say things about my friends without answering back.

Julian Harris told me at a dinner party not long ago in Atlanta that I was "dropping bombs on Georgia's peace." The particular bomb being the fact that at that time I was visiting the Benjamin Mays on the campus of Morehouse and speaking several times a day to the students. I told him in reply that once long ago when I was much younger, he had been one of my heroes when he so courageously denounced lynching.† It seemed to bother him. The rest of the evening he was quiet and rather gentle toward me . . . . .

You may be interested to hear of this "little drop in the bucket." Our county, Rabun, of which my brother is ordinary, has a maternity Home in which Negro mothers are admitted to have their babies on exactly the same basis as white mothers. One Negro mother has already been there. There was no riot. There was a little chatter, a few raised eyebrows. But not any reaction of grave import. The public county library also permits Negro citizens to enter its front door and take out books on exactly the same basis as other citizens. These two projects are my brother's and he has handled them very successfully and very quietly. He does the doing. . . . I do the verbal fighting.

*See McGill's editorial "One Word More," *Atlanta Constitution*, November 20, 1942, p. 2, col. 5. Strongly opposing the abolition of the poll tax, McGill lambasted supporters of the anti–poll tax bill and singled out Walter White as "the worst sort of leader any faction of the Negro people could have because he is, in my opinion, vain, personally and politically ambitious, and very much an officious show-off."
†As editor of the *Columbus* (Ga.) *Enquirer-Sun*, Harris won a Pulitzer prize in 1926 for his stand against the Ku Klux Klan and lynching. In 1930, while news editor of the *Atlanta Constitution*, he was a member of the Commission on Interracial Cooperation's Southern Commission on the Study of Lynching.[3]

Let Paula Snelling and me help you in any way we can. We are "all out" on this business of racial democracy. I came to the conclusion some time ago that I had to hit straight although good-temperedly. I also came to the conclusion that this is the right time to speak out clearly and unequivocally for racial democracy to all people at all times. And so help me, I'm doing it.

Good luck to you in all you are doing. And believe me, there are folks down here who admire you and are proud of you, and plenty of them are white folks.

tls, NAACP/LC

TO EDITORS OF PM

January 16, 1943

Sirs:

As a southern white woman I am grateful to *PM* for its efforts to persuade Americans to face and do something about the need to accord first-class citizenship to the Negro who is sharing so bravely in the defense of our land at this time. I have followed its editorials and news stories closely for the past year with increasing admiration for its honesty and intelligence. Especially do I consider Victor Bernstein's articles on the South a brilliant and fair treatment of the complex subject of the failure of democracy to work in the area of Negro-white relations.

It is, therefore, with reluctance that I find myself now criticising Mr. Lewis's editorial titled Another Open Letter to Paul V. McNutt. The readers of *PM* know, as do I, that John P. Lewis believes in democracy for all the people and works persistently toward that end. The purpose of his editorial was to urge Paul McNutt to support the FEPC* and to insist upon the hearings on discrimination against Negroes in the railroad unions. Yet I am deeply troubled by these sentences: "In peacetime, I'm not so sure but what a peaceful demonstration of that kind would be justified. . . . But in wartime, there is no question a march on Washington is not justified. It would seriously harm the war effort.["]

Is the war more important than the things the war is being fought for? If we are fighting this war to secure racial democracy for all the people then why is it wrong for the Negro to use democratic means within his own country to win this democracy for himself?

We must remember that it is not only to get something from his country

---

*Fair Employment Practices Committee, established to oversee President Roosevelt's 1941 executive order forbidding racial discrimination in defense industries.

but *to give something to his country* that the Negro asks for his share of democracy today and protests America's denial of his democratic rights and obligations.

In a democracy it is always the right time to give democracy; and always the right time to ask for democracy if the asking is done in democratic ways.

It must be subtly frustrating to an intelligent Negro to be told by his white friends, by those white Americans who honestly believe in and cherish democracy that although the Negro should be given democracy he hasn't the right to protest his lack of it. How is he going to get it if he doesn't demand it? How can he keep reminding us white folks (who forget the Negro so easily) that we still deny him the basic rights of citizenship unless he does protest?

The March on Washington plan is a non-violent and democratic way of protest. I too hope that it will never be necessary for the Negro race to have to resort to it as a protest. I agree with Mr. Lewis that we must face the Negro's needs *now*. But if we don't . . . let us then remember that such a protest is within the American's democratic rights. Let us not confuse the public by labelling it (should it ever come) as "unjustifiable" or "treasonable." Let's leave the calling of names to the demagogues and reactionaries North and South who will call plenty. Let those of us who believe in democracy use our efforts at that time and before that time comes to persuade the American people to understand what such a march is all about, what the needs are that motivate such a protest.

My own white South has used too often the phrase "it is not the right time" whenever the Negro has asked for his legitimate rights. We have used it as a club to beat him down whenever he has raised his head in dignity and self respect. Perhaps, when Mr. Lewis now suggests that "war time is not the right time" for a march on Washington the words remind me too bitterly of our southern traditional way of meeting the Negro's needs. I do not like to see the phrase creep into the vocabulary of other Americans, especially those who do so sincerely believe in the democratic way of life as does Mr. Lewis.

tlc, NAACP/LC

🦋 Smith's first major battle with censorship occurred over a year before the publication of *Strange Fruit*. The following letter to William Haygood of the Rosenwald Fund contains Smith's account of the events surrounding the attempted banning of *South Today* in January 1943.

Dear Billy:

[. . .] We aren't joking when we say we want you and your ideas on *South Today*—which is about synonymous (these days) with saying, "We like you fine . . . come on and go to jail with us." For man, man, them Klan and Vigilante folks have been tailing us around until we are about wore out. Just about the time it begins to seem real funny to me, another G man or Georgia Bureau of Investigation man pops up and gives me the creeps. But I now have in my possession a letter from the governor saying he is not interested in having us investigated and if he means it, I think we can relax a bit.

[. . .] Jimmie Tipton* and his young wife were spending the weekend with us in December; we told them how this lady at the post office kept us from getting a permit on the Spring issue and was now trying her tricks on the Winter issue, [. . .]. Jimmie offered to get the permit through in Atlanta and Betty, bless her, offered to see about the nasty business of addressing, wrapping, and mailing. So it went. Jimmie carried through the preliminaries with the Atlanta post office whose officials saw no reason why we should not have a permit (although the Clayton lady seemed to see plenty). Then Jimmie was called suddenly into the service. They were living in a place outside of Atlanta where he hesitated to leave Betty alone. So they closed up their own home and moved into a little house set in the back of a wealthy home on Peachtree Road. They rented this place, fixed it all up, moved in just before Jimmie left. Then trouble began. Betty seeing that she could not handle all the work with her job at the library at Georgia Tech, hired a professional wrapper to wrap the magazines. She is not experienced in running a subversive magazine and hence took no precautions. To her, bless her loyalty, it is the finest magazine the South has ever had the honor of letting go through its southern post offices and who would not be proud to wrap it? So she got a wrapper. When she phoned me what she had done, my heart sank a little for I know my beloved South and I gently asked her if she had investigated her man. Every one says he is reliable, was the answer, so I smothered my doubts. But I should have listened to my sinking heart which is often a very reliable barometer as to southern weather. The wrapper apparently read the magazine. Or somebody did while it was being wrapped in his office. Copies disappeared; many copies in fact, were stolen

---

*James Tipton, manager of Georgia Tech's bookstore, who had met Smith and Snelling through Glenn Rainey.

and passed around in Atlanta. The chief of police was given one and went into a foam. He said such subversive and indecent matter could never soil the name and virtue of Atlanta. He took it to the mayor. The mayor likewise gallantly defended Atlanta's purity by saying such indecency should never be permitted to be published there, nor allowed through the mails. Then he called the owner of Betty's house. Betty was using her new address as our temporary publishing address until we could find (and pay for!) a little office. The owner said he felt disgraced that a tenant of his had any connection with such indecency and subversiveness. He promptly got in touch with Betty—whose husband was far away in Indiana defending Betty's democracy etc.—and ordered her to give up her house. She had just spent a good bit cleaning, painting etc. but she said she had no desire to stay in it. He told her that she was just a front for damyankees and communists etc. and undoubtedly did not know what she was involved in. Betty did well with her reply. She is just 22 and quiet and reserved but she held her own well. She said that the editors and publishers were her best friends, that she had read the magazine for years and believed every word in this issue. He said no one could rent from him who believed a Negro should be called "mister" and asked Betty if she believed such a heinous thing. Betty said she not only believed it but practiced it. She held her own and with much quiet dignity—from all we could gather. He said he would not rent to her and she said neither would she rent from him—now that she knew how undemocratic he was. [. . .] Immediately after Betty's call I took the bus down to Atlanta. I found that at least half of the magazines were safe and that official Atlanta was quietly exciting itself to death about the magazine but nothing had been allowed to get into print. We found that they were urging the governor to have the legislature investigate me and the magazine "for indecency." [. . .] Then I wrote the governor a very calm and serene and tactful letter in which I told him how the magazine started, what its purpose is, and suggested that if he really feared his wife's camp director, to let me come down to his office and quietly talk things over with him. Then I wrote a mutual friend a letter that I felt would get to the governor. I said that I did not want an investigation but if one came, then I reserved the right to end it. And it would not be ended soon; that I would make it as big and as public as such things can be made. That when I was asked if I believed in equality I would give the public the answer that has not yet been given in Georgia. I would say yes, I believe in full social equality; and I would answer every question asked me in plain, unequivocal answers. If they wanted to hear those answers given by a well known and respected white woman, all they had to do was to have the investigation. I think that letter was enough to put the fear of God in the governor and in the Negro-haters in the legislature. The very last thing on earth they want to hear is one of their women say these democratic things. [. . .]

Anyway my brother was called by the postmistress (this is supposed to be confidential) and told that FBI agents were after me for breaking postal regulations. It really scared old Frank who ain't used to such notoriety (neither am I, of course) and he thought maybe through ignorance I had broken some law. But I knew I had not; or was reasonably sure that I had not and the whole thing sounded phony to me. So I went to the post office after I scrutinized my face to see if it looked peaceful. It looked positively benign—so I ambled in and softly asked the lady all about it. She tried to be mysterious but I pushed and probed and she said there had been an agent. Then I said I would go at once to Washington and clear the thing up, up there, with the Department of Justice. Her face went a little white at that and she said I could not tell them what she had told me etc. etc. In other words she began to back down just a bit. Then while I had her in a corner I quickly asked her if she was certain it was an FBI agent for I wanted my facts straight when I went to Washington. She immediately said no, that it was a GBI (Georgia). Knowing that she had deliberately lied to Frank I began to suspect the whole tale as being something she had concocted to stop our fight to get our second-class postal privileges. But we weren't sure . . . for there is a chance that those scoundrels in Atlanta might try to frame me with something—the three standbys being postal laws, income tax and sex. I rapidly surveyed the last twenty years and found poor pickings in sex so I don't think they can get far there; they might catch me on income tax, I am not certain, as neither Paula nor I (is, am, are) experts in accoun-tancy.

In the meantime I had placed a little of all this on friends and acquain-tances who are in the right places and who responded magnificently in most cases (although in a few the yaller streaks began to show up) and all in all enough pressure has been exerted to cause the governor and mayor to realize that maybe, just maybe, they have not chosen such a brilliant idea. [. . .]

Well, so the story goes. We've wasted time, money, energy, and emotion trying to get all these messy items cleaned up. We've worried Frank, who defends us valiantly and who naturally will, until he looks as tired as we both feel but so far Betty is the only one who has really suffered. Betty now has pneumonia and is in the hospital. Her friends turned her out of the house and I sent my colored friend Harley down for her furniture which is now stored up here. Jimmie, of course, is having a simply gorgeous time defending democracy while his evicted Betty is in the hospital. I shall of course do all I can to help Betty with all her troubles. While maybe she would have had pneumonia anyway, I doubt it. She lost 15 pounds and worried a lot and I am sure it helped wear down her resistance. I want to get Betty up here to help us. She believes so strongly in the magazine and is a highly intelligent and courageous girl. And she wants to come if she can. Anyway, we shall try to get her here for her convalescence—and decide later about her staying with us.

If we show these people that they'd better leave us alone, it will be a little triumph in itself. I shall be in Washington this next week and am planning to drop in for a talk with Rotnam of Dept. of Justice and with the postal authorities. I think it might be a good idea.

[. . .]

tls+als, RFP

According to Smith's notes, Frank Taylor, an editor for Reynal and Hitchcock, was in Atlanta searching for new talent when he met Frank McCallister (director of the Georgia Workers Education Service), who told him about *South Today* and the novel Smith was then calling "Jordan Is So Chilly." At the time Smith was speaking at a church in Durham, North Carolina, and Taylor flew to Durham to talk with her about the novel. Although Reynal and Hitchcock accepted the novel immediately and Smith signed a contract in April 1943, the editors urged her to change the title. The following letter reveals Smith's thoughts about both titles: "Jordan Is So Chilly" and her second choice, "Strange Fruit."[4]

May 15, 1943

Dear Frank:

[. . .]

I am thinking of names for the book. I still like *Jordan is so Chilly*, many other people like it, but I won't be stubborn. It has its real meaning though and I do want to tell you again (or remind you) of its significance to all white southerners and most Negroes (certainly all rural Negroes). Jordan to them (and to people who read their Bibles) is something you cross over into the Promised Land. The crossing over Jordan into the promised land of racial democracy is a chilly business. Yes, chilly, for understatement of such a difficult procedure seems to me truer (as art) than overstatement. Also the old song from which I took the line *is* "Jordan is so chilly" . . . I think it has overtones for many white and colored people and touches their imagination. But that is all of that. If you don't think so, that will just have to be one of my minor disappointments. And I am reasonable. Honest. And I hope terribly much, for I like you to a degree that has surprised me, that you won't think me too unreasonable about things. I have thought of another name. I am writing primarily about segregation—about all it does to the mind and heart and spirit as well as to the economy of the South. It does strange things to white people as well as to Negroes. Anything, *any* pattern as destructive psychologically as segregation, does things to people . . . How about calling it "Strange Fruit"? "I am the seed of hate and fear and guilt . . . you are its strange fruit."* Of course that song which somebody wrote for Bessie Smith† is called "Strange Fruit" also but perhaps that is all the better.

*Quoted from Smith's essay "Two Men and a Bargain," first published in the Spring 1943 issue of *South Today*.

†LS was confusing Bessie Smith with Billie Holiday, who made the first recording of "Strange Fruit" for Commodore Records in 1939, two years after Bessie Smith had died.[5] When the novel *Strange Fruit* was published, the copyright page contained the credit line, "Title from song of same name by Lewis Allan, courtesy of Edward B. Marks Music Corp." In her autobiography Billie Holiday wrote that "the germ of the song was in a poem written by Lewis Allen [*sic*]," and that she, her accompanist Sonny White, Lewis Allan, and another writer Danny Mendelsohn worked together to turn the poem into music. Holiday also claimed that Lillian Smith told her that "the song inspired her to write the novel and the play about a lynching."[6] In notes for her biographers Blackwell and Clay, Smith repudiated Holiday's story but also recalled that she had first heard Billie Holiday's record of "Strange Fruit" in 1942 when her camp dance instructor Carolyn Gerber, then one of Martha Graham's pupils at Bennington College where she had performed her senior dance on the song, brought the record to camp and performed her dance interpretation of it. According to Smith, it was at Frank Taylor's insistence that credit for the title of her novel was given to Lewis Allan because of his influence with a "leftist group" and, after the novel was a best-seller, it was Taylor's idea that he, Smith, and Mr. and Mrs. Curtis Hitchcock hear Billie Holiday sing the song. Afterward, Smith recalled, she "went backstage and spoke courteously" to Holiday, who seemed under the influence of drugs. Smith later regretted permitting Taylor to credit Allan and Holiday's song as a promotional device because she felt it distorted the focus of her novel, placing too much emphasis on the lynching as opposed to her concern with the destructive nature of racial segregation as a way of life.[7]

In the song, the strange fruit hanging on the southern tree is the lynched Negro. I imagine you know the song . . . I am still thinking of names and shall be glad to have your suggestions.

[. . .]

tls, HBJ

TO FRANK TAYLOR

July 26, 1943

Dear Frank:

[. . .]

You will by now have seen for yourself the various means I used to tighten up the book, to deepen character, and to give a certain symbolism to the story. It is not only a story of a love relationship between Tracy and Nonnie . . . it is the story of the White South and Negro South and their relationship to each other . . . the affectionate pull toward each other, the loss of esteem, always the loss of it just as it is about to be gained . . . the pull of cultural taboos against the desires of the heart . . . the pull of family against one's own personal conscience . . . I think it is first a love story of perhaps special tenderness, but I think it is also a racial fable that applies not only to the South but to the white race in its relationships the world over: the ambivalences, the conflicts, the love, the hate, the anger, the frustration, the terrible humiliations of the dark man's spirit . . . the gradual wearing away of the white man's civilized and humane feelings. Of course I think, psychologically, it is the story of a son in search of a mother . . . as is so much of life. And it is, too, the story of the conflict between our white culture and Christianity.

Chapter 4, I hope, added depth to the book in its portrayal of Tracy and its expression of the conflict between an individual and his physical and emotional desires, and the cultural taboos of his milieu.

I tried to give a feeling for him in this chapter, a sympathetic treatment that would carry over to other chapters. I also wanted another scene between him and Nonnie. In chapter 5, I shifted, pruned, cut six or seven entire pages, and tried to tighten up thus Mrs. Deen's chapter. It seems to me necessary to show her and her motivations, for she did drive both of her children into dead ends. You see Tracy enter his and destroy himself there; you watch Laura begin to enter hers; you know there is a chance for her however which Tracy never had. You see that Mrs. Deen too was driven by the hungers of her own childhood, and I hope you get a picture of the unending tragedy of parents and children who, driven by unconscious or unrationalized pressures, commit upon the "second generation" their own frustrations. I think the world has done this with its First and Second World Wars. I have tried to suggest universal implications in this way: by treating simply the individuals of two families and their conflicts yet in such a way as to suggest that their story is basically the story of mankind in its struggle to find a good life, in its obsessional failures etc. etc. Maybe no one but me sees all this in the book; but all the time I wrote it I felt that I was writing a kind of world fable. I hope I have at least made suggestive implications. I don't like books where points are pushed too hard; I wanted more than anything else to show the personal lives [of] two families in the South focussed so as to add certain highlights and shadows . . . . .

It is generous of Mildred to say such good things of the book. She sat here for several days typing with the tears rolling down her face as she typed. And once she left the typewriter and took a long walk, and told me afterward that she was so disturbed psychically by the book which was so much like her own childhood that she had been compelled to stop typing and get herself together. She said it all seemed like her own home town. This is very interesting to me, for of course it is *my* home town, not theirs that I am portraying.

[. . .] I pruned a good bit of the revival material but religion and race are so intertwined in the South that this seems definitely important to me, to show the deep ambivalences of our people; the guilts, the fears, the frantic attempt to grasp security by joining the church and talking about heaven. . . . And today it is as true as it was in 1920. All over the South people are growing more "religious." The more they hate the Negro, the more they fight wars, the more they pray and talk earnestly of heaven . . . this applies to the wealthiest as well as the poorest. The entire world finds holy reasons for its cruel deeds.

[. . .]

The idea of a movie still intrigues me. It seems to me almost a natural for a movie. The way it is written, the pictorial values, the scenes that suggest pictorial movement . . . all seem right. I know that it has only a slim chance now because of ideological reasons, yet there is movement on to portray the Negro honestly in the cinema and somehow I have one of my old hunches that this book might, just possibly might, ring the bell. As for the play: I know a play has a better chance of reaching the Broadway theater than of reaching Hollywood, yet I think it will have to be worked out more carefully in order not to destroy its original values. However, of course I want it in the theater if I can get it there. [. . .]

[. . .]

[. . .] I have been "written up" recently in many newspapers and magazines. . . . Perhaps this will help also. I have also been asked to talk (make speeches) in cities throughout the United States. Had to turn all such invitations down this summer and am going to accept only a few. Was asked to serve with Pearl Buck at the Peace Conference—on behalf of the Negro race. One of the invitations is to speak in November on a program with Wendell Willkie and vice president Wallace. This one I am accepting. [. . .]

[. . .]

The odd thing is that with all this radical publicity about me, I have more campers (nearly all rich little southern tories) than I have ever had in the history of the camp. . . . It is a strange, queer world.

tls, HBJ

TO VANDI HAYGOOD*

September 6, 1943

Dear Vandi,

I have discussed with several of my friends a little plan for a gathering in my home up here on Old Screamer Mountain during September. I have felt a great need to know more intimately those Negro women whom we would in a natural environment feel congenial with and whom we would want to have as personal friends.

You know without my going into the unhappy details, just how difficult it is to make such friendships. We can go to conventions and conferences and make speeches to each other, but the warm, personal comradeship that is necessary to the developing of any friendship is not easy to feel at a conference or convention; and the little gay, silly, heartwarming casual experiences which too have so much to do with the forming of personal relationships seem so terribly difficult under almost all circumstances.

So I have decided to have a party here on my mountain . . . . . and I shall be very happy if you can come to it. I am inviting eight or ten white women and eight or ten Negro women, all of whom are interesting and charming people who should enjoy each other.† [. . .]

---

*Employee of the Rosenwald Fund and wife of William Haygood.

†Among the letters of acceptance to the party were six from Atlanta: Sadie Mays, wife of Benjamin Mays of Morehouse College; Dorothy Tilly, secretary of the Georgia Committee on Interracial Cooperation; Dorothy McClatchey, former Laurel Falls Camp counselor and wife of Devereaux McClatchey, attorney and

Perhaps while we are together we shall as eighteen women of intelligence and ability and good will, work out with one another some interesting plans and projects that may be valuable to both races. I should like to think that out of this little gathering something very fine and beautiful would come. But it seems to me the finest thing that could happen would be for us as discriminating individuals to form with each other really warm and personal friendships. All the movements in the world, all the laws, the drives, the edicts will never do what personal relationships can do and must do.

[. . .]

As you of course realize the tensions today are most acute and troubling—something must be done and I believe this something will quite probably come from the women of the two races long before it comes from the men. I am not speaking as a feminist when I say this. There are valid historical, psychological and sex reasons for believing this. I am therefore

---

member of Atlanta School Board; Esther Smith (Mrs. John R.); Leala Kelsey; and Helen Bullard, publicist and civic leader. From elsewhere in the South came Constance Rumbough, secretary of the Fellowship of Reconciliation in Nashville; Belle Boone Beard, professor of economics and sociology, Sweet Briar College, Va.; Thomasina Johnson, attorney and legislative representative of Alpha Kappa Alpha sorority, and Mary Church Terrell, famed civil rights activist, both of whom traveled from Washington, D.C. In addition to Vandi Haygood, others who traveled from outside the South included Beulah Whitby, an official of Alpha Kappa Alpha sorority's National Council on Public Affairs, who also worked in the Detroit Office of Civil Defense, and Eslanda Goode Robeson, wife of actor Paul Robeson and a doctoral student in anthropology at Hartford Seminary Foundation, then living in Enfield, Conn.[8]

In describing the party to her sister and brother-in-law, Bird and Eugene Barnett, Smith wrote that there were seven Negro and eight white women as guests and further commented:

I lost five pounds during the two days . . . . . as I felt that I was doing a gay little tap dance over a barrel of TNT. The northern Negroes did not realize the danger; the southern Negroes did. All the white women were southern except one who is married to a southerner. It was a most interesting two days and delightful. It was purely "social"; we simply had fun together and got to know each other as human beings. Of course "race" was discussed and it was most illuminating to hear the Negro women talk; and also to discover their abysmal ignorance of white women and many of the problems of the South.[9]

inviting from the Negro race probably its most powerful and influential women leaders. I am inviting only white southern women (except for you) and only those whom I think have the courage to run a few risks for a good cause, and also the good judgment and tact that such a meeting requires of those attending it.

Do come, Vandi, it may be wonderful fun and maybe very interesting. [. . .]

tls, RFP

TO MICHAEL CARTER*

September 21, 1943

Dear Mr. Carter:

I liked your letter. Yes . . . I knew that you did not believe in me. So few Negroes in the North believe in the integrity or good faith of a southern white woman. It was a shock to me when I first realized this. You see—for a southern white woman to take a stand and speak out requires of her the willingness to run grave risks to her prestige, reputation, and so on. Knowing this to be so, I was naive enough to think that everybody would *know* that I was sincere if I said things which could so easily bring disaster to me and my family.

I admit it was naive; for I should have known (and I do know) how deep the antagonism of the Negro race is to white southerners, and how justified this antagonism is. I believe Negro men and white southern women in a very subtle way have much to be sympathetic with each other about. This is true . . . yet the historical fact of white southern women being made "sacrosanct" by custom, when Negro men know, of course, what nasty little animals some of them actually are. All of this sex business plays a psychological role that has not yet been fully analyzed or evaluated. I have now become accustomed to the cynicism of some Negro men; I expect to run into it; I understand it; and while I'm no angel, I am not usually upset by it. Sometimes, though, I get awfully tired of taking the verbal blows meant not for me, personally, but for Southern Womanhood in general. I don't blame anybody for giving themselves this satisfaction. I'd like to be treated simply

---

*The identity of Mr. Carter is not certain, but Smith's correspondence includes a letter from Michael Carter, special correspondent, Brooklyn office, to *The Afro-American* newspaper, in which he praised one of Smith's articles, reprinted in digest form in *PM* and *The Afro-American*, as "sensible and courageous."[10]

as Lillian Smith, a decent, intelligent, rather "nice" person and not as a "symbol." But on the other hand, I have met with so much generosity and graciousness and real "chivalry" (if you can bear to see the word in type without frothing) from Negro men that I feel my relationships on the whole (with both men and women) have been, and are, wonderfully interesting and pleasant. This *No Man's Land* of personal relationships is a strange country . . . we who plunge into it will at least have the fun of hewing out some of the paths. [. . .] I have a great fear and horror of unwittingly giving offense—and sometimes, remembering my childhood and the strange training given us in the South, I know I must do and say things that I am unaware of. If we can just keep our sense of humor—all of us! The thing I want to see happen is for us somehow to have fun with each other—to be gay and carefree. You say you have white friends in the North who are real friends—I hope some day that you can also say you "have white friends in the South who are real friends"—

[. . .]

fdr, UF

One of the women invited to the house party for black and white women was Bonita Valien, whom Smith and Snelling had met at Fisk University, probably in conjunction with work for the Rosenwald Fund. Valien wrote Smith, October 31, 1943, explaining that she had not received the invitation in time to attend the party because she had moved to Washington, D.C. In addition to expressing appreciation for Smith's efforts to improve racial understanding, Valien described a few of her encounters with white racists in Washington.[11] The personal feelings and attitudes revealed in both Valien's letter and Smith's reply offer glimpses of the value and quality of interpersonal communication that must have been present at the house party.

November 19, 1943

Dear Mrs. Valien:

It was very good of you to write me and I am so glad you did. I am especially glad that you wrote me so frankly about your Washington experiences. Sometimes I don't see how you bear it! Sometimes I want to shout at white people and shake them out of their blind complacency and stupidity—I am so ashamed of them . . . so ashamed of myself too, for I am blind at times also, blind to little things, to the nuances of human relationships. Of course this blindness is not limited to color. Blind people are blind to the feelings of their own families, to those closest to them. It is so easy to stereotype people! It is easy to stereotype one's own family—one's own husband or mother or child and see them no longer as human beings with dreams and fears and longings and hungers, but as names, and sometimes only as obstacles in our path.

The woman who spoke in the streetcar is a woman who would speak with equal crudeness and vulgarity and cruelty to her own family, her own husband probably, her own child, perhaps. She *spoke out publicly* because she believed the public was with her, would excuse her, or perhaps even admire her for doing so. It is this atmosphere of condoning that we must work on—as well as try to reduce hate to a minimum in human beings. No matter how much that woman *wanted* to speak out, she wouldn't have done it had she believed the other passengers would have turned against *her*. [...] The woman sitting next to her (if white) had a chance to speak to her quietly and rebukingly had she dared to take it. She probably was afraid to speak out. Afraid of an "incident"—we are all so afraid!

I was tired in Washington. I don't have much of a certain kind of physical strength. I am very good on the rebound but a series of speeches such as I was going through at that time is extremely exhausting to me. You see, I too am chained—by old fears, fears of "doing harm," of "making things worse"—and these chains wear out one's strength. I ignore them, I go ahead, but it is as tiring to the spirit as the chains of a convict must be to his legs. [...] It isn't conscious cowardice, nor is it "insincerity" which holds so many liberals back, but these old fears trained in them in childhood of "doing more harm than good."

[...]

tlc, UF

Wednesday [January 1944]

Dear Glenn:

[...]

[A]ll of my speech making, while fun and in a way exciting and certainly illuminating, has been very fatiguing for me. I am not emotionally very strong. I come in from these trips with the strangest kind of exhaustion that has not so much to do with body as with spirit. The way the Negro groups are beginning to depend upon me is frightening. I shall disappoint them, inevitably, as I have no desire to be a "saviour" and am not planning to let them make that kind of symbol of me. But I think there is danger here, for they are a people almost without hope, and desperately searching for "a Messiah." Even a white one! You understand how I am saying this . . . . . When I make speeches in the North, the halls are overflowing . . . there is something tragic as well as a bit funny in the way they cling to the idea of a southern white woman as being something "super." They weep . . . they are profoundly moved. . . . Oh Glenn, somehow white people must be shown what is happening to the minds and emotions of the Negroes. We have 13 million people on our hands who are heartsore and almost hopeless and desperate. They will surely be exploited by some national demagogue who will not have as many scruples as "Lillie" but more power! But I have learned a lot about Negroes. I've learned a lot about myself too. And I am glad, terribly glad, that I find myself without "ambition." I have no desire to be "important." And I am humbly grateful that I haven't. I wondered once, what it would feel like, to know that one had "power" over people. Well, I've learned enough to know that I don't want it. I don't want that insidious poison working on me. And it is so easy for it to happen! All I want is to keep enough courage to try to find the truth and to tell it as well as I can—with a prayer that as I tell it, I won't hurt too much the people I love.

[. . .]

Mr. Hitchcock always introduces me to his friends as "The little lady who has written a great novel"—which words he may some day have to eat in bitter silence, but anyway it is sweet of him and I am enjoying my pleasant, if still problematic "triumphs." I don't think it is "great"—but it is honest and I don't think I'll ever regret anything I said in it, although I hope to write a better book next time.

I dread what it is going to do to my family and Clayton friends and camp. It isn't a shocking book. If any one else had written it all of Clayton would take it in stride; but because I've written it, it will seem personal somehow to them, and every nasty "blue" word in it will be as loud in their ears as if I had yelled them from Dover and Green's drugstore. I've passed the age when notoriety can adequately take the place of commonplace and dignified relationships! Anyway, I'll have to sit and take it in now! I hope to have camp as all the children want to come back and are begging now to sign up. And I'm stubborn enough that I don't want folks to be able to say that I *couldn't* have camp. I really don't know. Maybe they'll be like the Lindley Camps who were heard to say in Atlanta that they didn't care "what Miss

Lil believed in race as long as she did as much for their child as she had done in other years."

[. . .]

tls, Rainey/EU

TO EDWIN R. EMBREE

February 24, 1944

Dear Mr. Embree:

Your letter touched me so deeply that it brought tears very near the surface. It was so good of you to write; so very good of you to say the wonderful things you said; so dear of you to be concerned about me. [. . .]

The novel is getting a generous amount of praise. To my amazement, the South is taking it quite well. That is, the previewers are. It is going to get a bad review in the Atlanta *Journal* Sunday but that is because Marian Sims is doing it. Frank Daniel himself liked the book and is giving it much space and a very good caption, in spite of the review. Rich's is featuring the book in their book store, sending out letters, having it reviewed over radio next Tuesday morning (29th). At first, Davison said they would not carry "that awful book" in stock. But . . . we put the pressure on (I'll tell you all about it when I see you for it is quite a tall tale) and now they are glibly telling everybody that they'll have the book and that it is "an honest book and a true picture of a southern town." Last week they snubbed Mr. Taylor, from Reynal & Hitchcock, and told him they were not interested in carrying a book about white men and "nigger women" sleeping together. In two days after we worked our rabbit's foot, they had changed their little song.

Clayton is taking it well. I decided that I should take my home folks into my confidence. So when the editor was here last week from Reynal & Hitchcock, I gave a party for him, inviting as many of Clayton as could squeeze in my library. He talked to them about the book; I told them frankly and as "eloquently" as I could, why I wrote it, what I wanted it to do, and how much I wanted my Clayton friends to understand my motives in writing it. They all wept a little, kissed me and embraced me, ate my chicken sandwiches and little cakes and went down the hill feeling that each of them had written at least one chapter of it. Bless them . . . I felt very loving too, and as far as I know now, things are going to be all right.

[. . .] I have written my camp patrons each a personal letter, explaining why I wrote the book, why it will be perhaps wise for the little campers not to read it (I hear that they've all ordered first copies of "Miss Lil's" nice book) and I have tried to tell them too what I want the book to do. I was shaken to the roots when letters began pouring in saying that the campers had ordered the book and that one teacher in Macon was going to read it to her class of little boys and girls. You see "Miss Lil" sends out those funny little stories about Buss Eye and the Triplets* and the children think I've written a book for them. I am doing my best to get my letters to them before the book goes on sale on Tuesday! The whole thing is completely fantastic. [. . .]

tls, RFP

On March 20, less than a month after its publication date, *Strange Fruit* was labeled obscene and banned by the Boston police commissioner. Twenty years later, in her notes for biographers, Smith recalled the events surrounding the banning and subsequent trial of the book:

It happened like this: A man bought a copy to send his daughter at college for a birthday present. He took it home and read it; was shocked by it; said it was the one four-letter word in it that shocked him.† Anyway, he was so shocked that he called the police that night and told them it was indecent and should be censored. The police went after it the next day, some of them looked at the word (and read the whole book undoubtedly) and they told the booksellers to stop selling it. As a gentlemen's agreement. And many of them did. Immediately. Then Bernard de Voto, of Harpers Easy Chair and Harvard, was outraged and decided to put it to a test. So he deliberately bought a copy at a Cambridge bookstore from a man who had been warned that he might be arrested if he sold it. The man said OK. It was a deliberate test case, you see. The man was arrested; so was Bernard de Voto; then the case went to court. My publishers, Reynal & Hitchcock of course defended it and the lawyer on the case was Mr. Joseph Welch of Army vs. McCarthy fame (later). I was asked if I would submit to having the word blacked out; if so, they said, it could be sold in Boston. I asked what else would they want me to do. Since there were many four-letter words in books I felt something else was bothering them too. They said it was. They wanted me to take out the famous "raping scene" and the famous or infamous preacher scene where the preacher tells Tracy to get

*The "Laurel Leaf" often contained references to Buss Eye, a trickster character, who with his wife Kita and their triplets, Cherita, Hersho, and Rango, entered camp life to stimulate the mythic imagination, as Smith wrote in her autobiographical notes, "to counteract in a sense too much reason."[12]
†The word, supposedly, for which *Strange Fruit* was banned was "fucking."

"some good nigger to marry her." And there were quite a few other scenes they wanted out. I laughed at them. And refused. Then is when it went to court. We lost the case and the book still cannot be sold in Massachusetts anywhere.[13]

Smith's concern for her reputation as a writer and that of her novel as discussed in the following letter to Frank Taylor was repeated at the publication of each of her subsequent books. Similarly, her suggested tactics for obtaining the desired prestige and recognition for the "real" concerns of her work invariably included appeals to that class of readers whom she saw as the major source of social influence.

Tuesday, May 2 [1944]

Dear Frank:

The party was gay and quite a success in terms of Atlanta, I think. Dot was very sweet about it, really spent a good bit of money on it, and everything looked very beautiful—wonderful looking tea table etc. etc. And they did break down and spike the punch. No one touched the tea after they found the punch was spiked but drank gallons of the punch. Even I began to feel a bit on the floaty side of life after three or four cups of the stuff and after standing for two hours greeting guests and struggling to think of the gay "bon mots" (sounds like Alice Dixon Bond!) that I knew were expected of me. The right people came to the party—except the Arnalls. I was disappointed that Mildred did not come. I do not think that Arnall* himself would have dared because of the political implications of such an occasion. But Mildred could have. However, the president of Georgia Tech came; a large number of church women and men, my brother; a number of well known business men; eight or ten socialites; and the liberals. And my friend Lindley Camp and his wife (crony of Gene Talmadge and well-known reactionary and prominent politician). There was a hush in the room when they walked in and the liberals whispered "For heavens sake, how does Lindley Camp get in on this?" Others whispered back "He is one of Lillian Smith's best friends." The answer was "My God . . ." I enjoyed it.
[. . .]
There is an awful lot of talk down here about the dirt of the book and the obscenity etc. What the trial has done has been to build up in the minds of the masses in the South (and elsewhere) a picture of me as an obscene

*Ellis Arnall, governor of Georgia, whose wife Mildred was a former LFC counselor.

woman who deliberately put dirt in her book to sell it. Regardless of the fact that the New York critics think otherwise, and a few thousand sensitive people, the masses have now about the image of me that they used to have of Aimee McPherson!!! [. . .]

I think it is very important, Frank, that we create in our advertising a new image of the book and its author. The banning has received more newspaper publicity than everything else put together. People say STRANGE FRUIT and nudge each other in the ribs. Here at Clayton they pass the book around to each other in paper bags—furtively, sharing a piece of "nastiness" with each other, just as they share their dirty jokes with each other. They aren't considering the racial problems laid bare in the book, nor the hypocrisy of the church; nor the strains in the family life; they are focussing entirely on the dirt. The book is cheap in the eyes of the middle classes—the very people whom we wanted to read the book and take it seriously for these are the people who can do something about both race and the church in the South—and indeed in our whole country. We can't dismiss them as the rabble, the fools. They are "our people" whether we like it or not; and they are the people who determine the quality of our national life. I think it is very important that we change their idea of the book. [. . .]

I think in our ads we ought to stop the passionate love story business. That thing has been run pretty much in the ground, it seems to me. There is a lot more about the book than a love affair and it continues to fix the image of "dirt" in people's minds. Let's put the book on its actual controversial basis: that of its racial implications, its criticism of a whole way of life that has crippled both white and Negro personalities, a way of life that has drained the richness from our culture. We want folks to argue, but we want them to argue about the real problems, the real psychological and social and racial implications of the book. There is a tremendous audience of readers whom we are missing because of the stress on passionate love and banning, and "the word" in all the newspaper stories. I had a wonderful letter a few days ago from a charming woman in Houston, Texas who said that she had definitely decided not to read the book thinking it not only dirty but cheaply sensational from the newspaper publicity it had been given. Then, she said, a friend brought it to her and urged her to read it. That she read it was purely accidental, but after reading it, she was deeply moved by it, felt its honesty and sensitiveness and what she called its "profound honesty and wisdom." She is an upper-class well-bred intelligent southern woman—the very kind who have influence in the South and can do things and change things. But see, she was not going to read what seemed to her from the publicity a sexy, cheap, sensational story about a white man and a colored girl. The publicity (except in New York City itself where I have had all the interviews and have talked at so many public gatherings) is giving people the impression that it is cheap and sensational.

[. . .]

Dorothy Norman* is anxious to do a piece on me, my real work, my philosophy, etc. etc. I think she will do it beautifully and I hope some time you can talk all of this over with her, telling her that you want to give the public a real picture of me and the book—that you don't care whether her story sells one book if it clears up in the public mind certain misconceptions. I wish she could do it for one of the women's magazines: the *Woman's Home Companion* or the *Ladies Home Journal*, or *Harpers* or the *Atlantic*.

[. . .]

tls, HBJ

June 12, 1944

Dear Richard Wright:

I hope some time you will let me call you "Dick," as do your friends, for I feel that you and I have a great deal in common.

It is difficult for me to explain my long silence. I believe you have some idea of the "blitz" that I have experienced. I found myself wanting to run away from all of it. I had no idea that I would hate publicity as much as I do, and it is good to be back now on the mountain where I can regain my equilibrium. Not that I actually want to run away from things, but I think too much attention, too much notice is bad for a writer or any other artist. I don't want to feel self conscious about what I do. I never have before, and I fear what this notoriety business can do to one.

I am very anxious for us to get together and have a good talk about the responsibility of writers to their culture and its problems. I see race as only one of these problems, and I think it is very difficult to separate it from other aspects of culture and personality. I am not in the least interested in political movements or in being any kind of a reformer or political leader. Hence, I find myself avoiding—too much, I suppose—organizations. I sim-

*Active in numerous civic and cultural organizations in New York City, artist, writer, and patron of the arts, Dorothy Norman from 1937 to 1948 was editor and publisher of *Twice A Year*, a semiannual publication of literature, the arts, and civil liberties.[14]

ply want to say what I believe and say it my own way. I have an idea that you feel much the same about this. Because you do, I believe we together might be able to work out some suggestions for other writers that might encourage them to do more creative thinking and writing about our cultural problems, and yet leave them free of any ideological ties.

If you are ever in the south, come by the mountain to see us. If you don't get down before next fall, I shall certainly make an effort to see you in New York, and I hope that you will have time for a long talk.

tls, YU

 While Lillian Smith had taken increasingly strong stands against racial segregation, Jessie Daniel Ames, founder of the Association of Southern Women for the Prevention of Lynching, began behind-the-scenes efforts to revitalize the largely moribund Commission on Interracial Cooperation (CIC) as a viable but decidedly more limited response to the increased pressure from southern blacks to end Jim Crow laws and practices. Enlisting the cooperation of the more conservative blacks, who evidenced concern about black militancy and a white backlash and cautiously liberal whites, the Southern Regional Council (SRC) was organized in 1943 and began official operation in early 1944 with headquarters in Atlanta.[15] In January 1944 Margaret Anderson, editor of *Common Ground*, invited Smith to write something on the SRC to appear with a critical article by J. Saunders Redding, then professor of English at Hampton Institute. Published in the Spring 1944 issue, Smith's article criticized the SRC for a "regressive" position on segregation and noted that she believed she had not been invited to participate in the council because of her public stance against segregation. Shortly after the article appeared, Smith received an invitation from Guy B. Johnson, executive director of the SRC, to serve on the SRC's board of directors. Smith sent copies of her reply not only to the SRC board members, but also to newspapers and other individuals whom she thought might be interested.[16] A copy was enclosed in the previous letter to Richard Wright with a note at the top saying: "Mr. Wright, I thought you might be interested in this. Lillian Smith."

June 12, 1944

Dear Dr. Johnson:

I want to apologize for the delay in acknowledging your very pleasant letter in which an invitation was given me to become a member of the Board of Directors of the Southern Regional Council.

I regret to say that I have already undertaken so much work and so many responsibilities that I cannot accept more at the present time.

I would also like to be quite frank and say that while I appreciate the invitation, I would not feel comfortable as a member of any organization working for racial democracy that does not deem it important to take a firm and public stand in opposition to segregation and in defense of human equality.

Do not misunderstand me, there are many individuals in the S.R.C. whom I esteem highly. Many of them have made valuable contributions to the South. There are a few who are among my closest personal friends. Some of these, I know, hold firmly to the belief that it is most urgent to face segregation and attack it directly. But these few have not been among the policy-making group in the S.R.C. [. . .]

[. . .] The white man himself is one of the world's most urgent problems today; not the Negro, nor other colored races. We whites must learn to confess this.

Segregation is not merely a southern tradition, a result of poverty, of certain economic patterns, etc., etc. Segregation is an ancient, psychological mechanism used by men the world over, whenever they want to shut themselves away from problems which they fear and do not feel they have the strength to solve. When men get into trouble they tend to put barriers between themselves and their difficulties. We white people got into deep trouble long ago when we attempted to enslave other human beings. A trouble we have never faced fully and never tried with all our strength to solve. Instead, we have tried to push it away from us; and in trying, we have used a mechanism so destructive that it, in itself, has become a menace to the health of our culture and our individual souls. Segregation is a way of life that is actually a form of cultural schizophrenia, bearing a curious resemblance to the schizophrenia of individual personality. It is a little chilling to note the paranoid symptoms of those among us who defend segregation: their violence, their stereotyped replies to critics, their desire to withdraw from everything hard to face.

Racial segregation, political and economic isolationism cannot be considered apart from man's whole personality, his culture, his needs. Neither can man's needs be considered apart from the destroying effects of segregation. Nor can the South's major problems be solved by trying to put a loaf of bread, a book, and a ballot in every one's hand. For man is not an economic or political unit. To believe that he is, by ignoring personality, we oversimplify a complex, subtle, tragically profound problem. It helps us sometimes to see this in perspective if we look at the restricting frame of segregation in terms of the needs of children. A child's personality cannot grow and mature without self-esteem, without feelings of security, without faith in his world's willingness to make room for him to live as a human being. Self-esteem and emotional security are to character what vitamins are to the body. No colored child in our South is being given today what his personality needs in order to grow and mature richly and fully. No white child, under the segregation pattern, can be free of arrogance and hardness of heart, and blindness to human need—and hence no white child can grow freely and creatively under the crippling frame of segregation.

[. . .] We simply cannot turn away and refuse to look at what segregation is doing to the personality and character of every child, every grown up, white and colored, in the South today. Segregation is spiritual lynching. The lynched and the lynchers are our own people, our own selves.

These are grave matters to me, troubling matters, which I feel must be faced, discussed, analyzed. For problems must be enunciated before we can know clearly what they are. We who do not believe in segregation must say so. We must say why segregation is unendurable to the human spirit. We must find the courage to say it aloud. For, however we rationalize our silence, it is fear that is holding our tongues today. [. . .]

[A]s long as the leaders of the S.R.C. or any one who speaks officially for it belittles those who take a firm stand against segregation, as long as they refuse as a group to come to grips with this urgent problem, I would not deem it wise to have any connection with it. I fear my efforts would be ineffective, smothered by the official attitude; and I think also that my presence would still be embarrassing to many of its leaders. Hence, with an expression of thanks I decline the invitation.

tlc, YU

TO: J. LON DUCKWORTH, CHAIRMAN,
GEORGIA DEMOCRATIC EXECUTIVE COMMITTEE

June 26, 1944

My dear Mr. Duckworth:

I have just read Mrs. Dorothy Rainey's fine letter addressed to you in which she urged that the high law of our land, as interpreted by the Supreme Court, be observed in approaching the primary. Specifically she urged that Negroes be permitted to vote in peace, exercising their right as citizens of the United States. Her letter was sane, democratic, Christian— the quiet letter of a thoughtful and honorable woman who cherishes democracy, who prizes all that is good in our southern way of life. A South Carolinian, she is southern to the bone—a southerner in the great tradition of Robert E. Lee, of Thomas Jefferson; a southerner in her respect for the Constitution and in her concern for our region's security and welfare; a southerner in her deep love for humanity.

She believes, as many thousands of southerners believe, that we must give all of our people, white and colored, their full rights as citizens. She believes that without a profound respect for its decisions our nation will fall into chaos and confusion. Regardless of personal prejudices, regardless of fear of change, we southerners cannot cheapen and disregard the highest law of our land. We dare not for whatever reason, belittle that which holds us together as a mighty nation.

There are white people and colored people who have not had the opportunity to become intelligent citizens. It is not their fault that they are ill prepared for this civic obligation. It is the fault of inadequate education, the fault of inadequate recreational facilities, the fault of inadequate homes. It is the fault too of poverty and poor jobs, bad housing, bad food, bad health, bad leadership, bad ideas. But there are white and colored people who are intelligent citizens, who will cast their votes wisely and well, who will contribute much to our region and its development. These people we need at the polls, regardless of race or creed. The Negroes who go to the polls are men and women who take citizenship seriously. Most of them have prepared themselves by study and thought to vote carefully and well. They are law-abiding, responsible people. They will do no dishonor to the South by voting. They are a part of the South, they are our citizens, our people. We cannot reject them as citizens without rejecting democracy, without rejecting the very foundations of our nation.

All through the state there has been a splendid response to Mrs. Rainey's letter. The decent, thoughtful, good white southerners want Negroes to share in our democracy. It is only the ignorant white who fears and hates; it is only a few demagogues and vested powers who keep stirring up trouble; it is only the mentally ill—the "lunatic fringe" who indulge in violence. The "haters" are the loud speakers, the ones who start fights. But we should remember this: we, the responsible citizens of our State have the "lunatic fringe" in our control. They will do only what they think they can get by with.

Today, all the world is watching America. Eyes are looking straight at the South. Let us show them a good South, a sane, decent, Christian democratic South; a Georgia we can be proud of.

I am writing to you because I believe you have it within your power to determine many of the events of the next few weeks. I believe your judgment, your decision, your faith will influence these events. I am writing to you also because I am a citizen of Georgia, because my family has lived in South Georgia for 150 years as active members of their communities, and because I believe in the goodness and fair-mindedness of our people. I believe the majority of Georgians want the Negroes to have their rights. I believe they respect the decisions of our Supreme Court. I believe they will, when put to the test, place democracy above prejudice.

tlc, Rainey/EU

TO JAMES DOMBROWSKI*

May 7, 1945

Dear Jim:

For some time now, I have planned to write you to tell you that I think it wise for me to resign from the Board of Directors of the Southern Conference. It would be easier to say briefly that my days are now so loaded with work that this added responsibility is too much for me. But the truth is that my days are never too full for something which has my allegiance.

My reasons for resigning are as follows:

1. I do not think we have a democratic organization which functions in a democratic way. I do think many of our goals are democratic, and a few of them are important. I think many of them are trivial, and one or two are positively dangerous but this I will take up in a later paragraph. Returning to our organization: I have always considered it undemocratic and hesitated years ago to accept a place on the Board when I was invited to do so because it seemed to me then, as it does now, that it is run about like a labor union. And I think most labor unions are run in a highly undemocratic way, although I approve, as you well know, of labor unions and strong ones. The organization is run by very few people: You and Clark,† mainly; Miss Mason has a lot to do with it, Virginia Durr, several of the CIO folks and one or two people whom I do not know. Things happen, new policies are initiated, that I know nothing about until I read it in the newspapers. Your answer may be, "But you don't attend the board meetings." And that brings me to my first specific point of criticism:

*Secretary of the Southern Conference for Human Welfare, 1940–46.
†Clark Foreman, chairman of the SCHW.

a. A group of busy people cannot meet regularly and with full attendance when there are no stipulated dates and places for regular board meetings. If the board met four times a year, on stipulated dates set a year in advance, at designated places, we could all be there—or stay off the board. But dates and places are set according to your and Clark's convenience largely and then we are written to and asked to attend. If certain people say that they cannot go to a certain place, then (if they are the people who are "in" on things) the place and date are immediately changed, however inconvenient this change is for the rest of us. I happen to be one of those persons whose schedule is worked out almost a year in advance. [. . .] This may seem to be a little thing. I think it is actually a very big point. We cannot have a democratic organization without *frequent meetings of the Board with full attendance. A person who misses two meetings of the Board each year should be automatically dropped from its membership.* Being on the Board should mean something both to the member and to the organization.

b. My second specific complaint is that we should have *at least an annual meeting of members of the Conference.* If, because of transportation difficulties, etc., we cannot have a full regional meeting, we should have local ones. State meetings and even city meetings would greatly help keep before the membership the important policies, the goals, the procedures used. The executive committee needs the strong light of group criticism on it. It is the only way that any group is kept democratic. It doesn't keep itself democratic; it has to be kept so by pressure from the members at large and by public opinion even of those who are not members.

My reason for wishing to see any organization function on a democratic basis is that those running things, after a time, begin to get a vested interest in it. Salaries get involved; certain pet projects of a highly personal coloration tend to flourish. Power begins to exert its influence. I don't believe any human being is sane enough to resist the pull and temptation of too much power. That is why I hate authoritarianism and totalitarianism. As the Conference has grown, as it now turns North for big money, I grow afraid of its lack of democratic machinery; I grow afraid of what power can do, of what special interests within the Conference can do if they get this power in their hands.

c. I don't think the composition of the group is democratic. I have always wanted to see the Conference a clearing house for the people of the South— the people, whoever they are; the Socialists as well as those who follow the C.P. line, the Negroes as well as the whites, the middle-class as well as the poor or rich, the professional man as well as the laborer. I think it has been a clearing house for everyone except professional folks and those democratic southerners who fight the Communists. The Socialists have had no chance to get into the Conference either as individuals or as groups. I do think there has been discrimination there. There is not a Socialist on the Board and there are certainly four or five people who follow the Communist line very closely whether or not they admit to being Communists at heart. There has also been discrimination against pacifists, conscientious objectors, and those who do not label themselves but who take a strong stand against the violence and stupidity of war. It is true that you have let me stay on, although I do not follow the war line. I have never been able to follow the line that we must get rid of racial discrimination, for instance, or unemployment, for instance, in order to "win the war." I think we must get rid of these evils because they are cancers in human culture and bring on wars. A war cannot be "won." Some day we shall all learn this, but God only knows when . . . However that may be, the trend in the Conference is toward the "war line," toward American-Soviet Friendship (why not American-China Friendship, American-India Friendship, even American-British Friendship?), toward all the forces in the world today that can be blanketed with a "get there no matter how you get there" philosophy. That, as I see it, is the strongest trend in the conference. I would not object to that trend being there, if there were strong counter-trends also that take a long-visioned view of life, that deem processes as important as ends, that are willing to grapple with the complexities, that don't hate any group of people but also don't glamorize them.

2. Now this brings me to the goals themselves and the means of carrying them out. "Win the War" has been the primary goal of the Conference. I don't think that means much. It turns the organization into a group of strategists and politicians. I happen to be a strategist myself—and I don't think a bad one when you consider that I live in the south and run a successful camp down here after writing *Strange Fruit*—but when one begins to politic, and to plan small strategies without valuing the *process itself*, one tends to compromise big ends for little ends; one tends to lose sight of the interests of all people and concentrate on special interests, special ideologies. I think that is being done in the organization. The boosting of Ellis Arnall is a glaring example of this kind of thing. He is being promoted by the conference, by certain southern liberals and by the entire Communist group. Why? I don't quite know. Everyone in the South knows he is a small man, an opportunist, a "compromiser," if there ever was one, a man of little social knowledge and almost no social vision. He didn't get rid of the poll

tax in Georgia, yet the conference officials say all through the North that he did. He made one of the most inflammatory speeches in his campaign that any one has ever made in Georgia—and he did it to get elected. Nothing he could do as governor could undo the damage that inflammatory speech caused the Negro in Georgia. He has never done anything to promote the Negro's rights in Georgia. He simply has better manners than Gene Talmadge, that is about all. Yet the Conference promotes him. And that is one of my strongest criticisms of it: this promoting of personalities rather than of issues themselves. It is this opportunist nature of the Conference that I think I object to most of all. The willingness to compromise big ends for little ones. I just don't belong on a board making such policies, Jim, and I think it is only fair to the Board for me to resign and say why I am resigning.

I would like to retain my membership so that I may be in a position to help on specific projects to which I can give my approval. I am now working hard *on getting rid of the white primary* (as an individual and as a member of various groups), and I am always willing to help the Conference on that project. I am already working to pass laws to prohibit discrimination in jobs because of race, nationality and religion. I am willing to work with you all on that. There are numerous projects that I work on constantly and many of these are also projects of the Conference. Toward any of these, as a member of the Conference, I shall be glad to turn my weight for whatever it is worth. But I cannot follow you all into the political field, the compromising, the little shrewd strategies that may become terrible boomerangs one day.

Well, this is a long letter. I am so fond of so many people in the Conference that I hate terribly to resign. But I have not felt comfortable since that meeting in New York when I heard you and Clark give Ellis Arnall such a promotion campaign and also when the Conference publicly claimed credit for getting rid of the poll tax in Georgia. That was really claiming something! And I couldn't swallow it, having worked as a Georgian for years on many other committees to get rid of the poll tax—many that had worked years before the Conference came down for their editors' meeting in December.

I am often called an idealist because I refuse to give up big ends for little ones. I *am* an "idealist," but a pretty tough one, I think, who believes that just to be smart isn't enough nor is it enough to be right. One must be both right *and* smart and one can be both. I think the world needs people who are willing to stand for what they believe without compromising. I think the world is sick to death of the little strategists, the little compromisers.

And it is this philosophy of the Conference, more than any specific defect in its organization, that I find myself completely out of sympathy with.

[. . .]

I have, however, agreed to work with the Atlanta group. I would like to do this. I think I may be helpful to them and they are people I know well—at least most of them—and with whom I am philosophically in agreement along most lines.

tls, TU

LAUREL LEAF   FOR PARENTS . . NO. 2 . . 1945 [June]

Lately I have been thinking—again!—about children. Thinking of my own mistakes with them and of a few successes too, remembering how I learned the "hard way" to understand the relationships between children and grown people.

I think, as I look back on my twenty-two summers with children, that I made all the classic mistakes that parents can make, that I had to do it the wrong way before I could find the right. The only thing that held me steadfast through all these years of learning—and I am still learning—was my respect for childhood filled with joys and love and delight but filled with fears and doubts and failures too—and dreams. This memory has kept my imagination awake throughout the years. I think it has made me feel the feelings of children, made me sometimes able to "see inside"—this remembering of the unverbalized longings, the disappointments for which a child can find no reason yet from which she suffers so terribly; the comparisons made between one's self and others; the shocks that hurt so deeply inside, yet are not formulated even in whispers to one's self. These memories and my respect for children kept me on the beam often when my knowledge was wholly inadequate for the relationships.

[. . .]

Of course I don't know all the answers. But it seems to me that the trouble is that we, who care a lot about children and what happens to them, tend to think so much about their "problems," their weaknesses, their needs, that we forget their triumphs, their strengths and their wonderful contributions to our own happiness. [. . .] I have my camp because I need children—I need their fresh enthusiasm, their wonderful energy, their immense courage at facing what you and I are often so afraid to glance at, their exhilarating honesty, and their crazy, silly, outrageous pranks. I learn from them every minute I am with them. Their roots are sunk in such fresh soil, their growth is so obvious, their minds so full of curiosity, so eager to learn.

Their emotions are not yet covered up by false pride and convention and hence their personalities seem so real and so right. These are the attributes that your children show me and that I as a grown person, feel a need to be near.

They give me wonderful gifts and I try in return to give them what gifts I am capable of: good, scientific, physical care; all the fun my imagination and my staff's ingenuity are capable of stirring up for them; a secure, harmonious environment free from physical danger and free from hatred and jealousy and suspicion; and then I try to give the understanding and insight and sympathy which my experience and knowledge make possible for me to give. [. . .]

P, UGA

In the spring of 1944 Lillian Smith had signed a contract with Jose Ferrer and Arthur Friend to produce a play based on her novel, *Strange Fruit*. Her sister Esther took two years' leave of absence to help with the technical aspects of writing the play, and Smith rented an apartment first at the Warwick and later at the Hotel Margaret in Brooklyn, where the two sisters lived while Smith wrote the script and both assisted with casting. *Strange Fruit* opened in Montreal in October 1945 and moved from there to Toronto, Boston, and Philadelphia before opening at the Royale Theater on Broadway on November 29. Reviews were mixed, praising Smith's honesty and sincerity but criticizing the length, number of characters, and staging of the play. Smith felt that the play failed in large part because of the criticism of left-wing reviewers, whom, she felt, fought her because she was as outspoken against communists as she was against segregationists; but she also blamed herself for giving in to Jose Ferrer's insistence on what she felt was a rather cumbersome and overly complex staging of the play. After four weeks on Broadway the play was in danger of closing when, on New Year's Eve, Smith learned that she had made $15,000 from the play. By investing her profits in the play, she managed to keep it open through January 19, 1946.[17]

As the following letter to the cast and subsequent letters to Paula Snelling indicate, Smith was as intimately and exhaustingly involved with the production of her play and its staff as she was with her camp, staff, and campers. Recalling the experience twenty years later, she wrote:

> You see, the play was from the beginning MORE THAN A PLAY. Never was it just a play. There were 35 or 36 in it; about half were white, half (or about that) were Negro; half were northern, half southern. Imagine that mixture! Caught up in that play! and under the pressures. Of

course segregationists were doing their nasty work, too; and American Nazis who at this time had stopped calling themselves nazi; but we were surrounded by pressures of all kinds; some of the reactionary churches were pressuring us too about obscenity, etc. It was really like casting and producing and rehearsing a play in a boiling cauldron.[18]

Emotionally and physically exhausted after the Broadway production, Smith agonized over the closing of the play but finally decided against letting it go to Chicago.

[Brooklyn, N.Y.]
January 15, 1946

To the *Strange Fruit* Cast:

I can not let our show close on Broadway without telling you some of the things that are in my heart.

I have sat in the audience night after night watching you act, seeing you grow from performance to performance, steadily improving, deepening your roles, going ahead, no matter how bad the press, how small the audience. Your workmanship, your faith in the play, your courage, your loyalty have been wonderful and something that I can never forget. When we were casting we looked for human beings as well as for actors and I think we found them. Your good sportsmanship, your decency, your good will, your cooperation in a thousand ways have thrilled me. [. . .]

Feeling this way, it is hard for me to bring up the incident of Saturday night but I think that I must both for your sake and my own. It was such a malicious lie, this rumor, so nasty really, that my first impulse was simply to ignore it for I've never liked to step in filth and that is the way it made me feel. This rumor, circulated by some one backstage, stated that the producers had set a "deadline" for some script and my failure to meet this "deadline" had closed the show. This is an absolute lie, without one shred of truth in it. I had nothing whatever to do with the closing of the show. On the contrary, I had helped, as many of you know, keep it open this long by putting money in it to swing it from week to week and by putting all my time into the job of swinging public opinion our way.

[. . .] The show closed *because we could not get a theater*. That is the only reason for its closing. [. . .] Our box receipts have been too low to guarantee our theater regardless, hence we have stayed on at the Royale through the goodwill of Lee Shubert who could have put us out at any week because our box office receipts were not up to the required minimum.

Now that is the truth and the whole truth. The person who started the lie against me did it to harm me and to destroy the faith of the cast in me. All I can say is "Try to forget it. It hasn't a word of truth in it." Apparently the person who told it was so upset and frustrated by the show's closing that he struck out in his anger. It is always easier to strike a woman than a man, if a woman is handy. And I was "handy." Now back to things that are decent and clean and sane.

Mr. Friend is doing his best to get everything settled for the Chicago run. The producers will of course take up business matters with you, but let me say here that the chances are good that we shall go to Chicago. My agent, who is also Steinbeck's agent told me what a success *The Moon is Down* had been out on the road and she is very enthusiastic about our trying Chicago. So we are all working hard to get things ready, hoping we can move quickly to Chicago.

Now one more matter! I know the show's closing is going to upset some of your financial affairs. If I can be of help, I shall be so happy to do it. I've set aside a little fund for the Strange Fruit Actors which you may feel completely free to use, if you need it. If you find you can some day pay it back, good; if you find you cannot, that is all right too. I want to be useful to you in whatever way I can.

Bless you all. You're a wonderful group of people and I've been proud to work with you and to become friends with so many of you.

tlc, cu

TO PAULA SNELLING

[Brooklyn, N.Y.]
January 21, 1946

Paula darling—

I know I haven't treated you very well but most—95% at least!—of the reason has been my hyperactivity and deep concern over the play. Now that it is all over, (and it is more like a death that one wants to mourn over than anything else) perhaps I shall soon revive something of my old life. At present I am tired and weary and sad and bitter. I am so bitter with these damnyankees up here that I have spoken out very sharply lately and my residue of good judgement (whatever of it my weariness has left me) warns me that they'll make me pay a thousand fold for every bitter word I say aloud. So I try not to say my thoughts but every once in a while they will out anyway.

I am sending you a copy of the *Amsterdam News*. I don't need to comment except to say that not one Negro has called me to express regret or apologize or anything else.*

The whole thing has been such a bitter and terrible fiasco that I find it hard to get free of it. It obsesses me—I can't sleep—things go over and over in my mind—and I know that *temporarily* I am not too well, emotionally. Physically I am all right, except for a touch of flu which has me in bed today with a week more of speeches staring me in the face.

As for coming home, I have planned to stay here mainly to get the apartment in some sort of shape and order. I have lived all this month with furniture piled high all around me, with not even one room in order. All this has been wearing too and to think of going home with so little privacy there either, just whips me. Perhaps it is hard for you to remember that for one long weary year, I have had no room of my own, no place that is really mine, no bathroom that is mine, nothing that is free from other people. My public life is so exhausting that I need desperately a private life of peace and personal quietness. I simply dread coming home and having dumped on my shoulders a thousand trivial matters that won't be dumped on me if I stay away. I have no resilience to take the trivial matters; none whatever. The elastic has at last been stretched so far that this time I fear it will retract very slowly.

You know I love you and need you and depend on you in a thousand ways. Relationships change. I think as you have leaned more heavily on me during the past few years, I have protested the weight. It is as simple as that. You have narrowed your friends and interests making my interests yours instead of holding on to a few of your own; you have made no friends of your own except Lou in the last ten years. That of course means that you depend solely on me and my friends for your life and that is hard on me— and terribly crippling of you. If you had one interest that was not mine I would feel better about it. Or just a few friends that you wrote to, and visited, I would feel better.

I know I am the kind of person who does this to people and so half the fault is mine.

*See "Abram Hill Writes Again on Strange Fruit: Lillian Smith Declines Offer," New York *Amsterdam News*, January 19, 1946, 24. American Negro Theater director Abram Hill wrote of his debate with Smith on December 18, 1945, at a forum held at the 135th Street Library on the merits of the play *Strange Fruit*. Hill claimed to be moved by the playwright's missionary zeal but bored by the play.

Perhaps we can work it all out on a better basis when I withdraw from this kind of public life. And I think I should withdraw. Whatever I could be as a leader, I am really an artist, a discoverer of truth. The world wants me to give that up and be a "leader" but there are too few people in search of truth. The world tries its best to kill the truth-seekers. The only way we can live is to withdraw from them. And I think I have learned my lesson.

Maybe when I try to live a quiet life of reading and study and writing, things will re-orient themselves. I know there is something precious and sweet and rare at the heart of our relationship and I know it would be a tragedy to let it be destroyed by constant friction. Maybe we can find the wisdom to work it out when I come home. I shall come just as soon after February 3rd as I can get my furniture in from New England and things settled up a little.

Esther wants to stay up and get some radio work and maybe do a little studying. She hates to waste this spring by going home and doing nothing. I think it will be wise too, if she can find something to do.

I love you dear. Just try to believe it if you can—and I am grateful to you for all you do for me.

alu, UGA 2337

TO PAULA SNELLING

[Brooklyn, N.Y.]
Wednesday—[January] 30—1946

Darling—

I still am in bed—still full of cold and aches and pains. Somehow can't throw it off. Have been here now 10 days. I was tired—but it was mostly emotional fatigue—not physical. I can't understand how this virus bug can dig in and keep such a grip on me.

I wish you were here to talk to me or be talked to! I miss you. [. . .]

I've been lying here reading—trying not to respond so emotionally to the demands constantly made on me by the public. You see I either feel I ought to do it or I'm furious because they're bothering me. I don't seem able to "not care." I need the pressures lifted. Where and how, I don't know. There seems no middle way. It is *all or nothing*, apparently.

I've read a few things lately that I know you would enjoy. Julian Huxley's book *On Living in a Revolution* makes very good sense. So does Reich's *Function of the Orgasm* although at times he does let his enthusiasm for orgasms run away with him. Still, I'm all for orgasms—and shall continue to argue that you should be! There's a daffy little number from Australia called *Schizophrenia, the Cinderella of Psychiatry* that is weedy with big words and a kind of bombastic air that purples up too many pages for me. Yet it is full of good things on the subject of schizophrenia and culture. Strange though how he takes Marx and smears him like a greasy finger across otherwise lucid pages. It has been worth reading however.

I tried to read Philip Wylie's *Generation of Vipers* but it was too much emotion and too little sense to make it good going for me. You feel that he's awfully mad about things but that it isn't the state of the world that's causing his madness. He's like a Mencken—with a date line 20 years too late.

I've enjoyed the Spanish philosopher Unamuno about as much as anything I've read lately. Just to pick up his *Paradoxes* and read a few pages has been good. He is wise—and that is as rare as a polite person in New York.

Bless you darling. I'd like to see you. I guess I "lean" usually only when I'm sick or miserable—but at least it's you I lean on at those times. Nobody else has the kind of strength I believe in. I'd be as happy as I'm capable of being, if you were to walk in now to see me. I wish you could. It would be fun to talk to you. I'm a little lonely in heart and spirit. I love you.

[P.S.] The sausage was, is, delish. Es says sending things to eat is a fine idea!

alu, UGA 2337

TO PAULA SNELLING

[Brooklyn, N.Y.]
Tuesday afternoon
[Postmarked February 6, 1946]

I was lying here, half asleep, half day dreaming, when I suddenly remembered that there might be a letter from you under the door. There was. And while you held back your pleasure and made it go through all kinds of acrobatic circumlocutions before you finally released it and let it smack me plumb on the lips, it was nice to feel it when it got there.

You are so funny—armouring yourself in full advance for whatever stones I may in my fury turn and chunk at you next!

I am still mixed up in my conscience about the play. My refusal to put the millstone again around my neck and drown in Chicago's dirty waters of hate and ignorance, does not leave me with the nice clean feeling that I'd like to be left with. That is I feel that the burden of decision was shifted to my shoulders so that the producers could say "Well if she would have taken it to Chicago, you backers would have got your money back." You know what a load of guilt haunts me at my weak moments always. I suppose my only real sin is my failure in my personal relationships—with you for major instance. Of all the people in the world for me to get dissatisfied with—the only person whose full mind and integrity I have completely respected!

I have just read Freud's *Leonardo da Vinci*—a second hard copy of which I obtained for $10.00! It is a slim little essay—a little bitsy thing packed to the last piece of type with great wisdom. I'll send it on for you to read. [. . .]

The *Living Thoughts of Freud* as collected by Robert Waelder is a fine skimming of the cream off of Freud. For a person who has only a slight acquaintance with Freud, it would be a very good introduction—like meeting Freud in just the right place with the right people, in the right mood. The new Kohler (Gestalt boy) book is hard going for me. You get your mouth full of jargon and keep trying to spit the damned mess out. I'm afraid it ain't for me in this mood. The gist of what he means can probably be summed up in five pages by somebody who can write. He can't. Words are to him just like fly paper.

There is the loveliest deep blue light that floats between my window and the towers each twilight. It is like a chunk of blue fire off the old Blue Steps that we used to see from the camp dining room. And the harbor has been at its most enchanting, these past few days.

My ticket home is for the 18th. I wish I could do better than that. I am very homesick and there is no good reason to stay except to get my apartment finished. Of course I shall be glad the next time I come up that it is finished. For I need to repay some social obligations. But now I want to go home—to you. Yes, to you honey, even if I hurt your feelings the minute I get there. Maybe I won't. Maybe I'll have the decency to take care of something precious when I get my hands on it again.

Tell K. to have drinks ready for us and some olives and some music.

It's difficult to know what one gains and loses by new and different experiences. All I have been through during the past three years has been of extreme stimulation—and you yourself feel that I'm thinking more clearly. Whether my fantasy life for creative writing is as rich as ever and as easily tapped, I do not know. I know the reform business puts the blink [blinds?] on the Id and unconscious. I think it smothers one's instinctual energy in favor of the damned old Superego. I also think too much intellective and "scientific" knowledge do the same. How to strike that beautiful delicate balance is the thing.

It is good to be writing to you. You think I stopped because I stopped loving you. I think I stopped years ago because if I write you I won't write books. I am afraid of not having enough libido for both. And remember when I am wholly in love I can't write a line! So there!

But I could do with a little loving for a change. Oh darling, if our full spirits and bodies could effect the marriage that our minds have always had—And that our integrity of spirit has had! Maybe the old wonderful Paula will come back too—the one so rich in ideas and feelings and inner vitality. The one who helped me through so many bad spots—so patiently and gently. Though you've never stopped helping me. I'd love to feel your lips on mine . . . and I can imagine other feelings too. [. . .]

alu, UGA 2337

LAUREL LEAF   FOR PARENTS

APRIL 1946

Since I last saw many of you up on the mountain, much has happened. Again and again I have thought of you and of each of your children for last summer was a very special experience for them and the counselors and me. It left memories with all of us that keep turning themselves over and over in our minds.

I left for the play rehearsal two days after the children went home. I thought I would be back within a few weeks and would then write you of our experiences at camp while they were still fresh in my mind. Instead I stayed with the play for six months. It was a fascinating and exhausting experience. [. . .]

As many of you know, we have for ten or twelve years at Laurel Falls, had what we call "creative conversations." That is, we talk with each other about growing up, about the world we live in. We share our childhood experiences with each other, we learn to develop a sense of humor about our difficulties, and we soon discover that tragedy quickly turns into comedy when we find out trouble is something everybody has had in one way or another. These conversations have given us insight into our little and big human problems, and that is good: but even more important, has been the resultant feeling of sympathy for each other and understanding, and the feeling that honesty is natural and right. Of course it gives maturity to our girls, a maturity of understanding and of mutual concern. It takes away from them feelings of hostility for "grown folks" and it gives to the grown folks a sense of the dignity of children.

[. . .]

I am now in the midst of doing a book for children about growing up.

The girls themselves call it "a psychology for children." Whatever its title, it will be a book written for young girls about all the things we have discussed here at camp for many summers. It will be hard to keep Buss Eye out of these discussions and probably he will get right into the middle of it before it is done. Which may make it more fun to read than it otherwise would be! I have not forgot the book I promised the young children several summers ago about camp and Buss Eye. It would be a kind of relaxation for me to write it after the last strenuous two years.*

Perhaps some of you remember that we talked a lot last summer about stretching our imagination world-size and about having with us some children from other parts of the world. I have decided that we cannot have this summer more than three and am at present arranging to have a little Russian girl, a French girl and a Chinese girl. I think the children will love these little representatives from foreign countries and I think it will add to our fun to have them. We call them "world campers" for our dream is some day to have many children from all over the world come to our camp. Perhaps it will be a long time before that dream can come true but anyway, we can keep dreaming it.

[. . .]

p, UGA

Although Smith had resigned from her position on the board of the Southern Conference for Human Welfare, she continued to support the goals of the conference and served on the board of directors of its Georgia affiliate in 1946 and 1947. In his study of the SCHW Thomas Krueger noted that the Committee for Georgia, one of the most active statewide organizations of the SCHW, "sponsored two test suits challenging the constitutionality of the state's county unity system, helped secure an equitable proportion of a school bond issue for Negro schools (increasing the Negro schools' share from $1,000,000 to $4,000,000), and worked quietly against Eugene Talmadge during the gubernatorial race of 1946."[19] Such quiet opposition proved unsuccessful, however, and because of the county unity system, despite a popular vote lead of 9,661, James V. Carmichael lost the Democratic gubernatorial nomination to Talmadge. Primarily because of financial difficulties, both the SCHW and the Committee for Georgia folded after 1947.

In political campaigns from Harry Truman to Lyndon Johnson, however,

---

*Although it never materialized, the idea for a book based on her psychology talks with children is one to which Smith returned throughout her life.

Smith continued to advocate a psychocultural critique similar to that outlined in the following letter. Her intense interest in child psychology and psychoanalysis informed not only her understanding of racism but also her entire political analysis. Always translating her philosophical perspectives into concrete practices, she repeatedly appealed to women, church leaders, and journalists to exercise their power as molders of public opinion. Just as she used the "Laurel Leaves" to educate camp parents about the importance of healthy human relationships, so her political involvement included not only working for a specific candidate but also, more importantly, trying to educate both the candidate and the public to a more holistic and long-range view of political issues.

Addressed to the Board of COMMITTEE FOR GEORGIA.
(Note: I fear it has almost turned into a speech!)

June 3, 1946

Dear Fellow Members:

I have been asked to go to India on the American Famine Mission at the invitation and expense of the Government of India. We leave by plane on June 17th. Until then I am so rushed that I cannot come to our board meeting. I am disappointed. But perhaps you will let me say a few things that are on my mind:

I am haunted these days by a little theme that says itself again and again in my mind: The campaign may be more important to Georgia than the election. Politics is a game over which we get excited and this is a race calculated to raise anybody's blood pressure. With Talmadge smearing poison wherever his voice can be heard, we take sides, and should. Most of you here will agree that Carmichael will make us a better governor than either of the others. Most of us are going to work for his election. Nevertheless, it may be that the campaign will be far more important in its effect upon our state than the man who is elected. After all, though we live in Georgia, we also live in the United States. No matter who our Governor is, we shall still have a certain protection.

But even the Constitution of the United States cannot protect us and our children from the hate microbes that Talmadge is scattering now from end to end of our state.

Lately, I have been thinking of children. Of white and colored children, sitting at radios hearing his words, reading them in the paper, listening to their elders talk. White children swelling with arrogance over having a white skin; colored children shamed to the bone over being "colored."

White children overhearing "nigger" jokes . . . colored children overhearing bitter reactions from their folks. It is not a good thing to think about.

We know also that ten-percent of our population are mentally ill or on the fringe of illness. They are people unable to cope adequately with their fears and guilts. Talmadge's words open a window within their sick hearts, giving a direction in which they may turn their hate—and without consciences hurting. We know too, that a lot of hate that once released itself on Germany and Japan is now back home again. Free-floating hate, just waiting for somewhere to turn; somebody to attach itself to.

Our state which we all love so much is fertile soil for Talmadge's words. And he knows it. He knows the loneliness of farms . . . the emptiness of the small town . . . the bitterness and lack of love in so many homes, and he is capitalizing on our weaknesses. He has appraised our spiritual and cultural and economic deficits and is exploiting them for his and his gang's advantage.

And we are letting him do it. We sit here and let him go up and down the state spreading germs of hate everywhere. Scattering bacteria over radio. If a mad man scattered germs by plane, he would be imprisoned. But Talmadge is free. I am not saying that he should have his civil liberties taken from him though I think the day will come when men will not be free to spread hate. I think the day will come when their madness will be recognized and they will be put into hospitals—not prisons—for treatment.

[. . .]

The harm now is in silence.

I think every minister in the state of Georgia should be approached, not politically, but from the point of view of the harm this kind of talk does to growing children, how it promotes delinquency and lawlessness, how it spreads hate and unrest among white and colored. I think we might persuade a group of church women to take over this project of writing to all ministers and appealing to them to stem the tide of hate and fear and arrogance. I think a man like Bishop Arthur Moore might be chairman of such a group, with ministers from other denominations working with him. But would he?

I think we could get nursery school teachers and social workers to help on this. For delinquency is tied up so closely with the hate talk and with racial arrogance and racial shame. If we could convince the people of Georgia that Talmadge is waging warfare against the emotional growth of children, we could get new allies on our side. Most white people do not think they and their children are harmed by racial discrimination. They think if they work for racial democracy, that they are working for Negroes. Our job is to convince them that they are working for themselves and their children's future.

[. . .]

Now for other matters:

1. I approve of the plan of sending Negro leaders into heavily populated counties to help get out the Negro vote. I think this will give hope and encouragement, will lift morale. Of course the men sent into these counties must understand rural white folks and rural Negroes and must work with wisdom and common sense and good judgment.

2. Other than plans we all are working on for off-setting the harm Talmadge is doing, and plans to defeat him at the polls, I have little to suggest. Except this one thing. I hope that we shall work in Georgia not only on political and economic levels but I hope that we shall make of the Georgia Committee a strong cultural force in our state. I want us to plow deeply . . . Not all our misery in Georgia is caused by poverty and unemployment; not all of it is caused by having the wrong men in office. Not all of it is even caused by poor health. Our ideas of child guidance, of rearing children, our attitudes toward sex, toward scientific knowledge of human relations have such a profound effect upon people and upon the security of the whole earth today. The haters will always find some one to hate, whether hater be rich or hater be poor. We must reduce the need to hate; and learn "sanitary ways" of using our hate—what children in my camp call "emotional toilet habits." Some of the poor and ignorant have great understanding and wisdom; and we all know Ph.D.'s as immature as children. So education isn't the answer either unless our emotions are educated. Facts are fine tools to use; but emotions are the driving force behind those tools. That is why I am so anxious for us to work on our mental hospitals, and to establish mental hygiene clinics throughout the state. This more indirect, but fundamental approach to our racial and economic and political problems may in the end prove to be the best and most efficient way to work. I know we cannot do much with this until after election.

I am sorry that I have to go away now. I wish I could see this campaign through to the end. I feel that I might be of help, somehow. Though I am sure that Mr. Carmichael would not want my kiss of death! But I have written pamphlets and if you think that a wide distribution of these pamphlets would be helpful I'll furnish them free if you will distribute them. I do think that preachers and newspaper men might pick up a good bit from *The White Christian and His Conscience*. And there is another pamphlet called *The Earth: A Common Ground for Children*; and another called *Humans in Bondage* (sent out by Congregational Church); and another called *There Are Things to Do* (of which 125,000 have been sold). [. . .]

tlc, LS/EU

LAUREL LEAF   FOR PARENTS

MID-SUMMER, 1946

Dear Parents:

[. . .]

Every once in a while, we look up from our magic Mountain where everything is so happy and gay, and suddenly realize that everything is not so happy and gay for other children in other places. And that worries us. The campers were very upset about the terrible lynching near Monroe, Georgia and have asked questions that are hard for a grown-up to answer. They want to know especially if the women who were lynched had children; and how those children are feeling, and who are looking after them; and how they must feel about living in America, and will they grow up to be good citizens and how can they feel good toward white people when white people have done these dreadful things to their mothers. I have not found their questions easy to answer and I am afraid neither would you find them too easy to answer. They want to know what they can "do." And it is hard to give them a good answer. I think the most heartbreaking and frustrating thing for all of us who feel decent inside ourselves is to know what to do. If we don't find some way for our children to express their kindly feelings I fear that they may find it easier psychologically not to have decent feelings but to grow instead a hard shell of indifference and blindness to protect themselves from questions that are hard to answer.

Well . . . we have not answered this for them too satisfactorily. But somehow we all, camp directors and parents, must try to find a real answer for these southern children of ours who are living with a problem that involves both colored and white and that cannot be solved by the shutting of our eyes. You know, I am rather selfish in my attitude toward race relations. I want to make life easier for all colored people; but I want to make it easier for us white people to live with our own consciences, and easier for our children to continue to grow as human beings. They can't grow very much if we surround them with fears and dreads and feelings of superiority and taboos that shut other human beings away from them. On this old mountain where our world is so gay and so full of fun; it hurts us to realize how many children in the south have never had even a taste of our security and our play.

We have this year a group of children of unusual intelligence and fine talents. They are children who already know how to ask interesting questions. And all of them make those comments about people and life that I find so completely fascinating. A few days ago, I asked a group to tell me what the word "personality" meant to them. One little girl, not quite eleven, said, "Well to me it means two things. It means your feelings about other people—that is, your social relations (those are her exact words). And it means your feelings about work. You see," she went on, "the way you feel about work makes you the kind of person you are. And that is your personality. For instance my Daddy," she explained, "His work means everything in the world to him. It is his life. If you took his work away from him, you would take a big piece out of his personality." We have interesting conversations together. I have always thought most grown people belittle children's ability to express themselves on fundamental matters. If we give them the chance, they usually say interesting and sometimes very wise things.

[. . .]

You will continue to hear from the counselors from time to time. In the meantime, we'll just keep growing, all we can, children and counselors together. That is all we are trying to do up here besides have wonderful fun: grow in our bodies and minds, in our feelings and our work habits and our relations with others, and in our imaginations.

P, UGA

 Deeply interested in applying Gandhian principles of nonviolent direct action to end racial discrimination in the United States, a small group of activist members of the Christian-pacifist Fellowship of Reconciliation organized the first Committee of Racial Equality at the University of Chicago in October 1941. In June 1943 representatives from similar interracial activist groups from nine cities attended a planning conference to create a national organization that, a year later, took the name Congress of Racial Equality (CORE). Although CORE founders dreamed of creating a national mass movement, the organization initially consisted of a federation of affiliates, located primarily in the Midwest, whose activities and finances remained localized. In 1945 under the direction of the first executive secretary, George M. Houser, an advisory committee was created to assist in direct mail fund-raising for the national office.[20] Although Smith's national acclaim as the author of *Strange Fruit* and a noted speaker against racial injustice made her an ideal candidate for such a committee, she declined Houser's initial invitation to serve on the advisory committee, citing doctor's orders to cut back on her commitments in the summer of 1945.[21] Having recuperated from the stress surrounding the play, she accepted a second invitation in 1946.

September 24, 1946

My dear Mr. Houser:

I shall be glad to serve on your advisory committee and feel honored that you have asked me to do so for I am deeply in sympathy with your aims and with your philosophy. I feel strongly that the steel network of segregation customs cannot be broken down by talk only although I feel that talk, thinking, the stirring of the imagination must come before much action can come. But I think that the mind, the heart, the imagination can be stirred through acting too and hence there is a reciprocal action needed, an interaction that operates on all these levels simultaneously. I especially believe the need for action in the North is pressing and immediate. Since for decades in the South we have lived in a psychological state where even words have not been permitted, we must first break down the conspiracy of silence. We must say out loud that we believe in human equality; we must say out loud that we do not believe segregation is just or democratic or sane. We have to say these things first. Then once saying them, we must begin to act. When one has "said enough" before attempting to act, is the unanswered question down here. How much one can act, before arousing a tremendous reaction of fear, is another problem of psychology and strategy. They are real problems down here of course. What areas to attack first, how many simultaneously, are questions we all need to find the answers to, by experience.

That is especially why I want to keep in close touch with your groups. I am of course glad for you to use my name for whatever it is worth to you; and I am glad to have another opportunity to "take my stand" on human equality. But I want especially to study your technics; to study each case of a successful breaking down of a custom for here in the South we have customs so deeply entrenched that the breaking of them is truly a profound problem. It is as difficult a job for us as military strategies are to the generals—it isn't something for ignorant people and amateurs to rush into. And that is why I like what you are doing. You seem to realize the difficulty of the job and to be using brains and imagination as well as good-will and self-discipline. By first working in the North and Midwest and West, you can develop the technics, the experience, the actual knowledge of human nature, needed for the thousand-fold harder job of breaking down these customs in the South. When they once begin to break down in the South, they will crumble rapidly elsewhere, as of course you know. It is the South that is holding white supremacy philosophy and practice intact. We are the steel-frame.

I especially like your philosophy of non-violence. I cannot see how means can be separated from ends, how the process (which never ends) can be judged in one light, and the goal (which one never attains) in another. Many of us realize that the man who is prejudiced is a man whose personality is sick and threatened. We know that racial hate is only a way of expressing hate that began to flourish long before the child's mind knew anything about "color." We know that anything that threatens such an unstable personality, increases his fear; and hence economic need does drive him to give racial expression to his hate. But the man himself is what we are working on. And if we want to change him, to show him better and more creative ways of using this hatred, we must win him. We must change his mind. Force doesn't change a man's mind; anger only reinforces his own, and increases his fear. You know this and I do. And that is why it is so terribly urgent for us to work out means, technics of changing people's minds, and allaying their fears about segregation. Your means, as used by your small groups, are a form of dramatic presentation. You are creating and staging a little one-act play (sometimes it goes on like a Chinese play for ever and ever!). This little play, this little artistic and creative act, is to change minds and to put before people's eyes a *new way of acting*. You are saying in this little drama that feelings about segregation are silly, that customs can change without disaster following, and that this is the time to change them. And you proceed to demonstrate. It is using drama for educating. That is what you are doing. But instead of putting your play on a stage, you take it to a real-life stage. It is rather fascinating to think about. It opens doors in the imagination—for here may be a method of teaching social change that even schools can use.

Because the strength of segregation *customs* lies mainly in the fear of antagonizing other people, rather than in the need to hate (though the people who need to hate are the ones who speak up so loudly for segregation) your little dramas—if they mitigate fear—have a big chance of success. We need to soothe the fears of our people as we would soothe a child who is afraid of a dog. And a smart mother doesn't do it by telling the child that dogs are nice and don't usually bite, but by touching the dog herself, and dramatizing her lack of fear.

tls, SHSW

In the 1940s the YMCA and YWCA were among the few civic and religious organizations working for racial integration, and Smith worked closely with YWCA youth and their leaders as southern college affiliates moved toward racial integration of their regional conferences. Not surprisingly, Brooks S. Creedy, industrial secretary of the Division of Community YWCAs (an adult division of the YWCA), wrote Smith requesting the use of her camp for an interracial industrial conference after an interracial student YWCA/ YMCA conference in June 1946 at Camp Highland Lake, Hendersonville, North Carolina, had been threatened with violence by locals.[22]

September 24, 1946

My dear Mrs. Creedy:

Please forgive me for this great delay in replying to your letter which came to my office two months ago but to my attention only recently. I returned from India the last of July, hastened to my camp where I tried to make up for lost time, and afterward suddenly did nothing but stare at the mountains and play with my three-months old nephew. I was so terribly tired .. not only from the India trip but from all I have gone through during the *Strange Fruit* episode of my life. I am trying desperately now to resume my old way of living, a quieter, more natural, more thoughtful way for unless I do I shall have no more creative effort in me—and I realize that. Indeed, I realize it so completely that I am frightened. So home I am now, writing, thinking, looking at the hills, trying to think things through and understand what our world has got itself into . . .

My camp is a sweet place and would be in many ways ideal for your group—if it is big enough. [. . .] I stand well in the town; I do not fear any one anyway. And there would be no violence. I think perhaps the trouble at Hendersonville may be arithmetical. I often think it is in the South. Too many mixed up at one time frightens people. It sounds ridiculous. But you are Southern, aren't you? The University of Louisville, quietly backed by Mark Ethridge and others like him, asked me to come for a three-day conference last year to talk to the Mayor's Group and the Governor's Group on Race Relations. I was to make a talk on the campus to all students (which I did) and then we were to have two days in town in a series of meetings with these two organizations. We did. But the first day, when the group assembled and saw itself almost 50% colored there was almost panic among the white folks.

It would have been funny, had it not been so pitiable to see otherwise sane stable men and women suddenly get scared to death—at their own shadow, or maybe the dark shadow of their consciences. Anyway, the grim look on faces was enough to make me weave as I stood there trying to talk to them, trying to win them over. I suppose I talked more frankly than any of them, white or colored had ever heard before. When I finished, I felt that I could hear glaciers moving and icebergs cracking. It was a frightening feeling, but I went among them smiling and chatting (we had a little 'recess') and then when we reassembled, I asked for discussions. The gates opened. On the colored side. I mean colored side for they had seated themselves automatically according to our taboos. The flood-gates opened. The colored folks had their day—for the first time in their lives in Louisville. They told the white folks of their hurts, of their shame, of their day-by-day humiliations, of the difficulty of moving, of working, of talking, of experiencing, of living the Jim Crow life. Lord, Lord . . . how dramatic the thing really was. Then the white folks froze. Their faces—most of them did not change expression during this out-pouring. It was terrific! Of course a few smiled, a few tried to be encouraging, a few tried to show agreement. But the group as a whole looked pretty rugged. Then I began to hold the Negroes down for by that time they were enjoying their little persecution spree. So I called them hard on their facts, injected a bit of humor where I could (it was like tweaking a corpse's ear, of course), put horse sense in where I could, scolded once or twice when I thought a Negro was being most unfair and gradually I began to give the whites a chance to regain some of their lost face. They began to feel that I was not on the side of Negroes any more than I was on the side of whites; but was for human decency, regardless of color. They warmed up—but almost imperceptibly. Well, I cannot tell the whole story. The next day everything was warm. Everything became decent and good feeling. And whites and blacks mixed in their own seating. It was like a sweet soft little miracle. Later, whites told me how that fifty-fifty proportion frightened them when they first saw it. Never in Louisville, they said, had that many blacks assembled with whites. . . . It was almost arithmetically, that frightened them. It is a pity that the director of Highland Lake did not feel that he could call his white group together and have a real talk with them about these matters. I wish I could have talked to them. You see, I feel that nearly always we can appeal to the white Southerner's sense of decency, his goodwill, if we can make him listen to us. If we can just make him listen long enough.

If you can use my camp under these circumstances I shall be happy to have you. I think maybe it would be worthwhile to do it even if it meant cutting down your number. (Especially with Talmadge as Governor! We must show him we are not impressed by his bullying.)

tls, Brooks Creedy, Bennington, Vt.

Confronting Limitations,

1 9 4 7 – 1 9 5 4

Between 1947 and 1954 Lillian Smith wrote the two books that together comprise her credo: *Killers of the Dream* (1949) and *The Journey* (1954). While writing *Killers* she made the difficult decision to close her camp; while writing *Journey* she underwent a radical mastectomy. At the same time, she continued to speak and write on behalf of the democratic ideals for which she had worked since the late 1930s. Thus, when the Supreme Court's 1954 decision in *Brown v. Board of Education of Topeka, Kansas*, declared racially segregated schools unconstitutional, Smith eagerly volunteered her ideas and skills as a writer to make it work.

In many ways, however, these years were for Smith a time of confronting limitations, not only those involving her own physical and emotional strength, but also those of the literary establishment who controlled, in part, her future success as a writer. Letters from these years document her struggle first to find focus and direction after the tumultuous *Strange Fruit* years and then to make a living as a writer.

Before becoming heavily involved with the production of her play, Smith had vague plans for a nonfiction book on segregation and white supremacy. In the fall of 1946, however, she had returned to her "Julia" manuscript, begun as a novella in 1935, and signed a contract with Reynal and Hitchcock accepting a $10,000 advance to rewrite it as a novel.[1]

The following promotional blurb for "Julia" was written by Smith for the May 1947 catalog of Harcourt and Brace (with which Reynal and Hitchcock merged in late December 1946):

> This is Julia's story and Maxwell, Georgia's story too, for Julia lived there. It is the story of a woman, self-contained, exquisite, who stirred an old dream in men's minds and fanned old doubts in every woman for women could not quite believe in Julia though every man did.
>
> It is a love story: of Julia and her father, Julia and her husband, Julia and her young confused brother, Julia and the shadowy procession of men who came to the library of the old Massey home, and left there increased in stature. For Julia made giants out of small men and they, seeing themselves in her eyes, believed in their tallness.
>
> But most of all, it is the story of Julia's love for the image of herself, which these men made and bowed down to, and which she clung to until at last she could cling no longer. For they who make images always destroy them. The day came when in sudden, horrifying violence the image was dashed to the ground and broken and lay there with the old repressed lusts and guilt of the community. Julia, looking at the fragments, turned away quietly and died. Women were glad and relieved for once more they could believe in their own sins and their virtue.
>
> Maxwell, Georgia, is here and its people, some of whom the readers of *Strange Fruit* will recognize. The old unpainted shacks of Colored Town are here also, but in shadow now, for Julia walks in the sunlight of College Street alone.[2]

From this description it is evident that in "Julia" Smith was again exploring self-destructive aspects of Western culture; but this time the focus was not on race but on gender, particularly as depicted in the image of the southern lady, that epitome of upper-class southern whites' attitudes toward sexuality and gender roles. Other evidence of Smith's thoughts about "Julia" as they changed through the years may be gleaned from her correspondence.

By May 1948, however, her letters indicate that Smith was working on a nonfiction book as well as the novel and trying to complete the nonfiction first. In her autobiographical notes Smith recalled the turning point in her writing of the novel that resulted in *Killers of the Dream*:

> After I got to the clergyman's suicide in *Julia*, I did his letter explaining why, and there was this phrase in it: I have killed my dream. Bang—. No more *Julia*. I knew I was going to write *Killers of the Dream* first. [. . .] I suddenly saw the South, and the USA, and all "white culture" in a different and much more profound way. The killers of the dream are ourselves as well as "the others" and we kill our dreams on so many levels of being: this became my theme.[3]

Although Smith's correspondence reveals more about her thoughts after the publication of *Killers of the Dream* than while she was writing it, her autobiographical notes describe *Killers* as "the hardest of all books for me to write; it stirred deep and dangerous memories." For six or eight months, she recalled, she "got lost completely and messed things up by trying at times to avoid the personal and use history." Significantly, it was only when she decided on the personal, confessional approach that the structure became clear.[4] That personal approach, the source of power for her writing and her psychocultural analysis, did not endear her to most literary critics of her day, many of whom were also political moderates in favor of maintaining the racial status quo. Accordingly, correspondence after the publication of *Killers of the Dream* reflects the beginning of Smith's conscious sense of battling for her life as a serious writer.

Her popularity as a speaker, however, was not diminished. During 1950 she lectured at Smith, Mount Holyoke, Yale, and Phillips Exeter; was awarded honorary degrees from Howard University and Oberlin; and taught at writers' conferences at the universities of Indiana and Colorado. Although she returned to the "Julia" manuscript for a few months in 1951, she also spent time studying contemporary art and "the effect of World War II and the atomic bomb on the creative mind" and became interested in "the anxiety-inducing effect of the body image," especially the latest developments in the field of physical rehabilitation. She visited rehabilitation centers and interviewed blind, deaf, paraplegic, and amputee patients and their doctors.[5]

Out of this interest Lillian Smith and Paula Snelling began their last joint writing project, an anthology on disabilities. The proposed book, as outlined in correspondence with Earl Miers of World Publishing Company, included autobiographical experiences of a number of disabled people, a bibliography of resources, and a list of relevant state and federal laws. Much of Smith's thinking on this subject may be found in *The Journey*, begun in 1951 and completed in the fall of 1953. Although work on the anthology continued, it was interrupted by Smith's cancer surgery (Spring 1953), the writing of *Now Is the Time* (Summer 1954), and Smith and Snelling's six-month trip to India beginning in December 1954. Finally the project was completely abandoned after many of the materials collected for the anthology, like so much of Smith's other unpublished work, perished in the fire of 1955.

TO LAMBERT DAVIS, EDITOR,
HARCOURT, BRACE AND COMPANY, INC.

March 21, 1947

Dear Lambert:

[. . .]

I have tried to withdraw this winter. I have shut and barred the door . . . but "those people" get at me I think through invisible cracks! I believe "schizophrenia" is better than the manic life I have been forced to live. But I am withdrawing steadily and surely. Soon I shall find not only peace externally but a little quiet place in my mind also. I have almost forgotten that I wrote *Strange Fruit* and that is good. I must forget a lot of other things too.

"Julia" has been fun to write. And bad, at times, for it tears down every wall in my memory leaving my childhood no shelter. Do you know—I keep thinking: "this is Lambert's kind of book." I hope you will like it. It is about a woman made so empty because her men filled her so completely with their dreams that she had no room to grow. In the big sense, it is a study of the role of Madonna worship in Western culture. In its personal sense, it is a quiet, subtle story.

tls, HBJ

TO EDWIN R. EMBREE

February 5, 1948

Dear Dr. Embree:

Sometimes I can scarcely understand how I can postpone the writing of certain letters. Strangely enough they are always the letters I want most to write, and herein lies the little seed of my big sin! It is because I am not willing to write a routine letter to certain persons whom I love and esteem, that I fail to write any at all. I keep believing there will come a quiet day . . . when I can quietly say what is in my heart: important things to me simply because I believe them or am troubled by them or want to tell some one who will understand what I am saying.

Well, the quiet days are stuff of which only dreams are made. This has surely been so for me for four hard weary dusty years in which little that is green has grown in my life. The coming of quick fame—how terribly destructive it is! One's friends should treat it as a disaster and mourn as for one that is dead. This is the truth. Though I should never have believed it until I was the victim.

Last year, after sleepwalking three years through a kind of long-drawn-out troubled night, I came "home," literally and psychologically. Of course I had continued to make this my legal residence, but was away in mind and body and spirit much too long. I came home, dismissed my big staff that had been trying to handle my strange notoriety and all the queer, artificial demands it had made on me, and settled down in my same little rock house, exactly as I lived when you first visited me here. I did as much of my own typing as possible, I put on old slacks and lived in them, I stopped answering the telephone (for a dreadful while I had as many as 20 long distance calls a day)[,] I worked in the fields with the men, I read, I talked to Paula, and gradually I found my soul again—its muscles a little shrivelled from disuse but still healthy I believe and pray. I began a new novel. It came slowly and with terrible pain and nausea, but it has grown and it is still growing. This week I have done the best writing of my lifetime—I think. I am terribly happy about it with that first blend of fool narcism and shining idealism that only the artist can embrace ruthlessly together in his mind.

The novel is about man teetering dizzily on an ever-narrowing ledge between his two worlds, his expanding inner world and his swift-shrinking outer world. They are crowding the poor fool hard these days. I have chosen what seems to me the basic dilemmas of law, love and the Church which our white culture has created and projected and which now we mortals are breaking our hearts and our future against in our blind stubborn agony.

Reading this over, it doesn't sound too amusing, does it? Well it isn't; but I believe it has as much narrative interest and mood in it as did *Strange Fruit*. I think, I hope most wistfully, that it will be a better book.

It is too late now for me to answer the specific questions you asked me. They concerned potential material for fellowships. I wanted my brother, Frank, to ask for one. He has done a miraculous job up here with rural people. Twelve long weary years of it, a brave and arduous and imaginative job. He was all set to write you, when the citizens of our county put his name up for re-election without asking his permission. He had said he would not run for this fourth term. He had fought so openly and hard against White Supremacy as no other county official in the state had fought (never mentioned in the Atlanta papers for they had included his name with mine in their ban of silence) and he felt after taking such a stand, after my inter-racial conferences openly held up here on the hill, that he would not embarrass his friends by running. So they rose up and put his name in the hat themselves—which is exactly what I expected them to do. I think one of the real problems in the South is the liberal self-defeating himself. He takes a stand, he is sure that there are not enough good decent people to support it. It never occurs to him that people are hungry for men who will take brave stands, who have integrity. [. . .] Well, anyway, the county proved to Frank that they valued his courage and integrity and re-elected him with a two to one majority with the largest voting ever seen in the county. Race was brought in; taxi cab drivers told how hundreds of "niggers" came to my hill, how I rushed out and embraced each one of them. My sister-in-law who fears these matters more than the Smiths do came rushing out to tell me of the nasty talk. I said, "Let them say it. We have decent people here who will not permit it to go undefended. And though I hurt inside for Frank's sake, you know how it hurts your brother for this kind of thing to be said in the South, I begged them to say nothing whatever either in my defense or his. And we didn't. But the people did it for us. The old female gossips of Clayton riz up and defended me, yeah by God they did! I never expected them to but they did. Most of them said it is ridiculous and let it go at that. "Of course she has a few Negroes out there at conferences," they said, "why not?" they said. "But she can't have hundreds, she doesn't have that much room." "As for kissing," one of them said, "Lil doesn't kiss anybody except an occasional child whom she's fond of. I've always said she didn't show enough affection. So I know she hasn't started a new habit in her old age." It was really very funny. One poor old sister who was deter-mined to do her part in my defense said "I bet it was Jews she kissed anyway; Jews and 'darkies' (her words) look a lot alike in the twilight. I bet it was that."

Well, we began to get hysterical as the comments were siphoned back to us through the rural pump. It was very funny. But a curious thing hap-pened. It was all hushed up in one week. Simply stepped on as if one stepped on a louse. I could not believe it myself; with all my faith in their essential decency I could not quite believe it could happen like that. Of course the real point is, where you are known, your whole life is known, your everyday acts and words are known, you can take any decent stand you want to take. It is only people who are "ready to be hated" who get the other treatment in a small town.

Tomorrow night I talk to the Music Club of Clayton on Writing Novels. I wish you could eaves-drop. And next week to the Cornelia (a town 40 miles from here) Kiwanis Club on Gandhi and India. It is only Atlanta that still snubs me in Georgia. Here in Georgia the rural people have treated me with more esteem than the so-called liberals in Atlanta. North Georgia completely accepts me. I talk to the various Women's Clubs, Men's Clubs etc. in all the little towns. They simply take me and my book for granted in an odd kind of way. It is all very interesting. It is only Atlanta that is still afraid to invite me to speak; only Atlanta papers that will not mention my name in the news or when they do only to pass on a bad rumor; only Atlanta. Birmingham, Richmond, various southern colleges have invited me to speak; not Atlanta. They have taken a stand against me and do not know how to crawl down from it, I suppose.

But I try not to feel the pricks and the pinches for these serve only to make you ill-humored and sore and hurt and vaguely "persecuted"; there is none of the spiritual or psychic catharsis, or "cleansing" of a real persecution. You can't feel like a hero if you're pinched, even if you are black and blue from the pinching. You just can't feel it, somehow. So it is best not to think about it—best for me—I have found.

Life is growing green for me again. For I am writing and growing, I think, as I write. I hope so.

[...]

tls, RFP

 According to Smith's autobiographical notes, the publication of the following letter in the *New York Times* (April 4, 1948, sec. 4:8), "infuriated Georgia and much of the South" and "tipped off a real battle" against her even before the publication of *Killers of the Dream*.

March 22, 1948

To The Editors of The New York Times:

As a Southern woman, I am deeply shocked that our liberals are putting up no real fight for human rights in the South. It is, of course, the same battle we are losing all over the world. Each day more ground is lost. In

Czechoslovakia—now in Italy we may soon be hearing the same old story. Caution, vacillation, no real program, no strong affirmations of human freedom—these are poor weapons to use against real enemies.

For weeks the front pages of our newspapers have been full of demagogic race fear, Yankee hate, affirmations of the "great belief" of White Supremacy, while Southern liberalism maintains its old grim silence. Not one Southerner has taken a strong stand in a Southern newspaper against segregation; not one has affirmed the proud fact that we Southerners are also Americans; not one has said that human rights today are not only the nation's but the whole world's business, and its first business. Even those of us who want to speak out are not permitted to. I cannot be heard in Georgia even in the letter columns. If there are honorable exceptions to this solid silence, I do not know them.

It is hard to understand such timidity at a time like this, unless we remember that Georgia, U.S.A., still has a lot in common with Georgia, U.S.S.R. Totalitarianism is an old thing to us down home. We know what it feels like. The unquestioned authority of White Supremacy, the tight political set-up of one party, nourished on poverty and ignorance, solidified the South into a totalitarian regime under which we were living when communism was still Russian cellar talk and Hitler had not even been born.

To keep us that way, our political demagogues used and still use the same tricks Stalin uses today: an external enemy to hate (the damyankee), an internal enemy to fear (the Negro), an iron curtain which was first forged out of the reluctance of the democratic few to take an open stand against such powerful forces. During those bitter decades liberalism was driven completely underground. Caution was a necessity, temporizing was virtue. This was the only way men could work for human rights under a system that exacted such heavy penalties from its "deviationists" as did Southern tradition.

Thus it came about that men took pride in thinking democratic thoughts and as much pride in never voicing them or putting them into acts. To speak out in those bitter years was truly the dangerous act of a fool (though a great fool); to speak out today is a mildly dangerous act of great wisdom. But it is hard for Southern liberals to believe it. Caution has become a cherished habit; conscience has been split off so long from words and acts that it is not easy to fill up the chasm between them. Into that chasm flow the energy of Southern liberalism and its integrity. We just don't love human freedom enough to take real risks for it.

It is incredible that demagogic oratory could hypnotize not only the poor and ignorant but our liberals into believing that the only way we can work out problems of racial segregation is to set up an even worse regional segregation which, like Russian denial of freedom of speech, book-banning, national isolationism, is so dangerous a withdrawal from the realities of the world we live in.

I believe it stems from two reasons. One has to do with our iron curtain, which is importantly different from Russia's because ours has a door in it. The Constitution of the United States guarantees that we Southerners cannot be cut off completely from the rest of the world. That makes a big difference to us and to the demagogues. Here at this half-open door the Dixie politicians have gathered for eighty-five years, trying to shut it, trying never to let it open wider. By veto, they have kept it half shut; by oratory, they have persuaded us that stepping across its threshold is taboo. Even the liberals half believe that there is something in this talk, for it has been a stiff indoctrination given us since babyhood.

Added to this vague uncertainty about the validity of human rights versus state rights, is the belief of the Southern liberal that "everybody is prejudiced but me." We live in a kind of schizoid world due to our self-imposed censorship. It is easy to be convinced—because we hear nothing to the contrary—that most Southerners (except ourselves of course) are so loyal to White Supremacy, so prejudiced against their fellow-Americans, that the only way they can be persuaded to move an inch toward racial democracy is by throwing them the d. y. [damn yankee] as a bone for their hate to gnaw on. It is a vast, though unintentional, libel against the whole South.

Our Southern papers and radio sustain this fiction. We are caught in a trap that we have contrived ourselves and now at this critical time for the future of the whole world, we are wiggling around like frightened little mice. We remember our psychotic 15 percent and our long, long Tobacco Roads, and say, "We can't change the folks overnight." No, we can't, but we can change liberals overnight. We must change liberals overnight, in the South, North, and all over the world if we want to save human freedom. It is our only chance now. It is only the liberal now who can win against the demagogue, whether Fascist or Communist.

We must remember that demagogues fatten on the poor man's vote and his loneliness, that they use the psychotic to do their dirty work, but they exist because we liberals let them exist. It is our caution, our lack of energy, our moral impotence and our awful if unconscious snobbery, that make demagoguery unafraid of liberalism.

Look at them today in the South: fanning hate, giving the green light to violence by their almost traitorous incitements against their own national government, while the liberals stand by silently. Silence is a poor way of changing people. It is a poor way of making people fall in love with an idea.

In parts of our South, our people have never heard talk of human rights and the dignity of man; they do not even dream that there are fellow-Southerners who would question segregation. But they hear, in every county, almost every day, on radio and in newspaper, the doctrines of yankeebaiting and White Supremacy; and they hear their "wisest" liberals repeating the old lesson "Whatever is done has to be done by us alone and has to be done under the segregation system." This is the "education" our people are receiving; this is exactly what the demagogues mean too when they say Southerners must change by education, not legislation.

Only the liberals, South and North, can counteract these doctrines. A concerted effort made by newspaper, radio and pulpit, could break the back of demagoguery in a year simply by giving Southerners something else to believe and making them fall in love with their new beliefs. Our long-range rural programs must be put in effect, of course, but it will take ten years to change our Tobacco Roads, even with hard work. We don't have ten years now. Things cannot go on as they are in Dixie. The Communists know it and they are not waiting for liberals to think it over—just as they are not waiting in other parts of the world. It is a tragic fact, but true, that people long used to one authority find it easy to accept another. The Solid South founded on the authority of White Supremacy, held firm by one party and a hatred of "those enemies outside," might not find it too hard to accept the authority and one-party system of the Solid Soviets.

Already the Wallace Party is gathering up many of our young idealistic Southerners while their elders are still saying "This isn't the right time," and the demagogues are still screaming about "our enemies in the North." It is the same old drama being played on stages all over the world today: liberalism squeezed to death between the Right and Left reactionaries.

p, *New York Times*

 In February 1949 letters to campers and parents Smith wrote that not only had her work on her two books kept her busy but also she had not felt really well since the previous spring and had been taking penicillin for a prolonged infection. Perhaps, she suggested, she should either take the summer off or have camp for only three weeks. Clearly, the psychic and emotional strain of writing her autobiographical critique of southern culture was taking its toll on her physical health. Not mentioned in her letter to camp parents was an added fear that the publication of *Killers of the Dream*—with its unequivocal denunciation of racial segregation including her bold discussion of its sexual aspects, or what Smith called the white man's sex secrets—might be more than her camp patrons could tolerate.

As the following letter indicates, her decision to bring to an end over twenty-five years of working with children was not easily made. Struggling with the idea of closing camp in her February letter to parents, Smith acknowledged how important the camp was in her life:

> My writing, the bit of success I have had with it, the somewhat stormy and exhausting years that have followed the book [*Strange Fruit*], all these have only made me more certain that from children come one's richest and most real experiences in life and one's final contribution to this world's welfare can be measured most truly by what one does for children everywhere.[6]

March 21, 1949

Dear Parents:

After much correspondence with many of you who have had your children in my camp for years, I have reluctantly concluded that we should make this a "sabbatical year" for Laurel Falls.

The three weeks' idea came perhaps more from my heart than from my mind. I cannot without much pain think of a summer without the children. But parents find it difficult to plan their summer around a three weeks' camp. It gives not enough time either for family vacations together or for a real camping experience.

Perhaps for me too it is better not to try it this time. It would inevitably mean that camp would have to be run at a heavier financial loss than usual; and also the overhead of preparation would burden me at a time when my health is still not good. I do need a rest. Both my doctor and my judgment urge me to take this rest now.

Twenty-eight years of memories are hard to close the door on. To tell myself that this experience of growing up with children is over, is a thing impossible to do. So impossible that I have to keep a crack in the door by whispering "Maybe we can have camp again next summer." But I know, and I think you know, that closing camp this summer will write "finis" to a chapter in my life that has been rich and creative and sweet and good. Of course there were hard moments and big mistakes but there were growth and triumph and experiences stirring and wonderful for all of us, and so much fun and gay silly moments. In a troubled world, whose children are in many lands lost and lonely and hungry, it is good to remember those years on Old Screamer Mountain and the dreams we dreamed there, so many of which have come true in the lives of girls now grown and mothers of children.

I hope that the idea of Laurel Falls will not die. I want to believe that we have started a chain reaction of dreams that will go on touching child after child in our South. And always I hope camp will not be full of just echoes, but that you and [your child] in the flesh will be climbing the old rock steps many a time to visit us.

I do not want to lose touch with you or the children. Perhaps even this summer we can have a reunion house party for a few days. I would like that.

A "Laurel Leaf" will come to the campers soon with news of Buss Eye's family. After all, we cannot leave them, unnoticed, on Magic Mountain. They would pine away in loneliness.

fdr, UGA

Smith wrote the following fund-raiser in her capacity as an advisory board member of the Americans for Democratic Action (ADA), a position she held from 1948 through 1964. Founded in 1947, the ADA was organized by New Dealers and union leaders to work for progressive political action free of communist influence.[7]

March 23, 1949

Dear Friend:

Once, years ago, I was in Arkansas at a meeting of sharecroppers. I am remembering it now, as I think of that evil bargain made which ended the filibuster several days ago.

It was a cold snow-bound day and icy winds tore at the little shack of a church where we were gathered. Bad things had been happening in cotton fields. Men had been killed. Thousands evicted from homes. Children everywhere were hungry. We were gathered, a few white and colored people, to talk about these matters.

An old Negro preacher led us in prayer. He stood and pressed his hard old hands against the chair in front of him, looked around him quietly, then turned away and in a low voice began to talk to God.

He told God about white folks, about a way of death in the South that had washed out the richness from land, souls and bodies; he told God about slaves and chain-gangs, about doodlum books and boss men, about cotton and long cold winters; he told God about human relations that had been eaten to the bone by men greedy as wild dogs; he told Him about hearts as hard as a stone in the fields on which rains fall and roll off again.

He paused and there was a moment of stillness as we pondered these things. Then came these words, "Break their hearts, oh God . . . give them tears. Tears," his old hand beat on the chair, "give them tears."*

I am remembering this as I write you to ask you to help us once more. Tears . . . yes; and sweat also for there are things to do; hard things, if we are to win civil rights for those of our people who have gone so long without them.

Last May, I wrote a letter asking for aid in the fight that Americans for Democratic Action, led by Hubert Humphrey, made for civil rights at the Democratic Convention. You know what a heroic fight that was and how he won it. Now as a senator in Congress and as chairman of ADA, he is beginning another battle to see that Congress takes action on the President's program for civil rights even if it has to stay in session all summer.

We need your help, and your money. Whether it is five dollars or a thousand that you can give, won't you send it in to us? It is not easy for me to ask for money. I do it now, only because I think that we are fighting not for a 'cause' or a 'political issue' but for our integrity as a democratic people and because I believe that Hubert Humphrey and the ADA will see this fight through to the end.

tls, ADA/SHSW

 According to Smith's autobiographical notes, after the first draft of *Killers* was not received favorably by Eugene Reynal she offered it to W. W. Norton Publishers, which accepted it immediately. George Brockway was then just beginning his career with Norton, and *Killers* was his first major project.

TO GEORGE BROCKWAY

Sunday [June 1949]

Dear George:

[. . .]

I hope to God I am through with race when I finish this book. I feel that I have had a thorough breakdown myself and I hope it purges me of certain

---

*In her autobiographical notes Smith wrote that *Give Us Tears* was once the title of *Killers of the Dream*.

guilts and so on, forever! I told my secretary—southern, smalltown, sweet and sensitive, and often whitefaced after a day's work on this thing—that my next book was going to be a cook book and she beamed and whispered, "Oh, yes, please!"

I find it almost impossible to sum up "what to do" so that the salesmen can talk about it. I am afraid anything I say would sound so distorted when they discuss it (not deliberately on their part but simply because what to do about race is tied up with what to do about EVERYTHING). Can't we leave it by saying that I deal with it plainly and explicitly first on the level of the South, then the nation, that I make a big difference between human rights and civil rights, that I see no possibility of great change taking place in the South until our mouthpieces (pulpit, press, radio) are willing to take a stand against segregation which not one southern newspaper does at the present time and only a few preachers; that the rural South is the key to the problem in Dixie and much must be done for it in order for it to be willing to give up the drug-like habit of White Supremacy; that I believe the whole problem of the peasant is a world-wide one stretching from Tobacco Road to the rice fields of China and the millet fields of India; that I believe white man's problem is a complicated thing centered at the core of our culture but that we could change the whole picture within a year or two if we wanted to and felt an urgent necessity to do so (I say in detail how I think this could be done); that I do not think the race problem is "economic" but that it reaches down to men's fundamental needs and dreams and values. I think our problem is not so much one of false beliefs but of a profound lack of any belief at all. I am summing up the 24 questions always asked on race relations and shall answer them quickly, briefly, and I hope without evasion. I talk about the symbolic significance of civil rights and why it is such dangerous strategy for us to delay and delay giving these rights once and for all to our people.

I say nothing that people in their hearts do not already know but I try to say it in such a way that their imaginations will be stirred and some of their energies released that are now tied up in conflict. That is why it is hard to sum it up. I am concrete and specific but I try to be a good bit more than that. In the last chapter I talk about communism and belief, belief and democracy, belief and a man's own soul. I'm trying not to let you down on it. Am feeling increasingly better. It is pretty wonderful to feel well again after nearly a year of ups and downs.

P.S. [. . .] [Y]ou are quite right, it has been only in the last 15 years that even our historians have been re-evaluating this portion of our history from the point of view of human rights. All the history concerned with the 19th century is very very white with the exception of two or three recent studies and four or five scholarly articles. It is strange to me how Beard ignored so much of this but he was so intent on selling his idea of the economic interpretation of history that he brushed off much that is psychological and human and "racial." Real history, in my opinion, has never been written and won't be until historians are willing to deal seriously with men's feelings as well as with events. [. . .]

tls, UGA 2126

TO SMITH FAMILY

October 11, 1949

Dear Family:

I have just put in the mail for each of you a copy of my new book. I hope that you will like it. If that is asking too much (!) I hope you will understand why I felt it must be written.

The first three sections are an analysis of the false beliefs which have combined to do so much injury to the whole of our people, white and colored and the fourth section suggests values and directions that I think we must accept if we wish to survive as free men on this earth.

It is written as honestly as I know how to write. This honesty will hurt many people. I hope it does not hurt my own family too much.

I am neither young enough nor old enough to be uncaring of the effect of my writings on the people I love. I hope that none of you will be too deeply embarrassed by my candor nor injured too much in your own work because of it.

There will be much criticism. Some of it will be as low and dishonest as the people who make it. Some of it will be made by stupid people, and some by decent people who fear me. And some of it will be deserved! Perhaps you can ignore it or perhaps you will remember that every one who suggests that profound change is necessary is always bitterly attacked. [. . .]

tls, Esther Smith, Clayton, Ga.

Smith's handwritten note at the top of one copy of this letter (to whom is not known) included the following: "You may be interested in getting a whiff of the smoke. The book made quite a blaze—but the blaze practically destroyed the author and her writing career."

REPORT FROM LILLIAN SMITH ON KILLERS OF THE DREAM

(in reply to hundreds of letters which cannot be individually answered now)

No—in answer to numerous queries—the Klan has not burned my home down. And people still "speak to me" in Clayton. Real friends are always friends; the others don't count.

Yes—in reply to the second question—I received my share of threatening, obscene, anonymous letters. But they have only nuisance value. One cannot take them too seriously, except to wish that we had a healthier culture and fewer people so confused and unhappy.

(A pleasant note: The librarian in my home town of Clayton reports that the waiting list for *Killers of the Dream* is so long it will be a year before all can read who have asked for it.)

As for reviews: Southern reviews, with the exception of Georgia, have been fairly good. In the North, the reviews have been more favorable than on *Strange Fruit*—though in at least half, *Killers of the Dream* was totally misunderstood and reviewed as a book on "the Negro problem."

But Atlanta—oh my! The book and its author are bitterly fought there. Not by Talmadge as you might think (at least, not yet), but by the conservative group, spearheaded by Ralph McGill and Jack Tarver, who with Hodding Carter of Mississippi, think of themselves as "the voice of the South." It seems to excite them when other southerners say things that deviate from the *Leave Us Alone!* line.

McGill and Tarver—both editors of the *Constitution*—have fought the book with few holds barred. Calling themselves "moderates" they speak as follows:

Atlanta Constitution editorial, February 9, 1950: "In last Sunday's issue the New York *Times* proved once again that the moderate Southern viewpoint cannot expect a fair hearing in Northern newspapers. The book review section of the *Times* carried a review of Hodding Carter's new book . . . Who wrote the review? Why, Lillian Smith, of course, the ex-missionary who has made a profession of writing stuff that purposely sets out to debase the South, with a fury that continually o'erleaps itself . . . Manipulation of 'reviews' according to the established prejudices of the editors is an unworthy deception by any standard. But Southerners long since have ceased to anticipate justice from intolerants. It is disturbing to find Mr. Carter's book reviewed by a person who is, in her fashion, one of the most prejudiced and intolerant persons writing today."

Here is Mr. Tarver's own "moderate" review of *Killers of the Dream*:

"Lillian Smith has written a new book and, brother, is it a stinker! It's not a novel. Nor could you call it nonfiction. It is, in short, neither fish nor fowl, although I must say it gives off the aroma of both . . . Talk about your devious demagoguery. Not only is this claptrap but very badly done claptrap. There is one chapter, or orgasm . . ." etc.

Here is Mr. Ralph McGill's column on *Killers of the Dream*:

"A thesis as warped as the Freudian cast with which she covers it. And although the Jung school now regard Freud as passe, he still is heavy stuff to swing about . . . With the zealot's zeal and astigmatism, she focuses her psychiatric magnifying glass on the South and comes up with her conclusions, magnified . . . A woefully unsound book. Miss Smith is a prisoner in the monastery of her own mind. But rarely does she come out of its gates, and then, apparently, seeing only wicked things to send her back to her hair shirt and the pouring of ashes on her head and salt in her own psychiatric wounds . . ." etc.

Many of the liberal leaders in the South—who cannot be confused with these conservatives—consider the book important and have expressed a warm approval of it. Others have been silent. This silence has troubled me, for I know they know that the book speaks truly of our South. I cannot explain it as an expression of "cowardice," or of "insincerity," as some do so glibly. These are real liberals, and real liberals are not cowardly or dishonest. Perhaps they are hurt; hurt not with me, for I did not call names in my book, but hurt by their own memories. The book is not only my biography as a southerner; it is theirs also. I think that many know in their hearts that to read it will be like turning the yellowed leaves of their own diary. Our past can punish us so painfully when we go back to it . . . Knowing this, they have left it unread; or reading, cannot yet talk about it.

Of course there are other people who are furiously angry that I told the "three ghost stories"*—that secret which "nice ladies" are not supposed to know. But the literate, sensitive, liberal group are not angry about this. They have too much honesty and humor and savoir faire to be caught in such an absurd trap of defensiveness.

*Part II, Chapter 3, of *Killers* discusses the taboo and unacknowledged relationships of southern society between "white man and colored woman, white father and colored children, white child and his beloved colored nurse."

Though a few men have exploded in wrath about these ghost stories, hundreds of women have written to say, "I am glad you told it." But many more—and this is good—have written of their deep concern about segregation's effect upon the growth of all children, white and Negro.

Do women like the book better than men? Yes, I think they do. But men like it also.

These men—and numerous others—have liked it:

JOSHUA LOGAN (A southerner. Of *Mr. Roberts* and *South Pacific* fame) wrote: "I have just read *Killers of the Dream* and I am on fire with the excitement and illumination of it . . . It was as though you had a private window somewhere under my shoulder blade where you could look inside of me. I'm sure most Southerners will feel that. What a great thing you have done."

MY YOUNGEST BROTHER wrote: "Many men will despise it; many more will throw it aside when they become aware of your reverse strip-tease act of making their souls naked. But some men will cherish it as they cherish vague memories of a mother's teachings of truth. I shall read it again but I wanted to let you know now that thousands of perhaps inarticulate men will think your labors have borne fruit—not strange, but familiar as every day, and heretofore ignored."

A MISSISSIPPI MINISTER: "The book possesses the fascination and charm of truth—a terrible but self-vindicating truth. It is beautifully written: clear and coherent; eloquent without being irrelevant. It possesses a poetic quality without being sentimental."

MAX LERNER: "You've done the kind of thing that very few people know how to do: to weave the strands of their intellectual and moral autobiography into the pattern of our times."

DR. KARL MENNINGER: "You have written something so keen and earnest and insistent and inescapable that there is only one recourse for the reader who doesn't want to find out disturbing things about his own self-deception and his own guilt feelings. He must close the book; he must say it is impractical, hysterical, exaggerated, Freudianized, etc. This won't relieve his feelings; he still knows you are right, and he knows that your rightness got under his skin and made him worry about something. For some readers, the net effect will make him feel better; he will say, 'At last it has been said; it has been explained, at least partially; it has been clarified.' . . . This is a social diagnosis by a keen physician who knows the disease from personal experience, and having cured herself, is pointing a way for others to follow, if they have the guts."

And the northern readers?

They tell me that in some northern bookstores, people go in, pick up the book, look at it, fascinated as if gazing at a rattlesnake, and walk out again. Why? Perhaps because they fear that they, too, will find in this book their childhood. It has been a luxurious thing to bask in complacency, seeing race relations as Dixie's problem. It comes as a shock, maybe, to realize that our American beliefs, north and south, are twisted together; that "sin and sex and segregation" do really have something to do with each other; that segregation and over-esteem of skin color have to do with our hearts and our bodies and our religious beliefs as well as with our money and geography and a war fought long ago.

Is it being read? Yes. 20,000 were sold immediately; then about 10,000 more. And suddenly, nothing more happened. It looked as if the blanket of silence had done what the book's enemies wanted it to do. But, a few weeks ago, it began to stir. People are getting over their first shock, are asking each other questions: "What do you think of that chapter on southern women? Do you agree with Lillian Smith about the lessons taught in childhood? Isn't she wrong about Two Men and a Bargain? Did you too have that experience in Trembling Earth? And so on. Ministers have begun to preach sermons on "the dream and its killers"; psychiatrists have begun to argue with each other about it; and teachers are discussing it in their classrooms, and maybe soon, those two college libraries in Atlanta will find the courage to put it on their shelves . . .

Since Christmas, many of its first readers have been asking: "What can we do to get the book read?" "It can bring about change in the only way that change should ever come: by changing men's minds and expanding their imaginations," said a college president. "But hundreds of thousands must read it to do this. And there is a curious ignoring of the book in North as well as South."

An author cannot compel people to read her book. All she can do is write it—and wait.

It is so close to me, too close to write about easily. I wanted it to do so much. Not "reform the South"—I am not interested in quick panaceas. I wanted, by laying bare my own childhood experiences, to help others understand this strange ceremonial we call "segregation": to see it not as racial segregation but as a profound withdrawal from life, a denial of reality. I wanted to say aloud that the concept of segregation has no validity for our new world; that we can no longer lean on walls that do not exist. This is the age of whole men, living in a whole world. I wanted my book to give insight, to stir imaginations, so that we can accept ourselves and all the earth's people as human beings, and once accepting, can go on with the job of making our new world—a world of open spaces with no walls in minds or between nations to throw their shadows across our children's lives. That was my dream.

Odds and Ends:

I am now back on my novel. It is a long novel and I have been willing to let it grow slowly. In between work periods on it I am writing a movie titled *Susanna and Her Sons*. It is about the Wesley family, the founders of the Methodist Church. I have fallen in love with that family, with John and Charles—who were so concerned with the common man's uncommon soul—and with their amazing mother.

A librarian at Wickenburg, Arizona, reports that a very young boy stared long at *Killers of the Dream*, and finally said wistfully, "Oh boy, I bet that would be a good murder story."

Publication rights have been sold in Italy, Denmark and England and the book will soon be in print in those countries.

p, UGA 1283A

TO STELLA S. CENTER

August 28, 1950

My dear Miss Center:

I feel deeply grateful to you and your committee for honoring me with the Southern Author's Award, and I do want to thank you for writing me such a nice letter about it.*

[. . .]

You may be interested in the curious sense of pride which many of my fellow Georgians seem to have in my having been given the award. The

---

*The Southern Award recognized "the best book on the South by a southern author" and was given annually by the Southern Women's Democratic Organization in New York, whose purpose was to honor southern letters. Stella Center, a native Georgian who had known Smith and Snelling through their magazine, was in charge of administering the award.[8]

book itself had aroused a terrific fight in the Georgia press—much more than *Strange Fruit* received. It cut more deeply into our southern memories, raised more troubling questions than did *Strange Fruit* and then it was autobiography not fiction—and hence gave readers no quick escape from its implications. I had had quite a winter of being beaten down by the newspapers when your award was announced. Then suddenly to my surprise the Atlanta *Constitution Journal* gave a very nice account of it with my photograph (one of the good photographs[,] not one of the bad ones which they usually use) and many Georgians wrote me letters of congratulations, my own county newspaper did a good job of it and well, I suddenly realized that Georgia was glad; glad that a fellow-Georgian had received it; glad to be able to say to the North "You see! We aren't so bad after all; after all, we've given Lillian Smith the Southern Award for the book. Now what more could we do!" They felt *they* had given the award; they felt that through you and the southerners who had adjudged the books that they had spoken to the whole world. It is really a curious thing. How strange and wonderful our southern mind is! [. . .]

tlc, UGA

Smith wrote the following letter to Paula Snelling after appearing on the NBC television show "It's a Problem," a thirty-minute panel discussion of "serious problems of daily life" aired weekdays and produced by Phyllis Adams.[9] The other guest on the program was Anna Arnold Hedgeman, a pioneer black leader in politics and public administration who was then assistant to the administrator of the Federal Security Agency.[10]

[Brooklyn, N.Y.]
Thursday [June 18, 1952]

Paulie,

[. . .]

Everyone liked the show. Bird called this a.m. to tell me she saw it in White Plains. And that many of her friends had called to say it was one of the best television shows they had ever seen. Of course those who didn't like it will be the first to tell Phyllis Adams how *they* felt. The nice people will not do it—unfortunately.

Elizabeth Otis and I had supper together last night.* It seems that I am on a list of "communists" that Congress has just "moved" to investigate

*Smith's literary agent.

because of the foundations who gave "us" fellowships are tax-exempt! You and Ralph McGill were left off the Rosenwald list (of communists)! I am on it, side by side with some *real* honest to god (like DuBois) commies, I am sorry to say. I was listed in the group of "Communists and Communist-front" people and since I was called one by Cox I may be able to sue him for libel. We'll see. All this is done by Eugene Cox from Georgia and most of it on a racial level.* Congress apparently has allocated the money for the investigation. Elizabeth seemed very disturbed (Steinbeck is on it too—on another foundation) but I laughed it off. Somehow it doesn't matter. They are doing it to try to kill out the liberal writers' audiences—that is the real idea, of course—so that magazines will be "afraid" to publish our work, and to keep readers from reading our books. And in that, they *may* succeed. But the issue is so big that one can't take it personally. Of course, I *hope* they will ask me to testify—or whatever you call it in Congress. What a wonderful speech I could make! Wouldn't it be fine to have the chance to tell the world how I felt!

[. . .]

Eliz. is anxious for me to do the piece on what America means to me. For several reasons I suspect! But it might be very good timing for it. So I am going to work on it today and tomorrow.

I miss you, darling. Your leg work! As well as your self and your beautiful clear mind and sense of values and comforting companionship. I always prize you especially much when I get off where I can see you whole and clear. You are a very fine piece of humanity—your faults are so awfully small—it is strange that I can get so bothered—but maybe you can understand if you remember how one gnat or sandfly or mosquito can bother you so much that you can't enjoy the moonlight and mountains and stars all around you. Sometimes it is like that with me when I stay too long too close. But it is my intolerance and my inability to accept the whole of those I love. Not your faults. My own are much more unbearable I honestly know.

[. . .]

Pauli Murray called. I am letting her come over maybe Friday night to

*Known for his opposition to New Deal legislation, Edward Eugene Cox was a U.S. congressman from Georgia's Second District from 1924 until his death in December 1952. At the time of his death he was heading an investigation into "possible subversive activities of educational and other tax-free organizations."[11]

talk over her book. After all, people have to help the beginners. She is a brilliant girl, a really brilliant one and maybe I can help.*

Have not done one thing about rehab. or Martha Graham. I thought maybe she'd call me. I suppose she isn't going to, so I'll call her soon. You know how I hate to; it is like calling camp mothers. I shall get out to Kessler too.† I'll *make* myself. [. . .]

I love you.

[. . .]

Thursday p.m.

P.S. It really was Ann who stole the show. Actually, my own part would have been better, more subtle in a philosophical way, but she got the bit between her teeth—she had a wonderful story to tell them—and I didn't ever get a chance to tell *my* story—not really. I told enough to surround *her* with the right attitude of sympathy. But white people *don't want* to think *whites* are hurt by segregation: *that* fact isn't as "important" to them or as dramatic as *Ann's* being hurt *as a Negro*. So it was she who got the attention, though I planned it and set it for her. Perhaps I should not mind. It was a terrific show. The *New Yorker* is interviewing Phyllis Adams on it. I am not going to get credit for planning it, I fear. It turned out too successfully. Phyllis will take the credit—though she gave it to me fully the day of the show—for the idea and Ann will get it for the show itself. So Lillie will take a back seat on this one—as she has on everything racial, during the past few years! [. . .] It was *such* a success and so completely my idea that I just sort of would have liked to be remembered as having originated it. [. . .]

alu, UGA 2337

The following letter is significant for its depiction of the relationship between Snelling and Smith, especially Smith's concerns for the quality and

*Correspondence from Pauli Murray to LS began at least as early as 1942, when Murray was a law student at Howard University, Washington, D.C., a dedicated civil rights activist, and an enthusiastic promoter of *South Today*. The Smith/Murray correspondence indicates that Smith had encouraged and advised Murray about her writing even before she began writing *Proud Shoes*.[12] In her autobiography Murray described the 1944 publication of her poem "Dark Testament" in *South Today* as "a great boost to my literary fortune."[13]

†Kessler Institute for Rehabilitation, New York City, was one of the centers LS visited for the proposed anthology on disabilities.

nature of their relationship after neither the magazine nor the camp existed as employment for Snelling. Smith's fear that her own success as a writer had stifled Snelling's creativity would continue until Snelling found her own work ten years later. Until then, Smith wrestled alternately with her need for psychic space, her need for Snelling's companionship, and, especially after cancer surgery, her increasing financial needs. Her suggestion that Snelling write about their relationship and that "*it* might be *the* masterpiece," while intriguing, seems somewhat ironic. It implies an awareness of the importance of acknowledging the significance of sexuality in creative work in a way that Smith herself seemed unwilling to explore openly.

TO PAULA SNELLING

> [Hotel Margaret]
> [Brooklyn, N.Y.]
> Friday [June 19, 1952]

Paula—

What a nice letter you write me! It did you good to go through the old letters, didn't it. The picture of you swung me back through the years. You were so darned cute and attractive. You are "sweeter," "finer" now but you had something then that was so *young* and—nice, that bi-sexual charm which no one dares admit is seductive—except in real life.

I am sorry my letters are burned, that is my ambivalence. My shame about something different and completely good. It has been that shame that has destroyed the keen edge of a pattern of love that was creative and good. Blurring it, dulling it. . . .

You wrote better, then, than I did. You attained your excellence early in life and held it. I was late even beginning to grow outwardly—and I still believe I have growth in me! But it is a shame that my growth stopped yours—or stopped your expressing yourself on your *already high level*. And that has been one of my deep disappointments and frustrations: for *you* have not profited as much from our relationship as have I, although in many ways you have been more content in it than I. But your contentment may not be as real as you think: its vegetative qualities cause me to think that perhaps it has been sometimes a facade. Not as deep as it should be. Yet, it may be your way of life. I am not sure. Still, it does not seem "right" or even "healthy" for you to try, through a kind of osmosis, to give to the world through me. A little, yes; even a lot. But your own unique experiences of life cannot be expressed through me or through my creativity. It is lost that way. Only that part of it by which you help me find my expression of my experience. Your own still remains unexpressed. Perhaps you want to go to your grave with your "secrets" but I don't think so. It is not in your family tradition to express. But you are different. And you should, once more, make the effort. When this book [*The Journey*] is finished, and the anthology, and we see a break ahead, you should begin. However esoteric or strange or special, you should put down your feelings about you and me and life. What it has meant to you. What this relationship has meant. *It* might be *the* masterpiece, not my poor little attempts to tell the world how to be good. I hope I can finally stop doing it. (telling it to be good) It is my vice, creatively. Yet I seem compelled [. . .]. You aren't. So why not try? Each evening before you go to sleep—or in the first hour each morning. If you write only a page, a half page, a paragraph. You need not show it to me. My criticisms blast you dry. I know it. I, at the moment, always think you can "take it," then I realize you can't. But don't show me—until you want to. But do it, for God's sake! Part of my trouble[,] my sudden pleas for you to "get on your own" is for *you*, darling—not just for me. I feel that I am ruining something delicate and fine in you, *your* creativity. (I know how much you help me but I don't want it at the price of destroying *your* individuality) and I use every precipitating issue to "say it again." The money issue is part of it, of course; but only a part. I know you more than "earn" all I give you which is a very very little bit. But it is what it does to the "inner you" that bothers me so. And the fact that your life narrows down to so small an orbit. You should have your own friends, your interests, your special group of appreciators who should not appreciate *you* by derogating me, as they now do but for you, yourself. And that is why I urge separations: we can see each other in the whole only that way. Not when we are tied back to back, or even front to front—postural positions that don't make for insight and clear vision.

[. . .] We should have, as Virginia Woolf said "a room of one's own." You need it even more than I do—though you don't know it. I take what I need when my need grows too intense—though I take it in the wrong way. And when I refuse to take it, I sicken, as you know. My sickening is always the sign that things are not well with me inside. Your "dependency," your refusing to make decisions is your refusal to assume the risk of making mistakes, is *your* signal that all is not well with you.

The separations are good and necessary and yet so hard to effect. But they could take place so easily if only we could see more clearly what *you* are doing for me and *I* am doing for you; and if we could see what we are doing *to* each other. Actually, I could not live on the mt. alone if you were not there. I would have to have a secretary live with me. I could not endure it, as you well know. But the thing that least fits *your* needs is for you to be "my secretary"—and it is a terrible title for a brilliant, wise woman like you. And that shames me and makes me feel that I am doing wrong to you—and yet— And so I grow angry and want to destroy us *both*. If you could do enough— anthologies—reviews—to make your own living so you would feel independent of me. Sharing the mountain with me—doing your share of the home chores. But independent. Then if I could pay you a definite sum of money for definite jobs: like, for instance, (a) $1000 a year for doing my income tax and gov. reports (b) (Maybe $2000 a year in the best years for keeping my bookkeeping records and income tax etc.) (c) $1000 a year for answering my phone calls and being my buffer and keeping up with speeches and things like that.

Then—if you *were* doing something creative on your own, like the anthologies—and a few reviews—for which you received a little money of your own—I'd have the feeling that you were building something for *you* and not all of you were going into my work—work that you weren't getting any "credit" for.

[. . .]*

als, UGA 2337

TO LEWIS GANNETT

Thursday, December 10, 1953

Dear Lewis:

[. . .] [W]hile I still feel that I am living on borrowed time, as the months pass the surgeon becomes surer and surer that he has outwitted the malignancy, at least for a while, anyway. It is odd to be "handicapped" and have to learn to use my arm with two thirds of my shoulder muscles removed. But it has been fun to see what I can do; how fast I can find new muscles to take over the old work.

I was writing this book at the time it was discovered. The one that will be out in the spring, called *The Journey*. I had been working on my novel, the one I have been on for many years when suddenly, two years ago, I laid it aside and decided I had to find out what life is about; what it is about for

---

*The remaining two paragraphs of the letter were written as Smith's "moral will," in which she left the royalties from her books and the property on Screamer Mountain to Paula Snelling for her use as long as she lived and which named Snelling as executor of her literary properties. The passage has been omitted to respect the privacy of family members also mentioned therein.

me, anyway. I knew what I did not believe; I thought I even knew what was "wrong with things" but I did not know what I believed nor did I know what is "right with things." So I journeyed forth to find out. This book is what I found. I was deep in it, when I began to realize that I was not well. I called it fatigue as long as I could, then went to a surgeon and was told that I had a malignancy of the breast which had gone too too long; only a radical operation could save me. I protested, wanting so much to finish my book and fearing the operation might be more than my old organism could take. As I went under anesthesia I can hear that surgeon saying: "Remember, it is going to be wonderful for the book. You will understand now what ordeal is really about." And that is all I remembered until I awoke, very much alive and part of the world.

Aren't these things strange? Cancer is the only big fear I had ever had. Always I had felt I could take anything but that. And that is what I had to take. But more strange is the strength that comes from somewhere, deep-down in the soma, maybe; deepdown in family tradition, maybe. I remembered, suddenly, Mother; remembered suddenly Dad; both of whom when faced with tragic events had always been so quietly assured and full of faith. I did not have their kind of faith. I had to make do with what we'd call "fortitude" I guess. But it helped, the remembering of them. And I began to see a bit more clearly what death is about; just a little; I am not inclined to be mystical and I have to talk and think in human words since I know no other. But some of it came a bit more clear, anyway, during those hard lonely months, the nights . . . such plain homespun experiences these matters are, this thing, death; this thing, maiming; this thing, constant danger; but we avoid and avoid and avoid, and then suddenly here it is: "Your turn now" it says. And you have to find something, then; something to take you through it without losing your nerve and your love of life and all the rest of it.

So—when I read your letter, and the enclosure about the young girl in Germany, I thought, Yes, she wants what we all want: peace, security, rest from ordeal. And yet life is ordeal; oh, God, yes, it is fun too; marvelous fun; but it is made up of crises; of sudden breaks; of trouble. And somehow, we have to learn to accept: accept the misery and poverty and ignorance and disease and the hate that tears a man's life to pieces; and in the accepting, try to understand its meaning. Shelley said it long ago but it is as true now as then that the imagination is the great instrument of morality. We cannot be good people unless we look at life at its highest and its lowest, its most absurd and most reasonable, at its cruelest and its most tender. Being human is becoming more and more aware of human experience, feeling it, probing it, sharing it. I believe that. I believe a good man is a man with a fine imagination. Without the imagination that can reach high and low and close and far, how can he be good? Without sharing, how can he understand bitter poverty and fear and cruelty and hate and ignorance and all the rest of it?

But of course there are times when we can take no more. We must have something to cheer us, to divert, amuse. But we should not ask our serious artists and novelists to be "good therapy" for us; nor should we ask them to show us the "best America"—whatever that is. It isn't fair to ask an artist to do anything but reveal to us human experience as he knows it; as he has felt it, dreamed it, experienced it. Faulkner is not America's press agent; which one of us would really want to play that role? Not I. For though we have tender, compassionate, loving, wise and mature people we also have the Joe McCarthys, the Jeeters, and the criminals, the psychotics and the lost children. . . . The writer, the novelist, the artist can only tell us about one man, one woman, one child; one experience—and always it is himself that he reveals. Faulkner does not "reveal" the South; he reveals his own deep dreams, and lets them walk through his pages costumed in southern dialect and southern clothes and southern incidents; but deepdown, it is Faulkner. And whatever greatness he has—and I am not sure that he is great though I know he is talented—lies in the beauty and terror, the utterly new thing that he makes of his vision of life. This vision he has given us I have been profoundly stirred by. I am grateful for him; grateful that he has given us his unique and, at times, truly wonderful vision of human experience.

Now to be helpful: I am not sure I can be. But I would suggest that this young German girl read:

1. Some of our autobiographies and learn to accept Americans as human beings, good and bad, lost and secure, groping and grasping and sometimes giving the best they have to others. Justice Warren Douglas's book, Mrs. Roosevelt's, [. . .], Lindbergh, James Weldon Johnson.

2. I would also suggest that she read some of our books written for teen-agers. [. . .] Your young German friend will get a good picture of pleasant American life from these books. It will not be true of all of us; but what is there, will be true.

3. The third kind of book I suggest is that written by people like Betsy Barton or Louise Baker about their special ordeal and how they came

through it. [. . .] They are success stories; America at its best, perhaps; for it is in this country that so much has been done to accept the different person, the so-called "disabled person." But when this young woman reads about Louise Baker's losing her leg when she was eight years old she must not think all American children lose their legs with their milk teeth. She must try not to draw broad generalizations about 160 million people from reading about one person, or ten, or fifty even. Perhaps she is at fault as much as our writers? Faulkner, for instance, does not claim that he is putting down a factual picture of a small southern town. He simply says, as all story-tellers say, "I have a story, would you like to hear it?" And you read it because you want to hear it. And when it is done, it may be just a story; or it may suddenly give an amazing X-ray of human nature; it may make you draw in your breath suddenly and whisper "This is *me*." Great story tellers show us an image of themselves, their deepdown selves, but they show us a picture of us, too. Always, like an after-image, a visual echo, we see ourselves as we listen.

[. . .]

I believe we shall develop a new kind of book, written largely for foreign consumption, honest, sensitive, real, which tells about ordinary life as it is lived by young men, young women, in various parts of the country. Something similar to the Rau books written by the young Indian about her home, her customs, her grandma et cetera. I doubt that Indians like that book. But Americans do. Nora Waln wrote in the *House of Exile* a wonderful account of her many years in a wealthy Chinese country home where she was the "adopted daughter." Do you remember it? I doubt that Chinese today would approve of it; but it was a valid picture of Chinese life in that particular home and was good for Americans. Everybody is so defensive, today; they do not want truth, they want an idealized picture of their country portrayed. [. . .]

tls, HU

Lillian Smith's friendship with Carson McCullers and her husband Reeves began in New York when they visited with each other several times during 1951 and 1952. Smith had just completed *The Journey* when McCullers came to visit her on November 17, 1953. Having recently left Reeves in Paris because of his alcoholism, McCullers was working on an article about Georgia for *Holiday* magazine. Her visit with Smith ended tragically only hours after it had begun when McCullers's sister called to say that Reeves had killed himself.[14]

In the following letter Smith takes the mundane occasion of writing a thank-you note to express not only solace for her friend's grief but also profound wisdom for living. Smith's advice to McCullers about heeding her inner knowledge concerning the reality of her relationship with Reeves, letting go what had ended in order to create something new, reflects the spirit and style of *The Journey*.

Undated [January 1954]
A new year has begun. I hope it will
be good, very good for you.

Dear Carson:

It is cold and bright like glass, today. Winds have stripped the trees clean and pale winy smoke color is drifting down on the mountain.

The kind of day when my tongue says "beautiful" and my heart mourns. Always those winds blow harder on my memory than on the mountain and I am driven back to an empty house and empty rooms that greedily spread over my whole life, sometimes; refusing to budge. Just taking over as if they have a right to stay. What happened on windy days long ago, I have no faint idea; but when such a day comes, I have to go back, like a ghost, to my childhood and wander it. Without map; without destination.

So, I write you from Clayton but really from a lonely corner somewhere in the past, to say hello and thank you and to wish you well. It would be nice to talk. I have never talked to you. Always we begin and there are—interruptions. Small ones, most of them; and the one big one which I pray you have somehow made your peace with. A hard six weeks you have had. I know this. I know there have been terrors and regrets, and sudden revelations, and grief, and a sadness that has no name. Always, if we could name the sadness, if we could find the word, we feel the sadness would lift. It is like stumbling across an old grave stone with no name and no date. Sorrow is like that. One can not name it. If one only could . . . name it and find a little date in time for it. Then we could drop a small flower, a tear, and compose our life around it.

All of this you have felt, I know. And more. And I have been glad that you were compelled to work hard; to write "about Georgia"; to meet a deadline; to "make a little money." It is harsh and right, this having to do the practical things when the deep breaks come. It glues us together; it drives us and pinches us back into some kind of shape. And while we are hardening ourselves, finding order in the chaos, we are at the same time growing within us new possibilities for life.

But it has been very hard. And I know this. I have thought of you, often. Paula has. We have talked about it with a profound sense of the pity of it, the sadness but, also, knowing a time comes when a relationship has ended. Death did not end it. You told me that, before you knew. It had ended before Reeves' death. You felt this; saw it with a clarity; felt it in the honest regions of your self; and I hope that you have not forgotten. For no circumstance, even so hard a one as the event that occurred, can break what was already broken. To forgive another and one's self; to accept all in another that one can and hold on to that. I feel you have done this; will do it; will cherish the bright moments; the gay, absurd, ridiculous and warm days; the tragic, too; and out of it all you will weave a new pattern, something real and Reeves will be a part of your words; and all this will hold that common past close and make you glad of those years. I feel that you are wise enough to be grateful for those years; and not to regret them.

The flowers were lovely. And there was a funny quirk to it which will amuse you, I hope. The florist called from Toccoa, misery loading down her voice. She had an order from New York for an old fashioned bouquet for me. But she did not really have the right flowers for an old fashioned bouquet, she said. And how on earth could she get an old fashioned bouquet to me in Clayton! Could I perhaps come over for it? The voice was troubled. Was I going to wear it Christmas day? No, I said. There was no special occasion. Then, she sighed in relief, would it be all right simply to send me cut flowers? Yes, I assured her. But how could she get them to Clayton? She thought over long distance, too miserable to count her dimes. Finally she said while I held the silent phone, Oh yes; the paper truck came through Toccoa and went from there to Clayton. She'd just put those flowers on the paper truck and he would leave them at the drugstore. Would that do? Yes, of course, I assured her. So the flowers came bouncing in on the paper truck Saturday; the drugstore called to say "Miss Lil, we have some flowers for you"; Paula went to town for them and that night beautiful red carnations and blue irises were all over my dining room and looked very gay and very Christmasy too. Thank you for thinking of me in such a very nice way.

Please give my love to your dear mother, to that very nice sister Rita, and my warm affectionate wishes for the New Year.

tls, UT

February 24, 1954

My dear dear Dr. Kallen:

A sweet and wonderful letter. Deeply moving and wonderfully good for me. It is always a joy to be with you, to feel your own profound sense of faith: a deep current that is beyond the mind, that must have somehow got into your bones and muscles and bloodstream—as it did in my Little Grandma. A curious thing: your belief, your faith. For I feel that it began as an intellectual skepticism and worked its way back and forward in time, in space, in human experience until suddenly it flowered! Manured, it may be, by doubt. And now it is so lovely. So strong and real.

I am coming along well, I think. [. . .] And remember, my chances are not too bad as one thinks of the human race: I have, they tell me, one chance in four of recovering completely. What more could a good gambler ask for? I used to be a gambler with a bit of nerve; so maybe I can still be. I try.

My book comes out in April. I was writing it when the crash came. [. . .] I think perhaps I could not have written what I said about death had I not been so close to it, one day; and were it not, that it slips in and out of my consciousness every day for a few minutes . . . We may become quite good friends, death and I, before it is all over. But the book, somehow, had to be written. I had to find out what I believe, what is meaningful in human experience, for me; what is the creative meaning of ordeal. [. . .] When I want to find out something: I write a book. It is my way of searching. Not to give the world "answers" but to find them for myself. So a book, for me, is a growing season.

[. . .]

What the book world will do to this book, I don't know. At present, in New York "the boys" are a bit hostile to me. Why? I am not quite sure. Because (for some) I am too anti-communist; because for others I am too anti-McCarthy; because for others I refuse to hate my own southern people; because for others I do not glamorize Negroes, I simply accept them as human beings like the rest of us. Because, it may be, I am a woman who is

*Horace Meyer Kallen (1882–1974), esteemed as one of America's leading social philosophers, a member of the original faculty of the New School for Social Research, a pioneer in introducing Zionism to the United States, a founder of the American Jewish Congress, active in civil rights and civil liberties organizations.[15]

trying to think through her human experiences and find something, some little something that is sweet and good and tough enough to cling to. But I shall have to accept what comes—and I am trying to, though it is a bit hard, this time, as I am so bitterly in need of money to live on. The years I was sick (before we knew what it was) ate up strength and savings and so on. An old familiar experience which most of us must go through at one time or another in our life. And what happens to my book is no more important than what happens to any other writer's book. We write our "prayer," we send it out to the world. What then happens is quite beyond us.

[. . .]

I hope, soon, to get back on my novel. Am doing a few magazine articles now to live on. [. . .]

tlc, UGA

 The following letter, published not by the *Atlanta Constitution* but by the *New York Times*, June 6, 1954, underlines the significance of Smith's stand against segregation: that is, not only her timing—that she spoke out as early as she did—but also her perspective and depth of understanding. Because she saw racial segregation as symbolic and symptomatic of many other aspects of human nature and society, it is not surprising that her first public response to the *Brown* decision contained broad and far-reaching interpretations of the new law.

Her passing reference to the ruling as a "powerful political instrument against communism" was not a new argument for Smith or for many others who for years had pointed to the hypocrisy of America's willingness to defend freedom abroad while blatantly denying the rights of citizenship to black Americans. While it is important to remember that Smith's anticommunism predated the end of World War II, her use of anticommunist language reveals her susceptibility to the Cold War rhetoric and a certain blindness in her otherwise clear vision of the relationship between means and ends in any struggle for social change. Although she may have intended to defuse the red-baiting tactics of those who labeled as "communists" the Supreme Court justices and all others who worked to end racial segregation, her willingness to use the anticommunist rhetoric—even against itself—left her vulnerable to charges of feeding the very red-baiting she would otherwise deplore.

In the remainder of the letter Smith's strategy was brilliant. To call the *Brown* decision "every child's Magna Carta" was at once to move the subject out of the realm of black versus white or federal government versus state and local school boards and to place it in the tradition of freedom for the individual that even the most staunchly Celtic descendant would have to revere. Simultaneously, she pushed beyond the stereotype of race by renaming skin color an "artificial disability" compared to "real disabilities" of physically or mentally disabled children.

Smith's knowledge of the legal, social, and educational plight of disabled Americans was grounded in the extensive research she and Snelling had conducted for their proposed anthology on the subject. Her perception that the *Brown* decision would affect disabled children as well as children of color was prophetic. Few, if any, of its defendants or opponents were even considering such far-reaching implications in 1954, yet educational historians now look to that decision as a major precedent for the extension of educational access to all children, culminating in the 1975 enactment of Public Law 94–142, the Education of All Handicapped Children Act.

Smith's confidence that "millions of other southerners" would "wholeheartedly" accept the challenge of the *Brown* decision reflected her basic educational strategy for social change. Believing that people would rise to the vision of their leaders, she always tried to embody the vision she held for the South. She would develop this appeal and outline specific creative responses to court-ordered desegregation in her 1955 book, *Now Is the Time*.

TO THE EDITORS, *The Atlanta Constitution*

May 31, 1954

Dear Sirs:

I have read, again, the recent decision of the Supreme Court. It bears rereading. For it is a great historic document—not only because its timing turns it into the most powerful political instrument against communism that the United States has, as yet, devised, but because of its profound meaning for children.

It is every child's Magna Carta. All are protected by the magnificent statement that no artificial barriers, such as laws, can be set up in our land against a child's right to learn and to mature as a human being.

There are, perhaps, 5 million children in the U.S.A. who are colored. There are close to 5 million other children who will be directly affected by this decision. I am not speaking, now, of "white children"—many of whom have undoubtedly been injured spiritually by the philosophy of segregation. I am speaking of disabled children:

Children who are "different," not because of color but because of blindness, deafness; because they are crippled, or have cerebral palsy; because they have speech defects, or epilepsy, or are what we call "retarded." These children we have also segregated.

There are more than 40 states with laws forbidding a child with epilepsy to attend public school—even though most children's convulsions can now be controlled by modern drugs. Little blind children are segregated in schools from sighted children; our deaf, from the hearing. Many cerebral palsy children are kept out of school not because they are unable to attend but because there are teachers who do not want to teach them. And yet, a basic principle of rehabilitation is that acceptance and a natural relationship with his human world is necessary for the disabled child, if he is to make a good life for himself.

All these children—some with real disabilities, others with the artificial disability of color—are affected by this great decision.

Then why are a few politicians protesting so angrily? Perhaps because they feel THEY will now be handicapped if the old crutch of "race" is snatched away from them.

It is true: this decision may shackle a few politicians. But it frees so many of our children. I, for one, am glad. And I believe millions of other southerners are glad, also; and will accept wholeheartedly the challenge of making a harmonious, tactful change-over from one kind of school to another. It will be an ordeal only if our attitude makes it so; there are creative, practical ways of bringing about this change. And in the doing of it, we adults may grow, too, in wisdom and gentleness.

tlc, UGA

 In Georgia's 1954 gubernatorial race Grace Wilkey Thomas, a well known Atlanta attorney, entered her first and only political race as a candidate for the Democratic nomination.[16] Not surprisingly, Samuel Marvin Griffin, who won the Democratic nomination and thus the governorship, had the backing of former governor and avid segregationist Herman Talmadge; but he was not alone among the candidates promising to maintain school segregation in Georgia.[17] Indeed, Grace Thomas was the only gubernatorial candidate who stood for racial democracy in Georgia in 1954. Lillian Smith's involvement in Thomas's campaign, as well as her analysis of it, was characteristic of the kind of political activism she maintained on local as well as national levels.

September 30, 1954

Dear Mrs. Roosevelt:

It was good of you to respond to my plea for help for Mrs. Grace Thomas. Your check was deeply appreciated by me and by her workers. They were thrilled about your interest. "Mrs. Roosevelt is helping us," they said.

But alas, it fizzled out to a small thing when the election returns came in. Almost nothing. Only 6200 votes out of about 200 thousand. We had nine candidates, it is true; the five big ones (men) made the big totals. Mrs. Thomas, the only woman, came next. The other men followed her, with very small totals.

It is the same old story of the liberals—at least, in the South. Thousands and thousands of them were for Mrs. Thomas. But they feared that she could not win; and some feared her simply because she was a woman. She is a fine lawyer; has held many big responsible jobs—but she *is* a woman. She has the best qualifications of any of the nine; but because she is a woman and was not well known socially, they said "she could not possibly win or maybe even be a good governor." But even so, a large proportion of them had planned to vote for her. To make a moral gesture—since she was the only one who had come out for the Constitution and obedience to the Supreme Court's decision. Then, the liberals began to wobble; they said "Maybe [Melvin E.] Thompson would be better." "Sure," they said "he is saying *nigger nigger* and says he will uphold segregation in the schools. But if he goes in, he will not. He will try to integrate the schools." Most Negroes voted for him, or for [Charlie] Gowen. Gowen is a fine man; Thompson is not. Gowen would probably have given in and obeyed the Supreme Court decision for he did not say *nigger nigger*. He said he was for segregated schools but would not abolish the public school system in order to maintain segregation. He said he "would find another way."

These two moderate candidates at the last moment, swung the liberal vote over to them. So: the liberals lost both ways, both politically and morally. Griffin (our new governor) is doing an almost treasonable job of trying to break down people's belief in their Constitution. It made it possible for [Herman] Talmadge to say over nation-wide television the following Sunday that only 6200 people in Georgia wanted integration of the schools. That is a lie; but the liberals helped make it sound like the truth.

I feel that I should not perhaps have told you that Mrs. Thomas had even a "slim chance." And yet, there were two or three weeks when the liberals could have been swung over to her if only she had had enough money to get on television and stay there. We got her on only one time: the last week. She has beautiful television presence; looked pretty and gracious and charming and spoke very well. Had it been possible for us to keep her there day after day, I do believe the liberals might have all swung over to her. We have about a 40 percent liberal group (if we count the Negroes, many of whom are not liberal; are only for themselves). We could have swung it. But we failed.

And yet, the old rule has been broken. A state-wide politician did, for the first time since the Civil War, speak out for democracy and human rights. Her campaign will not be forgotten. [. . .]

I do want to see you. I would love to have lunch with you and dear Mr. Golden if you have time for me.* I am staying at the Beekman Tower Hotel; and am coming up this next week for three weeks.

My warmest thanks for your help; maybe it was worth it just for the look that came on the youngsters' faces when they saw your check. "She cares," they said.

tls, HP

This copy of a form-letter fund-raiser for the NAACP Legal Defense Fund was enclosed with a letter to Smith from one of the recipients, Charles J. Williams, president of Moore Dry Kiln Company, Jacksonville, Florida. Adamantly opposed to the NAACP, Williams questioned Smith's authenticity as a southerner, saying that he could not imagine a southern woman who would sponsor the work of the NAACP.[19]

October 13, 1954

Dear Mr. Williams:

Three weeks ago, in hundreds of schools, Negro and white pupils were quietly getting acquainted in their classrooms. They were practicing together on football fields, talking together in corridors, young Americans learning.

Then suddenly an evil thing began to happen. Parents paraded the streets of White Sulphur Springs, West Virginia, protesting the presence of

*Eleanor Roosevelt had written praising *The Journey* and Smith's work paving the way for the Supreme Court decision on segregation and inviting her to lunch with John Golden, "the oldest producer on Broadway," who was almost completely blind and to whom she had been reading *The Journey* aloud.[18]

fourteen Negro children in the town's only high school. Parents in rural Milford, Delaware took up the chant, signed petitions, threatened school board members if eleven Negro tenth-graders were not removed from their school.

In a few days the contagion had spread to Baltimore, to Washington. The trouble makers stepped in: the opportunists who use such times to build notoriety and power for themselves.

We cannot blame the children. Children everywhere will accept each other if given half a chance. Nevertheless, prodded on by forces which they, of course, do not understand, they did let themselves go. It was an ugly thing to see. And frightening.

It was a relatively small outburst. But it is as much as any thoughtful American needs in order to know *something must be done quickly, and by every individual.*

We of the "Committee of 100" have pledged to raise a special fund of $100,000 to be used to stem this tide of bigotry and hatred, by sending experienced and understanding men and women into these towns to give what guidance they can in these emergencies. Some of these are southern white men; some are northern; some are Negroes; all are experienced. All can be of real help to both the Negro and white communities.

As a Southern woman, I ask you to do what you can. For now is the time to quarantine this contagion. We cannot afford its spread. Your works can help wherever you are; your dollars are needed too.

Won't you, today, send a check large or small, for the N.A.A.C.P. Legal Defense and Educational Fund? It will be used wisely. It will bring our country large returns as our people help the communities work out constructive ways of meeting this great challenge.

P, UGA

Lillian Smith's mother,
Annie Hester Simpson Smith, ca. 1931.
(Courtesy of Esther Smith)

Lillian Smith's father,
Calvin Warren Smith, ca. 1915.
(Courtesy of Esther Smith)

Left to right: *Lillian Smith, brother Warren, and sister Esther, ca. 1906.*
(Courtesy of Esther Smith)

Lillian Smith and sister Bertha Barnett, Mokansan, Sanmen, China,
ca. 1923. On the back of the photograph Bertha wrote: "We teased Lil
about her coy expression." (Courtesy of Esther Smith)

Lillian Smith as a young camp director, ca. 1927. (Courtesy of Esther Smith)

Paula Snelling and Lillian Smith at Laurel Falls Camp, ca. 1933. (Courtesy of Hargrett Rare Book and Manuscript Library, University of Georgia Libraries)

Paula Snelling on horseback, in front of the boardwalk connecting the cabins at Laurel Falls Camp, ca. 1930. (Courtesy of Esther Smith)

Laurel Falls campers, ca. 1940. (Courtesy of Esther Smith)

Lillian Smith dressed for a house party at Laurel Falls Camp, ca. 1940. (Courtesy of Esther Smith)

Lillian Smith, Mary McLeod Bethune, and Eleanor Roosevelt at a reception in Washington, D.C., given to honor the National Council of Negro Women's 1944 Honor Roll. Smith and Roosevelt were among the sixteen honorees. (Published in the Washington Star, *February 11, 1945. Copyright* Washington Post. *Reprinted by permission of D.C. Public Library)*

Lillian Smith at a party given in the home of Sarah Spencer Washington,
founder of Apex Hair and News Company, in Atlantic City, New Jersey, 1945.
Attendants at the party have been identified as follows: Standing, left to
right: *Rev. John Henry Hester; Shumpert Logan, Washington's husband; C.*
M. Cain, director, Artic Avenue YMCA; Rupert M. Chase, aide to Enoch L.
Johnson. Seated, left to right: *Emily Fowler, Atlantic City Department of*
Health; Nan Wooding, teacher; Sarah Spencer Washington; next three persons
unidentifiable; Lillian Smith; Martha Hester (behind Smith); *Mattie Lou*
Chase; far right person unidentifiable. (Courtesy of Hargrett Rare Book and
Manuscript Library, University of Georgia Libraries)

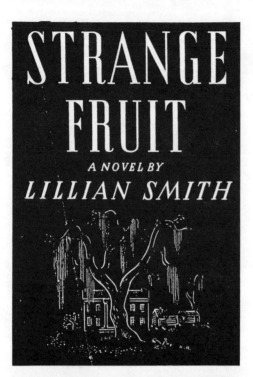

The book jacket for Strange Fruit, *published in 1944.*

The book jacket for Killers of the Dream, *published in 1949.*

*Lillian Smith being awarded an honorary doctor of letters at Oberlin College,
1950. (Courtesy of Hargrett Rare Book and Manuscript Library, University of
Georgia Libraries)*

Lillian Smith and Paula Snelling in their home, 1965. (Courtesy of Hargrett Rare Book and Manuscript Library, University of Georgia Libraries)

"the Chimney."
this is all that is left of the big camp playhouse
and theater. It was a very large building with
big stage, a huge fireplace, and room to dance,
play games etc. Underneath was where finger
painting and etching were done. We had the
building demolished a few years ago.

The chimney at Laurel Falls Camp where Lillian Smith is buried.
The description of the chimney in Smith's handwriting was found
with the photograph. (Courtesy of Esther Smith)

Lillian Smith's grave marker. (Courtesy of Esther Smith)

CHAPTER FIVE

Struggling to Be Heard,

1 9 5 5 — 1 9 5 9

Immediately following the historic May 1954 Supreme Court ruling on school desegregation, Lillian Smith wrote *Now Is the Time*, urging support for the Court's decision as a major weapon for democracy in the Cold War fight against communism and outlining specific ways southerners could work deliberately and calmly to end racial segregation. Written to reach a wide audience as quickly as possible, the book was published simultaneously in paperback by Dell Books and hardback by Viking Press in the spring of 1955. *Now Is the Time* crystallized approximately two decades of Smith's practice as well as theory about effective social change. Accordingly, thoughts of how best to bring about social change dominated her correspondence during the mid-1950s and especially in 1955 and 1956 as she dealt with reactions to her book and the increasingly violent resistance to efforts to end racial segregation in the South.

In keeping with her Cold War liberalism, Smith accepted an invitation to travel in India for six months with financial backing, though not official sponsorship, from the U.S. State Department to gather material for a book comparing India and China. Additional financial support from Smith's family enabled Paula Snelling to accompany her, and the two flew to Delhi in December 1954. With letters of introduction from Madame Vijaya Lakshmi Pandit, president of the United Nations General Assembly and the prime minister's sister (whom Smith had met in 1949 at one of Dorothy Norman's salons), Smith was able to meet a number of India's political leaders, including Prime Minister Nehru, Vice-President Radhakrisnan, and Madame Pandit's niece, Indira Gandhi, as well as a number of artists and writers. She and Snelling also traveled by car into rural areas, visited Welthy Fisher's Literacy Village, and were once stranded in an airport for several hours with Helen Keller, who was traveling in India at the same time promoting rehabilitation for the deaf and blind.[1] Although there are no extant letters written from India, Smith described some of her experiences there in subsequent correspondence.

Smith returned from India in May 1955 even more strongly committed to her prewar linkage of democratic ideals and movements for social change throughout the world with the emerging desegregation movement in the United States. In July, however, she found a recurrence of cancer, underwent extensive X-ray treatments, and was told by her surgeon in Atlanta that she did not have long to live. Unwilling to accept that diagnosis, she sought a second opinion at Memorial Center for Cancer and Allied Diseases, in New York, where she was encouraged to continue her work and plans for the future. With renewed determination, in the fall of 1955 she began a new novella and spent a month as visiting lecturer in the English Department at Vassar College. On November 16, shortly before her month at Vassar was scheduled to end, her home in Clayton was burglarized and her bedroom and study were burned. A few weeks later in December, as if to add insult to injury, Smith learned that despite steady sales through the summer and fall, paperback copies of *Now Is the Time* were being removed from bookstores and newsstands and Dell was not filling orders.

That month, as she tried to extract an explanation for the book's removal and fought to get it reinstated, some 40,000 blacks began their year-long boycott of the municipal bus system in Montgomery, Alabama. In February 1956, at the University of Alabama in Tuscaloosa, the first major test of court-ordered school desegregation in the Deep South sparked mob violence and rioting as students and townspeople protested the admission of

Autherine Lucy. While Smith argued in vain for the urgent need for her book to be available to college students and the public in general, *Life* printed a letter from novelist William Faulkner in which he, claiming to speak for moderate white southerners who opposed racial segregation, pleaded for the North to "stop now for a moment" the efforts to end segregation forcibly.[2] Smith wired *Life* immediately asking to respond to Faulkner's letter, but her request was denied.

Smith's response to that rejection was but one example of her ongoing battle with so-called liberal or moderate white southerners, most of whom were male writers, journalists, and newspaper editors consistently recognized by the national media as the spokespersons for the liberal white South. If she had felt "smothered" after the publication of *Killers of the Dream*, by the mid-1950s her sense of being smothered or deliberately ignored became almost an obsession. "Now, please sir," she wrote her friend Frank Spencer, "HOW AM I GOING TO BE HEARD?" And the question of "how" was accompanied by "why can't I be heard? [. . .] They can't think I am communist for no one has fought communism more than have I; that is the evils of communism." She questioned further: "Is it jealousy? Is it that I am a mere woman and my opinion is not worth anything?"[3]

Refusing to accept what she saw as efforts to silence her, Smith wrote letters to journals, newspapers, and friends seeking assistance in getting her ideas published in some of the larger magazines. Eventually, however, she returned to the course she had followed for years: that is, she accepted invitations to speak wherever she could, but especially on college campuses in the South where young people were discussing segregation and social change, and she directed her primary energy to writing her next novel, *One Hour*.

Smith's thoughts concerning *One Hour* dominated her correspondence from 1957 through 1959. In writing the novel Smith was, in effect, addressing her own questions about *how* she was to be heard and *why* her ideas about social change and human relationships were so strongly resisted. In *One Hour* Smith explored the relationship between what she called "mob thinking and mob acting," brilliantly depicting the destructive effects of mass hysteria and censorship associated with the McCarthy era while probing the dynamics of personal relationships in characters who resembled the white upper–middle-class intellectuals who populated her life—artists, scientists, business leaders, musicians, clergy. It was their silence, their unacknowledged fears, that troubled her. At its core, therefore, *One Hour* dealt primarily with sexuality, especially the power of fears associated with taboo sexual relationships.

Not surprisingly, her willingness to probe and question America's sexual fears did not win Smith the critical acclaim she sought. Indeed, the critics' negative responses to *One Hour* seemed only to intensify her struggle to be heard. That struggle continued, like the recurring bouts of cancer, until her death.

 Smith's correspondence from prominent New York psychoanalyst Lawrence S. Kubie dates from his highly favorable response to *Killers of the Dream* in the fall of 1949 and extends until her death. Because of his favorable comments about *Killers*, Smith sought his opinion of her subsequent work. In turn, he invited her comments on his professional papers and journal articles.

After reading *Now Is the Time*, Kubie suggested that she should reverse the order of the general and specific sections of the text. As a minor criticism, he also thought that her use of Washington, D.C., and Baltimore as examples of progress in racial desegregation might be misleading because, he felt, in smaller southern cities with a higher percentage of blacks "the practical and psychological problems might be different." His major criticism, however, was that *Now Is the Time* had failed to examine the deeper psychological foundations of racism, "the unconscious forces which are involved in fantasies of dirt and power."[4]

June 2, 1955

Dear Larry:

I cannot say I enjoyed your letter but I do appreciate it.

I wanted you to like my little tract. It was a tract, deliberately written as one; written with the purpose of persuading millions of white people to believe in their own capacity for meeting this problem, this crisis, constructively.

When a person is scared, when he is close to panic, we try, don't we, Larry, to encourage him? I know very well you would not tell me, were I to come to you in panic, what the roots of my trouble are. You'd reassure me, I think; help me relax a bit; help me find my courage, get hold of as many of my old defenses as possible. For instance, the night I told you I feared being in an automatic elevator, you did not interpret that fear to me. You reassured me, quite naturally; and offered to go down with me. Were I to come to you about it, you would gradually help me find insight and you would gradually lead me to see that the real problem is not the automatic elevator at all, but something else that has to do with my relationships to those I love and hate, or my relationship with my childhood, or with my present. But you wouldn't spring a full-fledged interpretation on me. And I know it. You would lead me steadily toward it until I saw it, I felt it, I re-experienced and finally recreated old relationships with others or with myself.

[. . .] [W]hen one writes a tract, a piece of writing deliberately to persuade, one tries to use tact, encouragement, to stress reasons that the public can accept and to play down (not evade or deny) deeper interpretations that will only arouse more anxiety.

I wrote *Killers of the Dream* to give myself insight; I hoped it would give it to a few others. I knew my audience would be limited. It was. I wrote *Journey* to find courage for myself; I found it. That audience was even more limited than the *Killers of the Dream* audience. I wrote *Strange Fruit* because I love above all else to tell a story that has levels of meaning. The story was in its deepest sense my own story, of course; the legend of my life. I see it, today, far more clearly than when I wrote it. It dealt with white and colored people because my childhood was white and colored and many of my most profound experiences concerned white and colored people. It was interpreted by my public as a book to help solve the "color problem." And I cried when I read the reviews! I did not even realize myself the urgency of the color problem until I was two-thirds through the book. My own book converted me to the importance, the urgency and, indeed, the universality of this "problem." But my book was a fantasy. Every character in it was myself or a mirror in which I looked at myself. Every tension was an echo of a tension in my own life. Not in the naive sense, of course. I knew as a craftsman what I was up to; I drew not only on my childhood but my mature experience and knowledge of life and let that wiser outlook stretch and distort, where such distortion would come closer to the truth.

In *Killers of the Dream* I explored the depths with some thoroughness, I think. I realized the symbolic significance of darkness, body openings, etc. I also stressed the interrelationship of the body image and Puritanism. I stressed the effect of our bi-racial childhood, our colored and white mothers, our proximity to the black breast of our nurse, the black hand that bathed us, etc. I stressed the ambivalence in white southern men and women who had had a nurse in childhood—and most did have, at least a three-dollar-a-week baby sitter. All this, I went into in that book. It was read by every southerner who felt up to the bitter experience for it received the best reviews of any book I have ever written. So I did not repeat that material in this little tract. I believed that people who had, up to this time, feared my books might (some of them) after reading this little tract go back to my "real" books and read them.

But this little book was for the purpose of reassurance; giving reasons for our trouble but exploring not further below the surface than was necessary—although I did mention the darkness, its identification with sin and with dread, etc. I did talk briefly in the book about body image—just enough for the reader to know in his heart that there is more to all this and much of this "more" he already knows, deep down in him. (And I had said so much about this darkness in *Killers of the Dream*.)

Now—about my optimism. We cannot come through this ordeal, Larry, without optimism. I am no fool. I know the difficulties. Heavens, I know them far more I believe than the Hodding Carters and Ralph McGills whose fears have always kept them from speaking out until it is safe to speak out. [. . .] But I also believe a southerner is the only person who can encourage other southerners and I know it will be those of us who have already been "punished" by our fellow-southerners (and northerners, too) who by keeping steady and cheerful can help the others. My nephew lost his job last week because his wife had written Herman Talmadge a letter; and he had preached against segregation. He is a very popular young minister whom the people love; but he was not asked back to Athens, Georgia. A young Presbyterian minister came by last week; he, too, has just lost his church in Virginia because he (a Georgian and from a prominent family) had let two Negroes come to his church. But neither my young nephew nor this young man is discouraged. They laugh and say "Oh well . . . we are in for it now." I, too, have paid a price most of my northern friends know nothing about because I don't like the martyr role. It is very hard, practically impossible, for me to get an article published in magazines like *Sat. Evening Post* and the better paying magazines. The pressures have been put on me. Mainly in the North. So that, today, I am depending on a local bank to keep me going until my bad time is over. Not my local bank; one 30 miles away whose president likes what I am doing! I have lost almost all of my old friends in Georgia—and many of my old northern friends. But I have found friends, too. And anyway—you can't help bring change about without paying for it. You also receive much. This I keep telling the young people. "What is the loss of a job?" My nephew has three children. But he is not afraid. And we want other people not to be afraid; we want them to see it as a challenge; as something worth doing, that can be done rather quickly if we believe it can be done. My brother was fired in Feb. (just after my book came out) from his position with the state. He was also Chairman of the Mental Health Association of Ga. Now he is in Florida.

As for my citing Baltimore and Washington. I think those success stories have had a tremendous effect on southerners. They know how southern both cities are. They know that Washington has more Negro children than white children and that there is no southern city below Washington that has more than one-third Negro. Atlanta has a bit more than one-fourth Negro. No city in the South that I have ever heard of has more than one-third Negro. I was reared in a small town that was 52% Negro, 48% white. But that is not true today. For migration of Negroes has siphoned off many Negroes from small towns, especially the young Negroes who have children. Up here in the hills we lost over 50 percent of our young Negroes and their children. They are all now in Philadelphia, New York or Detroit. [...]

We all expect the change to take place first in the southern cities. If Atlanta makes it successfully, then Macon, Columbus, Augusta will follow suit rather quickly. When these cities are desegregated, then the towns will not be scared to try. The border towns will have little trouble—once the cities begin to do it—for the population is small in border towns. The main thing is to create a hopeful climate of opinion—even if it takes ten years to bring the change about. In a few backward localities it may take 15 years. But one can never tell which cities or towns will do it first. It doesn't happen logically: it happens according to the leadership in the town. There are towns in Georgia whose Negro population is very large where, during the war, the only doctor was Negro. The white people accepted him, even letting him deliver their babies—and accepted him without protest. This prejudice is not deep; the fear of change, of "giving up" segregation is large, however. And that is why I was trying to reassure my readers.

[...]

tls, Kubie/LC

 Charles S. Johnson, president of Fisk University, had written Smith inviting her and Snelling to participate in a race relations institute at Fisk on June 27–July 9.[5] In this letter Smith replied that she was not physically up to making a speech but would be willing to be part of small group discussions at the institute; she ended by discussing her own ideas for eliminating racial segregation.

June 10, 1955

Dear Dr. Johnson:

[...]

I am trying to do a few things here in Georgia. I am inviting small groups of whites and Negroes to come up here to the mountain, have a meal with me and talk over this big problem of *how to begin. Now is the time to begin.* This is the emphasis to make, I think. Begin anywhere, I tell the young people who come by and who are so afraid to act. One young graduate from Vanderbilt came by yesterday with her mother. "What have you seniors done?" I asked. She said, "Oh, we are willing. Nearly all of us are willing to be unsegregated." "But what have you done? what have you said?" I prodded. "The climate of opinion must be changed. And it cannot be changed simply by you being willing inside you for the change to come. Who is going to bring this change about? God? Or you?" She seemed quite surprised. Began to ask how. And Lord help me if that nice young girl didn't ask that old question "How about dating? how about marriage?" I said, "Look. Get clear in your own mind, then try to help others get it clear: that you as American citizens have both public and private rights. Everybody has the same rights to live in and share the public life and public opportunities given all our citizens. But you also have a right to your own private life. No one has the right to make you have Negroes in your home; or in your club; or to marry one. No one can make a Negro invite you to her home, either; or to his club; or compel a Negro to marry you." She actually seemed to understand a little.

I am hoping that we can, this summer, gather up here in small groups a hundred Georgians of both races who have influence and opportunity to act. What will come out of these talks I cannot say. But courage may come; hope may rise; the imagination may be stirred. The apathy may be broken, at least. More individuals are coming by. That seems good to me. Some are coming because they did what *Now Is the Time* said for them to do and [they] got fired from their jobs! But they are not in the [least] dismayed. [. . .]

All this thrills me. There is more: The Baptists have a camp near here, a kind of Assembly Ground, like Junuluska is for the Methodists. The women have been meeting here. Two asked to come over to see me. I had them to tea and we had a nice talk. Toward the last we talked about race, segregation etc. They had books for me to autograph. Then they asked me over to lunch. I went. They gathered up quite a few of the women to meet me. We had two hours of wonderful talk. All about India, segregation, the South, what the churches are doing etc. Everyone was a Georgian; most from small towns; some were the wives of well-to-do textile men. They made it plain that they were working and were standing by *Now Is the Time.*

These things are what Hodding Carter and Ralph McGill know nothing about. They perhaps would not believe me, were I to tell them. They surely would not believe that the little rural (Holy Roller) church at the foot of my mountain is unsegregated. It is officially a white church. But they invite the Negro Baptists—over in the valley—to come very often to their church; and they go to the Negro church. I mean by "they": the entire congregation. Both Baptist rural groups (white and Negro) use my swimming pool for their baptisms. Last summer, the white group invited the Negro group to witness the baptism service. There were white and colored rural Baptists roaming all around my place. It was wonderful. On the Fourth of July, I had all the white and colored children (45) of my neighborhood to a hot dog and ice cream supper and party. Four pairs of white parents came, too—at my invitation. I wanted the grown folks to see what was happening so no rumors would get started. One of the white fathers said, "Miss Lil, this was so nice; why can't we have the grown folks up here, too?" We invited them for the next week and had 68. 36 were white; 32 were Negro. They had a "sing." Stayed in my big gymnasium singing and talking until midnight. I never saw anything like it. It was right in the midst of all the race hullabaloo stirred up by the gubernatorial campaign.

I shall, of course, have some kind of party for the children this summer. I am awaiting the arrival of the things I purchased in India for I got little souvenirs and toys for all the children. I shall gather them together to tell them about India and to give them their presents. We are not self-conscious about race. It is never mentioned in these groups I bring together from my rural neighborhood.

I tell you all this to let you know that things are popping here and there. The seeds are really sprouting. I think that somehow we must give word of mouth publicity to these things but see to it that they never get in newspapers. If we keep what we do too secret it does not encourage others; if we give too much publicity it subjects people to attack, people who are too naive to defend themselves and who might react and grow afraid. I let what I do happen in quietness; I say nothing for a few weeks. Then I gradually begin to tell a few people about it. The neighbors of mine might be threatened were certain roughnecks to know about these happenings. As it is now, people nearby know or half know and say nothing whatever about it.

But the big problem as I see it is to break down the apathy of the good people: those, like the young Vanderbilt graduate, who say "we, personally, are quite willing to be unsegregated." How can we get them to see that the door must be opened into the unsegregated life. It is not going to swing open by magic; it certainly should not be dynamited. How to find the key; how to pick the lock; how to loosen the hinges. . . .

The seniors at University of Georgia (a group of them) did do one small thing. It was rather naive, perhaps; perhaps not even very wise. But it was an act. They (this group, led by a Quaker) had 2500 placards printed. On these was printed something that read roughly, like this: What are YOU doing about segregation? No matter what you think about it, do something. Why not begin by becoming informed? We suggest you read the following books: (and they led off with *Now is the Time*). They called themselves the Committee for Creative Political Action. They put their names on the president's desk at 5 P.M. (too late for *him* to act). At 5 A.M. next morning, they scattered those placards in frat houses, dining halls, cars, etc. It created quite a stir. The Ga. papers hushed it up—so as not to give *Now is the Time* any publicity.

[. . .]

tlc, UGA

As the former director of Putney School, a private, progressive, ethnically diverse residential school in Putney, Vermont (a group of whose students and faculty had visited in Smith's home earlier in June), Carmelita Hinton wrote Smith on June 13, 1955, seeking financial assistance to enable a daughter of Alabama civil rights activists Clifford and Virginia Durr to attend Putney School. Smith had known Virginia Durr through their work in the Southern Conference for Human Welfare in the 1940s.[6]

June 18, 1955

Dear Mrs. Hinton:

It is always a pleasure to hear from you. I am very sorry, however, to hear that the Durrs are having difficulty in Montgomery. I suspect it will become a very familiar story during the next few years. For all of us are going to be challenged by this transition period. Those old veterans like myself have got used to the hard knocks; but it is never fun. The Durrs were in Washington for a long time. It is difficult to come back to the deep South and find people so fearful, so insecure, and so willing to let one down—even old friends.

It is especially hard for the children. And I am sorry about their young daughter. I wish they could somehow persuade her to feel that this transition has its glory as well as its pain and that someday she will be proud that she has been a part of it. But teen-age children, especially some children, want only to be a part of their social crowd.

I wish I could help in some way. I cannot help with money for my own economic condition is probably quite as insecure and depleted as is the Durrs'. We who have been working down here are subject to many pressures and reprisals—and I have had my share for many years, although I have tried to keep my troubles at home, where I happen to think trouble belongs. Threats to my life; loss of old friends; a curious kind of snubbing, of being left out of the important things taking place in one's state—all this is a common thing now to me. But the economic reprisals come from the North, mainly. It is the hostile critics (most of whom are northerners) and the refusal of the big magazines to take my writing that has left me wondering always about next month's money. You see, books make almost no money now for writers—unless they are really best sellers. Writers have to depend upon a teaching job or magazine articles. But when magazines like *Saturday Evening Post, Readers Digest*, even *Harpers* and *Atlantic* just flatly refuse to consider you, you are sort of left on the economic edge of things. *Time* and *Newsweek*, for instance, have refused to review my last two books. *Saturday Review* and *New York Times* gave the last book, *Now is the Time*, to Hodding Carter and Ralph McGill to review: two southerners who are gradualists and who are known to be extremely hostile to me. The northern magazines do this not because they have anything against me personally; indeed many of their editors call themselves my "friends" when they speak of me; they do this in order not "to antagonize the South." If you ask them "What South?" they grow vague and cannot reply. Fear of offending white people is in the North as well as in the South. This is the new state of mind we have to deal with, now.

Therefore, I am well aware of what the Durrs are up against, I have tried to think of northern friends who might help. But the need for money for urgent causes is so great that it would be difficult to find someone to whom one could appeal for money to send a child to boarding school when there is a good public school in her own town. I know about the difficulty for the child; but everybody working in the South against segregation has the same basic problems as do the Durrs. There would be hundreds of boys and girls to send north to school, were we to do something for all the children whose parents are working hard on this problem. For there are numerous young couples with two and three children who are going out on a limb on this issue of segregation.

[. . .]

Always, when it begins to feel too hard, I remember the Negroes: all the Negroes who have lived in insecurity in South and North; all who have taken snubs and humiliations day after day, sometimes for a lifetime. It is hard for their children to go to those segregated schools. It cannot be any harder for Virginia's child than it is for thousands and hundreds of thousands of Negro children. We must see it in perspective; and we whites must be willing to endure, willing to suffer a bit—not as martyrs but with a sense of humor, a sense of balance about the whole thing. Martyrs are awful, I think; they do us no good down here. [. . .]

[. . .]

I hope Virginia and her husband will spend time trying to work out good human relations with the white community as well as with the colored. Sometimes we liberals take up a cause and we forget that there are other human needs besides the one we are working on. To get along in a southern town, today, one must help the whites as much as the Negroes. I have always believed my success in my own home town (here, at Clayton) is due to the fact that I do as much to help the white community as I do to help the colored. I worked two years on the hospital board when we began our hospital and gave them also a very large sum of money which helped them build the hospital. I have always helped in the community projects. Then, when I do for Negroes or work hard against segregation, they are inclined to listen or at least "forgive." They don't turn against me. The friends I have lost have been my city friends: Atlanta, other places; not these village people.

[. . .]

[. . .] I know there are hard years ahead but we must take it with our chins up and teach our children to take it the same way; and somehow—and this is hard—we must still love the people we live among.

[. . .]

tlc, UGA 1283A

TO CHARLES S. JOHNSON

July 28, 1955

Dear Charles:

[. . .]

You know, of course, that I got much more than I gave while at Fisk. I loved every minute of it. I would not accept your check except for the fact that my future has suddenly grown a bit uncertain and my financial affairs are not very lush. So I am accepting it with gratitude but also wishing I did not need to do so. I think you know how the magazines have made me feel the pressure of their displeasure at my 100 percent desire for integration by never asking me for pieces and never accepting any I send them. [. . .] It is what any of us should expect—and especially a southern woman who has "betrayed" her white men folks, as they feel I have done. It is all extremely comic and sad, too; and vexatious. But the real disappointment is when they succeed, as they did with both *Journey* and *Killers of the Dream*, in keeping the public from reading the books, as well as from buying them. They have tried the same tricks with *Now is the Time*. Thurgood Marshall was saying that he was disappointed in the way the book had been buried in so many cities and towns. Somehow, we should do a bit of excavation but I have not figured out a good scheme as yet. If we could persuade a Fund or Foundation to send out 20,000 of them to groups who would promise to give them intelligent distribution such as Methodist women, Baptist women, etc. YWCA, young people's groups, American Civil Liberties etc. etc. This gush of books might act as a priming of the pump. And might do a really good piece of work. Perhaps some of us can get something started.

Please tell Marie that I am feeling quite well and stood my nine X-ray treatments even in the 94 degree temperature of Atlanta very well. I am home again now and trying to get into my Nehru book. The Indians are getting in touch with me, each group wanting me to write what they want said. They even are asking to read the chapters of my manuscript before it goes to the publishers! I think they fear my candor as much as the southerners do—although they know I am most sympathetic.

I am disturbed about our northern liberal friends who feel now that everybody should ease up on this integration affair since the Supreme Court has rendered its decision. They are deeply influenced of course by Hodding Carter's many articles and Ralph McGill's attitude that the change is brought about by "erosion" (Mr. McGill's words) and not by writings and acts and words. They take the attitude in their columns (these northern liberals) and in their talks with me that we are pushing too hard. The trend seems to be just now a sudden gush of sympathy for the poor white southerners who are having to go through the "ordeal" of change. What about the poor colored southerners, I ask, who have been held down for decades and decades? How about them? "But you are forgetting statistics," they say and then dare to quote Hodding Carter's absurdly distorted statistics to me. To ME. I gasp inside and try not to lose my temper. But they think Negroes have "won" the decision so why not be nice now and give the South at least 30 or 40 years to change itself in.

[. . .]

At Emory Hospital, in the Winship Cancer Clinic where I seem to spend a large portion of my time, there is a corridor where we cancer patients sit. It is lined with all those people, some almost dead, all sick, all worried even though trying to be tremendously hopeful. There we sit: malignant human beings. And down the corridor, a few steps, there is a drinking fountain with a sign over it For Whites Only. There is not a Negro patient in Winship. Yet that sign is up. And we cancer patients, gnawed on by our disease, sit there looking at each other and every once in a while one of us gets up and walks over to the drinking fountain for a sip of water. I wonder how many of them take pleasure in seeing that sign. How many of them, facing their dread disease, care now about white supremacy. I want to ask them, Do you care? Does it make any difference to you now. We are levelled down pretty low by this cancer business, do you still think you are superior because you have a white skin? But if I said it, I suspect the Emory authorities would think I had lost my mind and should not be there. Ah . . . what a world we live in. What a world.

[. . .].

tlc, UGA

Hallock Hoffman wrote Smith on behalf of the Fund for the Republic, whose work concerned civil liberties and racial and religious discrimination in the United States, to request a transcript of her testimony "before the Georgia legislature [where she] discussed [her] views on civil rights and equal opportunities for Negroes."[7]

July 28, 1955

My dear Mr. Hoffman:

I read your letter with a wistful smile. You don't know how I wish that I could talk to the Georgia legislature about human relations and civil liberties. I have never done so. I am sure it is the last thing in the world that they would want.

I have tried to check back in my crowded memory for the incident that has been reported to you. I have appeared before a legislative committee at the Capitol with a group of women from my county to protest the fight that was being made to keep Negroes from voting in Georgia and reported that meeting in *The Nation* (which at that time I still believed in. I find myself not being enthusiastic about *The Nation* during the past six years.) I was all set at that meeting to make a brief but I hoped, a really persuasive, little speech. But on the way to Atlanta, one of the women from my county whom I had corralled for this meeting, suddenly said, "We think one of us should make the speech. You are known everywhere for your views. Would it not be more persuasive if one of us, just women of Rabun County, made the speech?" I immediately said "Yes." I knew they wanted to feel that *they* were speaking out, not just "Lillian Smith." So one of them did it, shyly and sweetly and most eloquently and I sat there beaming at her. But we walked in together, the six of us, and everybody knew I was there and this was our group from Rabun County.

I am still exploring my memory: one time, about 1950 or 51, the United Daughters of the Confederacy gave a big award to General Longstreet's widow. It was held, the meeting, at the Capitol. To everyone's astonishment and I suspect the consternation of the UDC'ers, Mrs. Longstreet said she wanted me most of all to be there and to give one of the award speeches. The UDC had to invite me although they of course would have welcomed a nice cozy cobra from India far more than me, their fellow-Georgian. It was an amazing time. When the Talmadge crowd heard I was speaking, some of them hung in the doorway to listen. And I spoke of her, of our beloved Georgia, of the heavy shadow that segregation had burdened our state with; I spoke gently, humorously and with affection and the UDC'ers gave me quite an ovation. It is an occasion I shall never in my life forget. It is so characteristic of southern ambivalence and the ambiguities that twist our lives this way, and that.

[...]

My other big speech in Georgia that almost "caused trouble" was in Savannah in the spring of 1951, I think. The Ku Klux Klan and other ruffians began causing trouble as soon as they heard I was speaking at one of the churches. They threatened the lady (white) who was introducing me at the big Negro church; they threatened the Jewish choir that was to sing; they kept telephoning and sending anonymous letters to nearly everyone involved. Captain Frank Spencer (a truly remarkable citizen of Savannah) told me about it when I arrived. Asked me if I was willing to risk speaking with this possible trouble ahead. I merely smiled. Of course he knew I would go ahead. He had telephoned the mayor, the chief of police and the sheriff and told them the responsibility was strictly theirs to see that nothing happened. Savannah had been my father's business headquarters. I was getting close home with this speech. We went to the church. There were the ruffians in the cars surrounding the church. But there, also, were about 8 police cars; many police on motorcycles. We crossed the street and not one of the roughnecks dared come near. Several white ladies came together, got out of their car to cross the street. These KKK boys got out of a car, went up to the women, who never stopped their conversation, simply separated and walked around the KKK boys as if they were a mud puddle and quietly went on into the church. (There is really nobody like southern women when they decide to do something they think should be done.) I spoke for one hour. The Jewish choir did not appear—somehow, they felt a bit panicked by it all; but a choir of young Negro college students substituted for them. The church was completely still. I spoke softly, quietly, affectionately, of our common southern childhood, I reminded them of my own childhood under these same old oak trees, etc etc. I then talked about the harm segregation had done the little white children of the South as well as the little colored ones. A big tall man lounged in the doorway of the church. He never moved; never took his eyes off of me. I heard later that he was the sheriff. Not one thing happened. Everyone did exactly what they had planned to do—except the KKK. Next day, there was a very friendly account of my speech in the Savannah papers. That was all. When I left the De Soto hotel, the white men at the hotel desk suddenly shook hands with me, quietly, warmly, respectfully. That was all. That is a nice memory. I have that speech if you want it.

You did not know you would be at the receiving end of such reminiscences, did you? You are of course welcome to any of my speeches, my letters, my radio talks, my books if you wish them. My last book is *Now is the Time*: a little book that I hoped would encourage southerners especially (but everybody) to begin, even if it is only a small beginning, to bring about integration. [. . .] It has been smothered a bit, but more in the North than in the South.

I am proud of your work. I have been in touch with it.

tlc, UGA

 Although it was uncharacteristic of Smith to address people by their last names only, she wrote this letter to Denver Lindley, an editor at Harcourt Brace. It contains one of her more concise yet informative summaries of the extent of the destruction caused by the November fire and her initial response to it.

December 1st—or is it? [1955]

Dear Lindley:

It looks as if I am competing with Job these days: the last disaster being that my house, my bedroom, study, offices with all my files, manuscripts, letters, et cetera burned last week while I was still at Vassar. Two little boys set it on fire. But before giving you details I want to say at once that the manuscript of "Julia" was in the bank vault in town; and I had my notes of all my interviews in India with me at Vassar. So all is not lost; but almost all is. About 6000 important letters, of great historical worth; all my manuscripts of earlier writings, the two novels, the two novelettes, a half dozen almost finished short stories; manuscripts of the plays I had written for children etc. all family letters, documents, all business documents, all my paintings and drawings, photographs, the special things that had made my study and bedroom "mine" are gone. And all the clothes I own except those I had at Vassar. Thank god, though, for those for they were both my city clothes and my "campus" clothes. And that will get me through the winter here.

It is a gruesome and wholly absurd business: two small boys, strangers to this neighborhood (all the neighborhood kids are my buddies, you know) decided to come up to "that lady's" mountain to "see what was there." So, they said, they came. "And it all looked so pretty outside, we wanted to see how pretty it was inside; so we went inside." Yes, by God, they went inside. To get inside my kitchen and dining-room (and silver and china closet) they had to go through three heavy doors and three heavy locks which we had believed would keep out any adult except a real expert. But this 13 year old kid and his 9 year old brother, picked every one of those locks; then, once inside, picked every lock on every cabinet, chest etc. I owned. They went into everything in my dining room[,] handled my beautiful little Japanese sculptures (I have two very fine ones); handled my Indian sculpture, all the little carved boxes etc. in my living room and did not break a thing. But they took about $2000.00 worth of my sterling, coffee set, etc. etc. away and have hidden them probably in the woods on my own mountain. Then after opening food in the kitchen and eating what they could, they ransacked every drawer in there, pulled everything out, overturned chairs, etc., overturned this typewriter which was in the living room-diningroom, left a half eaten bottle of catsup near the overturned typewriter. Still, they did not break anything. They handled the china, the crystal, all my Steuben stuff, as if they were cats. They took quite a few beautiful pieces of Steuben crystal and hid them somewhere but still, never broke anything. Then, like Goldilocks, after trying the three bears' big bed, they decided to try the middle-size bed. So they went to the next house which happens to be my bedroom, study, and downstairs office. Upstairs is my bedroom-study. The steps are outside the house. Of course they were irresistible: those stairs. So they climbed them and found they could pick the lock to my enclosed upstairs porch where there is a fireplace. Then once inside there, they picked the really heavy lock of my bedroom door and went in. There they found a veritable treasure trove: little jugs, and strange carvings, naked ladies on the walls (Indian drawings and water colors), walls lined with books (all my important books and my beautiful books, my old ones, first editions, my fine *Finnegan's Wake*, all my own copies of my own books, all the scrapbooks of *Strange Fruit*, book and play, et cetera, my record player, all my records . . .) Can you not see them? Poor little fellows who were born on Tobacco Road and will die probably in a federal pen . . . they have never seen anything. They were undoubtedly entranced. So they decided to spend the night. It was freezing cold, my central heating plant was off (for we have never had confidence in its fire-proof qualities) but there was an electric heater there and also an electric burner on which I sometimes make coffee. So they probably plugged everything in and had a fine time all night, smoking my cigarettes, and maybe opening a can of something they had taken from my kitchen and heating it up on the little stove. What we think happened is that they left these stoves plugged in all night and that they were still plugged in all the next day. The boys apparently left my house and went back to collect their treasures (of silver and Steuben glass and Jenson ceramics etc) and spent the day hiding them in the woods. Then they got detoured somehow and did not get back. In the meantime, the heaters were becoming redhot and since they were directly on the pine (waxed) floor they were slowly but steadily raising the temperature. In the meantime, my care-taker (or rather the man who used to be but who has been ill for six months and is only now convalescing) walked through the place and saw that the big house (kitchen, diningroom and livingroom) was wide open. He at once thought of real thieves (there had been a gang of them in this region, lately) and fearing to approach my house without a gun, he went down the mountain and called the sheriff. The sheriff was tired from a long trip (hunting another gang) and said he'd come out next morning. So Kelton (my helper) got a young GI and with their guns they went up to camp in their car to look around. Apparently the house had been smoldering all day. Just as they approached it it burst into flames with a mighty roar. At first, they thought it had been dynamited but later decided the little boys had accidentally set it on fire. The boys admit opening the buildings and sleeping in my bedroom. They were horrified about the fire, I think, and are scared to death. Their father is a mean, dangerous man who will shoot anybody (in the back) and is now talking himself into a rage against me and Paula Snelling although we have been moderate and extremely concerned about the welfare of the two boys. So—

I came home Saturday afternoon. The wreckage had been cleaned up as much as the community and my cook and Paula could clean it before I got here. But it all looks pretty drear—especially on a cold, windy, afternoon with the temperature at 15.

The loss of my papers, my plans, my half projected books and all the rest of it is beyond a response of anything so irrelevant as suffering. One simply knows it has happened and lets it go at that. But I am trying very hard to look straight ahead and get very very busy on my two books, "India" and "Julia." Right now, I do not know which will hold me best. I need something to sort of mesmerize me and keep my sensibilities and mind focussing straight ahead. But the good thing is very good indeed: Dr. Randall at Memorial thinks the malignancy is at present completely stopped. He says it is a kind of miracle but he can find at present no sign of any activity whatever. He was fine to talk to for he understands fully the depth and extent of this other blow; but somehow he also makes me feel that there is inside me somewhere whatever it takes to pick up now and go on.

Well—I did not call you. For I took time only to see Dr. Randall for my check-up and come on home to help Paula. I completed my work at Vassar and left the campus in quite a dither. It seems that whatever else I do I always break everybody's complacency down and get them all stirred up, imaginations going at full tilt, etc. This scares some of the teachers to see the students so aroused, so full of questions, so quivering with new thoughts, new feelings, new intentions. But all in all, they liked me there and showed it to me when I left in deeply touching ways. It was good for me in that it challenged me to think afresh, to know not only that I thought this, that about art, drama, literature but why I thought it. It gave me a fine view of the fears and defenses of these college gals and a rather intimate view of their families. I am glad I went—even though my house did burn while I was gone.

[. . .]

tlc, UGA

 While teaching at Vassar, Smith had learned that *The Journey* had been selected by the Georgia Writers' Association to receive the Georgia Writers' Award for the best book of nonfiction with the most literary value written by a Georgian in 1954. Helen Lockwood was head of Vassar's English Department and knew of the award and the devastating fire. She and Smith had become good friends during their month of working together. The following thank-you letter to Lockwood epitomizes Smith's response to the circumstances that shaped her life and, in many cases, determined her perceived status as a writer. With such a friend Smith shared the sense of humor and awareness of life's absurdities that helped her survive the shock of the fire and fueled her continuing critique of southern culture.

Dec. 2, 1955

Dear Helen:

Please forgive the smudgy ribbon. I don't have the energy to clean it—and only thank God that the two little boys left me even a smudged ribbon. [...]

Now—let me say thank you. I think you know well how deeply grateful I am for you yourself, first; and for the hundreds of courtesies you showed me: and especially for the understanding you gave me and my efforts, even those that did not succeed very well. It was fun, being at Vassar. I liked it very much and I learned a great deal, not only about Vassar and the younger generation but about myself. It was one of the real experiences that one cherishes not only for its human qualities but for the stimulus to the imagination and mind.

[...]

The award was an absurd occasion—full of grotesque, the stupid, the sweet, the good—in other words: it was "the South" giving Lillian Smith an award with a trembling hand. I laughed until I was weak; I wanted to cry and didn't; and I suddenly felt proud, proud that these people had found somewhere the courage to do it. I did not attend the first day of the conference but came in the second day and attended the luncheon where Flannery O'Connor spoke; also attended a fantastic round-table discussion of booksellers who were telling writers "what the public wanted." It was so bizarre that it was unbelievable, this talk. The high point was reached when the booksellers agreed most gravely that what the public really wanted was a book about "how to meet sorrow." "A big book or a little book?" some one asked. They conferred about this, then the chairman said she believed that what the public wanted was "a dollar book on how to meet sorrow." Paula was in the back of the audience; I was midway in the crowd; but I could not restrain myself from turning and looking at her. It was altogether wonderful. I wouldn't have missed it.

The night I received the award there was a big crowd at the dinner. I had not been asked to speak; they feared I might drop a bomb of some kind, I suppose. I don't know. Anyway, I had not been asked. Hyman (*No Time for Sergeants*) who is a Georgia boy had been asked to speak. But when they met me Thursday morning they said to each other and even to me "Oh, she's nice; such a lady, isn't she? Oh my, and dressed like Park Avenue; let's ask her to speak; she must speak to us." Well, I must admit I had on my Sunday best and my Paris hat (the only one not burned) and my mother's manners. Well, I spoke (without preparation) and I melted most of them down. Not all, by any means; but MOST. Fully two-thirds of them came up after the dinner and shook hands with me. A Baptist minister said he was going to use some of my talk for his Sunday sermon . . . a young doctor said he had never read one thing I had written but now he was going to read everything. An old lady said I was so sweet and well bred, she knew I had the best intentions in the world, no matter what I said in my books. It went on and on. Afterward, I went to a friend's house (I don't have but two or three houses in Atlanta now that I am welcome in, but I went to one of them) sank into a chair and weakly asked for the biggest drink she could get in one glass. It was truly a whale of an experience. Flannery's talk was one of the funniest things I ever listened to. Do you know—I don't believe she had the vaguest notion how she shocked the crowd. She told em off; told Georgia off; told the South off; told would-be writers off. She is a little on the grim side in personality and not personally very attractive but she gave a hell of a good speech. There were about 30 of us there—they might not feel I should be so cozy as to include myself in the number—who enjoyed every word of it. But the stuffed shirts and the would-be writers (the place was full of them) began listening smilingly because they had heard she was "literary" and "talented" and nothing she wrote threatened anybody, certainly not on the conscious levels of their life. But after about two paragraphs they realized that a nice little snake was sinking her fangs deep into their complacency and they began to look at each other and shake their coiffeured heads and whisper, "Well . . . what do you know . . ."

Next morning, Friday, the WSB-TV actually asked me to be on the noon news spot. I dashed down and did it. First time, since *Strange Fruit* that my presence in Atlanta has ever been acknowledged. Everybody said everywhere, "Why, you nice person, have you kept yourself hidden away all these years, making us miss knowing you?" Honest to God, they said it. I smiled and said nothing during the first twenty times it was said to me (a new myth in this myth-making South is being created and that is that nobody knows me in the South because I have deliberately kept people away from me.) but the twenty-first time it was said, I said "I'll tell you why. It is because you have never invited me before. And I'll tell you why you have never invited me: it was because I write highly controversial books and you feared to do so. But now that you have, let's forget why and enjoy each other." The South cannot bear the truth—not even a teeny-weeny truth, if there is any lie, any fantasy, any myth they can grab hold of instead. When I said the truth, in a very soft voice, the person's eyes bugged out. She was as shocked as if I had said two dozen four letter words.

Well, it was fun. And I must admit it helped me get over the shock of the fire.

[. . .]

tlc, UGA

Following is the first of several letters between Smith and the ACLU regarding the suspected censorship of *Now Is the Time*. (In 1956 Smith was one of eight vice-chairmen of the ACLU's National Committee.) Alan Reitman, assistant director of the ACLU, reported that Charles Bolte, an ACLU board member and executive secretary of the American Book Publishers' Council, had investigated the matter with Dell and had determined that the postcard sent to Florida State University had been a clerical error and that *Now Is the Time* had not been taken out of circulation. While acknowledging that local book dealers may have been pressured to remove the book, Reitman also noted that the ACLU had not discovered an effective course of legal action against that kind of pressure-group censorship.[8] Disappointed with the ACLU's investigation and Frank Taylor's failure to respond to her requests for accurate accounting of the book, Smith remained unconvinced but also unable to pursue the case in any formal manner.

TO PATRICK MALIN

Neptune Beach, Florida
January 28, 1956

My dear Mr. Malin:

I don't like to break my very long silence by a letter about *my* affairs (when there are so many more important things to discuss) but I feel I must tell about the suppression of the paper cover edition of *Now is the Time*, hoping that the Union can advise me what to do next or give the case enough publicity to get the book back on the market.

Briefly, the facts appear to be these: during December Dell stopped filling orders for *Now is the Time*; and withdrew all copies of the book from the stores. I learned about this, not from Dell who told me nothing at all about it, but from a teacher at Florida State University (white) at Tallahassee. She had asked the bookstore to order 29 copies for one of her classes. They did so. They received in reply a card from Dell stating that *Now is the Time* is out of stock and they were not planning to reprint it. She sent the card to me and I am enclosing it with this letter. She was quite shocked for it was generally known in the South that the book was highly thought of by all thoughtful southerners and was being used widely by churches, colleges, etc. as well as by individuals who often bought 30 or 40 and distributed them to their friends. The book had not shocked the South as had *Strange Fruit* and *Killers of the Dream*; indeed, liberals were unanimous in saying that it was the best book of the kind that had come out. They felt it would do "a great deal of good, etc."

Then, suddenly, this happens.

Miss Snelling, who manages my business affairs, wrote Mr. Frank E. Taylor of Dell a pleasant note asking about the matter; enclosing a copy of the card from Dell and asking that the facts be given us as to what had happened. No answer, even though Miss Snelling and Mr. Taylor are friends of many years. Mr. Taylor, let me say, was the one who gave me the contract for *Now is the Time*; he had much enthusiasm about the book in the beginning. Whatever has happened is not of his doing, I think. At the same time, he does not seem willing to put in writing what has happened. He did, however, telephone me from New York two days ago and after some discussion of totally different matters he said quite casually that all copies of [the] book had been called in ("as we always do," he said) and he hoped sometime soon "another edition" could be brought out. I did not discuss the matter as I preferred to get my information on paper and not by means of a telephone call. He also said something rather vague about pressure having been put on them in the Atlanta stores, many saying they did not want the book.

He evaded the actual facts of the case which are that these particular books were ordered early in December and the order was not filled; and the bookstore was told there would be no more copies of *Now is the Time* for sale.

In early January, we began to look for the book in stores in Atlanta. No sign of a book. (In November and October you could find the book everywhere.) No sign of the book in Jacksonville, either.

Viking Press brought out the hard cover $2.00 edition. I do not know whether they, too, have suppressed it. I do not think so. I believe this is a strictly Dell affair. However, I can, as author, get no information whatever about it from Dell. Am writing Viking. I also asked for my statement of sales, due me in November. It has never been sent to me. (There is no money involved in all this; my advance covered the first edition of the book.) But I can get from them no written statement as to how many books have been sold. I was told once, in October, by Mr. Taylor, that about 130,000 were sold. I believe they printed 200,000 or 250,000. But his words were rather vague and I honestly do not know the sales of the book. However, it was widely scattered in the stores all summer and fall; and I rarely went into an Atlanta drugstore that I did not see a copy of it. Then suddenly, no more copies.

I believe some kind of pressure has been put on Dell. Whether this pressure comes from officials of Dell who do not like my book and do not like what some of them may call my "radical" position of not approving of segregation; or whether it comes from the stores themselves in Georgia and perhaps other southern states; or whether a group of powerful business men, encouraged by Mr. Talmadge who is called "Georgia's ambassador of industry," has persuaded Dell to withdraw the book in order to maintain Dell's "popularity" in the South—I do not know. All I know is, that Dell has stopped selling it even to white teachers in white colleges.

Is it possible for us to give this a bit of an airing? Or is it possible for the ACLU to talk with the Dell officials? Frank Taylor is probably pushed pretty hard by others in the firm; the book was his baby, he certainly wouldn't suppress it, but apparently he is in a position where he cannot talk frankly to me, an old friend, about it. Or what would you suggest? You know that I am mainly concerned because I believe this book, if used widely, can do so much good in the South among liberals and conservatives and help give them some answers they can use with their friends; help them also find courage to take a stand. I think it is helpful to northerners, too; but it is especially slanted toward southern psychology. I therefore hate to see it suppressed. It is also a matter of civil rights and freedom to be heard. When a paper book concern buys your rights to a book then refuses to sell that book you are completely smothered. I, at least, should have my rights back so I could offer it to someone else.

[. . .] Since the banning of *Strange Fruit*, the approach to me has been the one of smothering. It is much more efficient; you can keep a person from being heard much better by not selling her books, never mentioning her in the papers than you can by banning. [. . .]

[. . .] Can a few managers of drugstores decide what the public is going to read? And will a big firm like Dell withdraw a book from the entire nation and refuse to sell it even to colleges simply because a few storekeepers protested it? It is very interesting, as a problem.

[. . .]

tls, UGA

Smith wrote a review-essay of Walter White's *How Far the Promised Land* ("Negroes in Gray Flannel Suits," *The Progressive*, February 1956, 33–35) that was critical of White's perspective and by extension the focus and leadership of the NAACP. In response, Roy Wilkins, White's successor as executive secretary, and Henry Lee Moon, publicity director of the NAACP, wrote letters responding to her review, both of which, along with the following letter from Smith, were published in the March 1956 issue of *The Progressive*. In her review Smith had commented on White's "failure to show any awareness of how change actually comes about in the human spirit and of the meaning of ordeal in the growth of mankind" (p. 33). Her focus on the responsibility of organizational leaders to be concerned with means and ends, the process as well as the goals of social change, echoed her 1940s' criticism of the Southern Conference for Human Welfare and forecast a theme she would reemphasize throughout her involvement in the civil rights movement of the coming decade.

TO MORRIS RUBIN

Neptune Beach, Florida
February 7, 1956

Sirs:

Mr. Moon's letter distorts completely both meaning and intention of my review. I cannot do more than refer the reader to my original essay.

But Mr. Wilkins' letter is one with which I agree in large part. I, too, am deeply concerned with the black sharecropper and laborer in the South and with the poor white, also. I, too, think the work in race relations in this country is by no means finished. Indeed, it has just begun. For the roots go deep and sometimes a man's whole attitude toward life has to be changed in order to change his feelings about his body image.

We have much work to do with southern white college student[s], some of whom have been behaving so disgracefully. We have also much work to do up North, especially in Exurbia. Much of the pressure against the NAACP today is due to the whispering going on between northern Exurbanites and southern industrial promoters and politicians. They have a lot they agree about.

Now I happen to admire Roy Wilkins very much. We have often spoken on the same forum or rally; we have both been attacked (together) by the Atlanta *Constitution*. I have in all our work found him a shrewd, intelligent person. His good humor, his deep sense of justice, his never-failing courtesy, his clear understanding of the difference between "respectability" and "dignity," his honesty are qualities I value.

But I do think he used diversionist tactics in his reply to my piece about Mr. White's limitations as a leader. I did not criticize the NAACP. I pointed out certain failings, certain philosophical dead-ends of Mr. White's. I had only one reason for doing so: I want the NAACP to live, and to live it must grow, and to grow it must shake off certain small identifications, certain trivial enmities, which I honestly think Mr. White was guilty of. It must find a magnanimity of spirit. Success can destroy an organization more easily than can failure. This is the time for the NAACP to look hard at itself, at its past (triumphs and failures) in order to meet the challenge of the future. A cause no matter how good, shrinks to the size of its leaders.

No one knew better than did Gandhi that to win a fight you have to win it first with yourself. Some of his associates, among them Mr. Nehru, could not understand why in the fight for freedom from the British he felt he had to start fighting Untouchability. Why bite off so much, they asked him? What is the point of it? But Gandhi was wise: he knew freedom concerns all of a man and it concerns all men and one has to probe deep down and high up if one wants to achieve it. It is asking a great deal of leaders but leaders must give a great deal. This does not mean that the NAACP projects must cover the earth: it means simply that the leaders' vision must cover the earth.

tlc, UGA

TO PAULIE MURRAY

Neptune Beach, Florida
February 17, 1956

Paulie dear:

[. . .]

How sweet you have been about everything. Well, it was about as awful, the fire, as anything could be. I still cannot believe my little house is gone, my upstairs bedroom so big and simple and simply furnished too but just right for my work. [. . .] Everything about camp; all the special letters from growing girls and growing counselors which I had saved; poignant, real, so absolutely and completely irreplaceable. When I close my eyes I still see my room, every painting, every photograph, all my special books (my special ones were there), everything is painted indelibly on my memory for there it was that I faced cancer for the first time, and faced it for the second time; here it was that I lay awake wondering last summer what death would be like, what life on the old mountain would be like for Paula when I was gone, wondering, wondering, all night long sometime until the sun came over the mountain back of my window. [. . .] It helps to be down here on the ocean; so marvelously sweet and clean and wide and forever and ever stretching . . . I love it and it makes me forget. I keep saying It's no worse than what thousands, hundreds of thousands went through during the war; and two delinquent boys destroying something they understood nothing about is no more irrational then war destroying millions of people and their lives.

I have been working hard; studying about India; vacillating as to whether I really want to write that book now—or later. Still not quite decided about it. I want too to do a novella; and often think it would do me good to slip away into fantasy for a while instead of facing more and more and still more trouble. In my own life and vicariously I have been facing it a long time; maybe it would be better to slip away and imagine my next book: in other words, do the novella. [. . .]

Then back to "Julia." I delay on "Julia" because I have to make a living and I fear that once I get on "Julia" I'll have to stay on her a long time. Then, also, these pressing problems which seem to me to have such deep deep twining roots; and I keep wanting to feel in the dark and follow those roots and then once I see what is down there in our minds and hearts I want others to see . . .

I do hope "Proud Shoes" is coming along beautifully. I have great confidence in you and great hopes for you. I want to spank you when you become the lawyer or the sociologist or begin using the technical jargon which is not the words of an artist; so I scold hard hard hard to try to jolt you back. Don't cover up your heart and your seeing mind; see it, feel it, imagine it—and all will be well.*

*Upon receiving Smith's comments on the completed manuscript of *Proud Shoes*, Murray wrote:

I shall doubtless frame your telegram, or at least place it among my most prized possessions. [. . .] To feel that it met your standards—and I know that you would have indicated to me if not—is worth more than you can realize. We all want to make money on our books to keep alive, but the evaluation of masters in the field is equally life-giving to us.[9]

[. . .]

I was at Hampton Institute for three days. Loved every minute of it. Dr. Moton has done wonders there; he is wonderfully sensitive, keen, cute and funny, and brilliant with an incisive mind. I like him ever so much. The students were so much fun; more fun than the Vassar girls; more alive, more aware, less afraid, more questioning, less rebellious in a silly adolescent way, and heaven be thanked very sweet and mature now about white folks. They do not have the bitterness a generation ago (10 years ago) had. That to me is the sweet miracle. They have grown up on hope, real hope, and that is a sweet milk to be nourished by.

tlc, UGA

 Chloe Fox worked on public relations for the National Stevenson for President Committee. At the suggestion of Eleanor Roosevelt, who said it contained useful ideas regarding civil rights, Fox wrote Smith requesting a copy of her review of Walter White's book.[10] Subsequent correspondence indicates that copies of the review as well as Smith's letters to Fox were sent to Adlai Stevenson.

Neptune Beach, Florida
Undated [February 1956]

My dear Miss Fox:

[. . .]

I shall be happy for you to see the piece. And I would like for Mr. Stevenson to see it, too. While I don't think my piece will clarify the confusion raised by Mr. Stevenson's speech on civil rights, I think it might just possibly clarify Mr. Stevenson's own position on this problem of color and men's differences. I would be humbly glad if it gave him a more profound insight into the most complex problem on the face of the earth. And I do think it is that.

I suspect you have guessed that I was enormously disturbed by Mr. Stevenson's speech. I was. I felt, I honestly felt (and I was one of the first group to put him up for a candidate in the last election) that he made the biggest mistake of his public life when he made that speech. Much of the mistake came out of his lack of knowledge of the whole problem of color, of human differences. It is complex, subtle, profound and perhaps he has not had time to probe deeply into it. He depended, too, on the wrong southerners for advice. He also did this in his last campaign. He depends on the men like David Cohn, Hodding Carter, Ralph McGill who are "gradualists" and who are not deeply concerned themselves over the problem as it has injured white people's integrity. They were all for segregation until about five years ago. They do not, even now, understand the defense of segregation, why and when it is harmful; nor do they really think it would do us or the world any great harm if things were to stay like they are for another fifty years. At best, they think segregation is mildly bad; they would not mind seeing it go if it goes slowly enough not to inconvenience any white folks; they think any white southerner who fights the myth of White Supremacy is "queer" or "odd" or as Hodding Carter once called me in his column "a sex obsessed old maid." They are not real liberals nor are they even good at predicting what can or will happen in the South. Six years ago, everyone of them was saying "Never, never will segregation even be questioned in the South." They have blocked every step of the way by their doubts, spoken out loud always, by their negativism, their doleful shaking of head, and their actual arousing, oftentimes, of anxiety in quite decent, well-meaning people. Of course you can scare the hell out of anybody, if you want to, and if you go about it in the right way. These men have held the South back, have made it harder to change than it would have been had they spoken out bravely, hopefully and calmly. But it is men like these who advised Mr. Stevenson in the last campaign and who, we in the South hear, are advising him this time.

In each crisis of national and international affairs there is always a rational or realistic issue (maybe more than one). But there is also a symbolic issue. Now no demagogue ever fails to grab hold of the symbolic issue. The trouble with our "good" politicians is that they sometimes try to evade the symbolic and talk rationally about rational matters. But the symbol, whatever it is, cannot be evaded. How it is faced will determine the moral strength of a leader. The symbolic issue in this election—indeed all over the world today for color and colonialism are, unfortunately, equated in Asia and Africa—is segregation. This is IT. It would be nice if it weren't but it is. It is going to overshadow everything else because White Supremacy is a myth, and myths go deepdown in men. When that part of the mind which makes myths gets going it becomes less and less rational and more and more primitive. You don't hush a myth up by talking rationally about something else. There is only one way to do it and that is to talk on a high moral level. For religion and the myth are first-cousins; indeed they are on the deep level of us almost twins. To fight a myth you've got to fight with something that goes down just as deep inside a man. There is only one thing: religion. Or in modern terms a fervid morality. Mr. Stevenson is capable of that kind of talk. Indeed, he is a great preacher when he believes in his text. He can't meet this issue by talking of gradualism. He does not deceive the segregationists with that talk; nor does he win the Negroes; nor does he win that large body of white southerners who want to face this issue sanely and bravely and wisely—not gradually. Nor will he win the real liberals of the North. Of course all change comes about gradually; that is, some comes very quickly, other change comes slowly. The thing for him to say is that the change must be brought about without violence and as quickly as possible. But he should talk about the big things: the role of Constitutional law in our democracy; what it would mean to encourage lawlessness; what it means to the whole world for us to move over and make room for the little colored children in our schools. And so on. He must appeal to people's love, their sense of justice, their compassion, their sportsmanship, their need and desire to be law-abiding, to be good, to be fair, to do what is right. Only by substituting good feelings for bad ones, good plans for bad ones, can he hope to lead this country to a higher level of human relations. The whole thing is a matter of relationships: his relationship as a candidate with each person in this country; and with the colored peoples of the world. Mr. Stevenson is not running just in the United States. The colored peoples of the world are watching and will be voting for him, silently but in a very powerful way.

There have been times when segregation was not the symbolic issue. It was not when Mr. Roosevelt ran. The depression was the big symbol then. Starving children. Suicides. These were the images in people's minds. But this time it is segregation. It isn't war; it is segregation. The South's violence, its stubborn refusal to try to meet desegregation in a rational way has made segregation the symbol. The NAACP did not make it so. The South's refusal to abide by the Supreme Court's decision made it so. Now, the riots, the mobs, the dynamitings, the White Citizens Councils, the threats to black and white who want desegregation have created an atmosphere where primitive thinking flourishes. The South is facing the Return of the Repressed. But remember, most southerners are still decent; most are still sane: all they need is leadership. Leaders who calmly say Let's do what is right; let's do it as quickly as possible in the best way possible for all concerned. But we must do it. Mr. Stevenson could speak out like this and win hundreds of thousands of southerners to his side. They are frightened. They don't know, actually, what is going to happen next. They need somebody who is quietly unafraid to do the right thing; and who, speaking as a friend, can help give them the moral strength to do the right thing.

That is why we all felt so depressed when we heard Mr. Stevenson's speech. More gradualism. Well, we have seen where that has already got us. The word has a most insincere aroma in every southern dictionary. We don't believe in that word's good intentions. I do hope he will do a right-about face. If he doesn't, I think he will lose long before he is nominated. And the country will lose with him; for it is his opportunity to lift us all up with a grand grand moral gesture; he can do it; I still pray he will.

tlc, UGA

TO MARTIN LUTHER KING, JR.

Neptune Beach, Florida
March 10, 1956

Dear Dr. King:

I have with a profound sense of fellowship and admiration been watching your work in Montgomery. I cannot begin to tell you how effective it seems to me, although I must confess I have watched it only at long distance.

It is the right way. Only through persuasion, love, goodwill, and firm nonviolent resistance can the change take place in our South. Perhaps in a northern city this kind of nonviolent, persuasive resistance would either be totally misinterpreted or else find nothing in the whites which could be appealed to. But in our South, the whites, too, share the profoundly religious symbols you are using and respond to them on a deep level of their hearts and minds. Their imaginations are stirred: the waters are troubled.

You seem to be going at it in such a wise way. I want to come down as soon as I can and talk quietly with you about it. For I have nothing to go on except television reports and newspaper reports. But these have been surprisingly sympathetic to the 40,000 Negroes in Montgomery who are taking part in this resistance movement. But I have been in India twice; I followed the Gandhian movement long before it became popular in this country. I, myself, being a Deep South white, reared in a religious home and the Methodist church realize the deep ties of common songs, common prayer, common symbols that bind our two races together on a religio-mystical level, even as another brutally mythic idea, the concept of White Supremacy, tears our two people apart.

Ten years ago, I wrote Dr. Benjamin Mays in Atlanta suggesting that the Negroes begin a non-violent religious movement. But the time had not come for it, I suppose. Now it is here; now it has found you and others perhaps, too, in Montgomery who seem to be steering it wisely and well.

I want to help you with money just as soon as I can; I cannot, just now; I have had cancer for three years and have been unable to make much of a living during this time; also have found it an expensive illness. My home, also, was burned this winter by two young white boys; [. . .]. But I will have a turn of luck soon, I hope, and just as soon as I do I shall send your group some money.

In lieu of money, I send my encouragement and just a spoonful of advice: don't let outsiders come in and ruin your movement. This kind of thing has to be indigenous; it has to be kept within the boundaries of the local situation. You know the fury a northern accent arouses in the confused South—especially if that accent goes along with a white face. Keep the northern do-gooders out (sincere and honest as they may be); tell them to help you with their publicity in the North, giving you a sympathetic and honest press; tell them to send money if they are able to do so; tell them to try to use some of these methods in their northern communities. But don't, please, my friend, let them come down and ruin what you are doing so well. It will then seem to the country a "conspiracy" instead of a spontaneous religio-social movement. It has had a tremendous effect on the conscience of the people everywhere. But it won't have, if these people come in.

Dr. Homer Jack has written a most sympathetic news-letter about his visit. I was glad he wrote it. But I think his advice for northern "experts" in non-violence to go down and help is unwise. You can't be an expert in non-violence; it is like being a saint or an artist: each person grows his own skill and expertness. I think Howard Thurman could be of help, perhaps, to you. He is truly a great man; warm, deeply religious. Bayard Rustin is a fine man, too. Whoever comes should come only on invitation and should give only quiet advice. Except Howard Thurman. Mr. Thurman, as I said, is a truly great religious leader. Your congregation and that of other ministers in Montgomery would respond to him. He would encourage them in numerous ways and his advice would be wise and skilled. I think, instead of coming, if these leaders of CORE (with whom I have worked for years) would write you letters; send messages of encouragement to your group that that would in the end help more than anything else.* You have the awe

*At the time of this letter Homer A. Jack was minister of the Unitarian Church of Evanston, Ill.; Howard Thurman was professor of social ethics and dean of the chapel at Howard University; and Bayard Rustin was executive secretary of the War Resisters' League. All three were pacifists, promoters of Gandhi's ideas on nonviolence, and longtime activists with FOR (the Fellowship of Reconciliation) as well as CORE.[11]

and respect of many southern whites at present; they are genuinely touched and amazed at the discipline, the self-control, the dignity, the sweetness and goodness and courage and firmness of your group. It would break my heart were so-called "outsiders" to ruin it all. The white South is irrational about this business of "outsiders."

But please give your group a message from me: Tell them that Lillian Smith respects and admires what they are doing. Tell them, please, that I am deeply humbled by the goodwill, the self discipline, the courage, the wisdom of this group of Montgomery Negroes. Tell them that I, too, am working as hard as I can to bring insight to the white group; to try to open their hearts to the great harm that segregation inflicts not only on Negroes but on white people too. Tell them, that I hope and pray that they will keep their resistance on a high spiritual level of love and quiet courage; for these are the only way that a real change of heart and mind can come to our South.

tls, BU

TO O. C. CARMICHAEL,
PRESIDENT OF THE UNIVERSITY OF ALABAMA
[Neptune Beach, Fla.]
March 10, 1956

Dear Dr. Carmichael:

I know that you have been greatly harassed by the recent events at the University. At such times, almost nothing seems quite the right thing to do. But I do want to congratulate you on the action of the Board of Trustees in dismissing the young man who apparently was the ring leader in the mob violence. This will help clear the situation, I think. People felt—and I shared in the feeling—that the dismissal of Miss Lucy was unwise and a bit unfair. It seemed to us, watching from afar, that it lacked a certain sportsmanship and a certain fairness. I am glad, very glad, that the trustees tried to balance her dismissal with that of the ring-leader. I hope, as feelings simmer down a bit, that some small group discussions can take place: not arguments, not debates, but a quiet and humble thinking things over. Growth can come out of this ordeal; and growth cannot come without pain. The fact that the students have seen what mob thinking and mob talking can lead to is of great worth to them. If they can realize that under stress it is dangerous to identify one's conscience with that of the group; that at such a time one should hold on tightly to one's personal conscience and listen only to it, they will mature both spiritually and intellectually.

[. . .]

Last spring a little book of mine was published by Viking Press and the paper book by Dell called *Now is the Time*. This book was written by me in anticipation of the upsurge of mob feeling and acting that I felt might come after the decision of the Supreme Court. I was for that decision; in the state of the world today no other decision could possibly have been made without wrecking the peace of the world; for the Asians and Africans and Europeans were watching this great nation. The Supreme Court did the right thing but it, also, had no alternative. It had to do what it did. Yet, I realized, knowing our South, that we should have trouble. So I wrote this little book to try to show quiet ways in which we could begin to work our way into the future. I do believe this little book might be of great value to many of your students and faculty members. And to the Board of Trustees, also. I merely mention it. I am asking that a copy be sent to you.

Once more, let me say Thank you for dismissing the young mob-inciter. This will put a quietus on the professional haters and those slightly psychotic people who throw gasoline on a fire just to see the blaze. If they know they cannot get by with it, they will be more cautious next time. I still believe that there were outsiders who helped stir up the trouble. I personally think the heads (national heads) of the unions should be asked to investigate their own unions down in Alabama to see if any of their men took part in stirring up trouble on the campus. Perhaps you have already asked them to do so. It would be too bad for the University to be penalized for their acts.

tlc, UGA 1283A

Dorothy Canfield Fisher wrote Smith on March 5, 1956, on behalf of a group of Quakers in her hometown of Arlington, Vermont, who wished to express their concern for the increase in racial tensions in the South and ask what they could do to be helpful in "the great moral crisis of our country's history." Following is the first of a series of letters Smith wrote Fisher in the spring of 1956.[12]

Neptune Beach, Florida
March 10, 1956

My dear Dorothy Fisher:

How good you are to write me. I am deeply touched by your letter. And by the thoughts of the little group of Friends of whom you wrote. Yes I do, I think, understand something of their way of life and thinking. I have always worked with them, especially in the field of human relations, and have developed for them an immense respect and admiration. Whatever real religion I have finds its psychological home in their way of life.

The situation is, of course, quite bad down here. As I see it, much of our difficulty is due to the fact that the real leadership of the South cannot be heard either in the South or in the North. [. . .]

I think of the creative work going on down here: the fine sermons against segregation, against mob violence, against disesteem for the Supreme Court which so many of our young preachers have preached; I think of the small groups of women who are working steadily, persistently day by day in their home towns trying to give insight, to illumine the situation not with angry arguments but by talk of children and their growth, by stressing the moral aspects of the segregated way of life; I think of the teachers who are quietly discussing this in their school rooms. This is spiritual and mental yeast and it will have its effect. But people in the North know nothing about it; and people in the South who depend upon their newspapers for what is happening down here know nothing about it.

For instance: there is the Till case.* We all, all of us who are decent people, were deeply shocked. But in the papers, only the angry Mississippians were given a voice. One child who came South to visit his grandparents was killed. But every summer, thousands of little colored children come South to visit their grandparents and go back home unharmed. This is a custom of Negroes who have moved North, to send their children back South to see Grandpa and Grandma out on the farm, etc. Last August, I went to New York from Georgia. I boarded my train at Toccoa, Ga. Two old colored people were sitting there in our new integrated waiting-room. (But who knows about these integrated waiting-rooms in the small towns?) They had with them two small colored girls. I got on the train and went to my roomette. The two children got on and were put by their old grandfather (a farmer, and rather ignorant and "country") into the roomette opposite mine. I invited the children over to talk with me. We had fun for an hour or two. Then they went back to their roomette and read comic books and played games. The conductor came by, spoke most pleasantly to

*While visiting relatives in Money, Mississippi, fourteen-year-old Emmett Louis Till, a black boy from Chicago, was brutally murdered for saying "Bye, baby" to a white woman.[13]

them (he had a Georgian accent) asked them if they'd had a good time visiting Grandpa, asked them what they had done. They had learned to milk the cow, they said, and had fun helping Grandma gather eggs each day. He laughed and told them not to worry about getting off next morning in Philadelphia, he would help them. He was very kind. At supper time, I asked them if they'd like to go to the dining car with me. We were now in South Carolina. They said they would. So I took them in, we were seated together. The steward (also white southerner) looked a bit surprised but said nothing and treated us exactly as he did everyone else. No one seemed to resent this; I saw not one expression of shock or resentment and everybody in the dining car was probably a southerner. We ate our dinner, went back to our compartments. Later, they went to bed. After they had undressed, I heard a chanting of little voices. I opened my door—and there they were, kneeling in the aisle in their pink and blue pajamas with their heads on the bed, saying their prayers. Now I lay me down to sleep . . . if I should die before I wake, I pray . . . But you see, they did not die. They got home safely and they had a pleasant, comfortable trip back North. They had also had a fine vacation, a completely secure one, down South. There were thousands of these children who came South last summer and returned safe and sound. That does not justify the death of the Till boy, nor does it make it less cruel and barbarous; but it does help us see the total picture in an honest perspective to be reminded that after all, murder came only to one of these children.

I am completely without defensiveness concerning the South. I think, however, that it is dangerous for the pseudo-liberals and the scared people to be the only ones heard at this time. Faulkner [in his *Life* article] was trying to make the North believe we are worse than we are. He was suggesting in his piece that we are all Snopses[,] that even he is, when pushed too hard. I was profoundly shocked. For I think we are tested as thoughtful human beings by a time of ordeal. It is then that we must show ourselves to be persons, individuals thinking constructively and creatively and critically, not members of an emotional and mental mob. What William Faulkner has succumbed to is mob-thinking. Now, there will never be mob-acting until leadership has broken down into mob-thinking and mob-talking. This prepares the people, the crowds for mob-acting. Hodding Carter, all the other gradualists and separate-but-equalers are guilty now of merging with crowd thinking. At the very moment when every writer of the South should be thinking, in alone-ness, as a person, here is our Nobel prize winner thinking with the mob. It is too too bad. But the worst part of it is the reluctance of so many northern editors to let the individuals who have not succumbed, who are still thinking with critical intelligence, to speak out quietly. [. . .]

I do think, dear Dorothy Canfield, that you might be of help at this time in persuading some of the mass-circulation papers to let me speak quietly to the South and the North. I can't be heard in southern newspapers; certainly not in the Georgia ones. But through *Look* or *Life* or *Colliers* I could be heard by southerners and northerners. What I want to write is several rather brief pieces; pieces that are simple, plain, quiet, hopeful, down-to-earth. I want to do one called Don't Say It—Just Now.

I wish to list eight or ten stereotyped defenses that are being used by nearly every southern editor (and northern ones, too) and those asked to speak out in northern papers. These stereotypes are cluttering up the processes of quiet, rational thought. We should not say them any more. Each one I am puncturing, showing how ambiguous it is, how without real rational content. One of these is talk about the "extremists." Putting everyone who speaks out plainly against segregation in the same category with the demagogues who speak out plainly *for* segregation. Mark Ethridge was guilty of this in his otherwise fine speech at the University of Florida recently. He put the NAACP and Senator Eastland in the same moral category stating that both were "radicals."* He made no moral discrimination between the NAACP working for the rights of Negroes and Senator Eastland working for white privilege. I was shocked by the muddiness of this kind of thinking. We might as well put the completely honest man and the habitual thief in the category of "extremist." If we are going to ignore values, what will become of us? [. . .]

[. . .]

If you can help me get a hearing I should appreciate it. Here is the *New York Times* (who often published pieces by me until a year or two ago) doing a big feature on the South. They sent 10 reporters down here to talk with people. Not one has talked with me.

I wrote *Time* a letter about the Mark Ethridge speech. I believe they are going to print it this week. If so, this will be the first letter *Time* has ever printed from me. I believe they are going to because they called the editor of the Jacksonville *Journal* to ask him to check a word that had gotten in my

*Mark Ethridge was publisher of the Louisville *Courier-Journal*. Excerpts from his speech were published as "A Southerner Faces Facts" in *Time*, March 5, 1956, 21. James Oliver Eastland was the senior senator from Mississippi.

letter by mistake. They did not have my street address and called on the *Journal* to help them find me.

I wish I could tell the country about the fine courage of our young preachers and of some of our older ones. And the women, bless them, how steadily they work down here. This confusion is caused largely by white men, not by white women.

The paper edition of *Now is the Time* is no longer on the market. [. . .] I do think individuals writing cards or letters stating that they cannot find the paper book anywhere might help us get it back on the stands. These individual protests help. I also think letters from various prominent and not prominent Americans asking *New York Times, Look, Life* etc. why no article or opinion of Lillian Smith's has been printed might smoke them out, a bit.

[. . .] Since this whole problem of segregation is a world problem I do not think the good people of the North should let themselves be intimidated by the angry voices from the South. It is not making protests that anger[s] southerners. Good southerners are glad to know that good northerners are on their side, helping them work for a better, a freer, a more harmonious world. It is only when a protest voiced by a northerner is voiced in a holier-than-thou tone that good southerners are upset. [. . .] But you see, I have hope; we must keep white southerners hopeful but above all else we must keep Negro southerners hopeful, too. As long as they have hope they will have self-restraint. How beautifully 99$^{1}/_{2}$% of them have behaved, as compared to the white southerners.

[. . .]

tlc, UGA

In response to Smith's request for help in getting her ideas published in the larger magazines, Fisher wrote editors at the *Saturday Review of Literature, Yale Review,* and *Reader's Digest* on Smith's behalf. In her April 6 reply, however, Smith wrote that she had been wrong to ask for help for herself and urged Fisher's group to send money and letters of support to Dr. Martin Luther King, Jr., and the Montgomery bus boycott. Smith ended her correspondence with Fisher in a May 30 letter that stated that instead of humiliating herself by begging northern editors to let her write about the South, she had decided to do her own work as a speaker and writer. As indicated in the following excerpt from that letter, while expressing her appreciation to Fisher for her concern, Smith also let her northern friends know that they had their own work to do to bring about an end to racial segregation:

I am working very hard down here to help our people change; I have decided that this direct work *as a person* (not necessarily as a writer since I have already written three books on this subject and dozens of articles and given hundreds of speeches North and South) is what will now count the most. I did a great deal of work in Jacksonville; spoke to numerous small groups; they were all reading my *Now is the Time*; I felt the work planted some seeds that will sprout. Next fall, I am working on the college campuses for a while. This is the way I now feel I can contribute the most to this phase of human relations.

In the meantime, since I am a writer I must write and I am busy finishing up a short novel for Harcourt, Brace. [. . .] I do deeply appreciate all you have done. I am sorry that the North and West are not getting the clear story but they could get it if they chose; they don't at this time choose. There are many reasons for this but they are complex and difficult to define clearly in a brief space. In the meantime, the old South is going to have to suffer and grow and grow and suffer its way through to a real understanding. I am not too worried about it, actually. I think there are so many white southerners who are risking and sacrificing for the cause of human dignity and freedom and integrity: it is bound to count in a very real way. I have begun, in recent years, to believe that a belief is not worth much to a person until that person has suffered for it, has risked his life or his job or his work or his popularity for it. Southerners are beginning to risk. And this heartens me. And I believe it will spread for it is powerful: any idea is powerful when people begin to risk for it.

Gradually, the North will learn to risk, too. It hasn't had to risk anything, really, in the name of integration. But it will have to and it will, later. In the meantime, I believe the South is going to keep changing and growing. It won't be the Faulkners who make it change and grow.

tlc, UGA

TO ELEANOR ROOSEVELT

August 15, 1956

Dear Mrs. Roosevelt:

My long, more personal letter will come later. This is only a note to tell you once more—in addition to my telegram sent to Chicago—how deeply moved I was by your presence and your speech at that convention.* You

*For an account of Eleanor Roosevelt's speech at the 1956 Democratic National Convention, see *New York Times*, August 14, 1956, L12.

were, as you always are, a very great human being; and as such, a symbol to those sometimes cynical and smallminded politicians of what it means to be a real leader in these troubled changes now taking place throughout the world. I know there are other idealists there besides you; but perhaps never was there so great an idealist fused with so practical a sense and know-how of "the possible."

Bless you, my dear dear Lady. I shall write you soon and tell you many things on my mind and heart. Both your letters have meant much to me. [. . .]

No, I am not resting: I am working seven days a week on a novel. Called *One Hour*. It has to do with the silent, invisible mob in men's minds and hearts that is waiting to burst out into spiritual violence and sometimes physical violence. The plot has to do with an eight-year-old girl framing a young scientist on a sex charge. That is a mere plot; it goes on from there into deep places in the human heart and out to the ends of the earth. It is concerned with innocence and guilt; with suspicion; with goodness, too; and knowledge and truth. It has something of the quality of *Journey* in it but is a hard driving, dramatic novel, too. I hope you will like it.

Take care of yourself. I hope you will rest a bit after this strenuous week. My own health seems fine; after my second go-round of the malignancy last summer when the prognosis was poor, I went to Memorial in New York; I got well again; I have continued to be better than I have been in three or four years; I believe I'll manage for a few more years, anyway—maybe quite a few. Anyway, I feel fine; and strong and full of energy. And am having fun, a deep kind of joy, in writing this book.

Of course I want to see you and talk with you; thank you for asking me to. I shall let you know when I come up.

tlc, UGA

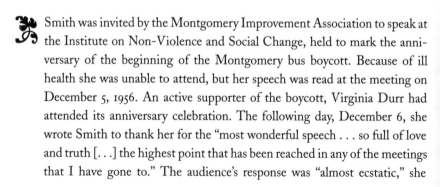

Smith was invited by the Montgomery Improvement Association to speak at the Institute on Non-Violence and Social Change, held to mark the anniversary of the beginning of the Montgomery bus boycott. Because of ill health she was unable to attend, but her speech was read at the meeting on December 5, 1956. An active supporter of the boycott, Virginia Durr had attended its anniversary celebration. The following day, December 6, she wrote Smith to thank her for the "most wonderful speech . . . so full of love and truth [. . .] the highest point that has been reached in any of the meetings that I have gone to." The audience's response was "almost ecstatic," she continued; 50,000 copies of the speech would be printed and distributed.* In closing, Durr expressed her regret that she and Smith had been divided in their ideas about the Southern Conference for Human Welfare and had not become friends.[14]

TO VIRGINIA DURR

December 8, 1956

Dear, dear Virginia:

Your letter touched me deeply. I am so sorry, too, that we never quite understood the other, although I think I liked you much more than you liked me! But never mind that . . . the letter brought back, too, the old memories of our resurgence of hope and the feverish desire we had to "do something," to change things. We knew, in a way that the younger people will never know, the pain of it, the wrong of it. Our differences were that some of us felt it could be done in one way, and others of us felt it must be done in another. Because of my years in China when young and my coming under the influence of Gandhi in those years, I held on rather grimly to the importance of the means we used. I made big mistakes, too; we all did; but we shared something very real, together, and I tried to say so in *Now is the Time*. Maybe you have seen that little book.

I was sorry that I could not come to Montgomery. I had counted on being there; and even until the last day I thought I could go. But I was feeling not good at all that week and finally, at the last, Paula Snelling (co-editor of *South Today*, remember? and my long-time helper and companion) begged me not to undertake the long drive, the strain of that kind of speech. I am not, however, as ill as the N.Y. *Post* said I was (Ted Poston.) I have been; but I am not, just now. In fact, I am going through one of the smooth times; the only thing is lack of strength, lack of endurance. [. . .]

[. . .]

*The speech, "The Right Way Is Not A Moderate Way," was published in its entirety by Atlanta University's *Phylon* and the Fellowship of Reconciliation's *Fellowship*; excerpts appeared under different headings in the *New York Post* (December 23, 1956), *Civil Liberties*, *ADA World*, *Community*, *Congress Weekly*, and a number of black newspapers and major southern newspapers. For the speech, the Americans for Democratic Action gave Smith the Franklin Roosevelt citation, which was presented by Eleanor Roosevelt. Eugenia Rawls received it for Smith and read her acceptance speech.[15]

The meeting sounded wonderful. Your account of it was beautiful. Thank you so much for describing it to me. I had asked that Dr. Lewis read it [Smith's speech] for me.

They are truly wonderful people. As I have talked to young white people—and they are beginning to come and talk to me now when once they were so afraid of me down here in our South—I try to tell them what the Montgomery group is doing, how this is the only way it can be done, how we as white people must humbly seek our way, too, by forgiving ourselves first and going on from there, in humility, and truth.

A reporter phoned me from Montgomery to ask if the speech was really mine. "Did you write it, Miss Smith?" he asked. I was so amused. But I said quietly, "Yes. Why?" And he said, "Well, we were not sure. And we did not want to say you had said these things if you had not actually said them." I then said to him, "What troubled you the most?" And he said, "Well, I was wondering if you had really said the white people had lost their freedom, too. Did you say that?" I replied, "Yes. Why don't you read it to me, the part that puzzles you?" All this over long distance. So he did. "It is true, isn't it?" I quietly asked. And he said, "Yes'm, in a way, yes it is. But—" It was an almost touching conversation.

I have heard, indirectly, of the troubled, difficult, heartbreaking times you and your husband have had. And I am so sorry. I, too, have had my blows. The worst of all for me—in a way, it is worse than cancer—was last winter when two white boys burned my bedroom-study and office. [. . .] It was really the big blow of my life. Knowing my years were probably going to be curtailed, this blow seemed at first just too, too much. But I turned away from it quick, quick; and put my mind on this new novel and have never let myself think too much since.

Other than these traumas, the years have been eventful and rich. [. . .]

tlc, UGA

TO LAWRENCE KUBIE

January 30, 1957

Larry dear:

[. . .]

My book still has a strangle hold on me. I was getting so anxious, so tense about it that my fantasies went dead on me. So I had to stop completely, and begin all over again in a different rhythm. I postponed the publication of the book. [. . .]

Yes, I'd like to talk with you about distortion; what you call "neurotic distortion."* I don't think all distortion is neurotic; I think it can be art. I think this rhythmic pull or stress or "cold war" or maybe coition that occurs between the imagination or mythic mind and man's reason can go either into neurotic illness or into art—and it doesn't have to be neurotic art. That is, there is a place for distortion in well, let us say: metaphors, word symbols; in sculpture, art, even in a novel if the author can handle the two different kinds of logic involved. There is a dream logic (this you know far better than I do) that extends throughout the mythic mind; then there is the logic of conscious reason. For instance, in Ralph Ellison's book *The Invisible Man*, he fell on his artistic face (I think) because he did not know the difference between the two kinds of logic. For instance, if I did not distort by stressing only certain aspects of human experience I, at best, would write pretty flatly, wouldn't I? It would be an imitation of life which isn't life but a kind of embalmed something.

I agree that much modern art is neurotic but I don't think it is because it is distorted. I think for instance that Faulkner's writing is not only distorted but limited. And I think it is this limitation that gives the aroma of illness to his and so much writing, so much painting and sculpture. It isn't that they distort: *it is that they have no vision of anything beyond that deliberate distortion.* They have felt the edge of ugliness but they have not felt the beauty that lies on the other side of the edge. They feel the harsh lie—but they themselves have no glimmer of the shape of truth that is so close. They don't see it. It is lack of vision, lack of clear intelligence, lack of love—and of course, lack of wisdom. And we shrink from it, we turn cold; we are not shocked, we are not afraid to look, but when we look we are staring at an emptiness that is I think worse than illness.

This is the way I see it. For instance, Kierkegaard; why is he popular with the avant garde today? A schizophrenic, of course; obviously so. Why do the young turn to his writings? because he is distorted? I don't think so. They turn because he is empty—fundamentally empty and they do not want to be filled. They shun wisdom, vision, love, compassion, hope. As I said of the Vassar girls (after working with them last year) they want above

*Kubie wrote Smith on August 30, 1956, from Seattle, Washington, where he was attending a meeting and reading a paper on the topic of "The Vulnerability of the Creative Process to Neurotic Distortion."[16] In the deleted initial portion of this letter Smith thanked Kubie for a telegram he had sent during the Christmas holidays. Presumably, in it he had expressed an interest in having her read his paper.

all else security from hope. If they have hope, then they will have to assume the responsibility that lies before them, of making a wholeness out of clashing fragments. But as long as one is hopeless, one need do nothing, be nothing: hopelessness can pay high dividends (especially in that world we call art, literature, etc. etc.).

There is a good deal more to say about Kierkegaard of course than what I say here. He *lived out a fantasy* that so many only dream of.

I am talking off the cuff; writing it down almost before it turns into words. Am sure I am saying things badly; because I am not taking enough time. But your paper is important and I want to see it, of course; for always you say so much that is penetrating and very right, indeed; and I always respect everything you say, even when I sometimes differ with you. And I may agree entirely when I see it!

[. . .]

tls, Kubie/LC

TO LEWIS MUMFORD

February 14, 1957

Dear Lewis:

Thank you for that wonderful letter. It came at a moment when I needed it. I am hard on my novel now and I go through periods of cruel self criticism. Your words gave me a little nudge that put me back on a more confident path.*

Of course your opinion is valued by me in a very special way. Because of your books and my long hours spent with them. They speak to me on so many levels of experience: mind, yes; imagination, yes; heart, yes yes; but on another level, too: vision? I grope for the right word here. For vision is not quite what I mean. It is the wholeness of your view that I respond to. I think that is it. There are a few people who see things close up, in detail, but who can also turn quickly and see the whole of human experience, brushing away detail, never forgetting it but brushing it away, as they embrace with reason and mythic mind and poetic imagination and heart the big movement, the ebb-flow of the human experience. You do this: when you speak of man you never are speaking of Western Man, alone—as do most Euro-

---

*Mumford had written Smith thanking her for writing *The Journey* and expressing his appreciation for her writing, her sense of the ultimate realities, her characterization and atmosphere, and her capturing of the pathos of the South.[17]

pean and American writers. You are aware of the others, too, the Asians, the Africans, the Arabic world. When you speak of life you are thinking, too, of death; when you talk of man's rational experience you are profoundly aware that the rational would be meaningless without the irrational; you know sin is meaningless without the concept of goodness; that goodness is as nothing without an understanding of sin . . . But there are so few who think, feel, dream like this.

When you mentioned van der Post, you made me happy. And excited me a bit, too, for you see I feel exactly the same way about him. Along with you, he is a writer I have responded to with all of my mind and imagination. I have never met him except in his books. I remember how I felt when I read *Venture into the Interior*. I was very near him as I read: this, too, is the way I look at things, I said; this is my feeling about night, darkness, the mountain, our mythic mind, and so on. When I read *Dark Eye in Africa*, I felt he understands it as I do: he understands the white man's fear of his personal and collective unconscious; he knows that the darkness is filled with the terrible for white eyes and the natural and ugly but the necessary and the good for Africans. He understands "the dark eye"—and so do I. And I felt it was an important book so I asked the *New York Times* to let me review it. I feared it would get in the hands of a "race relations expert" and God help any book that does. So they gave it to me. But Harvey Breit told me that they had not planned to review it at all until I asked for it. You see Francis Brown had not even recognized its worth and importance. Then when I did it (he limited me to such brief space that I could not even begin to deal with it adequately) it was hidden in the back pages.

His publishers invited me to a party to meet him but I was here in Georgia at the time and felt that I could not take the time from my book to go up. When I read that sentence I am shamed. For why couldn't I take the time? What was more important, actually, than to meet this man whose writings mean so much to me. Perhaps I feared that when we met we might find it difficult to talk. That is true, sometimes. Many writers have a self that can come to others only by way of the written word. I am an old talker; I find it quite as easy, or easier, to talk than to write. But only to those who can understand. With others, I am mute and dull.

Thank you so much, Lewis, for sending me *The Transformations of Man*. I think it is a wonderful little—and very big—book. It is remarkable in its simplicity; remarkable in its profound grasp of the rhythm of the growth of man's spirit and mind; remarkable in that it is a portrait of a man in depth.

It is, in a way, the cream of your thinking, feeling, study, understanding. But because it is written so simply I suspect many will think of it as "superficial." And that is when I shout hell and damnation. These people who value erudition so much that they never recognize the profoundly erudite mind! They bother me very much. The people who pile their minds up with words; they talk about form and they have no sense of form; they talk about knowledge and they have no knowledge; they talk about art and they mean esthetic ideology. It has (your book) so much imagination in it; imagination fused with tenderness. I value my copy from you; and I have, in turn, given it to others who I know will value it as I do.

But *Condition of Man* is in its fragments, richer, more subtle, thicker in texture. *Transformations*'s quality lies in the book as a whole; *Condition of Man* appeals to me, paragraph by paragraph. That is really a remarkable book.

My novel is coming along. It is a small book, perhaps not an important one. I don't know. At times, I find myself wondering how in the world I got into this book. But I felt that way about *Journey*, too. It is called *One Hour*. It concerns, in its headline story, a young scientist who is accused by a small girl of "an immoral act." But the headline story is nothing; the real story moves from person to person, from level to level of their lives. I think of it, too, as a fable of our times. The irrational quality of this atomic age. The modern primitive who lives on the mythic level of his mind surrounded by his scientific gadgets; the ignorant, the naive who accept science as a new superstition; who having lost axial religion is searching for new idols to worship. It is, in a sense, also the story of man against the mob—the mob inside his own mind as well as the mob outside. Well . . . we shall see what I finally make of it all.

[. . .]

tlc, UGA

 Correspondence between Smith and Mozell Hill began in March 1957 after *Phylon*, Atlanta University's review of race and culture which Hill edited, published Smith's Montgomery speech, "The Right Way Is Not the Moderate Way," and received requests for five hundred reprints. Smith's following invitation for a group to gather on her mountain as a first step toward creating a more effective climate for racial desegregation in Georgia is reminiscent of her 1940s house parties. It is also noteworthy that Smith was actively encouraging young people to create a new movement three years before the student sit-ins mobilized the civil rights movement of the 1960s.

March 11, 1957

Dear Mozell:

I'd like to call you that, if I may—and if you will forget the "Smith." Thank you for your letter.

I should be hard at my book but the more I write about this problem of the mob inside a man's mind and outside on the street, the more concerned I become about many things. Just now, I want to mention only two thoughts: (1) Why don't you and your wife and two others come up on a Saturday (or Sunday) and have lunch with us? Saturday is better, in that my cook can come and help me a bit with it; and also because on Sunday there is a big crowd at the little church which is down at the foot of my hill, therefore all visitors are studied, commented on, and gossiped about by the church-goers. Saturday is strategically better. Or shall we come straight out and say "safer." Once here, we could talk, walk around the hill (it is a lovely old mountain) and you could leave in time to arrive home by seven or seven-thirty. There is no risk in coming. At least, up to this time none of my visitors has had trouble. But always, I suggest care and caution to avoid trouble. Once trouble comes, it is hard to deal with creatively; I prefer never to give in but always to do what I do in as tactful a way as possible.

(2) I think—and I imagine Grace Hamilton would agree—that we need rather desperately in Georgia to get together a group of honest people of both races, with fresh minds, fresh points of view, to form a nucleus of the most creative thinking and acting on this issue. I think we need the group in order to fuse the truly liberal elements in our state; I think we need the group in order to communicate and to develop a feeling of camaraderie; I think we need it also in order to devise ways of meeting problems and creating a new spirit in our state. [. . .]

The very fact that the first interracial work in the South began in Georgia has proved recently to be a deterrent to progress.* The old-timers are dogmatic; they stirred up a lot of dust in their day; all right, they say, that is the only way you can stir up dust, paw the ground the way we did. You can't move them. Some are dead now but their ghosts are still around. I appreciate what they did and what those still around are doing. But we need a fresh approach. Something younger, more vital, more risky, full of fun and ardor. We need to get the youngsters involved; they haven't got sense enough to know there is danger, so they'll go ahead and do what even you and I would

---

*Reference to the Commission on Interracial Cooperation and its successor, the Southern Regional Council, both founded in Atlanta.

gulp over. But we've got to let them try. If the young white men and women and young colored men and women of Georgia can't do something, it just can't be done. The rest of us have broken down walls, filled up ditches, defined problems, put a sharp edge on dilemmas, we've shaken everybody's souls with the moral issue—now something more has to be done. And what we who are more experienced, more aware, can do is encourage the young ones to try, to take over, TO DO SOMETHING. Their apathy is shocking. It was shocking at Vassar. They all fell back on their tolerance. We are tolerant, they said, we haven't a prejudice, but that is enough. And when I told them it was not enough, they had to believe in something with their whole heart and mind, they had to *commit themselves* to bring about a new world, they did not like it much. They long for *security from hope*. [. . .] At the YW conference at Spelman I thought a little of the same thing. There were the young white and colored girls together, eating together, sleeping in the same dorm, often sharing the same room. They felt pious as—hell. (Forgive me, but honestly that is it.) So tolerant of each other. The whites had not found it easy to come; parents had opposed them; some of the colleges wouldn't permit them to come and a few had slipped out. So they felt they had done enough. And when I suggested that they hadn't even begun, they did not like it too much. I said "You've got to create a new South; a new state of mind; a new place to live in; you have to fight for your freedoms because they're slipping away from you." But they said to me, "We are all right; it is our parents, it is the older people; it is their fault; we'd be all right if they'd leave us alone." I used to say it too, long ago. I was really a rebel; these children are sort of playing dolls with it. But when I said "That isn't enough: to blame it on the parents. You, and you only must change the psychology of the South, the spirit of things, the quality of human relationships,"—they didn't want to risk anything. Both these white and Negro girls have been too sheltered. Well: this is, at least, part of our problem.

It would help if a few of us could get together and talk things over. Shall I write Grace Hamilton?*

tlc, UGA

*Hill's response to this letter enthusiastically endorsed Smith's invitation to visit and talk about new directions in the desegregation movement, especially the need to involve young people. Cautioning against recruiting persons who he felt were obligated or connected with old institutions and agencies, Hill wrote that he had not mentioned Smith's proposal to Grace Hamilton, then executive director of the

The following two letters to Denver Lindley are representative of the way Smith engaged her editor in the writing process. Correspondence with her editors during the three years of writing *One Hour* provide a richly detailed portrait of a writer at work, her fears and inhibitions, her commentary on philosophers, theologians, artists, and writers whose work influenced her thinking at the time.

March 19, 1957

Dear Denver:

[. . .]

Part of my enormous interest in technic just now is an escape from my book's unique problems, not all of which are technical. I am captive in my own tangled nets. I have let Mark's nature and Dave's and Grace's take them into tight spots where I dread going.* What is so ordinary, actually in real life, sounds sometimes so damned perverse when put into words. I have never been afraid of life—at least, I don't think so—and the unnamed places, the forbidden experiences have drawn me toward them rather than away from them. But I find it difficult to say things in print that I say in daily conversation. I know a number of young ministers intimately enough to know quite a bit about their love affairs, and their somewhat perverse and "abnormal" affairs. And yet the moment I write honestly of a young priest I am going to have seven thousand devils let loose on me. Not that I mind—but maybe I do. Maybe I had too much of it with *Strange Fruit* and *Killers of the Dream*. Maybe I've got scared of my own shadow. I just don't

---

Atlanta Urban League, but had invited Jack and Betty Gloster, young people working with the Greater Atlanta Council on Human Relations, who were completely enthusiastic about the proposed visit with Smith. Hill also invited Smith to become a key consultant on a proposal initiated by Atlanta University's Department of Sociology to develop a project for leadership training for a new society, which he felt was in keeping with her ideas.[18] Subsequent correspondence, however, indicates that conflicting schedules may have made the proposed visit impossible. There is no evidence that the Hills or the Glosters visited Smith in the spring of 1957, nor that she was involved in the proposed leadership training project. Their conversations may have continued in June, when Smith gave the commencement address at Atlanta University.

*Three major characters in *One Hour*: Dave Channing, Episcopal priest; Mark Channing, scientist; and Grace Channing, painter, dancer, and Mark's wife.

know. But I think some of my problems are psychic, or moral ones which I am going to have to battle out with myself.

[. . .]

tls, HBJ

Sunday morning [April 1957]

Dear Denver:

We are having some fine New York weather down here: cold air and wonderful sun. [. . .] It is difficult to stay indoors and work on the book; and I don't succeed; I have spent several days after eleven o'clock outdoors digging and spading and wondering what Grace was saying to Dave and how she let him know how she felt and how he found out the trinity-level of her act: that she needed love, needed to give love, needed to hurt Mark while giving love to someone else. And yet he has to see all this even as he is accepting what she gives, knowing he wants it, that his body image needs it, that she needs it, that she at the same time feels she is giving more than she is receiving—and always Mark there in the shadows. I dig in the earth and I think and dig some more. And then I wonder if her child, the child she wanted, did she want it by Mark or Dave—and if not by Dave why . . . and if by Mark why. . . .

Lawrence Kubie (my friend, the psychoanalyst) and I have almost lost our friendship over this book: he is stunned over my interest in the Cross, in faith, in the church, in the cross-relations of science, religion, art. The symbol, the rite, the myth. First, he resents my "drifting" away from the "sane rational world of science" into all this business of religion, value in the mystical sense, etc. And second, he is a psychoanalyst who literally does not feel the weight of the symbol. To him it is a sign[?]. That is so strange to me: how any sensitive human being can turn away from myth and symbol; when he told me he despised dancing: "How can any woman fling her arms and legs around, letting her legs do what her arms should do and arms do what legs should do," I cringed in a kind of mammoth distaste, and we decided we had passed each other in a pleasant place in the road and now one traveler was going this way, the other that. It is so sad, though, to have had a friend and feel suddenly that either the part of you who cared for him is dead or the part of him who cared for you is dead. But the evening we spent together was like that, this time. And he is the kind of friend who likes your mind more than he likes either your personality or soul—and he thinks my mind is not what it used to be.

So—even before publication I am losing friends because of *One Hour.**

Denver, if you have not read Tillich's *Dynamics of Faith,* may I send you a copy? I liked it very much. There is a chapter in Frithjof Schuon's *Transcendent Unity of Religions* which I also found of great interest, an interest sharpened because I agreed with him only in large part, I could not agree on some of his definitions of the word "tradition." This is the chapter called Concerning Forms in Art. The book as a whole I find difficult. You have probably read it. The Tillich book is a little masterpiece in that he knows his subject so well that he has found his way into simple earthy words and handles them deftly and with tremendous integrity. It is as if he is communicating with one earnest honest sensitive intelligent man who wants to understand the meaning of faith. And this great scholar, this fine thinker reaches back through a lifetime of thought and study and brings out his answers, addressed not to fellow-theologians, not to a scholarly group whom he might, quite humanly, want to impress a bit, but to this one quiet, earnest, solemn, sensitive, intelligent fellow who "wants to know." I wanted to know, too, so his book has meant a great deal to me—and to Dave. I think this book which Dave read after the trouble helped clarify his thinking about it—as it helped the author.

You remember you talked to me a bit that Saturday about O'Hara's book which I was reading while in New York and mentioned that he had great hopes for the book, believing he was writing something of genuine importance and worth. After you said it, I completed the book and sat there one night a long time thinking about it and your words. How could O'Hara have had such a dream and turned it into such a tawdry thing! This is the horror, the nightmare of the writer. Inside me is such a fine big dream: will it turn out to be commonplace, ordinary, dull, maybe vulgar? I felt about the O'Hara book as I feel about Erskine Caldwell's books: there is a denigration of—something, of the human spirit, for everybody. The writer as he tells about empty people spills his own blood and spirit out on the ground. How to get what one is thinking, dreaming, feeling down on that damned paper! I feel what Grace is going through . . . then I translate it into words and I read them and I see I didn't put down what Grace was really thinking, feeling, but what a part of the world thinks she was thinking, dreaming. Are we such slaves of language that we cannot free ourselves

*The feelings expressed here about Kubie were only temporary; their friendship continued throughout Smith's life.

enough to put it together in the way we want to use it? I know that is what Gertrude Stein and Joyce were trying to get at. I want to communicate but I want to communicate what I know and feel not what the world thinks it knows and feels. And most of the time I can't. I am like O'Hara: the profound turns into the trite, the subtle into the gross . . .

I know you'll be glad when you're through with this book and me. Paula says I'm hard to live with; and I know I'm not an easy author to have to put up with. I pour my problems out to you without telling you what the problems actually are: what I do is pour my pains out to you. Don't feel you have to sop em up. Just bear with me. I'll be a pleasanter person when it is all over. Then *Julia* . . . but I am surer about Julia than I am about this book. So maybe it won't be so hard on you, the completion of that. [. . .]

tls, UGA

On September 24, 1957, President Dwight D. Eisenhower ordered federal troops to protect the entrance of nine black students into formerly all-white Central High School in Little Rock, Arkansas. A copy of this letter dated October 4, 1957, was sent to Ralph McGill at the *Atlanta Constitution*. Neither paper published it.

TO THE EDITORS, *New York Times*

Undated [October 1957]

Sirs:

There are valuable lessons for the entire country in the painful experience Little Rock is going through:

We realize, as we watch that situation, how dangerous silence can be. For it is the silence of law-abiding people that gives the green light to the mob and to the demagogue. No mob ever came out on the street until enlightened public opinion had left it. No demagogue will talk too much unless the good people talk too little.

We know the great germinal ideas have civilized mankind. But Little Rock reminds us that good words and good feelings are necessary every day. For when we become mutes, in the name of moderation, we slide toward barbarism with shocking rapidity.

We need, as individuals, to say aloud that we will not tolerate mob rule or disrespect for our Supreme Court. We need to speak out for obedience to our highest laws, for loyalty to our basic form of government. We need to remind each other that the welfare of our country comes before that of any state; that it is our President's sworn obligation to maintain the peace when law enforcement has broken down in a community, if the State fails to do so.

Some one said to me, last week, in New York, "But it was a terrible thing for the U.S. Army to have to take over." Ah . . . but you don't know how secure it makes some of us in the South feel to know if the demagogues in our state go berserk, if our officials indulge in the madness of Governor Faubus, that the good old U.S. troops will come in and protect us. Some of us southerners do not feel too well protected at the present moment. Those of us who stand up for human rights down here, who refuse to defend segregation are not too sure that in a crisis we would have the protection we might need.

We have a sense of sadness that it was necessary for troops to go into Arkansas. But we are proud to know, as a prominent woman of my town said yesterday, that President Eisenhower will move fast if law and order break down in our state.

The good, creative things happening in Little Rock can teach us some lessons, too: Here is a brave editor who stood for law and order, who was determined to keep down mob violence, doing all in his power to help protect those nine children who went to school because the Federal courts told them to go; here are a few ministers working day and night to awaken their church members' minds to the urgencies of the ordeal; here is one Congressman who made valiant appeals for law and order. But where are the others? where was Senator Fulbright? why did he not speak? where was Senator McClellan? why did he not go home and help? where were the civic leaders? the Jaycees? the Rotarians, etc? Could the trouble have been avoided if the leadership of the state had begun to work earlier and in much larger numbers? Is this good leadership, even today, saying enough?

I am not sure. It is urgent to say we must obey the law whether we like it or not. But a free, independent people want to feel that it is a reasonable law, that it will help their children and their country. If they obey the law without becoming convinced that it is both necessary and good for the nation, their resentment will, inevitably, slosh over.

Knowing this is so, it is our obligation now to persuade and to clarify. All of us must say aloud, if we believe it, that segregation is not a sacred way of life. It was not handed down as a revelation from God and cannot take precedence over our religious beliefs, our human rights, and the prestige of our nation.

I cannot see how segregation can be defended from any point of view. In the old days, it made money for the few; today it loses money for everybody.

It certainly aids and abets the southern politicians but it has never made one southern child a better person or given him a better life. The segregation system itself puts rigorous pressures on us, strips us of freedom of speech, and above all else, of our freedom to do what is right.

It is an exorbitant price to pay simply to help the demagogues build themselves up. Then why do we let ourselves be exploited so cruelly?

For one reason only: the fear of intermarriage. As Senator Eastland said on television a few days ago, "Segregation is to keep down intermarriage and prevent mongrelization."

Yet, a glance at figures and facts, will show us that the system of segregation has always encouraged illegal miscegenation. This is an inevitable result, of a system where there is the master race and the slave race. But under the system of integration (a word I dislike very much) there will be much less illegal miscegenation—which is the result of irresponsible sexual adventures—and very few interracial marriages. Why? Because (a) educated girls who are accepted in the community are not interested in concubinage; (b) marriage is a social institution which carries with it heavy and public responsibilities. Few young couples in the South would want to assume the double load of marriage responsibilities and the burden of social taboos that would surround them were they to cross the racial line in marriage.

If the fear of intermarriage is the only reason people can find for their support of segregation, then how tragic, how truly mad it is to be risking so much for so little.

This kind of fear is not fear at all: it is anxiety. It is the result of mob thinking; the result of old memories that have festered in our minds; old superstitions that have not been analyzed, old taboos given us in childhood.

We, North and South, need to substitute for these sick anxieties a few real fears: fear of mob rule, fear of the breakdown of our national government, fear of the loss of America's moral prestige throughout the world, fear of moral delinquency, fear above all else of the demagogue who has certainly thrown the gasoline on the fire in Arkansas and will do it in Georgia, and other southern states—and in the North also—if we don't get busy now to prevent the mob from gathering in people's minds: where it always has its first clandestine meeting.

Rational fear is a technic of survival; once we fear the real dangers we can get to work to do something meaningful and constructive about them. And the first thing the North can do to help us is to open their magazines and

TV forums to the white Southerners who oppose segregation and who know why they do so. Let them speak; only in this way will others find the courage to break their silence.

fdr, UGA

TO LAWRENCE KUBIE

October 10, 1957

Dear Larry:

[. . .]

Let me tell you what happened to Dave Garroway's show on Integration, scheduled on the NBC network for October 2nd. Because I have been working on the networks, urging them to let the more intelligent, "Americanized" citizens speak out from the South, they asked me to be on this program. Indeed, I was the first one asked, I think. They told me they were having me, Senator Eastland, perhaps Senator Long, Harry Ashmore, Jonathan Daniels, a young white minister from Kentucky who had quelled the beginning of a mob (if they would come): in order to give the arc of varying opinions in the Southland.* Daniels refused to come; Ashmore refused; don't know what happened to Senator Long; Senator Eastland agreed; I agreed; the young white minister agreed. Then they filled in with white northerners and northern Negroes.

When the program was announced in the press, NBC began getting telephone calls from the South. The pressure put on them must have been terrific. They told me it was; and I saw their anxiety and something closer to terror than anxiety. They heard from TV stations in the South; they heard from big-name businessmen; and heavens only knows who else. It was not a spontaneous reaction from the people: it was a concerted intensive drive put on by an interested few.

The show was to be on Wednesday. I arrived in New York Tuesday morning (leaving my novel on which I am working day and night now because I have a November deadline.) They began getting the calls on Monday. Tuesday, they got more. I was in the office of a prominent New Yorker who is from the South. While I was with him that day he received four calls from the South, asking him to use all the influence he had to kill

*James Oliver Eastland, Mississippi; Russell B. Long, Louisiana; Harry Ashmore, editor, *Little Rock Arkansas Gazette*; Jonathan Daniels, editor, Raleigh *News and Observer*.

the show. He refused to do so; he is a real liberal; and happens to be one of my closest friends.*

Now: this is what happened. I was to have a nice spot on the show; they had asked me to prepare a four or five minute statement on why I felt segregation was harmful to our people. I spent two days doing so, trying to make it firm, clear and at the same time, tactful and considerate of the southerners' feelings. But it was plain, all right. They refused to let me give it; they did not even see it; they just said it was off; but they let Senator Eastland give his on mongrelization. I fought softly but persistently for some intelligent questions to be asked me; they finally promised to ask me one on segregation. They were to ask me four. When I got there and went on, they had cut it down to two: both of them off the segregation subject. One was silly; the other was on the mob. I answered them both with as much wisdom as I could. When they did not ask me the segregation question, I raised "hell" after the first show. (There are always two shows in daylight saving time. The second one covers most of the South and mid-West.) They promised me once more they'd ask it. They did not. Dave asked me two questions, hurried my answers and said Thank you and cut me off. No one even thanked me for being on the program; no one apologized for my wasted five days: two to prepare the little speech, three to go up and return. I got no money for it, of course. Was promised my travel expenses, have not yet received it.

It is, to me, Larry, one of the most shocking experiences I have ever had. Not alone the easy quick fear and terror which a giant of a network like NBC falls into from a few telephone calls; but the curtness, the indignity shown me, the lack of consideration of what it meant to me to come up and give, for nothing, five days. My really liberal friends down here were shocked to death that I didn't "speak out." They even called me up; of course I was sick over it; I could have outwitted him had I believed he was going to cheat me. This is my weakness: my belief in the innate decency of people. I lean backward to try not to feel persecuted, not to let myself believe "everybody is against me"—but I should have known. Of course I should have known.

We white southerners run risks every day of our lives. What discourages us is the fact that so few white northerners will take even small risks to help us.

*In other accounts of this experience she names her friend, Donald Seawell, her lawyer and literary agent.

I wrote the *New York Times* a letter about this conspiracy of silence. They refused to print it. I called no names, gave no specific instances but wrote about the danger of this silence, how it must be broken etc. It was a very long letter, it is true; but in 1948 they published a letter from me just as long and Sulzberger wired me he was honored to have it appear in his paper.*
But the *Times* has been worked on by these southerners too. The "line" on me is that I am "a queer," a fanatical "old maid who lives by herself up on a mountain" etc. Hodding Carter in one of his columns called me "a sex obsessed old spinster" . . . although he had never met me in his life. Ralph McGill who wrote about my being "a fanatic living on a mountain in sackcloth and ashes" has never met me in his life. He has never met me because he refuses to: if he finds out that the two of us are on a program he refuses to go. I suspect Jonathan Daniels reacted the same way when asked to be on the NBC show.

[. . .]

This smothering has crept into quite a few odd places: for instance, if somebody writes about best-sellers in this country during the past fifteen years, *Strange Fruit* is never mentioned; although it broke, as you know, ALL RECORDS for a serious book. If race books are mentioned, I am never included. Yet my books on the problems of race and segregation have sold more than those of any other writer in the world and are known all over the world. And if I am not the South's best writer I am certainly among the first two or three; and surely my books have made history and will make history.

This is my story. You don't know how I hate to tell it. I saw Evelyn Scott smothered to death (one of our early and best southern writers) and I saw her go into paranoia. Ah, maybe she would have gone, anyway; I don't know. But I saw this happen, watched her turn even against her best friends believing that they, too, "were against her." W. J. Cash, whose book certainly was not shocking in any sense of the word but was one step forward for a southerner[,] committed suicide, afterward. Cason committed suicide.† People have hoped I would; well—I don't know . . . guess I'm too curious about what will happen next here on earth! No southerner has ever, since the Civil War, spoken out as I have and *insisted on staying here.* This is what they hate so. If I'd only leave.

*Arthur Hays Sulzberger, publisher of the *New York Times*.

†Clarence Cason, author of *90° in the Shade* (Chapel Hill: University of North Carolina Press, 1935).

Well—I'd like to, all right. But I think I am needed here and as a novelist here is where I see things in their most distorted and exaggerated mode: and I like to watch it.

Now: if we can somehow persuade a few influential northern friends to work with us: we must open up more newspapers, more programs on the networks, and see to it that some articles by white southerners who oppose segregation get in the mass magazines.

I must confess I live in fear of what the *New York Times* will do to my new novel "One Hour." If they kill it, it won't have a chance. And it lies in Lester Markel's power to do this.* He used to like me. But he "advised" me once to stop writing on racial problems and "use that marvelous talent of yours for real novels." I didn't follow his advice. Lester doesn't like you if you don't genuflect to him. So I just don't know what to expect. [. . .] The southerners have infiltrated every paper in New York; and while a few are truly liberal men, most are barnacled with prejudice and body anxiety.

So: here we are, down here, slowly smothering. We really need help. This problem of freedom of speech is far more important than either the mobs or segregation. For if the southerners could speak out we wouldn't have the mobs, and we would soon not have segregation either. But all our poor people hear is the brainwashing the demagogues and fetid-minded politicians like Dick Russell give them.† No good talk. No questioning of segregation in any public places, except in the pulpits: here there is a crack: we are hoping to see this crack widen. We would like to see Dean Pike, for instance, have two or three (or even one) of our ministers who oppose segregation (and know why they oppose it) to be on his program.‡ I can give him, or anyone else, a few good names. I believe some of these ministers are brave enough to speak out. To me, the sad thing was that Harry Ashmore when asked on *Meet the Press* how he felt about segregation would not answer. He said he felt "it was irrelevant to the situation." They pushed him hard but he wouldn't answer. I see why: in the crisis in his city; but it was sickening just the same. So like the good, thoughtful Christians of Germany . . . from 1930—to 38.

*Lester Markel, editor, Sunday *New York Times*.
†Richard B. Russell, U.S. senator from Georgia.
‡James Albert Pike, dean of the Protestant Episcopal Cathedral of St. John the Divine in New York City, conducted a weekly half-hour discussion program on ABC-TV each Sunday.[19]

Well, this is surely a long letter. Forgive me. But maybe it should be set down somewhere, even though I am burdening you with it.*

tls, Kubie/LC

TO CONSTANCE MCMILLAN CARPENTER†

November 14, 1957

Dear Connie:

It is always good to hear. And recently, I heard from Ann—which was nice. I'd like so much to see both of you. I have the feeling of a vast isolation [. . .]. I was with Dorothy Norman a month out at East Hampton this past summer. Nevertheless—I feel isolated from the people I want to be with, the currents of feeling, thought, creativity that I feel I belong to.

While at East Hampton, I met Ossorio—the Spanish-Filipine artist. He is a fascinating young man; with the rigorous conscience, the austerity of the Spaniard and the sensuousness of the Spaniard, and that curious remoteness of the Asian. I like his painting. He introduced me to the French painter, Dubuffet—his works, I mean. Alfonse is rich; he inherited his father's sugar plantation fortune; his big rococo house on a lagoon at East Hampton, or three miles from, is full of Pollock's paintings and his own, and many others of the school or half-school which these men belong to. He has crucifixes all over his home. One large one hangs over his bed. Alfonse tries to forget Picasso. It is difficult to forget Picasso because of his giant virtuosity. I saw his retrospective show in New York; went twice. The scope, size of the damned thing is enormously impressive. I feel that nobody can draw as well as he—except you. I really think you can. I don't think he ever conceived much on a profound imaginative basis. It was his craftsmanship, his enormous talent with pencil and paint and things, things, things, putting them together in new shapes, new designs. But rarely rarely has he created an image that can extend from one's mythic mind to one's poetic mind. And a big artist must do this. Or rather,

*In his response Kubie offered to show parts of Smith's letter to Reinhold Niebuhr and Dean Pike and to appeal to Niebuhr to approach Edward R. Murrow about building a story around the suppression of the liberal in the South, using Smith's experiences.[20]

†An instructor in painting and sculpture at Laurel Falls Camp in the late 1940s whose paintings Smith greatly admired and encouraged. Her sister Ann had met Smith through Connie.

a great artist must. But I think these younger men I met at East Hampton this past summer reject him in order to give themselves courage. Of course, just now, they actually are not painting at all: they are dabbing, finger-painting, only now and then do they stumble on even a new image—much less a new vision. Ossorio has a two-story studio on his grounds full of the paintings of the mentally ill of France and Spain. It is a monstrous and raw and fascinating collection; some of the paintings show more originality, more insight, more vision than that of the best known artists of today. Technics are poor; but some technics are excellent. And there was much beauty.

Alfonse has living with him and for him a former dancer, named Ted. Ted has a last name I am sure; but he was Ted to all of us; he is lovable; we got along fine together. He is a beautiful cook. There was a young pianist who had recently finished at Dartmouth, whose sister fell in love with a woman when she was at boarding school and followed the woman to Paris where they now live. The young pianist of course had to tell me all about it. He was leaving for Greece (Fulbright) to do some research in Greek poetry, perhaps, but his real reason was to get TO PARIS, SOMEHOW AND STAY. [. . .]

While at East Hampton—Dorothy Norman has an exhibit on the myth, she calls it the Heroic Encounter going up at the Willard Gallery in January—not paintings but photographs of paintings, artifacts, sculptures, et cetera . . . now back to the beginning of that sentence: While there, I met the Willard woman; she is nice; I want her to be sure to see your paintings; I mentioned you to her; and she listened; I also want you to meet Alfonse. [. . .]

[. . .]

I must get back to the book. I am on the chapter in which Grace tells Dave (the clergyman who is in love with her) of her first love for a woman she met at camp when she was fifteen. I am trying to do this memory as a child would remember it, not as Grace the wife of Mark, the mother of Andy would remember it. Yet as she tells it she must overlap her mature memory with the child memory. It is interesting to work on. And hurts, too, at times. The whole book hurts, at times. The few who have read it say it is fascinating—but I feel dissatisfied with it most of the time. As if I stay too near the surface but when I skin-dive I seem to lose my oxygen mask; and have to pop back up again.

tls, Constance McMillan Carpenter, Ann Arbor, Mich.

December 19, 1958

Dear dear Helen:

[. . .]

Your letter was almost as good as a talk with you. Not quite—for those talks are something rare and wonderful and unforgettable. I have thought of you so often: wondering where you were, what had happened. Of course I could have written—or could I?

The past year . . . since June, full of the book and nothing but the book, day and night, almost. I tried so hard to meet a deadline of October 20th so that it could be published this spring, but failed again. Now I am trying to finish by January 20th for a mid-August publication. It is very long. Long for me. About 725 manuscript pages. I am wondering what you will think of it and I know no one whose opinion would be more precious to me. The president of the firm likes it very much, he says, and wants to make it his "big" book for the year. The editor he sent down—I lost Denver Lindley when he left the firm after a stormy session with the president—seems to love the book: he is a sensitive guy, nice to know, not—what does one say? He is sensitive and subtle, aware, warm, "liberal" and loves *Killers of the Dream* (which is a test I give people!) but has not—suffered. I suppose this is it: has not the tragic point of view. Or perhaps he is not philosophical in temperament. Anyway, he loves the book, *in his way*, came down in November, read 620 pages of it and seemed deeply moved, almost stunned by some of it, and "respectful" after he read it. He came fully expecting to help me get the "hard" chapters together. I wouldn't let him see a chapter that I did not consider completed. When editors begin helping me write my books, that day I cut my throat! That is one trouble with this firm: there is not now one person in it who knows me, or who remembers anything about *Strange Fruit* or *Killers of the Dream* or *Journey* or anything else. All the ones I knew have left; and now the "younger ones" are in command. Bright boys who know so little.

[. . .]

About us: Paula and I are both well. I had my third malignancy this past spring and came through it quickly and apparently successfully; no more surgery; just very heavy radiation. It left me worn and tired, of course; but I am all right. Paula had a skin cancer on her eyelid that happened to be one of the dangerous types; but so far, no return; and Dr. Brown at the Clinic thinks she is now beyond danger of a return.

Did I write you that "the rough ones" set our place on fire twice this past February? The first time, they almost succeeded: they set the woods down in the cove, the wind was blowing straight up toward the little rock house where you stayed. When I discovered it, Paula happened to be in bed with flu; I was down in the dining room writing; saw smoke gathering on the mountain but had a slow reaction, thinking it was mist; suddenly realized it was smoke. When I stepped out of the dining room the entire hill was black with smoke, I was afraid Paula was in a burning house and ran there; then I realized it was the forest and I could hear the fire just below the parking space. Paula was asleep! We called fire department and forestry fire dept. and since Clayton is headquarters for the forestry conservation corps in this area, they were here in ten minutes with all their modern machinery for handling big fires. They worked hours and got it under control. Once, they told us they were afraid they couldn't save the houses; so all the time they were working, Paula and I were packing the car with our manuscripts and boxes of letters we prize most. Not much, you know, left—after the other fire. We didn't say a word to each other: just packed. Put in our heavy winter coats. And waited—ready to start down the hill when they told us to. But they got it out. The forestry chief told me the fire had been set in four different places. Until then, I honestly thought someone stealing wood had dropped a cigarette. Then two weeks later, when I went to the hospital for my malignancy treatments, it was set again. But this time, all our neighbors helped put it out—and the town seemed truly shocked. Yet no one *mentioned* it! Complete silence. The real shock came to them, I think, *because I was sick with a malignancy* in the *hospital*—this touched their hearts—had I been well and at home, they would not have cared so much. Oh God, aren't we made of strange and wonderful stuff? The sheriff even had the Georgia Bureau of Investigation up—which seemed pretty funny to me, because you know how much those boys love me, but anyway, they did; and seeing the GBI prowling around was enough, apparently, to put the fear of the Lord in whoever did it.

Somehow, it broke me up rather badly. I wanted to leave and never come back. It was difficult for me to remember the *majority* of the good people, the sweet neighbors, who worked to help us and protect us. I could think only of the evil ones—who, as you know, are always in the minority (which of course is not the real point; the real point is that these things can happen only because we live in a moral vacuum.) Well, we'll talk about that, sometime or other.

We went to Washington and Eastern Shore and stayed two months to try to find some peace and rest. And it helped us both. When we came back in May, we both felt all right about coming. And ever since, I have done nothing but work day and night on the book. I am coming to Washington to use my sister's house in January, and I do hope we can have a visit with you while we are up there. Perhaps you will come down to Washington?

I have much to say about Atlanta; and Georgia; and so much else. Thank you for the wonderful Rilke poem—I have sort of lived off of Rilke the last two years . . . I think of my month at Vassar, with you and the others, with Mary and Mary Ann, with so much joy. [. . .]

tlc, UGA

TO LAWRENCE KUBIE

June 29, 1959

Dear Larry:

[. . .]

I think the scholarships for Negro students at Johns Hopkins an exciting thing. Am so glad this has happened. Changes are coming everywhere . . . it is a pity that such changes (at least, in the deep South) seem to come only after battles when the human spirit is so wounded and scarred by conflict that the results hardly seem worth the spiritual cost. This disturbs me greatly: the hating, fearing, resistance to small changes. It is, of course, because of the symbols. Our people are afraid to give up their cherished symbols. The reality changes will be so small; they will affect the white man's external life so little: then why does he fight so desperately for the old way of segregation? Because, of course, it is changing his dream life; his symbolic experiences, all his psychic defenses are challenged. "The Negro" has gathered up all the white man's dreams about his image and his intimate relationships and darkened them and distorted them. The *word*, Negro, I mean, the "myth" of the Negro. The actual Negro in the South is a source of pleasure to most white southerners; they like Negroes, they really do; they enjoy them, they are concerned about individual Negroes but—Whatever a demagogue says is always so full of truth! This truth is distorted because it is shaped by feelings and motives that are unacknowledged. But always, there is truth in the demagogue's lying words. The worst segregationist in our town (he is from South Georgia but now lives up here) the one who aroused so much fear of me two or three years ago when my study was burned, and last winter, when the woods around my home were set on fire twice—this fanatic (and he is that) spends most of his time visiting with colored folks in our small Negro community. He lives near them and he takes them baskets of his vegetables and sits and chats with them. He likes them; he feels at home with them; they were his "best friends" in his boyhood; now at 89, he chooses them to spend his time with rather than the white people. This ambivalence, interesting to me as a writer, fascinating (I never tire trying to understand it) tears the white minds of the South to pieces. [. . .]

What the South is going through is a revolutionary conflict inside its people's minds. To change, they must change on a hundred different levels. The Minute Women (a group of fanatics who in their words and acts seem almost insane) have grasped (as many mentally ill people do) the essential truth of our situation. Now they are fighting the mental health movement. Their slogan is: Mental Health is communistic! My brother, Frank, is executive director of the Mental Health Association of Georgia. On his board are many strong segregationists. They have never yet seen that when mental health comes to Georgia, segregation must go. But the Minute Women see it and are fighting the Mental Health movement more bitterly than they are fighting segregation. They have put a great deal of pressure on the legislature and on the Mental Health board of directors—and they have converted one or two of them. Our governor, Vandiver, a stubborn segrega-tionist, is still working hand in hand with Frank for mental health. Frank just hopes he will not see the close relationship between good race relations and mental health—for if he does . . .

Most of the psychiatrists in Atlanta, Larry, are being pretty cagey about desegregation. Sometimes it makes me ashamed of them. I suppose they are afraid. Or perhaps they feel they can do more for healthy relationships by concentrating on each individual they come in contact with. It is true, most of them signed the statement last winter "for public schools;" a statement that said a democracy must hold on to its public schools; Georgia must not sacrifice its public school system etc. etc. A good state-ment. I realize their position. I know its difficulty. But I wish all of the leaders would come out and take a moral stand against segregation. But they'll never do it now. They lost their one chance the summer after the Supreme Court's decision. Then, they could have done it. But they with-drew into silence, instead. This gave the rabid segregationists their big chance to arouse the people's memories and guilt and dreads. After this state of mind was developed—a state of mind close to acute illness—it would have been suicidal (as the leaders then said) for them to speak out. This must be similar to what happened in Germany. There was a time when the liberal sane people of Germany could have fought Hitler. But they let their big chance pass. After that, they were as helpless as they claimed to be.

The bombing of the Jewish Temple last fall in Atlanta, did a wonderful thing for much of Georgia. The damage was a small price to pay for bringing about the sharp change in the moral climate that occurred, afterward. People who had been morally paralyzed stirred, spoke out, protested. The cagey ones stopped being quite so cagey. Most of Atlanta's best people had been moral zeroes. They began, at least, to say they were "against bombings, violence, and for obedience to law." They felt terribly brave to do so.*

Isn't it a grisly commentary on our nation and its present state of mind that people are called "brave" when they take a stand against mob violence and for obedience to the Nation's laws? It shocks me to see the national committees give their Pulitzer prizes and other accolades to those who have dared speak up against bombings and violence. I find myself rubbing my eyes: I cannot quite believe it is happening. Have we really sunk to such a low level? Are we really a nation of moral cowards, are moral values so rare that we award people for taking stands against violence?

The country's attitude about segregation fascinates me, too. [. . .] North and South, our people have raised an altar to moderation. It is our new god. One must not be completely honest. To be so, places you in the category of the "extremists." Be only moderately honest, be only moderately decent, moderately good, moderately EVERYTHING. I wonder when we'll wake up.

I am having a copy of *One Hour* sent to you. It will be published in October. The books will soon be off the press, I hope. I am not sure you will like it: it is told from the point of view of an Episcopalian priest. There were things I wanted to say that could be said only through his mouth, I felt.

tls, Kubie/LC

*The Temple of the Reform Jewish congregation in Atlanta was bombed on October 12, 1959.[21] The psychological effect of the bombing, which Smith sensed, was dramatically portrayed in Alfred Uhry's 1988 Pulitzer Prize–winning play, *Driving Miss Daisy*.

July 20, 1959

Dear Bob:

[. . .]

About India and books on India. I know, of course, how shoddy *Mother India* is in many ways. I was speaking rather lightly of it when I said "it had its point." Before making my two trips to India I did not think highly enough of it to read it. Yet afterward, I saw some truth in its distortions. She misunderstood, exaggerated, distorted—yet she said some true things, as Gandhi once told his followers. He said, "We must so live that *Mother India* will not be true. Unfortunately, it does hold some truth now." But Gandhi thought "wrong" much that I think deeply "right." That is, about the body and its intimate relations with other bodies. Of course I admire him in other ways tremendously but I always thought he was wrong about food and sex being "evil."

The fascinating thing to me is India's asceticism, rather than its sensuality. It is natural, of course, that natures capable of such deep sensualism should be capable of an equally deep asceticism. But part of my interest lies in the fact that the cultivated Indian feels there is a time in life for all things: a time to play and learn as a child and boy; a time to have intimate relationships, as in sex life and family life; a time to achieve, do business, become an erudite man, perhaps; then finally, a time to withdraw, especially from one's concerns with sex and appetite for food and hunger for money, and spend the rest of one's life in contemplation and deep, rigorous thought. I like this very much. The fact that the Indian accepts his body and emotions and their appetites and then feels capable of renouncing them for a deeper, more mature pleasure, the pleasure of becoming wise, seems rather wonderful to me.

What I liked so much in "The Loves of Krishna" was the candid discussion of the Indian man's understanding of women's sex life. The Indian man—at least ideally—understands that the woman has as deep a sexual hunger as he has; he also understands that in love-making the woman need not always be the passive one; he also understands (all this is theoretical or in his "ideals") that he cannot meet her needs save by great tenderness. I

---

*His letter to Smith, written July 15, 1959, on Atlanta University Graduate School stationery, thanked her for a wonderful visit and conversation that he and his friend Allen enjoyed with her.

found this interesting and what my cultivated Indian friends had told me confirmed it. The other aspect of sex that interested me was that in their legends, their symbols, the images they made of their gods and goddesses, their spirits and near holy ones (such as the Boddhisatvas) they created a kind of neutral sex. It was as if they understood the bi-sexuality of men and women. The Indian's subtlety is what impressed me most. In Zimmer's books on Indian art, especially the one (two volumes) called *The Art of Indian Asia*, I found the sculptures, frescoes, cave paintings enormously fascinating. But most of "The Loves of Krishna" has to do not with sex analysis but with the actual legends of Krishna and the schools of painting that used Krishna and his loves as a major theme. The discussion of sex was entirely secondary and the "handbook" I mentioned was named here almost as a footnote. I shall try to get the author's name for you and the name of the "handbook on marriage."

I think Dube's book on caste and class in the Indian village about as good as anything that has been done. *Behind Mud Walls* is warm and most interesting and written by two people who have lived in villages with the Indians for thirty-five years. Zimmer's books are of course interesting. But this is enough: the others are on the list.

The other thing about the Indians that especially interested me had to do with their art. Because of the Hindu all-inclusiveness their art with its whirling concentric movements bedazzled me. It was a relief to turn to Burmese sculptures for there one finds a rigorous selectivity which the Indian art totally lacks. I think this is the Buddhist influence but I also think it is more: some of the Chinese influence and perhaps Japanese has drifted down to Burma and Java and the rest of Southeast Asia. But of course Buddhism greatly influenced China and Japan. There was interaction, of course; a concurrent two-way flow. But by accepting all things, all ideas, all philosophies Indians become too lost in details; there is a restlessness in their art and their thought, sometimes, that breeds a final negative blackness. I feel they sometimes by accepting everything find a big zero in their minds. But these are small reactions; don't take me too seriously; when I write my book on India I'll weigh every sentence carefully!

tlc, UGA

July 30, 1959

Dear Bill:

[. . .]

I am almost afraid to keep "Julia" out of the bank's vault. [. . .] Only the first sheets were in the bank. All my various versions were burned. But I think this is to the good. I want to dive into it almost as if what I have done is only raw material for the book, finding now its real form, its real shape. I see it more and more as a story of Julia and her relationships with men: for her relationships with the two women in her life were not significant to her, although terribly so to her author. The relationships with men, with every one of them: her father, her criminal brother, the U.S. Senator, her poet-husband, and all the "young men" who adored her were real to her because of their basic unrealness; her relationships with women were unreal to her because they were in essence too real for her to accept. These two women were her mother and her daughter. It is going to be a study of "shadow and substance" in one sense: of the inner reality that transcends the outer shell we call reality. Her brother who kills the husband of a woman he liked (he never loved her, never slept with her) because he recognized in his relationship with this "husband" something homosexual is a weak, loving evil scamp for whom she slowly sloughs off her image of herself in her attempt to save him from death in the chair. In one sense, Julia is Western man's concept of "the white goddess[,]" of the Madonna, of his dream of woman, a vase into which each man poured his dream; her final dissolution is the death of that old dream.

Well—enough of this. Mr. Cohen of Cresset press wrote Don† a wonderful letter about *One Hour*, ending with "It is a great book." I appreciate his enthusiasm, of course. Mrs. Fischer of Germany (her editors—non-Jewish—turned it down) called it a brilliant piece of writing, "important" etc. Her editors, I hear in a most roundabout way, felt Germans would not "like it," and were opposed to publishing it. It will be that kind of book: people will go off the deep end for it or they will resent it with a terrible resentment. I seem to plunge too deep for some of them.

tlc, UGA

*President of Harcourt Brace, publishers of *One Hour*.
†Don Seawell, Smith's lawyer and literary agent.

October 25, 1959

Dear Sidney:

I have sent you today a copy of my new novel *One Hour*. I hope you will enjoy reading it.†

All reviewers have ignored the big issues of the book: the framing of an innocent man, the anti-intellectualism, the anonymous powers, the forms of seduction that may be even more evil than that of seducing a child. But Alger Hiss apparently understood what I was writing about. My lawyer gave Hiss's lawyer a copy of *One Hour*. After reading it, Hiss's lawyer sent it to him. The report is that Alger Hiss loved the book, said it had deeply moved him, that he felt it was one of the most important books he had read in years. He told his attorney he was reading many of the books I had mentioned in *One Hour*. I treasure this for I have always believed Hiss was a good man, a truly good man. Whether he was "innocent" I don't know because I don't know what "innocence" is. But as I was writing about my young scientist I kept thinking of Hiss; again and again I would suddenly have the feeling, "This story is saying something important about the Hiss case." I did not actually write it because of Hiss; but as I wrote his case began to haunt me and I believe there is much in the book relevant to his experience and ours, as Americans.

[. . .] The reviewers really cut my throat this time but I see why: to them, I am "an enemy of the people." I fooled them with *Strange Fruit*: they thought it was about the South but they realize *One Hour* is about all of us in this hour we are living through. Next time I come to N.Y. do let's get together. I have not met your wife yet and I do want to.

tlc, UGA

---

*Smith described him as "once my doctor, but we became such good friends that I found it difficult to continue to go to him as my doctor."[22] He was also on the faculty of New York University medical school.

†He wrote Smith that he found the novel "very great and very frightening."[23]

November 17, 1959

Dear Dr. Tillich:

Your very fine letter is cherished by me, of course.* I know no one whose praise of this book could mean more to me. It was difficult for me, yet seemed almost from the beginning a search I must make. All my books are journeys, searches, explorations into the unknown complexities of human nature and human relationships, into the depths of our spiritual life. I agree with you completely that religion is the dimension of depth in all our spiritual functions. It is so right and you have said it so beautifully and so convincingly in your new book which I am reading now for the second time.

Thank you for sending it to me. I read it carefully, marking it up outrageously as I do all your books! Now I am doing the second reading, and sometimes I find myself in awe of your profound understanding, sometimes I am delighted (just that) with a sentence here, there, a phrase that suddenly opens up new depths of human experience. Now and then, I question you just a little, and then I realize that what puzzles me is probably simply the fact that you are writing in your second language. What an amazing achievement that is! To be able to say so cleanly and clearly the complex things you are saying in this second language of yours! It is impressive as an intellectual and psychological achievement.

In many ways this *Theology of Culture* has been your book most helpful to me. Or is it that, after living through with my David in *One Hour* his search, his question, his bemusements and confusions I am now just exactly right for your book. Perhaps I am only now asking the questions that *Theology of Culture* answers for me. It does say things that I need to hear; things I want to hear; I have always since I was eleven or twelve years old struggled with God and my own nature, asking clumsy, crude questions, then achieving a kind of amnesia about God and religion and asking nothing at all; then beginning again: to ask questions that maybe are more valid and therefore can draw forth valid answers. You and your books have meant a very great deal to me. I have a profound interest in existentialism, but not

*Tillich had thanked her for sending him a copy of *One Hour* and praised her "profound psychological insights," her knowledge of the "ambiguities of life," and her "theological outlook," which he felt was near his own. He had also sent her a copy of his *Theology of Culture*.[24]

in Sartre's perversion of it. I feel there is something diabolical in Sartre, something that is destroying the young of his country and ours who hang on to a few of his perverse statements and make of them their "foundation." I also feel this: that we have had a dehumanization of the novel for 50 years. Now the time has come to restore his humanity to man. I feel that every existential question must be explored, examined, lived through in a metaphorical sense and lived with but I feel that there is a need to write novels about characters who are thinking, suffering, hurting, yearning, longing to find meaning—instead of simply concocting the sleepwalker (without conscience, the blank spirit without the moral imperative in his nature) for the rest of us (the readers) to feel superior to. My criticism of Faulkner is that never has he had in his books a character that is his moral or intellectual equal; nor has he ever shown the future in his books. I do not mean that a novel should give answers. I don't really think it should—although characters in the novel may try to. But I do think part of the awful complacency of today comes from the fact that the novels being written and deemed of literary worth are those whose characters are one-dimensional, empty-hearted, without moral imperative: hollow men, sleepwalkers, faceless men, and the readers of these novels, the reviewers of these novels all feel morally superior and emotionally superior and intellectually superior to these characters—with the result that they become complacent and terribly afraid of any writing that "disturbs" *them*, that comes close home, that compels them (as I think *One Hour* does) to enter the novel and be the invisible, silent character in it. [. . .] I try to involve my reader, as I think every existential novel should do: not only should the characters come alive but the reader must come alive, too. There must be as Karl Jaspers once said, "the beating of the other wing."

[. . .]

Kafka had the great gift of showing us existential anxiety and despair but interlinearly one always saw the shadow of the real human being, the whole man or the man who can be whole, if only—if only—And that is the pathos of Kafka. Perhaps the word pathos is wrong. Perhaps the word is tragedy but I have always felt pathos, too, when I read him. I understand Kafka and respond fully to him. But Faulkner, no; Sartre only sometimes. Faulkner does not know the human being; he may know about him but he does not know him; therefore, there can be no shadow of this human being, no echo of him, no vision of him even interlinearly. The man who walks in and out of his novels now and then, is Faulkner himself who is superficial philosophically, immature, too; and unknowing of real goodness and compassion. His *Requiem for a Nun* is a diabolical travesty, a blasphemous piece of writing. Faulkner does not want to know God—using that phrase in the deep, mystical sense but also in the sense of "ground" and concern for ultimate things. Faulkner does not know what "ultimate things" are—nor do I; but I yearn to know, I am concerned, I have a glimpse now and then. So—I protest the nihilistic novel. I am searching for depth in my own writing, more and more depth; perhaps I have not found it, as yet; perhaps I do not as yet express it with as much artistry as I should. I write passionately but I believe in passion, I think a writer should write passionately.

[. . .]

tlc, UGA

As acting head books researcher at *Time* magazine, Joan Titus was present when *Time's* books editor, Max Gissen, discussed *One Hour* disparagingly and inaccurately summarized the book in the weekly discussion of new books with the senior editor. Titus recalled that she naively "corrected Max on a couple of points" and "thought the book, good or bad, deserved to be reviewed because of the author's reputation." *Time*, however, did not review *One Hour*, and Titus never again worked in the books section. Not long after the fateful discussion of *One Hour*, in September 1959, Titus took a trip with her friend, and former Laurel Falls Camp counselor, Connie McMillan Carpenter. On their way to Myrtle Beach, they stopped in Clayton to visit Smith. Subsequently, Titus became friends with Smith and decided to write a critical study of her writings. Some weeks after she returned from vacation, Gissen summoned Titus to his office and told her: "I don't like southern women writers, especially Georgians; my first wife was a Georgian." So, according to Titus, although Gissen's attitude had nothing to do with Smith as a person or writer, because of his position of power, his personal bias damaged her reputation as a writer.[25]

TO JOAN TITUS

Thanksgiving Weekend [1959]

Dear Joan:

I have waited to thank you for the beautiful record for the silliest of reasons: until I could change my typewriter ribbon. Since this happens to be one of the small things of life that I suffer over in existential despair I keep postponing the dread day when I must virtually wrap myself in yards of smudgy stuff while I figure out the intricacies of how it coils and uncoils. I can do it, of course; but it is one of the hard things of life—not easy like having cancer and watching a good book get vile, dishonest reviews.

[. . .]

One Hour continues to surprise me. The worst reviews came out of New York City—which, in my estimation, means that the reviewers rely heavily on stereotypes for their praise and blame. If a book is not fashionable, or they cannot see it as so; if it has not been hailed by "the authorities" or the avant garde then it is poor—especially is it poor if it is serious. That I may be a part of a new "avant" (don't you like that phrase?) has not occurred to them. [. . .] The philosophic group in New York is recognizing the book and writing me warm, encouraging letters about it, but the literary group— no; like your Max Gissen, they have not read me, and they do not want to. But they hate me; why?

On the other hand, the South has read the book with understanding. The South has suffered; its people are passionate; its people know ambiguity not from reading Empson* but because we live so ambiguously; they know the tragic by the way their blood slides through their veins, not by having read or misread the existentialists. They know fear; anxiety; they know courage, too, as few New Yorkers can—for we live down here with courage or without it every day of our lives. We have the country's lowest cowards and we have the country's most courageous right here at our doorstep. Therefore the literate South has responded, in Heinemann's phrase, to this book. [. . .]

But Boston did well by the book, too. There were two good reviews in the *Globe* and *Post*, one of them (the *Globe*'s I think) of unusual awareness and sensitiveness. A very fine one from Providence, R.I., two excellent ones from Detroit. Paul Engle did a fair one in the *Chicago Tribune* but he reviewed it merely as a "good story" not as the philosophic and psychological analysis of our times that it actually is. He missed the point; but then, of course Paul Engle would until someone told him what the point is. He is not the brightest critic in America.

There are three ideas about me that everyone in America chooses one of and hugs tight. Not any of them is right. One is that I am a dirty, nasty purveyor of obscenities; a cheap sensationalist. Remember *Forever Amber* was cleared in Boston and permitted to be sold; *Strange Fruit* is still banned

---

*Literary critic William Empson, author of *Seven Types of Ambiguity* (1953).

in Massachusetts. These people who think this way about me have not read *Killers of the Dream* (or maybe they have!) or *Journey*, or my various analytical studies of racial concepts, or the old *South Today*—a magazine that was published for ten years and whose circulation list read like the top-cream of Who's Who. But many reviewers feel this way, and editors of book pages and never read me, really read me. Perhaps they can't, psychically. Then there are those who think of me as an odd, funny "little rich southern woman" who goes out parading around and defending Negroes, and tearing down the wall of segregation. There is a tiny bit of truth in this stereotype, of course; I am not rich and have never been, having been "on my own" without a penny from seventeen on. But I have taken a stand against segregation in all my writings, one way or the other, but always a complex stand, a philosophic position that many Negroes do not understand. I am not popular with Negroes because I have never been "for" Negroes: I am for quality people, regardless of color; I am for getting rid of barriers that stunt and dwarf human growth. But many Negroes think I should be "for them" and for the stereotypes they are now building up of themselves which give them comfort, but which are as silly, perhaps more so, than the stereotypes built up by white people of Negroes. The third stereotype of me is an odd one: it is that I have been a "social worker," a sociologist, that I rely on sociology, that I go around working with groups in the social sciences, etc. and that I think it is through the mass that the world can be improved. On the contrary, I have never taken a course in social sciences in my life—I was always interested in literature and music and art—I do not like the social scientists I have met, I mean they tend to bore the hell out of me and I think they think smudgily, and overrate their damned little "experiments" etc. and their "objectivity." I am deeply concerned about the human race but I am for the person, the human being; his quality is what I am concerned about; and I don't think organizations can do what must be done by the individual himself, but I do think each of us can be deeply concerned and can care what happens to people. So, what is left for me to be? What I think I am: a creative worker, a human being deeply concerned about human beings; an aristocrat in a sense that I value quality of mind, spirit, taste, etc. and do not want it destroyed by any mob, visible or invisible; a democrat in that I value the rights of all people to reach out and grow and to enjoy their rights as citizens and their "human rights" as breathing people and therefore any authority is in my eyes to be viewed with suspicion and kept control of by "the people;" an artist, in that I value the creativity of man and believe in the redeeming power of art, of music, poetry, painting, sculpture; I am a philosopher in the sense of being profoundly concerned about the human experience and its significance, and man and his potentialities for evil and good; and last of all, I guess I am just a plain human being who believes in the power of love and compassion and acceptance, and would like to have a little of all three one of these days.

tlc, UGA

Mothering the Movement,

1 9 6 0 — 1 9 6 3

Profoundly discouraged by the low sales and lack of literary acclaim for *One Hour*, Smith wrote numerous letters to explain and promote the novel in the year following its publication. Correspondence from this time also indicates that the process of writing the novel had heightened her interest in writing consciously as a woman about a woman's thoughts and experiences. That interest found expression in her subsequent magazine articles, book reviews, and speeches and in her analysis of the rapidly growing civil rights movement. While reviewing Betty Friedan's *Feminine Mystique* in January 1963, she wrote Ashley Montagu that "the attitude toward women is at the heart of the racial matter."[1]

Throughout the middle and late 1950s, when not writing *One Hour*, Smith had devoted a great deal of energy to speaking and writing on behalf of the emerging nonviolent civil rights movement in the South. Characteristically, she had worked to increase whites' awareness of the destructiveness of racial segregation and had especially urged young people to become active in working for social change. Consequently, when in February 1960 college students in Greensboro, North Carolina, staged sit-in demonstrations to desegregate public lunch counters at Woolworth and other chain stores, Smith was ready and eager to support the students in the sit-in movement spreading throughout the South. In keeping with her emphasis on educating white community leaders, she wrote James Robinson, executive secretary of CORE, suggesting that he send copies of CORE's booklet explaining nonviolent protests to North Carolina's attorney general, mayors, chiefs of police, newspaper editors, leading ministers, and local TV news commentators in Durham and Greensboro, where picketing and sit-in protests were then in progress. Ever mindful of the movement's financial needs, she also enclosed a check to defray mailing expenses.[2] Despite a recurrence of cancer and another round of radiation treatments in the spring of 1960, Smith's correspondence through 1960 and 1961 was dominated by her activities on behalf of the movement. Excerpts from a letter to her sister Bertha Barnett provide a glimpse of the extent and rationale of her involvement:

It has been a most active fall and winter for me: the South is in turmoil, the young people are turning to me for help all down the line; they've never known who I was before; most have never read my books but somehow they've heard I'll help; I do. At Richmond, I believe my two long talks were the only ones that gave the white students any real help in understanding what the problem is in terms of the human being, and how to find the insight that will help them also find the courage to act. [. . .]

[. . .] I talked with students at University of Ga. after the mob on their campus; they asked for me; and it was a brave, solemn, deeply moving meeting to see these youngsters trying so hard to find the courage, the willingness to risk and suffer. They know they must—but they are having a battle with themselves. A letter today from Emory was urging me to come talk to them—the students wrote it—and I shall do so on my return in April. Perhaps, right now, is my one unique opportunity to speak to this decisive moment, in the right way. That is why I am trying to do so many different things: some are just to make a living; others are to help the young South; others are to push forward with my literary and philosophical writing. I wish I were ten or fifteen years younger![3]

If most of the young activists had not heard of her books when the sit-ins began, their actions helped create a receptive climate and a new audience for her work. In the fall of 1961 she wrote the preface for James Peck's *Freedom Riders* and Norton published a revised edition of *Killers of the Dream*, which became a classic among the movement volunteers who traveled to Mississippi in the summer of 1964 to conduct "freedom schools" and voter registration drives.

The fall of 1961 also saw the publication in *Redbook* of "The Ordeal of Southern Womanhood," for which Smith had interviewed a group of white New Orleans women about their response to the desegregation of public schools, and for which she received the Sidney Hillman Award for Best Magazine Writing. In December 1961 *Life* published her "Memory of a Large Christmas." The following spring, while undergoing cobalt treatments for lung cancer, she completed the book-length version published by Norton in the fall. On a 1962 Christmas card Smith thanked Frank Daniel of the *Atlanta Journal* for his "elegant piece about my little book" and included the following:

> I shall always be glad I skimmed off so much good, clotted cream from my childhood memories. There was much sadness in our home after Mother became mentally ill and Dad never admitting defeat, finally died with a broken heart, although he whispered at the end, "I have fought the good fight, I have kept the faith." So—as you can see, my own family are all deeply moved by the sweet good memories which for so long were hidden behind the tragic ones about which we all were completely silent. (Daniel/EU)

The changing social climate also contributed to a renewed interest in Smith's other works. Her 1961 correspondence reveals extensive negotiations for film rights for *Strange Fruit*, and in the fall of 1962 she was the subject of a television documentary, "Miss Smith of Georgia," produced by Time-Life Broadcast, aired in Los Angeles and New York, and sold to the BBC.

Along with a genuine excitement about the movement and a sense of being "let out from the smothering blankets," as she wrote George Brockway, her correspondence from the early sixties also reflects the financial and psychic pressures resulting from her own deteriorating health and concern for the health of several members of her family, all of which invariably interfered with her literary and philosophical writing.[4] In a moment of frustration she wrote her friend P. D. East: "I am tired of mothering the whole damn South as I have mothered the Smith family for thirty years!"[5] Even as she vented her frustration, however, Smith also frequently made her correspondence the vehicle for theorizing about her own writing and the creative process, the dangers inherent in all organizations working for social change, the future of human life in general, and—as the bouts with cancer grew increasingly severe—reviewing and reclaiming her own life.

TO JAMES R. ROBINSON[*]

Alexandria, Virginia
[March 1960]

Dear Mr. Robinson:

I shall be grateful to you if you will send me the names of the presidents of the five or six major variety stores and their addresses; also any names you may have of managers of the stores where sit-down protests have been made. I should like to write a letter to these men urging them to let the Negroes use the services of these stores in the same manner as do the white patrons.

[...]

I also am writing an Open Letter to Southern Students and shall appreciate any names that you may be able to send me. I should like to send copies of this letter to one young leader in each of the Negro colleges whose students have participated in the sit-down protests. This letter will also be released to some members of the press.

I am having lunch tomorrow with Edward Morgan who is a radio commentator here in Washington and its environs. He is anxious, and eager, for white southern leaders who approve these protests to speak up; and I think my interview with him may be of real value. Through him, I hope to arrange to talk with David Brinkley of NBC and Howard Smith of CBS; I can at least give them a full orientation and perhaps clarify the legal, moral and spiritual values involved. I can also urge them to tell the country that thousands even millions of white southerners are sick to death of segregation and want Negroes to have their full civil rights and their full human rights.

Talmadge has been put on networks three times in the past three or four weeks but no white southerner, however well known, has been asked to state the case against segregation—and no one can state it more eloquently than a white southerner who has accepted himself as a human being.

*Executive secretary of CORE.

Somehow, we must fight this; a false dichotomy has been set up, largely by the press and TV and radio pitting the Negro against the white southerner and the white southerner against the Negro. This is dangerous and even evil and pressure should be put on the networks and the press to give the white southerners who oppose segregation a hearing. Only those who are for segregation get a hearing; or those who are so "moderate" that you don't know what they are for or against, except they don't want violence.

I think my speech at All Saints Church (Unitarian) has now been set for April 21st. The Unitarians are trying to get the American Friends and CORE and the Council of Churches and some of the Jewish groups to cooperate. All the money will go to CORE; I am contributing my speech free on the condition that the money go to CORE. This speech I shall also release to press and *N.Y. Times, Herald Tribune*, and the small magazines. Some of them will pick it up, I am sure.

The Chapel Hill students made a fine statement about their sit-down protest and the Council of Churches in Chapel Hill also made a forthright statement approving the students' statement and their protest. Every white minister in Chapel Hill, N.C. signed this strong statement. I shall show this statement to Edward Morgan as one proof of the strong public opinion in the South for opening up services in the stores. Have you a copy of it?

I believe, if you would follow up my speech and activities in Albany, a good bit of enthusiasm for CORE's activities and philosophy would be engendered. I have never spoken more plainly nor have I ever received a warmer and more thoughtful response. This Interracial group knew very little about your work. I told them a good bit, not in the detail I should have liked to make use of, but enough for them to feel that here is a place for their money and their help. Mr. Edward Kennell is director of the Interracial Council and is a good worker. He has many friends (white) on press, radio and TV and he could use strategically ten or twelve copies of Color Line booklet. Albany is not only the capital of N.Y.; but it has a fairly good racial feeling; a good bit of integration exists; and this particular group leans toward non-violence, avoidance of all hate and resentment in their words and acts and are philosophically a mature group. They could be most useful to CORE and CORE could be most useful to them.

I may set up a speech at Howard University, if they want me to speak to the students. I think it might help in this business of communication; I have good, encouraging things to tell them about the constructive, creative white groups working in the South; I can say a good bit on the Gandhian philosophy. All this might be helpful.

I think to speak out to both white groups and Negro groups in the National Capital is a strategically good thing to do at this time. If handled well, these speeches can be reported to radio and TV audiences of the South and will do good.

I am doing what I can, hoping to find a way that will not close the door to the white communities of the South, at this important time when I need to communicate with them, also.

tlc, UGA

George Sion, editor of the journal *Booklover* in Bombay, India, wrote Smith requesting background information to use in promoting *One Hour*, which was soon to be distributed by Signet in India. He had heard her speak at the India Book House in Bombay in May 1955 and had printed excerpts from her speech in *Booklover*, which he quoted back to her. Admiring the three-hundred-year-old cubism of the Jantar Mantar, according to his letter, she had suggested that viewing the caves and ruins of India could be the source of a new creative movement for Western artists.[6] Smith's response contains one of the more cogent summaries of her thoughts about *One Hour*.

July 11, 1960

Dear Mr. Sion:

Your letter was most interesting, and very pleasant to read. Thank you for remembering me and the visit and the little speech which was spontaneous and totally unplanned. I do, indeed, think of India as a place for artists to go for glimpses into the depths of man, for understanding of the complexities of good and evil, for the elegant and wondrous images one's eyes are filled with. The archaic, the momentous, the deeply questioning: all this is good for the Western artist.

One Hour is, I think, a better novel than was *Strange Fruit*: it goes down into human vision and dream and motivation more profoundly, it appeals to any person who realizes that he is living in 1960 and not the 19th century, that he is a watcher of the cosmic skies and of the vast, chaotic changes taking place in the depths of man. This is a time when man's image of himself has broken to splinter; some are putting it together again as a machine, others are making only a rational animal of it, but few, a few in every country are spectators of the New Being, the New Man, who is perpendicular, whose feet are in ages so far gone that none of us can actually feel the vastness of the time and whose eyes and soul have stretched into another infinity beyond him. We are witnessing, I think, the miracle of

Man Creating Himself, making a terrible mess of it, at times; falling into awful error; but creating himself: as if God, the Creator (and Preserver and Destroyer) has said, "only in you, Man, lies the potentialities of life and death; you, now, are my Son and some of my creative work I have turned over to you to do. Whether you create, preserve or destroy is now up to you."

These words describe briefly the feelings I have now and had while writing *One Hour*. I deliberately chose a young priest or minister to tell the story for this young man is still honestly searching for a relationship to the word, God; he is trying to fuse science and art with feeling for God; he is a product of this scientific age, he knows the godlessness and nihilism of this age, and knows them well but he still searches, he still longs. This book, using him as the teller of the story, a most exciting and hair-raising story, searches modern man's heart and mind, looks at the "dangers" of democracy, knowing that it, too, has its terrible dangers, different from those of communism, but dangers, just the same. The danger of the mob dominating the few who are artists, intellectuals, priests; the danger of the eight-year-old mentality of the masses drowning the poetic vision, the scientific knowledge; the danger of primitive and ignorant masses oversweeping what the few have made throughout the ages, the few poets, the few artists, the few Men of God, the few scientists, etc. etc. Communism leaves few doors open for human growth; and has dangers that are gross and easy to see; democracy leaves many doors open for human growth but has, also, insidious dangers when power is put in the hungry, anxious, terrified and hating hands of the millions who for so long have been totally deprived. Actually, our biggest world dangers are the same in USA and India, in every new country that is hoping to find "freedom" and a good life for humans.

I think ONE HOUR may be the first American novel that has dealt directly and on many levels with the problem of the human being caught in his many traps called silence, art; God, freedom, the importance of the masses, and yet the dangers inherent in proletarian rule; the new authoritarianisms, etc. etc. It is a book whose characters are real, four-dimensional, not abstractions. For twenty years it has been fashionable in the Western world to reduce man to an abstraction but while I see its validity for art, I do not see it for writing and I refuse to write that way. I think we are just going around a curve now and do not need more abstractions. We need to find man-in-depth and man-in-height. A more poetic vision is needed. I hope I have done some of this in *One Hour*.

It will not sell with the speed of *Strange Fruit* for it is a more profound book, although madly interesting, even hypnotic the reviewers say, but it does make you stop and think hard, very hard. Still the story, itself, of a little eight-year-old (symbol of the eight-year-old mentality of our masses in USA, Europe, Asia, everywhere) makes a false indictment of a scientist, which is (in the parable) false accusation of science, seems to be so interesting to read page by page that most people have to read it the second time to realize the parable, the allegory, the myth back of it. But you feel it as you read even though you may not see it with the mind.

I hope India will like this book. The Indian intellectuals should for they are in many ways less tied down by our sick fashion of dehumanizing man (this is part of the West's illness, a *malaise* I trust Indian intellectuals will escape) and I hope they will see that I am talking not only of that hour of accusation, not only of Dave's terrible and beautiful hour (and hours) with Grace, but the hour we mortals are now living in.

I have never done my book on India because I respect India too much to believe I was fitted to write on deep levels about it after only two visits, even though one was a six-month visit. I came home and read a hundred or more books on Indian religion, Indian art, Indian symbols, Indian myths, prehistoric India, more and more, then I had it out with myself: You must go back again now, after this background of reading, after long months of remembering your other two visits; then after the third visit maybe you can say what you feel you have in you to say. I feel the same way about Mr. Nehru: I want to say frankly and honestly what I think, and I need to think more about him before writing of him.

I have had three more sieges with cancer since I came home. [. . .] But I am well, now; and feeling strong and getting ready to begin a new book this week. And still have a deep, warm feeling for India and my Indian friends. I hope to return; and I hope to write the really good book about India that needs to be written.

tlc, UGA

 Referring to the following letter, Smith wrote to her friend and Atlanta journalist Margaret Long:

On the spur of the moment I wrote the *Journal* a letter about the new laws the police force in Atlanta want set up in order to protect Atlanta from rioting. They published the letter and omitted the dynamic why of its motivation. It reminds me of the time the *New York Times* published my article against Joe McCarthy (when nobody else had really spoken out) and left in the part in which I told why I believed in the United States (and didn't think McCarthy actually did) and left out all reference to Mr. McCarthy! It was the queerest piece of writing that my name was ever signed to. I felt not that bad, of course, about the *Journal* piece; but my real point was that we needed the creation of a good, strong public opinion: and if we had it we wouldn't need any new improvised laws to protect us from "the mobs."[7]

TO THE EDITOR OF THE *Atlanta Journal*

September 5, 1960

Sirs:

How long are we going to let ourselves be dominated by the five percent of our people who are haters and hoodlums and moral riffraff? Each day, I wonder. Frankly, I'd like to see in our region a little aristocracy; aristocracy of mind, of spirit and soul: what Socrates spoke of as arete.

We could use a little of it. And surely it is here. Surely there is another five percent—maybe, even ten or fifteen or twenty percent—of our people who are too proud to be bullied by these ruffian groups; too sure of intellectual and moral values to waver when an illiterate dares tell them what to say or read or think or believe.

Plato warned that this is where democracy inevitably ends: on the mudsill and in terrorism. But he was wrong: It is not democracy but demagoguery that leaves us fouled up in filth and violence. Not too much freedom but too little responsibility is the cause of our region being taunted and terrorized by this criminal trash, who, in turn, have been given a green light by the words of political demagogues—and our own silence.

Why don't we turn on these tricksters? They dare to speak out. Why don't the rest of us? Why are we afraid to stand up for human dignity, for compassion and love and honesty and justice? They are such beautiful words: why do we shun them? Why don't we say, "We cherish the human spirit more than our skin color; we honor the sanctity of the person, we believe in decency and goodwill, we know segregation is dehumanizing and therefore, wrong." If we said these words, if thousands of us said them, we could break this hypnotic spell that is on us. Words are magic: they can whistle out their evil in a man, but they can also persuade the sleeping angel in him to wake up and speak its wisdom. But silence can never create either excellence or virtue.

Our police force does not need a new law forbidding nonviolent sit-ins and picketing. Such a law would be more dangerous than is risk of violence, for it would take away from all of us our inalienable right to protest injustice. What the police force in every town and city needs is a strong public opinion that places value where value belongs. If we, the people, say "We shall tolerate no hoodlum's holy mission to maintain hoodlum supremacy," then the police force will not find their job too hard—as it is now without our moral support.

tlc, UGA (Pat Watters file)

In the spring of 1957, at the recommendation of Dorothy Norman, Ruth Nanden Anshen, editor of the World Perspectives series published by Harper Brothers, invited Smith to contribute to the series a book on the philosophy and psychology of color and race. Feeling honored to be associated with a list of authors that included Paul Tillich, Jacques Maritain, W. H. Auden, T. S. Eliot, and Lewis Mumford, Smith promised to write the book after she had completed *One Hour*.[8] Subsequent correspondence indicates that it became a repository for her philosophical musings about the larger meanings of race and the human experience, in much the same way that the "Julia" manuscript received her thoughts on gender and human relationships. Although she never completed the World Perspectives book, at least some of her ideas for it became part of the revised edition of *Killers of the Dream*. The following letter to Anshen contains her first major outline of the book.

September 9, 1960

Dear dear Ruth:

I am full of the book and am going to tell you something about it—for I see it now shaping up and I feel that it will continue steadily to do so.

Since I am not a scientist, nor a philosopher, nor a theologian, nor a psychiatrist, I feel that the worst possible thing for me to do would be to try to be one or all these specialists. I am a writer, a woman, a southerner who due to birth experienced in early childhood the ordeals, the psychic and spiritual ordeals, and the intellectual ordeals of a life lived in a culture split and broken, full of abysses and not many towers, full of estrangements; a region that leaned its weakness against the past; that lost its vision of God as it stared at its "whiteness."

I know brokenness deep down; not because it is the existential fashion to speak of it but because in a sense it was my fate to know it; and yet, at the same time, due to the ambiguities of family versus culture, I was aware of the possible wholeness of things; I knew that one must take the leap in the dark—not alone to reach God but to reach whatever creative life was within me. I must, in a sense, leap the barriers and find the dark places inside where all is illuminated, even though there is darkness, always.

[...]

And so, out of this turmoil and heaving past, out of my own personal suffering as well as mankind's suffering, my searching, I shall write my little book. It is going to be in the form of four (maybe five) long letters (about 30–40 pages each) addressed to a young man; it will deal with the five great encounters modern man must make or refuse to make; it will be informally written, fused with my own feeling about the human condition, sensitive to his blank spaces (and my own); I can by using this form, draw easily and unselfconsciously on my knowledge of painting, music, poetry, literature, life in Asia, visits in India, life in the South with its brokenness and estrangements; I can use my talent for direct and personal communication and communion. At the same time, there will be within these five letters a firm structural continuity as I search for faith and hope, as I form my world view, my belief about the phenomenon of man: my view of why we are here, what in a sense has been turned over to us by God, by his command to continue with our own human evolution. As I talk of the person versus the individual, of the person versus the mob, versus the "collective," I shall seek for means of making clear the interpenetration of human thought, the dependence of men one upon the other. In my letter about the encounter of man with the body image, his and woman's, I shall have a great deal to say about race fear: I shall show that it comes from our emptiness; from the fact that we have become hollow men; that it is caused by the loss of our own spiritual identity; that we break our ties with other human beings only when we have broken our ties with our own Self and with God. I think this may be the best thing, a going-on so to speak, that I have done on segregation and race: and one of the best parts of the book, since it is what I have thought about, suffered over, studied, dreamed about, written about for so many years—even, in a way, from the day of my birth. I think, also, my letter on time may be one of the best things I have ever written.

There is one letter called *Beyond Existentialism* which I believe I am doing a good job on. So it goes. And Beyond Science may turn out to be pretty good. These are tentative titles for these chapters or "letters."

By writing in the form of letters, I clear myself from any presumptuous claims of being an expert in science or psychology or philosophy, etc. I am simply a human being, a woman, a writer who has, perhaps, experienced more deeply than most, who has traveled and lived in faraway places both on this earth and inside my own spirit; one who, since childhood, has been asking the unanswerable questions, and hearing no answers has kept reformulating the questions, hoping that someday the right question will be asked, knowing when that happens it will answer itself.

[. . .]

I am, at the same time, working on a little book for children; for teenagers about our famous conversations here at camp on the human being. [. . .] I started it this summer, at the urging of my family, when I was too weak and tired after X-ray therapy to tackle my "big" if small in size book for World Perspectives. This returning to children in my imagination gave me immense relief and rest; I still miss their love and belief in me; no other group, in my South, or even in this country has ever given it to me. But these children did: for twenty-five years; and sometimes when I am weary and worn it is good to call them together in my imagination and renew our old bonds. Their book is doing this for me; and it seems in no real way to be interfering with The Letters. Indeed, some of the old love and warmth may be seeping into those five letters.

What title to use for the letters, I still don't know. I think of In the Presence of Others; I think of Unfinished Man (the old Nietzschean phrase); The Double Mirror; Irreplaceable Man; The Mysterious Gift (of existence); Man is the Arrow; etc. etc. I have jotted down in various places innumerable titles. These are only a few of them! But let it move on further; then perhaps I can have the sure feeling that one should have about a title.

[. . .]

tlc, UGA 1283A

 Smith was asked to help with speech writing for John F. Kennedy in the 1960 presidential campaign by Chloe Zerwick, formerly Chloe Fox, with whom she had worked in 1956 for Adlai Stevenson. Subsequent correspondence indicates that she wrote specifically for Kennedy's speeches in Warm Springs and Harlem and encouraged Kennedy to appeal especially to the young and to women.[9]

Undated [September 24, 1960]

Dear Miss Zerwick:

[. . .]

I would like to suggest, if I may, some of the weak points in the campaign as I see them from the vantage point of an observer in Georgia. Perhaps these points can be remedied by the speech writers, or passed on to the speech makers, etc. (I shall do a piece for the N.Y. *Post*—at least, I think they would like for me to—I have done pieces in the past for them for Truman etc.)

These are the points I want to stress:

a. The real liberals and "moderates" in the South have no place to go! Nobody they think they want to vote for. To my horror, two weeks ago, in Atlanta, I found strong Stevenson admirers in favor now of Nixon. When I expressed not only amazement but a kind of numinous horror, they merely said, But is Kennedy a real liberal? I said I felt he was, and I knew he was an honest man while Nixon was a man still in search of a soul. I startled them a bit by my language for I was astonished. How could Stevenson's admirers flop over and hang on Nixon!

b. I think the one man who could swing the decent element in Georgia over to the Democratic ticket would be Stevenson; if he could come down and talk to a group in Atlanta, not necessarily a political group, it would do worlds of good throughout Ga.

c. The second point I wish to stress is that our present governor does not have much prestige among the thinking Georgians. It is not only his race attitudes, it is a certain mental sluggishness that makes us laugh too much at him. Kennedy will make a tremendous mistake to leave things to Gov. Vandiver who cannot influence the eggheads, the sophisticated, nor the real liberals. Most of the bland old conservatives are going to vote for Nixon; they smell a conservative, you know; and they have had adequate opportunity to sniff Nixon's secret beliefs or tropisms.

d. We have got to do something about the Negroes. Many ordinary literate and non-literate Negroes are voting for Nixon. They say, "He will keep us out of war." They mean more; they mean they can depend on him, if on anybody, for racial alleviation.

This is a problem not only in Harlem but down here: The Negroes have lost faith in the democratic party; not all of them, but far too many. For that reason, Johnson cannot help too much in the South because no matter what he says he is a symbol to the Negroes *of what has not been done for them.*

The most powerful Negro from the symbolic viewpoint down here is, of course, Dr. Martin Luther King, Jr. I am hoping he is working for the democratic party. I shall try to see him; he and I are good friends. But also, it would help the Kennedy campaign if some of the young Negroes of the South, those who are now feeling their oats having had so much success with their nonviolent movement if a man like Hubert Humphrey could address them. To do any good he would have to speak plainly. There is no longer any question in the silence of holding the Democratic Party together. It is rapidly breaking into three parts: (a) the liberals, who are still clinging desperately to it but with sick hearts; (b) the real conservatives who are boldly now bolting to the Republican party; (c) the Democratic machine which is rapidly losing its prestige and rapidly going to pieces. This is so obvious that even the politicians are silent: They just don't know what to do or what to say. If the people are swinging toward the removal of segregation barriers, then they'd better not say much; if they aren't—well, but they are not sure. At present things are about 60% segregationist and 40% "non-segregationists" and things are changing every day.

We need somebody to talk to the white and Negro intellectuals, artists, teachers, welfare workers, etc. and this should be Adlai Stevenson. We need a straight from the shoulder talk on race and nonviolence etc. and this should be from Hubert Humphrey. If Kennedy himself could come down his charm and honesty (both growing from day to day on TV) would win a great many of the young whites. But he should not pay too much attention to the old political party which is almost in shambles—at least in Georgia.

If you can pass on this information, please do. Perhaps Bob Kennedy could have it; perhaps Jack Kennedy himself should. I'll send a copy to Hubert Humphrey, a close friend of mine. Whatever is done down here must be different from the past for we are different: the South is about to [be] reborn and is going through rather loud screeches of birth pains. [. . .]

Tell me if there is anything special I can write or do.

tlc, UGA

 Smith's correspondence with Marvin Rich, community relations director of CORE, documents the variety of ways she worked to support and strengthen the work of young civil rights activists. At the time of this letter the national CORE office was heavily involved with court cases stemming from lunch-counter demonstrations in New Orleans, but Smith was reporting on her speech at the October 14–16 conference of the newly organized Student Nonviolent Coordinating Committee (SNCC), after which Atlanta students had organized major demonstrations to desegregate downtown Atlanta.[10]

Dear Marvin Rich:

[. . .]

I am so involved in the Atlanta affair right now that I don't think I can take on New Orleans. When the regional meeting of the Sit-in group was held in Atlanta I did their big speech at their mass meeting on Sunday afternoon. It was well covered by AP, by both Atlanta papers, and by TV. The reports in the Atlanta papers of all the meetings, including my speech were friendly and fair and for the most part accurate. They had copies of my speech so they couldn't go far wrong although they made up some odd and wholly imaginative headings such as (in Ralph McGill's *Constitution*) Miss Lillian Smith urges Sit-in Coup. That was just to stir people and make them restless. As a matter of fact the coup came yesterday; but the group were so anxious to keep it secret that they did not even tell me! I came home Tuesday afternoon; and Wednesday the coup was pulled off. The students did a fine, well planned job of it. Dr. Martin Luther King, Jr., at their request went along with them but he was careful to say that he was not leading it, that the students were: they had planned it, and carried it out. Last night, there were 36 of them in jail including Dr. King. All 36 have refused bail which I personally think is the way it should be done, when it is possible. One hundred took part in the demonstrations which included not only Rich's and Davison's (our two biggest department stores) but Sears, Woolworth and many other variety stores. Nobody had anybody arrested except Rich's. The group arrested last evening are going to stick it out in jail. Fortunately, they have been put in Fulton Towers which is newer, cleaner and much more modern than city jail. I hope they keep them there. Today, there were other demonstrations but no arrests until the students reached the Terminal Station (our big railroad station). Then they were arrested. About 25 more; I am not quite sure of the number. Tomorrow they plan to march and demonstrate again. They are using a good technic. They are being arrested only when they do not leave a store when asked to by the top management. So today, when asked to leave, they left; then in twenty minutes a new batch was there; they left when requested to, then a new batch came. To me, this is a terrific war of nerves and might work beautifully anywhere. It can go on and on until Rich's nerves break.

Governor Vandiver offered state troopers to quell the "mob" and to protect people's "private property" but nobody took him up on it.

I called Mrs. Martin Luther King, Jr., last night and we had a good cozy talk during which I tried to reassure her of not only my support and sympathy but of that of many others. I shall keep in touch with her and I shall write some of the students, many of whom I know. About three weeks ago they spent Sunday here with me on the mountain (ten of the leaders) and we discussed many things. Then I was with them for the speech, and afterward some of them and I went to the Negro restaurant Pascal's for dinner. I shall do what I can for them and I'll see if I can stir some of my white friends to help by writing letters to the stores, and to the mayor (who so far is all right, although he seems to find it hard to understand that the young Negroes really mean it; he tries to think of it as a kind of half-serious lark which should not be built up by white hysteria into something big.)

I wrote Dick Rich of Rich's, today. A three and a half page letter. I think I made some strong points; hope so. I sent a copy to the editor of *Atlanta Constitution* and the editor of *Atlanta Journal*; also, a copy to the Atlanta mayor. I shall send a copy of it to Rich's chairman of the Board tomorrow.

Now: here is something that I hope you can help me do. Davison's (the second biggest department store in Georgia) is an affiliate of Macy's in New York. They should quietly open their restaurants to Negroes; if they did, then Rich's would have to. Dick Rich is not too bright a fellow; Walter Rich was a splendid man; but Dick inherited the business built up by his grandfather and father and uncles. He is just wrong-spirited. He is Jewish and he knows how white and Negro Christians stood by the Jewish community when the Temple was bombed; but he does not see what he is doing is a bombing of the spiritual structure of human beings. I wrote him rather plainly about this. Rich's is so firmly established in Georgia (since the Civil War); so beloved and popular that its management could do anything they wanted to and Georgians would accept it. Yet, here Dick Rich is faltering as if he had just opened this giant store last year.

[. . .] But we shall have to put pressure on Macy's which is the mother store. Can that be done? Have you the people, etc. you need for it? Macy's will hate this for their own policy is now good; but they have been behind Rich's down here until a few years ago when a bombardment of letters (managed by a friend of mine) got out the "White" drinking fountain, in Davison's. [. . .] Publicity in New York would push the management down here. I'll try to get a bombardment of letters to both Rich's and Davison's as soon as I can, from white Georgians. They both have a large number of wealthy Negro customers. We'll work hard on them, too.

tlc, UGA

The following letter was sent to Eugene Patterson, editor of the *Atlanta Constitution*, as well as to Jack Spalding, editor of the *Atlanta Journal*.

October 22, 1960

My dear Mr. Patterson:

At times of crises it always seems that we tend to regress to old cliches and verbal reflexes. I suppose this is the most human thing about us: to depend on old learnings that once upon a time worked.

But it may be dangerous for us to do so. Do you mind if I point out a few cliches, a few somewhat wobbly defenses that have appeared in editorials in both *Constitution* and *Journal* and in WAGA-TV's Dale Clark editorials? Some of these were in one, some in another, some in all.

Let's take them one at a time:

1. "There are better ways to work for one's rights." May I ask what are better ways? None was suggested. There is the alternative of taking cases to law, one small issue after another, through the weary and slow procedures of the courts. The Negroes do not have the money for this; and we whites do not have the time. And who likes it? White southerners hate the NAACP because they do use court procedures. When I say the white race does not have time, I mean that the international situation is so delicate that we are going to have to hurry on this righting of racial wrongs. We are still running things on Confederate time but the countries of Africa and Asia and the Communists are running things on world time. This is where the Communists are beating us: they've got their watches set up to world time, and we haven't. We are not only using spurious values, "Confederate money" as I said in my speech last week, but we are setting our watches to a time that no longer exists.

(b) Another alternative to the sit-ins is talk, mediation. The students in the nonviolent movement always try this first; it is only when this fails that they try sit-ins and picketing. The mayor is now mediating but only because the students staged their sit-ins.

(c) There is also boycotting; and this movement is of course, growing; but it, too, is an outgrowth of the nonviolent movement; and a stage of it.

(d) The fourth alternative is violence: mass violence on the part of Negroes. You wouldn't want this nor would I, nor would any sensible Negro. We are indeed lucky to have Dr. Martin Luther King, Jr., leading this movement instead of a southern Adam Clayton Powell. Think of what that would mean.

Suppose we did not have this nonviolent protest movement in the South? Suppose our young Negroes were being trained to hate, to do violent acts and say violent words? You know their slogan, do you not? "When you are slapped, do not slap back; when you are cursed, do not answer back. Use only kindness, courtesy, compassion in your encounter with whites." Are we not lucky? I doubt that we deserve such luck but Fate or God or Strange Accident has given it to us and we should be using it to bring about a constructive, creative, democratic change. But no; these young students are jailed, and Dr. Martin Luther King, known in every corner of the world as a symbol of freedom for the dark races, is jailed. And yet, none of it had to happen. All could have been avoided with a little foresight, a little insight, a little imagination, a little give-and-take. But unfortunately, many white men grow very emotional about this matter and do quick, impulsive emotional things. And then we are in trouble.

So, today, Atlanta's good name is blackened and is being pushed by many people in the world, nearly two billion of them, right along with Little Rock's.

As I am writing this, WSB-TV news has just said Rich's has withdrawn charges against Mr. King. This is good; but alas, it comes too late to do the prestige of the United States any good. Or Atlanta's name much good. Why didn't Dick Rich and Frank Neely do this last Wednesday? Was it not that the white reflexes worked too well and too swiftly?

[. . .] We cannot keep counting on good sense, and self control, and even wisdom from Negroes when we whites are showing so little of any of those qualities. Why do we think they will be more reasonable than we are?

But let me return to the clichés, if I may:

Let's take the one about nonviolent protests calling forth violence, therefore it should not be used. There is nothing more specious. Are you going to let a child's tantrums make you do the wrong thing? Are the hoodlums of Atlanta going to determine what can or cannot be used as a way of protest? They may decide, the Klan may, and the hoodlums may that Negroes must not protest at all; they must be slaves, silent slaves to the cult of segregation. But are you going to side with the hoodlums? Are we going to say to Negroes "You musn't do anything that will upset our psychotics and our criminals and our crackpots"? Is this not a genuflection to insanity and crime that not one of us would want to make? I think this old argument (we used to hear it in the Gandhi days—in fact the British imperialists used it— they were imperialists in those days, as they went about flogging Indians on the streets during their protests, putting their leaders in jail) is about as solid as a marshmallow: the argument that nonviolence causes violence and must not, therefore, be used. How on earth can nations work for their rights without physical fighting except by the use of mediation, symbolic protests, and a lot of give-and-take.

Now the argument about stores being "private." No store is a private affair. It is neither a home nor a club. It is licensed to serve the public; all the public, not the white segment only. In America, we have "one price for all." An American custom that has gradually spread to Europe, and is slowly now spreading to Asia. We are proud of it. We would not like it if Rich's for instance, had a price for whites and another price for Negroes. But to give whites special comforts and conveniences and to exclude Negroes from them is as bad. I don't think this argument holds up morally and in our country, what doesn't hold up ethically won't hold long legally.

And about breaking a law that everyone knows was set up just to discriminate against Negroes. It is a law that won't hold up if it is carried through the courts. This is exactly the way the old segregation laws were slapped on the statute books: in a time of confusion and hysteria; and we are still paying a terrible price for those unConstitutional statutes. Let's don't defend that phony law put on the Ga. books last year.

In 1942, I wrote a piece called "Buying a New World with Old Confederate Bills" in which I talked of the African and Asian nations which were sure to gain their independence. This piece was reprinted in many papers and magazines. Last week, in 1960, I repeated in a speech much of what I said in 1942—and it still is relevant, still seems "new" to many people. Why can't we catch up with the times? Are we caught in a nightmare? Are we going to sleepwalk until it will be too late to act in any rational way?

Please forgive this long letter; and forgive my appealing to you so often. I am supposed to be hard at work on another novel and a book of nonfiction. But I cannot, like Faulkner, and some other authors, tear myself away from this great moment in history and pretend it has nothing to do with me and my art. It seems to me what is happening or failing to happen in the South may determine our and the free world's entire future. I find it hard to sit here on the mountain writing about philosophical matters at such a time. So once more, like dear old Cassandra, I must cry out a warning to my beloved people.

tlc, UGA 1283A

 The daughter of a white Baptist minister from Virginia, Jane Stembridge was a student at New York's Union Theological Seminary when she was recruited in June 1960 to manage the SNCC office in Atlanta. Correspondence between Smith and Stembridge began in September 1960 when Smith was invited to give the closing speech at SNCC's fall meeting. One of several student activists from Atlanta whom Smith invited to visit on the mountain, Stembridge was also a poet who admired Smith as a writer and looked to her as a mentor as well as a source of support for the movement in the early sixties. In turn, as SNCC's first office secretary and editor of its newspaper, the *Student Voice*, Stembridge was for Smith an important source of inside information from SNCC's perspective on the civil rights movement. The following letter was written in response to Stembridge's of October 20 in which she had questioned whether she should be participating in the massive sit-in demonstrations and subsequent arrests of students in downtown Atlanta, rather than working in the SNCC office.[11]

October 22, 1960

Dear Jane:

[. . .]

We are so proud of you and the group; I am; and Paula is, too. We have hung over TV and have scrutinized the news carefully. The WAGA editorial last night disappointed me. I wrote Dale Clark today; I'll send you a copy of the letter, tomorrow. I tried to set him straight on what it is all about.

I have also written Mr. Dick Rich of Rich's a long, and I hope, persuasive letter. I told him to cancel my account unless Rich's can soon find a way to open the lunch counters and Magnolia Room. I tried to be persuasive in a real way; and I hope it will help. I sent a copy of this letter to Mr. Frank Neely with a personal note to Mr. Neely. I also sent a copy to Mayor Hartsfield with a personal, friendly note to him. I suggested that the lunch counters could be opened; and the Magnolia Room opened quietly, without publicity—simply by telling a few Negro leaders. I am afraid by "leaders" Mr. Hartsfield thinks of the older generation. But I thought I'd try to remind him again that he should deal, and the stores should deal, with the students, also.

I rather think the WAGA letter is a good one, so I may send Mr. Hartsfield a copy of it, too; and perhaps to two or three of Atlanta's businessmen. I also want Dr. Martin Luther King to see it, so I'll send him a copy of both letters. I have also written Davison's a briefer letter; I didn't have the same kind of contact with Davison's that I have with Rich's. I have also written CORE in New York (Marvin Rich) [. . .] to go to Macy's and try to push them into putting a bit of pressure on Davison's. This kind of thing will be good; and will also give the sit-ins in Atlanta more publicity.

Now publicity for a job that is being done is exactly what a movement must have. Gandhi was good at getting it and using it shrewdly. What we all want to avoid is publicity for ourselves. Sometimes, as in Dr. King's case and perhaps my own, because our names are known all over the world, we have to let our names be used in a way that will help the movement. So don't worry about using Dr. King. You are not "using" him; he is a symbol and he wants to be one, at this time. This is right.

Everything seems to me, at this distance, to have been managed beautifully. And this is YOU, Jane. Here is where you are participating and being. One acts in the mind, in the imagination, in the heart as well as out in the world with one's body. You are making impact with your ideas, your guidance, your suggestions, your restraints, your values. No one in the movement seems to me as important in the Atlanta situation as you. So don't worry about it. You are exactly where you are needed; what you do can determine whether the movement fails or succeeds. I know how you feel about going to jail; I feel I should go, too; it is very hard for me to stay up here and write letters to important people, and phone others, and write speeches, etc. and keep in touch with news media. It would feel better to me to sit-in and go to jail. But by doing so, I fear I would split the sympathies of white people. The sit-ins are a symbol or rather they are symbolic acts which white people can respond to with their hearts and minds if the young Negroes do it. When a white woman does it, or a white girl, the symbol splits; it is still a good symbol to those who understand that segregation hurts the whites as much as the Negroes, but since most whites do not yet understand this, we confuse them in their symbol-making. (I'd like to talk about this more with you.) You keep on where you are, doing all you can inside and outside the movement; I'll do all I can up here; and if the time ever comes when our sitting-in will have symbolic significance, then we can and must do it. It does not, at present, in my thinking, have that significance.

Anything else I can do day or night, call me and I'll help.

tlc, UGA

TO JANE STEMBRIDGE

November 21, 1960

Dear Jane:

Dr. Henry Crane and his friend have gone; Paula and I have played solitaire for a half hour to ease us down a bit; and I am thinking now of all the things I meant to say to you two, and the questions both Paula and I wanted to ask you, and the check I meant to give you; sitting here regretting that I protested too long and too much about the Southern Educational Fund, etc.* Etc. For after all, this kind of thing is a matter of intuition, not proof, a matter of judgment, not morals, a matter of strategy rather than an ethical choice.

Let me say the small things I want to say, first: Here is a check for $30.00 which I meant to give you and Donna; it is from my dear old, very aged friend who knows she has only a year or so to live, maybe less, and wants to do what she can to help with the nonviolent students' movement.† She knows about you and her last letter spoke of "your dear Jane," for I had told her of your fine mind, your quality, your sensitiveness, your integrity, etc. This dear old lady who has no strings tied to anything she gives, wants you two girls to use it for yourselves for whatever you need: rent, food, clothes or whatnot. [. . .]

What are we trying to do? I am trying by nonviolent means to persuade people that change is inevitable; I am trying to persuade them to value not only human freedom and human rights but the creative methods, and means, of achieving freedom and human rights, that I think are necessary in order to bring about change. I believe with all my mind and heart that only nonviolent technics of conciliation and exchange of information can bring about the kind of change that will make human beings more aware of their responsibilities, and more aware of the purpose of human life. I believe there is purpose in our being on this earth but I do not dare to know what that purpose is, save that we have now reached the stage where we, as

*The Southern Conference Education Fund (SCEF), originally part of the Southern Conference for Human Welfare, from 1947 on was a racially integrated organization devoted entirely to antisegregation work in the South.[12] In the late 1950s SCEF came under attack from the press when one of its representatives, Carl Braden, refused to answer questions before the House Un-American Activities Committee and was sentenced to a year in prison. Despite Smith's and other Cold War liberals' suspicions of the leftist origins of SCEF, SNCC students found trusted supporters in Braden and his wife Anne. SCEF's newspaper, the *Southern Patriot*, gave early coverage to SNCC's activities, and, largely through Anne Braden's influence, SCEF provided funds to hire a white field secretary to recruit southern white college students to work with SNCC from 1961 to 1963.[13]

†Anna Grace Sawyer of Forrest Park, Ill., wrote Smith in August 1960 asking where to send financial support for the nonviolent sit-in movement in the South.[14]

the human race, are bringing about our own evolution. Pierre de Teilhard has said very fine things about this in his *Phenomenon of Man* and I intended to ask you if you would like to take my copy back to read. I also meant to offer you and Donna any books you wanted from my library. These intentions all got sidetracked in the sudden pressure of personalities and overlapping visits.

I do not know if I am right about Jim Dombrowski; I wish I had proof; I have little; but I have felt a deep split in him, somehow, and this has disturbed me from the beginning. He seemed an idealist who at the same time saw little that is good in his own country and too much that is good in Russia. It is not a matter of love of country, or loyalty; I criticise my South and my country and have been doing so for a long time, but I also criticise Russia when I think it is wrong. And I never heard Jim, in my life, criticise Russia and its dictatorial leaders, and its slave camps, its firing lines, its censorship, etc. I cannot see how we can take this kind of position: I criticise evil wherever I see it, knowing it is in me, also; therefore I try to do it humbly. I do not always succeed. But how can we criticise it in our own region and our own country and not in other countries in the world. You know, Jane, I, too, loath red-baiting and McCarthyism; I happened to be one of the first writers in this country to speak out against McCarthy, long before it was "the thing" to do. But he was not actually against communism: He was against the future, against change, against all kinds of free, creative search for truth. That is why he was so dangerous; and that is why he pulled so many people to him. He was a hater of the human spirit. I fought him because of this, and I fight the red-baiters because they are dishonest; it is not the communists' evils that they dislike but their virtues. And these virtues you and I *like*. I have never known a red-baiter who disliked censorship, or curtailment of personal freedom; or dictators, or the infringement of civil rights. No; what red-baiters dislike is the human search for truth, the value we put on man, the person, and man the human being. That is why they seem dangerous to me. They dislike in communism their concern for the physical welfare of men, and their attempt to abolish poverty.

All these things get twisted together so that when we use the word, "red-baiter" we are involved in inconsistencies and conflicting ideas; and it is true when we are afraid of working with American communists. What I fear in working with them as a group is that they don't let you know where they stand; they say one thing and often mean another: they are devious and tortuous and this I do not like in anyone, Methodist, Baptist, Catholic, Communist. [. . .]

Now—enough of that. I want to apologize to you for saying so much about it when you were here. As an old veteran in these matters I grew afraid for you, respecting and admiring you as I do; I did not want you to be trapped when it was not necessary to be trapped. I don't want your usefulness stripped from you by your having to battle all kind of accusations of being a Communist that would wear you out and use up your energy fighting the red-baiters instead of fighting against segregation which as symbol and symptom is a very big "war" for us to engage in. It is a shame to use up one's time and strength on the wrong battles. Of course you will be accused. I have had letters circulated about my being a Communist by a fascist group; and these letters injure and hurt. On the other hand, I refuse to get detoured into fighting my own causes celebre. And one thing I dislike about some of these people who have seemed to be strangely close to the old Communist line is their tendency to think of themselves as martyrs and to ask others to fight for them. Nobody need fight for me; what I want is for them to fight the big evils.

[. . .]

How are you and Donna managing financially? Have you any money to live on? Perhaps I can persuade my dear old lady to help you more. This $5000.00 she wants to give to extend an understanding of the principle of nonviolence could be used well down here. Will you jot down any ideas you have? I'd like to know what you think after these six or eight months of working and talks? through your little paper? just how? How can we get information to the newspapers so that editors will understand what nonviolent action is? Will you write me what you think? And will you both come again and have a real visit? [. . .]

My warmest regards to both you girls: I have real admiration for you, and Paula and I both are fond of you, and concerned, and proud of you, too.

tlc, UGA

TO PAUL TILLICH

[December 1960]

Dear Dr. Tillich:

It was most kind of you to acknowledge the speech. I sent it to you because I want to keep you au courant with what I am trying to do down here with the sit-in movement, and what the young students are succeeding in—and failing in.

It is the first movement in the South that I have ever had a sense of excitement about. It seems to me, as we relate the racial crisis here in our country with the new African nations, we tie these, in turn, to nuclear war or the possible chance of it, this attempt on the part of the young to use nonviolent technics of dramatic acting-out, verbal persuasion, with insistence on conciliation and the redemptive power of suffering for others, reveals itself as a spiritual catalyst. The people involved are bound to become different, bound to grow in spiritual awareness; and this, in turn, is bound to have an effect on international affairs for here is a way, a technic, an attitude that can be used in a larger framework.

To watch the Negro students, to see the slow working of ideas in their minds, to feel their inner tensions building up and then to watch these dissolve in feelings of love, compassion, and decision to risk, to endure—all this is rather wonderful.

[. . .]

It is sad, it is grievous to watch the lack of imagination in the whites. Segregation has frozen their mental resources, as well as their spiritual resources. The heads of a great store—the biggest in the South, Rich's—could think of nothing more creative to do when Dr. King and the three young men asked to enter the Magnolia Room (the more expensive restaurant) than to arrest them for "trespassing" and send them off to jail. [. . .]

A month passed. The managers and owners had withdrawn the charges against Dr. King and the sit-in students. They asked for a month in which to come to some agreement. The students promised not to picket or sit in during this month. The month ended. Not one thing had been done. So, the students began sitting in again. Now all the restaurants, tearooms, lunchcounters in the stores of downtown Atlanta are closed. And the managers, owners, etc. are being congratulated by the KKK and the GUTS (a rough, crude, sex-ridden group of men) for their brave stand against Negroes! It delighted me when I read that last night in the Atlanta papers. I am glad Dick Rich—a Jew who has tried to become completely identified with white Christians—is now hailed not by the best element of the community but the worst as a "brave supporter of white rights." I am sure he is embarrassed but he deserves every bit of it. The other stores in Atlanta are ready to open if Rich's will. Up to now, Dick Rich has been only angry, stubborn, and determined not to change.

And as this was going on, here came the New Orleans mess. These white women are of course behaving like Maenads and Furies and Eumenides because the white legislators have asked them to do so. But it is an awesome sight to watch them on TV attack the white minister for insisting on bringing his child to school; to see them pinning signs on their two and three-year-olds which read, "We don't go to school with niggers."

Well—this is my South; the South I was born in and still love. Full of cruelty and blindness; stiff and rigid in some of its ways, so resilient and warm in others: dragging itself and the whole country toward chaos. Sometimes I am not confident that we shall make it. Sometimes, I feel that the white race has had its day; its chance; that it cannot measure up to the ordeal now confronting it. I say this only to a few; I rarely say it at all; but sometimes as I write, talk, work trying, like a Cassandra, to warn my people, I feel the words breaking to pieces against my own face.

[. . .]

My life, this fall, has been busy and full of things. After my fourth bout with cancer, I did not begin to get my strength back until in September. But I am now feeling fine and have been able to meet the demands made of me. Such strange ones, sometimes. A young woman, cracking up, had read one of my books. She called me long distance, saying she had no money, no friends, was completely alone, and felt herself going to pieces. She was at an airport and had been wandering around from airport to airport until she had used up all her money. I had to hold her calm by my voice, while I tried to get enough information to help her. The Western Union was closed in this small village, so I telephoned New York and asked my lawyer to send enough money by Western Union to pay for this girl's ticket to Washington D.C. where she said she had a friend. I then called the airport and persuaded them to put her on the plane even if the money had not arrived by the time the plane was to go. They finally promised to do it. Then I phoned Washington and found that the friend was not a friend, but just someone she had met with whom she had no real relations. This person was frightened by my call and refused to help the sick girl. I then asked her to call Travelers Aid and ask them to help the sick girl. She refused. So I from down here in Georgia called a Unitarian minister I know and asked him to help the girl. He phoned the airport, found the plane was just landing, got a policeman to get the girl to the phone, and told her to come to his church in a cab. She did, and he found her almost physically dead, as well as mentally collapsed. He with the help of the police put her in General Hospital in Washington; and there she is at this moment, critically ill, and none of us can find out who her family are or where they are. This hangs over me: How can any one person meet the needs of these strangers who call? and yet how can you ever refuse to? I am as distressed about the stranger lying there, unknown, in General Hospital, as I would be if it were one of my own young nieces. She told me, as she sobbed out her story, that she had called her brother and he hung up on her. I could not get his name from her. So—

Why on earth am I writing you this? I don't quite know. Except, sometimes, the vast misery of so many wraps around you and pulls very hard at the heart, the mind; and you hear yourself telling it, again, to one you know will reach out and accept the misery as "his own."

tlc, UGA

TO EUGENE PATTERSON

December 21, 1960

Dear Mr. Patterson:

May I thank you for the line in yesterday's editorial which said, "It seems not only dangerous but wrong to celebrate Christ's birth in a spirit that his death condemned. Atlanta lies hurt and passing men look the other way."

I was moved by this, and felt in it your sensitiveness, your awareness that Atlanta's dilemma is both a moral and a spiritual one.

Because it is a moral question, one based firmly on the dignity of men, on the rightness that all men be treated as human beings, it has seemed futile to me—even dangerous—for the question of "breaking the law" to be wrapped around this deeper, more fundamentally moral question. The legalistic question chokes the moral question. Men's minds are shifted from asking what is right to asking what is legal. There is something Pharisaical about this, although I do not think you Pharisaical. I feel in you only an honest, compassionate mind searching for the truth. Nevertheless, you, too, have stressed this legalistic angle; and have—although you have not meant to—driven men into a quiet, comfortable corner where they can shield themselves from the moral question.

I think this has been easy to do because many of us have stressed to the public that they must obey the Supreme Court's decision of 1954 whether "they like it or not, or whether they think it is right or not." In a sense, this was an easy way out, this legalistic way; it seemed to avoid dialectics; it seemed to avoid all talk about segregation which some hold too sacred to be discussed. But actually, while easy, it was perhaps not a very wise thing to do. For now, the mob, the GUTS, can throw it right in our faces. They can say, "You said, Obey the law, right or wrong; all right, say it to the Negroes, too. You jumped on us; now jump on them."

In a time of change it is very hard for any of us to think clearly, to probe deeply, to disentangle the small threads out of which is woven the web of men's beliefs. The heavier threads are easy to see and to deal with. But the finer threads, the ones which actually create the designs, are more delicate and more firmly woven together. It is easy to say, "Obey the law." For 999 times out of 1000 this is the right and safe thing to say. It is much harder to say, "The law is sacred, it must be obeyed—but only when based on morality, only when it adheres to the principles of our democratic Constitution." When we say this, we immediately step into an area of uncertainty; we must think, we must move carefully among invisible things, and that is hard to do. [. . .]

But I think we should welcome this challenge to think with more subtlety, to move through complications not as a bulldozer moves but as a human being stepping carefully here, there; recognizing and naming the chasms, the mud puddles, the quicksands that surround us. Out of this kind of thinking and feeling will come a new South; and this will be worth all our sweat and tears and brain exercise.

[. . .]

The difficulty lies just here: Our people do not agree on what is moral and what is spiritually right. If they did, our troubles would float away. [. . .]

I remember saying this once to my sister. She had said, "But we should obey the segregation laws, even though we don't think they're right because they are the law." She is something of a Puritan so I said to her, "Would you still say this if a law were passed requiring your daughter to walk on the streets without her clothes?" She stared at me. "But which is more immoral? to walk without clothes on the street or to strip Negroes of their dignity and worth as human beings?" She saw it at once. She said. "Of course, we don't really believe it is wrong to segregate Negroes, do we? even those of us who think we do." And I agreed; for it is true, most of us who say segregation is "wrong" do not honestly think it is gravely wrong; we do not really understand what it does to a Negro's spirit and mind; to a little colored child's feelings about her own importance.

This is our trouble: We do not really feel it; we almost do but we don't actually let ourselves hurt with the hurt of the Negro and his children. If we once felt his anguish, his humiliation, if we identified with his little dark child as we identify with our own children, we could never let this Thing, this Terrible Thing, we call *segregation* continue. Or if we could see what it has done to our own minds and spirits, how it has blurred our capacity to think, to search for the truth, to feel compassion—we would turn away in revulsion.

[. . .]

May I say just this? [. . .] If the lunch counters are not open to all citizens, there will be no possible chance of keeping the schools open. Eating in restaurants and lunch counters is a "sometime thing." Going to school is *every day*. If Atlantans cannot move this one small step by opening their lunch counters and restaurants then God help them next fall. The GUTS and White Councils will have won; they will grow strong on their victory; the good decent people of Atlanta will already have lost. If we can't win this small battle, the big battle next fall will be inevitably lost to the mob. If we win on this small thing which 128 other southern cities have already achieved, then we shall be prepared morally, psychologically, strategically to carry through our hope of open schools into a reality.

Once more, forgive this long letter. I write it because I respect and like you, as you know. And want for our people a season of peace which has, of course, to be created not "won."

tlc, UGA

Gerda Lerner wrote Smith after reading Smith's December 24, 1960, *Saturday Review* essay, "Novelists Need a Commitment." While expressing her appreciation for Smith's writing, Lerner wrote that her personal experience as a writer indicated that more than a commitment was necessary to get her work published. She described a novel she had written (which she had been told was out of tune with the literary market) as being in keeping with Smith's concepts of dehumanization and fragmentation in human relationships. Feeling blocked as a writer and in need of affirmation, she asked Smith if she would read the manuscript.[15]

Smith's response not only documents one of the many instances of her willingness to help younger writers; it also provides an excellent example of the way her correspondence became more autobiographical and philosophical, especially in her later years, as she reiterated or reinterpreted her life and thought to those she felt would be a receptive audience. Significantly, just as her support of political activists included challenging their understanding of the process of working for social change, so her support for other writers included both networking efforts and theoretical discussions about writing and the creative process. Such correspondence demonstrates once again the consistent interrelatedness of theory and practice in her life.

Sunday [January] 22, 1961

Dear Gerda Lerner:

I was deeply moved by your letter. Warmed by your appreciation; hurt by the sudden glimpse you gave me of your own frustration; troubled and brightened, shocked and encouraged by vistas your words opened up. I am going to answer now, for fear that things, THINGS THINGS will keep me from doing so, later.

This sharp edged, cutting, upthrusting age we are living in makes inhuman demands on human beings. I think this about my own life. I am by nature shy, quiet, withdrawn; every move I have made in my life toward people, toward relating myself to my external world has hurt behind it; something pushes; sometimes, my conscience, my awareness of the hurt of others; sometimes, my own blazing rebellion against the false, the hypocritical; sometimes, my simple, almost childlike curiosity about people, things, customs, defenses—I want to read, to brood, to study, to think. I want simply to look. Just look. At mountains. At a face. At a painting. I want to listen to the music that was the only real joy I had for the first twenty-two years of my life. I was absorbed in it, covered by it, hidden by it, exalted by it, excited— All my life was involved in music, except my two sharp eyes that kept staring at people. Then, in my own life, things happened; parents crumpled with psychic burdens and financial ones; I had to come out of myself and help them, take over. This call on me from them gradually spread and became a call[,] a silent call from the South on me for my help. Only the poor South did not know it needed me. *I* felt it did. Not southern people. And so, a conflict began which has never for one year let up: the conflict between my deep desires, my instinctual needs, my hunger to create something, to make a thing—and this crying, pleading but even-now silent cry of my people, Come over to Macedonia and help us. The tragic knowledge that they have not known they were crying for help and resented the help I have tried to give is one of the wounds of human life.

What I mean when I say an artist, a writer must have a sense of commitment (by the way that title was not mine, but the *Saturday Review*'s: my title was more accurate: *Out of Creative Tension Comes Peace.* They subtly altered my real meaning by that title which they used without my permission.) is that the artist must have a sense of vocation, a sense of being "called" to his work; it is something he must do; he must listen when he is told to "make a new thing." This is what I meant, truly. This is my belief. But since this artist lives in a world of people, a world of surging life, ambivalent life, aching, passionately hurting life, he must make his "thing" his "new thing" out of this life, out of his own personal experience of life. Because my experience of life has to do with chasms and walls, with "a trembling earth" which literally was true since the earth near the Great Swamp of my childhood does actually tremble when one walks on it—

because my experience was in the actual living a kind of metaphor of the white race, of all his grandeurs and all its errors; because I also lived with Negroes, close to them, not as problems but as people, because I saw the cruelties, felt them abrade me as well as my Negro friends, I could write of nothing else. How could I! I had to explore the meanings of the trembling earth beneath my feet: the philosophical and ethical meanings, the psychological meanings, yes—the esthetic meanings too. I have always looked at racial segregation as something that has spelled out a doom for white people that black people may escape. I have always seen our human dilemmas from the point of view of the corroding effect of arrogance and hate, of moral blindness and intellectual obscurantism rather than from the point of view, "Let's help the poor Negro." The Negro has had a hellish time: he has been bound outwardly by many bonds, but the white man has bound his soul and mind and heart until they are abject slaves to this sick worship called White Supremacy. Always, I have looked at things this way.

As for problems: There is neither a white nor Negro problem. There is no racial problem; no "problem" of racial relations. These matters are not simple, sharpedged problems which can be solved. The only thing that can happen is for us to "make a new thing," to do, as does God the artist "create the new." We abandon human dilemmas, we never solve them. And that is why I say even the young writer (although I did not say this in the *Sat. Review* article) must have a commitment: a commitment to make something new of the life around him. But does he see this life? I don't think Faulkner, for instance, really sees the life around him or even inside him. He has made something new, something interesting; but nothing great, nothing that can find its place in the future of mankind. As I said of him, twenty-five years ago, he is truly a great finger painter. That was the term I used then; today, I'd say, Faulkner has tried to do with words (but has not succeeded because words have set meanings) what Pollock and de Kooning have tried to do with the drip method. With him, not quite abstraction for words are symbols not abstractions and he cannot make pure abstraction out of them. But he has used a method something like theirs. But there is a fallacy here: The writer and the painter are not in the same creative category; they can never be equated with each other. Not even the poet can be equated with the painter. The painter is much closer to music and when he tries to achieve pure abstraction as music does often achieve, then he is on solid ground. But the writer can never do this. He cannot take a word and drain all its old meaning from it, mash it into pulp and make "something new out of it." He can try as Joyce tried but he cannot do it. The word is there. In the beginning was the Word. It has meaning; it has ten thousand layers of meaning, maybe; but meaning which human beings know is there; and so you cannot begin as if you were God and make the material, too, with which you work. Your subject matter can be personally yours, and should be. If it also happens to affect the whole world as my material does, then that is both good and bad. Good because it is important. Your treatment of it may not be; but the subject matter is important. It is "bad" for the writer because readers are always reading into your words and your subject matter what they want to see there; or what they fear to see there. You cannot get esthetic distance from subject matter that involves "race" for instance. When Melville wrote *Moby Dick*, no one read him; reviewers sneered at the book. Why? Because whale hunting was an actual business at that time; they couldn't get esthetic distance. They felt he was dealing with a "problem" although actually he was not, as every reader today knows. But then, it seemed so; and only Hawthorne grasped his real intent. But never said so publicly. Only privately to Melville.

As a citizen, I have sometimes used my writing talent, my talent for finding a simple way to say something that is hideously twisted and complex, to help view a fragment of "race relations" more clearly. I have even suggested, as a housewife might during a thunderstorm, that there are ways to shut windows, and doors, and put pans under the bad leaks; and call the children in out of reach of lightning, etc. But as a serious writer, as I think of myself in *Strange Fruit* (yes, even that first book) and *Journey* and *Killers of the Dream* and *One Hour*, I have always tried to make something new out of what was before hackneyed, trite, and false; I have always tried to show invisible things (in this sense, I am a realist. I do like to dredge up what even my own eyes have never seen before). I have tried. I do not think I have quite succeeded in making a new, wondrous, shining thing out of the big Nightmare. And I want to do this. I want to do as Auden and poets before him have said, "teach my terrors to sing." When I do this maybe I can take a nasty, obscene, hating, panting monstrosity and show it in a way that even it, even it, takes on some of the luminous quality of first creation.

I am sorry that your books have been lost in the awful, crazy shuffle of our times. Yes, I'd like to read your book. Our reviewers and critics are to blame. They are men lost in the present; talking of nihilism as if they had discovered it. It would make us laugh, except it is no laughing matter for serious writers. They now talk of "total rejection"—and one moans, Oh God. Dostoevski did all this 80 years ago and did it so well, always setting the nihilism cleanly against the great shadowy Affirmation. But they have nothing to affirm. Why? Because these critics and reviewers do not see the actual life we are living. They see what the 19th century saw; they see even what was seen up to 1940; but they don't really see the invisible things. This kind of realism is the realm of the creative writer: to show the invisible things actually present in contemporary life. This is one duty; one that we can commit ourselves to. Then we have another duty, another commitment to make. And that is to show it reflected against the future; and the past. Then we have a third commitment: to show these visible and invisible things as they look to each of us, in the dim depths of our own heart and mind, as they link on to what they find there. This is art as the writer deals with it. Art as the composer deals with it is something different; art as the painter and sculptor deals with it is different, too. And the painter's art is clearly different from that of the sculptor. Actually, writer and sculptor are closer together in their needs, their materials, their actual results.

Thank you for writing me. And thank you for letting me write you.

tlc, UGA 1283A

TO BERTHA BARNETT

April 18, 1961

Dearest Bird:

We had a fine if strenuous time at Oak Ridge. I stood it much better than I thought I could. I spoke Thursday night on the southern situation to an audience that was city-wide. And they had the biggest crowd, they say, that any speaker has drawn. It was a highly intelligent audience and fun to speak to for they were responsive and argued with me about important things. Many of them were scientists. The next night I spoke at the Institute of Nuclear Studies to the Friends of the Library. I spoke about writing and my own books, etc. We had a full house then, too. One day, the day after the first speech, there were four features in their little daily paper on me. I practically consumed the space! Actually, the account of my speech was the most intelligent one I have ever received. He bungled it a little when speaking of the unique contributions Western culture had given the world; it was hard for him to remember them and to get it straight; and he, as do many others, confused segregation with racism and in doing so rather spoiled my imagery. But never mind that.

One of the scientists—the one who handles all the National Laboratory seminars and their special public relations—spent five hours with us showing us reactors etc. etc. and the various plants. We had lunch that day with the director of the National Laboratories and the next day I had lunch with the director of the Institute for Nuclear Studies. Both are interesting men but I found more rapport with Dr. Weinberg, head of the National Lab (all the atomic business) who is not only brilliant but a most sensitive man, keenly aware of the human aspects of nuclear science. He came to hear me speak after I had lunch with him, and his wife asked me to tea the next day—so I hope he liked my speech. I couldn't go to tea[;] there was too much else brewing. They always work me to death at these places but I took it better than usual this time. After my first speech I got up early the next morning and went to the Negro school and told the children stories; and I really wouldn't have missed it. This school is segregated. The children did the salute to the flag and then piped the usual "sweet land of liberty" and I watched their faces and wondered how much longer can we endure our terrible blindness and hypocrisy! They were darling kids and while talking with them I found that all from the third grade up are studying French. And they have seen some French films etc. And seem to have excellent teachers. There was a reception the first night (Wednesday) but I also rather guess they do not have too many visitors who are not scientists and perhaps it was a relief to be with a plain writer. I certainly enjoyed it all. I had dinner with a young scientist (and his wife who cooked it!) who had that day returned from MIT where he had read an obviously important paper on theoretical physics . . . Bright. But I got the feeling that the very young, brilliant physicists did not have as many misgivings about things as did the older men. One thing that impressed me was the sadness in the older men's eyes. It was startling. So many sad faces I have never seen before. But the younger men were full of beans and brightness and did not seem to worry about what all this might be going to do to the human world. They seemed rather to accept it. The men in the cancer lab were also sad; and this sounds depressing but it actually wasn't. It was enthralling and I was almost overcome by the new beams of knowledge that came my way, and the sudden new thoughts I had about all this. I had to brush it out of my mind with a real effort in order to make my speeches. I'd like to go again. For one visit—even a five hour visit—is not enough.

[. . .]

tlc, UGA 1283A

The following letter is to Marianne Fink, the niece for whom Smith had moved to Fort Pierce in 1925. Marianne and her husband Omar Fink were ordained ministers in the Methodist church and, at the time of this letter, were missionaries in Africa. In 1955 they had been asked to leave a pastorate in Athens, Georgia, because of their stand against racial segregation.[16]

May 2, 1961

Dearest Marianne:

[...]

The mob on the campus of University of Ga. was really something. 2000 students pushed down on that dormitory and stoned the windows of this one girl, Charlayne Hunter. It was a terrific bad time. But I want to tell you the good things that have come about since then. The people in Athens rose up with moral indignation against the mob; the Athens police did a fine job of protecting the girl and holding down the students. The State Patrol was there—sixty strong—but would not lift a hand to help, saying they had not been ordered to by their superiors. When this happened the people of Athens really rose up. Since then, the girl and the boy have been invited into numerous families to eat a meal; think of it! And many nice things have been done for both students. Also, people spoke out; there were telegrams, hundreds of them to the Governor, expressing disapproval of the way he had handled things with his State Patrol. The mayor of Athens, the chief of police, the sheriff—all three—acted with courage, and wisdom, and plain decency. You see, you and Omar did a good job in Athens; it may have seemed wasted but it wasn't; and I have heard several people mention you during this trouble. You both should feel that your stay there prepared many people for this Great Moment in their lives. The Athens people are to be commended highly.

After it was over, I was asked to come to the Presbyterian Center, the new Westminster House, to talk to students and faculty members. Only about fifty or sixty came but they were extremely grave and concerned and we had a beautiful three hours of discussion together. Then some of the students asked Paula and me to go to some place (it was Sunday night) for coffee and talk some more; and we did; until one o'clock. The next day, Popovic (I think I have his name right) of the speech department gave me a thorough briefing on all that had happened before and since. He and other faculty members (nearly three-fourths of them took an open stand against the mob, against the two students being "suspended" when they had done nothing wrong, etc.) have been very active on the campus, organizing faculty members and students into groups who are working for Good Will on the campus. Some of the teachers, the morning after the mob, refused to teach the mobsters who entered their classrooms. I thought that was terrific. There was real moral indignation on that campus. There is now a group of about 400 (when I was there the last of January, just ten days after it happened) working hard not only to accept the two students but to arouse the moral outrage of those who were "nice" but neutral during the situation. The mob itself had a hard core of only 100 fascistic-segregationists but just see what one hundred can do! This shocked everybody to think only 100 could stir up this much trouble and pull in another 1900 of so-called neutrals. I talked with the splendid Negro lady with whom the boy lives; he is not yet on the campus; and found her to be iron-willed, strong, powerful, sane, courageous, sure sure sure of her righteousness. She was wonderful. She told me how the police had protected her home, how the city put a powerful light in her backyard (free) so that intruders would not dare come there; how they kept patrolling her block night after night; while she and three Negro men (all with guns) sat up at the windows throughout each night. She had 20 Negro men, good solid citizens, who took turns coming to sit up with her each night. The boy, they said, just calmly went to bed and to sleep! This amazed her. But I think he could take it only by blocking himself psychically from it. The girl faced it all but with a fine, forgiving, understanding spirit but she lost weight rapidly and has had a hard time of it emotionally, I am sure. I talked with both of them for about an hour and a half. Both are fine looking, well bred, well educated, with excellent spirit and good minds.

[. . .]

There is a piece in *Redbook* (May issue) on the New Orleans story by me. I did get good pay for this and have lived on it for three months. I haven't had time to tell my family yet to watch out for it. But will try to do so right away. I think the story is plain in it—and I won't tell it here, except to say I was warmly welcomed by white people in New Orleans, many of whom entertained me. I hope they like the story. It is optimistic and hopeful but I also tell the ugly side too. I would have emphasized the ugly side more had they let me but they wouldn't. Still, I think it is a fair and well balanced story. By "they" I mean *Redbook*. The North is guilty on this subject of not letting us white liberals tell the full truth. But we have to tell it straight where we can, then tell it "tactfully" in other places. The point is: get it told!

I talked at Emory University this past week to the Students and Faculty Colloquium. When the Administration heard I had been invited, they raised the roof and told the students they must not let it "get in the papers" that I was there. The students asked Why? This was the answer, "Because the Klan wouldn't like for Miss Smith to be on our campus." Isn't that something? I told the meeting about this and they roared with laughter at the Administration. They had allotted to Colloquium only a small room; they did everything they could to keep it from being a success. But they had the largest crowd they had ever had at a Colloquium meeting, many students who had never attended a meeting before. The crowd was warm, appreciative, deeply touched by much that I said. My subject was The Mob and the Ghost. I suggested, as I talked of ghosts in the mythic mind and how close the mob is to this primitive mind of ours, that maybe I, too, am a ghost in Georgia; perhaps I have never been seen as a woman, as a perhaps important writer, but as one of these ghosts wandering around everywhere in the southern mind. I told them the trouble about ghosts was (a) not enough people believed in them (b) not enough people knew how to treat them because they didn't really believe in them—at least, they wouldn't admit they did. I told them that ghosts must be carefully segregated; they must be kept in their "place." And this place is in the mythic mind, out of which come novels, stories, art, even scientific hypotheses, even certain elements in religion. But ghosts wandering through the rational mind and out on the streets could cause a lot of trouble. It was a totally new approach to the students and they loved it. I compared mythic mind with rational mind and said how dangerous it was to segregate them from each other: they must be connected, related, but never never merged and fused. And the Klan always merged the two minds together and let ghosts wander all over the place. Also, mobs did this kind of thing. They, too, let ghosts out, and turned living people into ghosts, into symbols. I then said the University's mob at Athens was stoning not a real girl but beliefs. The group listening to me got the point very quickly. I said all mobs let their ghosts out or transferred them or projected them on to living people—then they went on a ghost hunt. [. . .]

Now—Atlanta is about to desegregate its schools in September. Much good creative work has been done to prepare people for it. But not nearly enough. Atlanta is too damned complacent. It is already saying it has practically done the job when the job is only now approaching us. Some of my friends, and others, in the liberal white organizations have been going to Negro schools urging the young 11th and 12th graders to apply for places in white schools. To date, (in two days of applying) 140 students have applied. The white community is horrified. They expected three or four and hoped they could throw out the applications. Now they will have in all at least 500 applications—maybe more—and now what? So there was an editorial against the Negroes pushing so hard yesterday in the *Constitution* (which has prided itself on being so liberal). It is funny to watch but it scares me too. Anyway, I got $1500.00 for the group of white women who have done so much, so they can continue working through the summer. Their money had completely given out. But this $1500.00 will keep the office open and the work going.* So—this is the way things go. [. . .]

tlc, UGA

Correspondence in the spring of 1961 contained frequent references to financial pressures—no money from *One Hour*, civil rights work interfering with writing, no insurance to pay for cancer expenses—and renewed efforts to find employment for Snelling, some of which included Smith's seeking research positions for Snelling with the CIA and the State Department. Fortunately, Snelling was hired as librarian at nearby Tallulah Falls School for the fall of 1961. To prepare for the position, she took library science courses at Emory University in Atlanta that summer. The following letter summarizes many of the concerns Smith had written to other friends and family about financial pressures and reiterates her analysis of her relationship with Snelling at earlier times of separation.

TO PAULA SNELLING

Wednesday, June 20 [1961]

Dearest Paula:

I am so proud of the shrewd way in which you manoeuvered things at Emory. I am also glad you have the librarian on your side. All your work will be in that department so if you make friends there it will prove advantageous in numerous ways. Perhaps, even in helping you get a better job—if you later discover that the Tallulah Falls job is not pleasant or too limiting in some way. I hope you will become friends with all of them and I know they will recognize your worth immediately and like you very much.

Honey—I know it is hard as hell. But any new step is. It was terribly hard for me to go out and speak after being sick so long with cancer and a fluttery heart. I felt I couldn't do it; and as you know, I often panicked. You are bound to have hours and days when you, too, panic a little; or feel it isn't "worth it" or something. But in the end, I believe you will be deeply thankful that you took this step. It is a step toward saving our deep, good relationship; it is a step toward taking care of your financial future; it is also a step toward freeing your personality from the pressure my personality

*One of several gifts from Anna Grace Sawyer.

puts on you. You realize this, but you hate to acknowledge that my personality does weigh yours down. I have known it for years; and sometimes I have managed to deliberately lift that pressure from you; but I have had too many things to manage; I just can't work when half sick, make a living, and change my personality all at the same time. At least, I have not been able to. I know living with me has extended and expanded your life in a thousand different and fascinating and rewarding ways. I understand all this. But my "fame" and loss of fame, my position, my special work, and my kind of personality have pushed you in the background when you should not have been pushed back. And at the same time, it has made people look down on me for putting you in such a difficult position. And this has seemed unfair to me; and I have resented it. This kind of moral-psychological-physical-spiritual-financial tangle can destroy both of us and our relationship with each other. When such a situation gets like this, there is one thing to do: change it. Not destroy it. But change it. And this is what you and I are now trying to do. First, by your getting a job so you can share in the financial pressures. This I shall deeply appreciate and you will feel my appreciation and this will, in turn, make you feel better. Second, by giving you a means of livelihood that might sustain you were something to happen to me. Third, by putting you "on your own" in many ways so that you can make your own friends, make your own decisions, choose what you want to do and buy; plan things without always consulting me, etc. You do not yet realize how much you will welcome this freedom from a kind of subservience to me and my life. You will like it fine; you will have growing pains for a while; but you will like it. For I have at times felt your resentment toward our way of life. It is one reason you have been smoking so much. You are under tension here on the mountain. This tension will disappear when you have your own work, your own money, your own liberty to do as you dam please.

[. . .] It will be hard on both of us: we shall miss each other dreadfully; and I shall certainly miss the thousand ways you have lifted details off of me and the work you do around the place. But in the end, it will be better for me and better for you. Each of us will feel more free and let ourselves do what we sometimes need to do as persons and want to do. By your taking half of Ulmer's debt* off of me, we can repay it. And since it was basically for our own livelihood, your sharing this seems right. I have already paid

---

*Kathryn Ulmer, a former camper and counselor at Laurel Falls Camp and farmer from Valdosta, Georgia. Her lifelong friendship with Smith and Snelling included financial assistance during Smith's cancer years.

back thousands of dollars in interest and some capital. But this division now of the rest of it will be most helpful. Then, if gradually, you can put the roof on the Little House and remodel what needs to be remodelled there, you will profit from that in having a delightful place in your old age or else selling it if later you decide you want to. I'll try to put the roof on the diningroom and kitchen if I can. Then you can buy a dress when you want to, buy your cigarettes without my needling you (which I shouldn't do but do do because of too many burdens on me) and spend your money as you please.

Later, after you get through summer school and get on to your job, we'll need to work out some kind of division of our housework and chores just as any two people do who live together. But Big Anne* will be here this summer and will take some of it off of me so this is not anything you need to worry about or think about, as yet.

Most of all, it is going to bring our relationship in the clear: we shall have a chance of making it the deep, rich, mutually rewarding relationship it has been. Money will get out of it; and "working for me" and all that which in your heart you have never really wanted to do. But all that has been frustrating to both of us will be *cleared up completely*.

I love you better than anybody in the world. I want you to know that. I respect and honor you as a person. I have realized even in my angriest moments, my weakest times when I felt I could not work another hour or take another step, that you wanted to help me in every way you could. During my cancer years you were a tremendous help to me; I leaned on you heavily at that time; very heavily. I always lean on you as to your criticism of my work: your criticism is the only one I truly want or value. I think you leaned on me during your years after the accident and after the hysterectomy. We have been mutually helpful to each other and mutually understanding. [. . .] And I want you to know that I could not do without you as a beloved person; nor do without your criticism of my work and your encouragement and psychic support. I need all that desperately. And I hope to give you what you need from me in a personal way. Everybody in my family loves you greatly, and deeply respects you; each is grateful to you for living with me when I was sick. They appreciate all your fine qualities. But they are glad *for your sake*—and for the unknown future—that you have a job for they know my income is dwindling. Or seems to be. And they have worried about your future. I love you very much and care deeply.

tls, UGA 1283A

*LS's older sister, Annie Laurie Peeler.

Dear Jerry Bick:*

I know my silence and my hesitations, my insistence on this change and that in the contract must make you think I either do not know my own mind or am a most difficult person to deal with.

Let me explain my hesitations, my real doubts about the contract:

First, I hesitate to sell it so cheaply because I know that *Strange Fruit* is an American classic and will in literary history and social history be considered so. Just now, it is being pushed aside, covered with silence, because it struck so deeply into white culture, laying bare so many of our self-destructive values and intellectual habits. But it will come back, find its own—just as *Moby Dick* did. When Melville wrote *Moby Dick* he was a popular writer. He was the first writer as you know to popularize the South Sea islands. He was an early Michener, so to speak. And people liked him, just as they like Michener. Then what did Melville do? He turned around and dared to write about man's future, about man's depths; he dared to probe the weak spots in the white man's way of life. His whale became a million times larger than a whale—and the reader knew it; Ahab became the prototype of something in the culture that had better be watched. The whale—what was it, the reader asked? Evil, itself? the mythic mind of man? Was the struggle between the mythic mind and man's reason? Who is Ahab? Just the Master of the ship out for a personal revenge, or is he the white man trying to subdue Nature? He failed, you know. Had he succeeded in killing the whale the book would have been a best-seller. But he failed. And this frightened the readers and the critics. Then, also, at that time whaling was a major industry: Some thought he was writing a book about the evils of whaling, the treatment of sailors, etc. Mothers probably read it and shivered and forbade their boys to sign up on the next whaling expedition. Etc. Anyway, the book got not good reviews; and was buried in a heavy silence.

Something of this nature happened to *Strange Fruit*—but it was a "second thought." The story got people with its drama, its warm people, and they read it and liked it. Then thinking about it, they began to see its real implications. And they tried to bury it. [. . .]

Now—this is how I feel about *Strange Fruit* as a movie: It should, under no circumstances, be a "race" play. It should avoid this stereotype like poison. It wasn't written as a "race" book; it was interpreted as such. It was from my point of view a book about two families, walled away from each

*Jerome Bick, an agent for Film Artists International of Beverly Hills, Calif.

other and themselves, blocked off from life itself by powers, forces they could not grapple with. It was basically a book about two lovers: Nonnie, a girl who knew how to love, not just how to be sexy; Tracy, weak, yes; but made so by a dominating woman who is a symbol of our own era, needing the love Nonnie could give him—and only Nonnie. Here they were, Romeo and Juliet, a modern Romeo weakened by a mother who sucked the life and courage out of him; a Juliet, a modern one, who could maintain her integrity only by withdrawing from the world she actually lived in. Nonnie lived in her own private playhouse, so to speak; and invited Tracy to live there with her. They both were escaping from reality, an "unreal" reality, a false reality, it is true but the only reality they knew; and tragedy struck—as it would have anywhere in the world under those circumstances. The two families are prototypes of two forces, two complexes in the world, today. Their relationships with each other within the family are fascinating. And it is these relationships plus the across-the-barriers relationships of one family with the other that I consider the real story. For instance, Eddie, Nonnie's brother. Eddie thought he hated white folks, he thought he hated Tracy, but Eddie was jealous of Tracy (and of all white males); he loved Nonnie too much in the wrong way; there was something incestuous about this love (and the actor who played this role on Broadway felt this and played it like that until it became so shocking that it had to be toned down a little). He killed Tracy because *Tracy was his rival*. Nonnie felt this passion for her in Eddie and always kept pushing him from her, from her. In the white family, there was Tracy's sister, Laura, pushed by the same mother into the by-paths of Lesbianism. This, too, is interesting; and I used it in the book as a deeper shadow of the deviation which the mother forced on both her children. Both cultural deviations, but one (Tracy's) less deeply rooted than the cultural deviation we call "homosexuality."

All the characters in *Strange Fruit*, are as Malcolm Cowley said about them, "four-dimensional." And should be played this way. The relationships are subtle, dramatic, powerful and should be played this way.

I see the movie as a strong, powerful, mature movie that might measure up in quality to Ingmar Bergman's movies. He is the greatest film artist in the world in my eyes. I have seen all his pictures shown in this country and studied them carefully. Our characters should be four-dimensional as are his. They should be sur-natural; super-symbolic. And this can be done. But we should avoid trite racial comments, statements, etc. etc. Of course, my view of human relations in general and racial relations in particular is that the aggressor is the one who is always destroyed, he and his children pay the great price—not the victims. Therefore, I have always stressed that race prejudice and the fear of the unconscious, the fear of the depths of human nature (which is really what race prejudice is) are harming the white people far more than the black people of the world. And the whites are going to do the most suffering before it is all over. But race is to me a symptom and a symbol of the white man's struggle with his own nature, his own God, his own world. I see these matters poetically, mythically—never politically.

And *Strange Fruit* can be done this way: its drama should be the drama of relationships even more than the drama of events; the poetry in it can be the poetry of events if these events are seen in their depths and heights and with awareness of all the nuances of the events. I think a great picture can be made of *Strange Fruit*.

It would break my heart if a poor, trite picture were made: another one of the awful "race relations" things. I, personally, do not like these movies or plays. They miss the big philosophical point, they miss the myth, they evade the symbolism. And all this is plain stupid. But few people in this country see these matters as I have always seen them.

Now—you will see why I hesitate. First, I think I should have a better percentage of the movie—in case it is a success. Second, I think I should be asked to participate as advisor and writer of words; someone else may be needed too to help with the more technical aspects of picture making. But I should have a role here; others who have dickered with me for the movie have always offered me the job of writing the words and advising about the show. Third, I'd like to see the actors chosen not because they are white or Negro but because they can play the role. I'd like for either Audrey Hepburn to play Nonnie or I'd like for Sophie Loren to play it. They are as different as can be—and each would interpret Nonnie in a different way, but both could really interpret her and give her stature. Since she is the silent type, the actress who plays her role [must] be able to use her body, her face, her hands in such a way as to fill in Nonnie's feelings unexpressed in words. If we can find some good Negro actors, find them; but don't take them just because they are Negro. I am sure the part of Nonnie could be played best by a European or even an Asian; the role is too hurting for any American Negro to do well.

It seems to me that before a contract is signed, you and I should somehow get together: you need to take my measure, I need to take yours. I don't know how this is going to come about. But it should.

Jack Warner has always been interested in *Strange Fruit*. It is possible that you could interest him in financing it, if he were shown what I have written about it. He was, also, interested in *One Hour*. He gets close to doing something—then he shies off. I don't quite know why.

[. . .]

tlc, UGA

Smith spoke on the "Importance of the Freedom Rides" at the national meeting of CORE, September 1–2, 1961, in Washington, D.C. Afterward Marvin Rich wrote apologizing for the divisive fights at the convention but praising her speech as magnificent and helpful in the ensuing debate.[17] The following letter to Rich reflects Smith's long-standing practice of critiquing the organizations she worked with and foreshadows her later break with CORE when it officially abandoned its commitment to nonviolent social change.

September 10, 1961

Dear Marvin:

Thank you for your nice letter. I enjoyed the conference—the messy things as well as the good ones. All organizations are basically dehumanizing: the very structure of an organization makes it impossible to keep the edge on individuals—(my book is about this, here and there). What we need to do always is to keep holding on to the persons, the individuals and forcing them to do the same. The moment they combine numbers to seek power, then the real purpose of the organization begins to become corrupted. I wish your New York delegation were more thoughtful, more self-critical, more aware of the meaning of nonviolence and the danger of organized power, even when it is in a "good" organization.

I found myself a bit appalled at the lack of understanding of nonviolence as revealed by the talk in the group who had been to jail in Mississippi. Some of the northern young whites seemed to me only rebels clinging to a new, dramatic cause. They have so far to go. And yet, the young we have to depend upon simply because they are reckless, are impulsive, are in a sense, thoughtless.

I was a bit shocked, too, that some of Core's members can so easily use stereotypes and masks. Wanting "a southern Negro" for chairman, for instance; wanting one to speak (instead of me, I hear!) Who and what is "a southern Negro?" We are such stupid people when we use phrases like that. What we want is a good person to make a speech, one who can and has the kind of experience and background that can be useful to Core. This same kind of thing I have seen in New Yorkers who hate "a white southerner."

Any white southerner, apparently. Many hate me in New York, simply because I am a white southerner, regardless of what kind of person I may be; regardless of what I have done in the segregation fight. It is stupid and dangerous, this kind of silly generalization, this placarding people. I feel there is a strong disposition among many New Yorkers to be opposed to real integration. Many liberals want Negroes to dominate white southerners. I'll bet they don't want them to dominate white northerners. This is a troubling psychological confusion that I think many white northerners are now involved in. They hate the liberal white southerners because they know they are risking more than the white liberal in New York, say, is risking. There is jealousy, here. They hate to think, too, that there are many white integrationists in the South—so you can't damn the entire South anymore.

The South for so long was solid evil, in the minds of northern liberal[s]. Then when I first stood out, they acclaimed me because I was "the only one." (There were, of course, more; but they were not known.) Then, gradually, as the northern liberals began to realize how many white southerners are risking everything for integration, this confused them; they tried to hide it from themselves and concentrate on making southern Negroes heroes. [. . .]

We are going through a most peculiar time of intellectual confusion. *Partisan Review*, for instance; its policies; the New Critics (now old men) who trained young college students to wear white gloves and stay away from the political and social arenas of the world; the Ezra Pound cult; all these factors have worked together to make heroes of Ernest Hemingway (who never engaged in any cause except war) and William Faulkner who lives in his mythic mind and when he strays out, makes a fool of himself. But the fact that his work has no contact with the future has won him a Nobel prize. It sickens me. How can any writer be first-class without using both his mythic and his rational mind! How can he be important unless he has seen both past and future! There is no future in Faulkner's work. And nothing he has done is of real importance save his short stories. He has done excellent work in that field and that field only. While Hemingway wrote nice escape stories for the fat, paunch middleaged organization man who wistfully gazes out of his 35th floor office toward the veldts of Africa.

Well—this is fragmentary and impulsive, this little outburst. I have real things I want to say maybe in my Harpers book on this subject. All our writers, poets, dramatists, critics and reviewers need to be held up by the feet and shaken hard. The fashionable admiration for Genet, for instance.

The Balcony is such a phony—really; oh, you have to look at it sharply to perceive that it is but it is basically nasty and foolish and dishonest. I haven't seen the *Blacks*; it may have something really interesting—at least, its presentation may be. I'd like to see it.

[. . .]

 Because of her public stand for desegregation, Margaret Long lost her position as columnist for the *Atlanta Journal*. Smith saw her as carrying on her own tradition of speaking the truth about the South to southerners, and their correspondence reveals a strong mutual support for each other as women writers. At the time of this letter, Long had taken a new position as editor of the Southern Regional Council's magazine, *New South*. Sissy was Long's daughter.

September 10, 1961

Dear Maggie:

What is all this I hear about your being with Regional Council, about our Sissy being jailed with the Freedom Riders, about the *Journal* pushing you out, etc? I presume it is all true but I've heard no details. [. . .]

Carson McCullers's new book—*Clock Without Hands*—is funny and tender; good and full of one kind of cockeyed truth. And I sent her a blurb saying so. But somehow it bothers me too: it has all the ingredients for a New York success: interracial sex: be sure to make it white woman having baby by black man; politics: be sure to make it exaggerated and stereotyped so that you can't take the old Congressman seriously; adolescence: be sure to make it vaguely homosexual and beatnik and "full of compassion;" when people are killed or hurt, be sure it seems to happen without reason and sense or even evil. And have no real characters that any reader would think of identifying with. With this exception: she plays all this out against the background of a man slowly dying of leukemia and wondering about life and death, fearing death and then being too weak to fear death. It was touching this: and this background of a man grappling with the meaning of life and death was moving and good. Then why do I half resent this book? I think because these ingredients are basically reassuring to people who do not want to get involved with life. She talks of passion but she doesn't really mean a passionate concern with life or death. When I was told I was going to die by Christmas I did not fear death; I feared the end of what I was involved in, the end of what I wanted to do. I feared especially, or thought about it a great deal, that I could never hear any music again. But if I, with cleverness and a certain lack of honor, deliberately set out to write a success- ful book that would sell in New York (and if it doesn't sell there it won't sell anywhere) I'd put all the ingredients in it that she did. Oh yes, she also had enough antisemitism to interest the Jews in it. It seemed to me, in a way, a strangely cynical thing to do. Could she, perhaps, be so much a part of the intellectual and psychological climate of New York City that she did this unconsciously—just following the New York line about southerners all being evil or fools or idiots, and the line about sex, and the line about having only absurd characters which no reader would ever need to identify with. I don't know. But I think it is the least real of any of her books. I stumbled across bits of *Strange Fruit* in it, bits of *One Hour*, bits of *Killers*, bits of Truman Capote's *Breakfast at Tiffany's*, bits of *Finian's Rainbow*—and oth- ers up here at Clayton say it is like in spots *To Kill A Mocking Bird* which I have not bothered to read, although I have a copy. That is, it seems like a melange of hearsay and what one has read rather than something out of one's own experience of life. Hence, there seemed a basic dishonesty about the thing. I wrote her the nice things[;] then I did say it seemed to me that it was as though she had clipped items from the papers for 15 years and stirred them up, then pulled out those that particularly appealed to her. And I do feel this way about this book. There is no deep organic wholeness about it. On the other hand, it was good technic, excellent structure and patterning, to play the idiocies out against the background of a poor ordinary man dying of leukemia. The only blunder she made here was to say he picked out of the reading cart in the small city hospital in a Ga. town one of Kierkegaard's books. She also wrote as if from memory of her childhood in the 1930's and what she has picked up in New York about recent happenings in the South. And the two do not click. But it was interesting to me, in this sense, that she like all the creative, especially the mother bird, made her nest out of the bits of life that had strayed across her path. She has never been in north Ga. except the time she visited me; yet she remembered Tallulah Falls, Flowering Branch, and used the words in her book; the dying man's wife was a little like her own mother; the dying man was a pharmacist, so was her father; the young Negro beatnik probably like one she has met in N. Y. etc. etc. But we all are like that: just busy-busy birds picking up threads and cotton wherever we find it.

I still cannot decide why this book on one level offended me. I see it as the good farce it is, the absurdity it is; and no one knows better than you and I how absurd and foolish and crazy this old South is. It will make a crazy, funny play which everybody will enjoy. If it were comedy, it would have to have real people; but farce is successful only when its people are a little unreal; only when they seem to be something you pasted together. Then everybody can enjoy without hurting or bleeding anywhere. Maybe—well, I don't quite know. Maybe it seems to me incongruous to be writing farce in this tragic age when we shall die if we do not look at what is happening to us; all the earth will die. Maybe this is why it seems somehow false and wrong and escapist to me. At the same time, we do need to laugh. Oh God, I just don't know. Maybe, too, it seems wrong to me to pander to New York's complacency. Laughter in this age should *hurt*. I think this is my point. You laugh and you don't hurt. It is sad but sad only as you view it intellectually.

tls, SRC/AU

TO DAN WICKENDEN, EDITOR, HBJ

October 16, 1961

My dear, dear Dan:

[. . .]

I have been busy helping the sit-ins; I felt that this was definitely a place where I might give some special insight and encouragement [. . .]. But it was like helping one's family: one is glad to, one wants to, one wouldn't do anything else, but one's own dreams, one's own life just sort of dwindles away. As I have told you before, Martha and Mary have been fighting inside me since I was fifteen; it is a losing battle for Mary (with whom I am more deeply identified) I am afraid, but I always keep hoping that I can be myself, write the way I want to, do what I want to—and not what everybody else seems to need of me.

And too, I felt an urgent need to think, and feel, all by myself for a while—and when I have had a chance I have done just that; also reading many books that I wanted to read and think about such as Father Teilhard's *Phenomenon of Man* (a terrific book—maybe the greatest of our times) and that odd but to me most interesting book, Poulet's *Studies in Human Time* and Otto's *Sense of the Holy*—I suppose the classic on the subject of the numen and the numinous; and a dozen others on ritual and symbol and symbolic acting, and the mythic mind; and I did a lot of poetry and a lot of modern plays, and pondered a great deal of modern art—Then, suddenly, this summer while W. was so ill and our family life because of him was in turmoil and early mornings seemed unbearable—I began to write: lightly, almost gaily, certainly with a smile on the lines. Why? I can't tell you. I just did. I wrote a little book called *Don't Take A Ghost Along Unless—* About 110 pages. It is the first time, since *Strange Fruit*, that I have written anything without having a signed contract before putting the first line down. It was sort of nice just to be writing—for me. It is light; I hope it is deft; it says quite a lot of maybe significant things about ghosts and the mythic mind, and symbols and symbolic acting, and the reason—all this is dotted here and there with sudden experiences from my childhood. [. . .] I [. . .] laid it aside [. . .] because I had promised my agents to do a piece I've planned to do for six or eight years but kept putting off. [. . .]. It is called *Memory of a Large Christmas* and is a sort of montage of the Christmases of a big family—there were nine of us plus two parents plus Big Granny and Little Grandma, plus the cousins who to this day are fairly anonymous in my memory as they came and went to our good school. It is silly and absurd and funny and more about highly imaginative children than about Christmas; and I like it. There is a hilarious and wacky scene in it when two of my brothers and their colored friend decided they might give the parents a coffin for Christmas. It is absurd and full of male fantasy and I think it is sweet and wonderful. But I let a northern friend—passing by for a brief visit—read the whole thing. He loved it; I could see that; was amused, stirred, moved. Then he said this, "You know, yankees don't give coffins for Christmas." I think this is the funniest line ever said to me about anything. I replied, " They don't? You know, southerners always give coffins." I was so aghast. Afterward, Paula and I tried to reason why. All we can come up with is that I have been so stereotyped that people get self conscious and think in terms of North and South and race and—well, I suppose the poor dear thinks that my new concern is about coffins and that I am fighting for the coffins' right to be given as presents at Christmas. And by this time, I truly feel that I am walking on my ears and my eyes have slid to the back of my head, and my hair has elongated into crutches. So. There was nothing for it but a cool long drink of Tennessee Mash.

[. . .]

I wrote Bill recently about "Julia." [. . .] I think the main trouble may be that as the years went by I used "Julia" as a sort of bag into which to stuff all sorts of bemusements and grave concerns. So now, I want to strip it down, clean it out, and leave a simple strong line. Last week, as I was thinking of man, the deep split, I saw the old Eve story in a slightly different way: that is when man split in two, his slightly different fragment became Eve; and for the first time he became man for now Eve was his mirror and he could ask her those old questions: who am I? where did I come from? where am I going? who is God? Eve: man's awareness of himself. And as I was thinking this, I suddenly saw Julia as just that. It wasn't sex that held the men; in fact, she was afraid of all that sex really meant; it was the mirror: she was the mirror in which each man found himself. I knew this was the beginning, but somehow turning it into this simple image made me see really what Julia is all about. And what happened to her when her brother Clem smashed that mirror to pieces. I think it is now coming to me in terms almost as simple and profound as poetry; and if it does, then I can go back to it and find my real book—which is in all those chapters but which somehow is buried under too much else.

Of course, I am working on the Harper World Perspectives book which will say in nonfictional terms much that "Julia" will say in strictly fictional terms of look, gesture, symbol, image, and the double and triple vision of a world pulling against a person, of a man pulling against a woman.

tlc, UGA

October 27, 1961

Dear Jerry Bick:

After studying your last three letters I conclude this: you are not really ready to commit yourself to even an option of $500.00 (payment) for eighteen months. You do like my book, I can see, but you don't feel anybody else does. When we come close to agreeing with your terms or you come close to agreeing with our terms then you suddenly back out. [. . .] Then you keep telling me how little people think of the book; how few first-class people would be interested in directing it or acting in it. I am not sure whether this is because people have discouraged you or because you want to discourage me!

I am not at all disturbed about it; for I really appreciate your interest. But neither have I the slightest desire to low-rate myself. I have never had to. There is a group in this country who have done all they could to low-rate *Strange Fruit* and every other book I have written; there is tremendous anger against me felt by many white men not because of racial ideology but because I told their sex secrets—and secrets that are not too bright and honorable to look at. There is this sex jealousy and I have known it for many years. But I have never low-rated myself or my book, nor do any of my contracts. You see I don't need to sell *Strange Fruit* as if it were a bankrupt property; and I do not intend to. Its day will come; and I do not want to tie myself up with a contract that essentially offers me nothing but ties me up tight. That is, when the time comes to make a picture out of

Strange Fruit, the offers will be good. Until that time comes, why should I tie myself up with a contract that does not even carry any option money along with it? I can't get the point of this. I think you may have a lawyer who is just a bit too smart, too shrewd. I think it might be well to remember, too, that as a writer I get the top royalty paid any writers. I am not quite what you and Hollywood think I am: a has-been. As a matter of fact, my books are selling all over the world at present and selling better and better all the time. In my own opinion, some day I rather think *Strange Fruit* and *Killers of the Dream* plus my other writings will give me the Nobel prize. I am patient; I know my worth; I know my historical value to this country; and I just don't have to sign that kind of contract.

[. . .]

You see, you become discouraged more easily than I. I have had to fight my way from the beginning: I am different from other American writers, more profoundly dissenting, more disturbing, therefore; and Mr. White Man hates that image I gave of so many men in poor Tracy (whom I happened to love and feel only compassion for) who was, after all, what a segregated culture had made him. Hollywood, or those you have talked with are crazy and ignorant if they think the Freedom Riders made things worse. What are they talking about? When *Strange Fruit* was published things were terrible racially; not one person but me in the South had ever spoken up publicly against segregation; now, all decent people do. This book, *Strange Fruit*, changed the South: shook it to its heart; then came *Killers of the Dream* which finished the job. Segregation was broken then; I didn't do it all; but I did the symbolic creative job that had to be done by some white artist. Things are better racially in the South than they have been in a hundred years; very few people believe in segregation now except poor white trash and Mississippi! Even the old demagogues are changing their tune. Sure—Mississippi wouldn't want to show *Strange Fruit*, but who cares about Mississippi? The trouble is, some of those Hollywood people have been so isolated from the world that they think things are as they were—or worse—fifty years ago. They are ridiculous. People would love to see *Strange Fruit* in the South. Somebody consults with the Birchites or old southerners who've been away from the South twenty-five years and don't know how the South has changed. Nobody who is anybody is afraid of intermarriage; just the poor white trash who've never had anything in their lives and cling to their skin color as a drug addict clings to his drug. Are we catering to them? I am not and never have and don't intend to. But upper class and middle class white southerners are as sophisticated as they come.

Remember, the South never tried to ban *Strange Fruit*; they loved it—except the demagogues and their mobs. It was Boston, not Atlanta that banned it. And you have just been talking to the wrong kind of people. If Audrey Hepburn would refuse to play Nonnie just because Nonnie was colored then to hell, my dear, with Audrey. But you malign her; I would not believe that. If she refused, it would be because she didn't think the script was good or the director was poor; nothing else.

[. . .]

It may be that I'll have to die before the Hollywood crowd will be willing to make it; then they'll have the fun of knowing I reaped nothing from it. This happens again and again to writers; just look at Melville who died virtually unknown after he annoyed the world by writing *Moby Dick*; and Bach, remember whose nephew stole all the glory from him; and he died with his manuscripts selling for twenty cents a piece. These things happen; I realize that I have questioned deeply most of the moral foundations of the white race; during this time of change I am not their heroine. I have dissented more profoundly than any writer in this country; read my books, you will realize I have. So—why should cheap Hollywood value me? They value the absurd, false, truly spurious histrionics of Faulkner—because he spits in the face of all upperclass women. I answer back. Yes. I am not mad. Just proud.

tlc, UGA

TO MARVIN RICH

December 1, 1961

Dear Marvin:

Here is a check for $100.00—half of the collection taken up at a church in Chicago where I spoke. The other half they kept to help with interracial affairs in Chicago. It is not a gift from me, but a gift from the church where I spoke. So please send the receipt to Miss Anna Grace Sawyer [. . .].

[. . .] The Atlanta situation is to me most depressing. With an awful roar the mountain brought forth a mouse. Nine kids taken in school; Memphis did much better with no to-do at all. And since then, there has been a terrifying quiet needling of those kids in the schools—with everybody keeping absolutely dumb about it; so that one finally announced she wanted to go back to her old school—which sent the governor into snickers, nasty to see on TV. I blazed up as I watched; I suddenly wanted to stop being nice and gentle and quiet and firm but instead I wanted to rage at them, to shout aloud like the old Judaic prophets warning them that even God would not put up with this kind of thing much longer. And there is, too, a quiet and sinister police tyranny abroad in Atlanta: when whites and Negroes are seen together on the street, coming out of a private home, the whites are at once arrested for "disturbing the peace." We do not want to break this until we try first to get the new mayor to put a stop to it. My close friend, Helen Bullard (a real liberal) is the new mayor's assistant at city hall. We are going to gather up all the facts and take them to Helen; she is a good friend, also, of the chief of police. We'll see first if Helen can handle it through the mayor and chief. If not, then we must gather all the facts and blow it in a big way—letting *Time* or *Life* do it, or *Newsweek* or all of them in such a big way that it will shame Atlanta to death. [. . .] (I am getting down to this this next week; I have been so busy trying to make a living—am badly in debt— and haven't had a chance to get on this scheme.) I've done a piece about Christmas in our big family in the first decade of the century. It is warm and sort of quaint and amusing. I did a very long piece but it had to be cut for *Life*, who to my surprise took it. I had to whack it almost in half so some of the wackiest scenes are out: it is strange how the big papers are afraid of anything off-beat, wacky, absurd and wonderful. Not the editors. They've loved the whole piece—it was unanimous. But they were afraid of "the people." The people won't like this, the people will be offended at that, the people won't get the point of that. I live in a small town: and *these* people would get all the fun and wackiness in the piece and thoroughly enjoy it. The rule of the proletariat might not be so bad; but the rule of the Ivy League boys who think they speak for the proletariat is something pretty terrible. But anyway, *Life* took the piece; it will be in the Dec. 15th issue (the one with the cathedral on its cover) [. . .]

There is an odd kind of truth in the juxtaposition of this merry, gay memory of Christmas to my *Killers of the Dream*. People will say, But how can both be true? That is the magic and wonder and horror of life: that both can be true, and are.

I talked about Freedom Riders, of course. I did it in Jacksonville, Florida, too in October. I went down there as a North Floridian made a big point of my "coming back home." I talked to 500 whites and Negroes (about half and half) at one of the best hotels in town. Everything fine that night. Nobody heckled me, although the Birchites were there in full force to do so; my talk was so philosophical and also so moving, since I said much about my childhood in north Florida (which is their childhood, too), that nobody had the nerve to take issue with me. I came home. I now hear that the Birchites and some neo-nazis stayed up all night afterward answering my speech. They have a scandal sheet down there called the *Herald* (I think); also, they got out a six-page mimeograph brochure on my evil past: people tell me it is quite awful. I am writing and asking them to send it to me; how can I do anything about something I've never seen. But these Human Relations people tell me that when I spoke in my speech about the great, unanswerable questions: Who am I? where did I come from? where am I going? what is death? who is God? this group said in their brochure that this proved I was a bastard. They apparently said a lot of other sewage. [. . .] My two brothers (eldest, 76, youngest 58) were there that night—the first time they've ever heard me speak. They were both moved and said they were impressed by it and highly approving. They felt the audience was warm and moved and troubled but at the same time lifted up. But the Birchites and the other mad ones got to work on me, apparently. What has happened to my brothers (it was in the papers that they were my brothers— they are businessmen in Jacksonville) I do not know. I hope nothing. I shall try to find out; if they don't know about the brochure and scandal sheet, I'd just as soon they didn't—why trouble them? But at the same time, I feel that they may need to be warned that these maniacs may try to cause them business trouble. They can't harm Austin, the elder who is too highly thought of in Jax. But Wallace, the one who has been so ill, they can hurt—

tlc, UGA

 Margaret Long had written Smith about the difficulties she had getting northerners to believe in the reality and sincerity of southern white liberals who actually fought for an end to racial segregation. The flavor and length of Smith's reply were characteristic of their correspondence, about which Smith once wrote: "You and I are about the only two people on earth I know who can talk on paper."[18]

December 3, 1961
My dear Maggie:
    Settle down with a drink or a pot of coffee for I'm likely to be long-winded—after this long time of not writing you.
    [. . .]
    I want you to know John Howard Griffin who wrote *Black Like Me*. Did you meet him when he came to Atlanta at the end of his six weeks of "being" a Negro? His book is deeply moving; I felt that I was bleeding all over when I finished it. It had been here for months (they all are sent to me, or most of them) and I didn't much like the title so hadn't read it. Then he

wrote me a beautiful letter about *Killers of the Dream* which he had never read until this new issue. It was so moving, so generous. Then P. D. East sent me another copy of *Black Like Me*. And I sat down and read it—in one sitting, I am telling you. I felt a knife was turning in my heart and mind. I sat here, afterward, feeling we white southerners do not deserve even mercy; we do not deserve life; we are soft and rotten to the core, we put sugar in rotted wounds and think we are doing something highly healing and civilized, and bow down to our own futility.

It is enough to ruin us all: this self torment every time we think seriously about things. And how seemingly ambivalent we are. But it is only *seemingly* with people like you and me and John Griffin and P. D. (and some others, too). We do live a three and four-leveled life; we have a private, personal life and we have a life lived in groups—and here we run into our troubles. We think and talk in lumpy words: the South, "Negroes," "The North," "we southerners" etc. etc. This gets us into our trouble; but we do move around those words every day as though they were mountains. We cannot ignore them: they are here, they are protuberances of hills or mountains (if you will) and we either painfully climb them or bump our brains out against them, or go around them.

And, curiously enough, just as you said in your letter, sudden, quick loyalties spring up between southerners regardless of a certain understanding and intuitive meeting of minds felt by southern whites and Negroes, when together. Northerners find this difficult to understand; difficult because they resent it; look, they say, here we are working for those Negroes and instead of feeling at home with us they feel at home with those white southerners who should be their enemies. God . . . how beautifully intricate and complex is the human being. For this, I give paeans of thanks each day. We are so difficult, thank God, so twisted, so divergent, so deviating, so absurd, so irrational—isn't it wonderful to be that way? I often kid the young beatniks on the college campuses where I talk now and then about their mourning the absurdity of the human condition. I tell them, I rejoice that this is true; wouldn't it be horrible if we were not absurd? Why should everything be reasonable and subject to proof? why should everything make sense? Absurd? Thank God that the human condition is absurd; how would it be endurable if we knew for instance why we are on this little earth? wouldn't it be a thing of terror to believe we had "seen God?" wouldn't it be too cruel to be endured if we needed to prove everything and what is worse, actually did it? The kids take a deep breath, and then suddenly they begin to understand what I am getting at. What many beats have done, and more of the Sartrian type of existentialist, is to accept the old scientific assumptions of the 19th century that everything is subject to proof. But if we really belong to the 20th century, as I often remind them, we would know that only one small area of human experience can be "proved," and even then, scientists have finally to accept the uncertainty principle which Heisenberg writes about so elegantly. How could you prove anything about art? how can you about anything creative? how could you prove that when you fall in love you have "found the best one for you?" How about the millions of others you've never come in contact with? Proof is so silly, so stupid a thing to cling to, except in a limited area of "natural events." "What man hath wrought" . . . his dreams or his books or his paintings or his vision of God—how could these be subjected to proof!

What does this have to do with Negro and white? Probably not a dam thing. But I think we get into a great deal of our trouble by leaving the concrete (with its innumerable differences) and settling for the abstract which is seemingly so simple and clear. We know that we talk nonsense every time we talk about "the Negro" or the "white man" or the "South" or the "North"—and yet, we keep doing it. Maybe our real problem is how to keep brushing off the lumpy words and concepts and holding only to each individual who is different thank God, from every other individual. This individual (with light skin) and that individual (with dark skin) once went barefoot, once ate boiled peanuts, once gathered pecans in November, once pulled sandspurs out of their feet, once watched blue smoke curl out of little old windswept cabins, once got scared of snakes back of palmettos. Were these two individuals to meet each other at a bistro in Paris, they would almost embrace each other, after a few minutes of talk. Yes, we are individuals, their minds would whisper, we are even persons, maybe; but once, long ago, we shared the same kind of experiences, our bodies responded to the same stimuli and the same memory designs are etched on our brains and so, behold we call each other *brother* . . . *sister*. We love something in each other. [. . .]

This is the wonder of our southern lives; the magic and the terror; and I, for one, wish to God we could be free to be our own selves reaching out for what we know is valid for us, is true for us, and what we cherish. I wish I never had to hear the words *race relations* again; or *segregation* or *integration*, or *rights*. I long to be free to be human—and I have never been, and I know it.

This is the pathos of our southern lives. Sad and beautiful and terrible and—Well, why say more? There are thousands of us who feel this and are drawn to each other because of mutual losses which we know we have endured.

As for the youngsters reaching out for dates: our caution warns against it; but how do we know? maybe it has to be; maybe the only way people win their human rights is by accepting each other personally and intimately. Maybe it is right for some, even though it plays straight into the dirty minds and scary power of others. We may have to go through all this; I just don't know. My "judgment" says, Why not wait a little? but they may be right in risking what we have been so bitterly conditioned not to risk. I have the feeling that the old lying demagogues are always partially right: in every lie they stuff a smidge of truth; if they did not, the lie would die; only truth can keep a lie alive. And they may be quite right that as segregation goes, love and marriage are going to come; but they are wrong to think it will come to many; only the few who are somehow courageous enough to cross the taboos and live the new way, accepting the responsibilities of the new way. The old dirty boys had their sex and gave the colored women babies without ever accepting their responsibility for this human relationship. Sometimes, I think morality can be summed up simply as the full accepting of the responsibilities that arise from every human relationship. I suppose that is all morality actually is, or could be. No rules.

Well—I do want to see you, soon; Paula does too. We must get together and not wait too long.

tls, SRC/AU

TO ROCHELLE GIRSON*

March 5, 1962

Dear Miss Girson:

[. . .]

Please mam, send some really first-class books my way. I wish I could have done Dorothy Baker's *Cassandra at the Wedding*. That is a first-class book in a minor genre, perhaps, but a thoroughly good book and one on a subject that has never been treated in fiction before. (At least as far as I know.) It is a witty but profound tale of narcism, of two girls who find their images in the other's face; it is complex and subtle in that it reveals a most interesting symbiotic relationship. It is highly contemporary and that is welcomed by me; its homosexual overtones are fresh and muted tastefully

---

*Book review editor at *Saturday Review*, for which LS wrote a number of book reviews in 1962 and 1963.

but intertwined with the symbiotic relationship: an astute revelation of female homosexuality which is, in my opinion, as different as day from night from male homosexuality. There is no such thing as "the homosexual" anyway; but here, in this lovely little book about the twins Dorothy Baker says in print for the first time some revealing things about the feminine nature. (The one subject I think I know most about is the subject of women and girls and their symbiotic relationships, their narcism, their curious attachments, and their equally curious snipping of these attachments.) Do give me a chance at some female stuff now and then; I hate to be stereotyped as a race specialist or Civil [Rights] specialist or South specialist. I do know a goodish bit about such matters but what I really know best is women and their curvatures of soul and twisting relationships—and I know a good bit about contemporary art, music, dance. I am part Mary and part Martha: as Martha, I have written about segregation, the South, etc. etc.; as Mary, I know best girls, women, artists. So.

[. . .]

tlc, UGA

TO BERTHA BARNETT

Atlanta, Ga.
April 6, 1962

Dearest Bird:

It was sweet of you to send Frank a check for a gift. They bought me a box of candy which they know I like—but it happened that day I lost my appetite for chocolate. It seems the cobalt I am taking plays tricks on the appetite and I am finding it hard to think of things I'd like to eat. But they used only a part of it this way—and I haven't told them that I've turned against candy for I can offer it to friends when they drop in to see me—and the other part I am going to spend on two or three papercover books. Emory has a fine papercover bookstore with thousands of excellent titles; I picked up seven when the doctor put me in the hospital for observation; have about finished them so shall be glad to indulge in buying a few more.

I finished the Christmas story this week and have sent it to Clayton to be typed by Katherine who does all my final typing. [. . .]

It does not tire me (much) and does not pain me at all to use the typewriter. This, to me, is wonderful. I am in more pain when I am lying down. But I have to lie down a great deal in order to offset the cobalt weakness. So.

[. . .]

About the only chance I have of surviving this is my own resistance to cancer which, as we all know, is very strong. It pulled me through the second time and I hope it will do the same favor for me this fifth time. We don't know, as yet, how cobalt is doing for me. [. . .] The malignancy is not in my bones, they tell me; and as far as we know, not in any of my organs beside the right lung. If they can contain it there, I can live—at least for a few years, or months. The problem is: can it be contained? I am going ahead with all my work just as if nothing were wrong, except for the extra six hours in bed; I hope to get well; if I don't I am thankful for the nine years I did have after it first came. And thankful I have got so many books written; I hope to write four or five more but we'll just have to see. I am not in the least depressed; I see all the funny macabre things about life as I've always seen; I entertain my friends with my stories of the cobalt patients and they spend most of their time with me laughing *hysterically* at the funny pitiful and brave patients. I am fully aware of what may be ahead and aware, also, that I can take it whatever it is. I am not arrogant, I am simply accepting that everyone's life must end and life without death would be a strange monstrosity; so death holds no fear for me although I don't try to envisage anything so fuzzy and ephemeral as immortality which the rational part of man's nature cannot understand and which we simply from my point of view have to accept the uncertainty of. What matters from my point of view is how richly and in-depth I have lived; and what I have made of what was offered me: a mess, part of the time, but perhaps not wholly so. This is not stoicism: this is a recognition of the basic uncertainty of the human condition: that we cannot prove or know surely what we long to prove and know: we have simply to act and keep searching for truth even when it may be disguised in strange dirty garments. That the wise things come to us from a deeper part of our nature than the reason, this I know; whether from mythic mind or from the transcendent spirit or from both, I cannot know—most likely from both. I know faith is not something one wills but something that comes, like happiness when one loves deeply and is concerned deeply with others.

The big party given me, an autograph party given by the Southern Regional Council and other groups, was a big affair at the Biltmore Hotel last Saturday. My doctor—I invited him—scolded me for the party but of course it didn't do me a bit of harm. There were 600 there: 200 Negroes, 400 whites from the top levels of the society of both groups. The Ku Klux Klan was in front parading up and down on the street where the Biltmore is. Upstairs, in the mezzanine floor, we were all having a big gay time. I autographed books for nearly three hours; would stop and talk with people who came up and go back to the autographing. Many of Joe's friends were there, and Frank's friends and my friends, churchwomen, Freedom Riders, Sit-inners, college kids, high school kids, five or six big politicians, journalists (of course not Ralph McGill nor the top men of the papers, although Jack Spalding, editor of *Journal* had said he would be there. But measles is all over town so that may have kept his wife from coming.) A lot of socially prominent people plus many fine people who are not socially prominent. But imagine 600 people! The funny thing—they had begun to plan this in January before any of us dreamed of cancer; they felt the new *Killers of the Dream* was being smothered to death—(it was not reviewed in that dirty boy Ralph McGill's paper) so they decided they'd make people recognize its existence plus pulling off the first social bi-racial party in the whole South, I suppose—certainly in a hotel and on a city-wide scale. It was all lots of fun and I wouldn't have missed it. I told the women who planned it that it almost turned into an Irish Wake but skimmed by a little, anyway. We all had great fun about it. Maud and Frank thoroughly enjoyed it; some Clayton people came; more were coming but it was a terrible, stormy day.

I won't be able to write much. It takes so much strength and time; and I do have to make my living while I am taking these cobalt treatments, so I *must write* things to sell! [. . .]

tls, UGA 1283A

The following thank-you letter to her friends Tom and Laurina Needham of Jacksonville, Florida, contains Smith's entertaining account of the response to her speech, "Autobiography as Dialog between King and Corpse," delivered in May 1962 at the University of Florida in Gainesville.

May 23, 1962

My dear Laurina and my dear Tom:

It has only slowly dawned on me what a very big and gracious thing you did for me to leave your house and all going on there to take me to the University. You were so casual about it, and so completely relaxed about leaving everything, that I accepted it without feeling I was accepting too much. Well, I still accept it that way, for your own grace makes me do so. But let me say thank you again, a very real and deeply felt thank you. You did much more for me than simply convey me to a point in geography: you by your calm cheer caused me to find much more confidence within myself that I could go through what I had committed myself for. I was not at all sure when I left Clayton that I could even manage the train trip to Jackson-ville—much less all that speaking et cetera. But along the way, as we ambled here and there, talking easily about small and big things, I began to feel strong and certainly well enough to do what I had to do. Thank you for that, too.

I was very sorry I did not invite you both up to my air-conditioned room for a cooling-off period; but I did not know I was to have an air-conditioned room. [...]

But—when I got there, the phone began to ring. First, the loquacious young man at the desk who carried up my bags told me the students from Jasper were so "excited" that I was there. Then a young man phoned to say he was from Jasper and was so thrilled about my being on the campus because his great aunt was in *Strange Fruit*. He spoke of it quite factually as though she had played a role in the play. I asked who she was in *Strange Fruit* and he said the little telephone operator. I then asked him who his great aunt was and he said, "Miss Ada Reid, of course." And of course it is true, I did base "Miss Sadie" in the book on this little dauntless lady who tried to stop the mob. He is now as proud of her exploits as can be—and I do not think it has ever occurred to him that none of it actually happened. There were many sweet, naive things that happened to me—all of which I liked very much. But alas for me, they had planned drinks (I wanted the drinks all right but not what went with the drinks) and dinner with people who had met me in Bombay (and who speak of you rather intimately but I don't really think you ever met them—maybe but no more than that). They had somehow con-vinced the committee that they were intimate friends whom I would want to see at once; so I swallowed hard, asked if it had been settled—it had—and went. Then late that night I was informed of a luncheon in my honor the day I was speaking at four; I gulped again; then one hour before the luncheon a phone call informed me that of course I would be expected to speak twenty or thirty minutes to the librarians at the luncheon. I quaked, What about? Silence. Then, cheerily, "Oh, you'll think of something and we are sure it will be charming." I should know how these things go: it is like this on every campus; they pay you for one speech and all the others are sort of tucked in your pocket along with the soon-to-materialize check.

I did all these things. Then I did my speech. Since they were taping it, I read it (I was going to, anyway) but I read as though not reading so all that was OK. My speech was about the mysteries of autobiography (which mysteries are gripping me so hard that I now think I'll do my World

Perspectives book on this subject). I talked a little about Adam and Eve (one of my favorite subjects) and how Eve outwitted Adam by learning all about him while keeping herself a big secret; then I soothed male feelings by saying that no woman had ever written a great autobiography but I wouldn't tell them why for that would be another speech. Then I dropped into my story (Hindu) the King and the Corpse, I do actually think it is the best ghost story ever created and so did the audience: the proverbial pin did not have a chance. And it was fun to tell the story to an audience who was holding its breath. Once the story was told, it was easy to make my various points, especially the one that no great autobiography is ever a monologue carried on by the King, but always a dialog between King and Corpse. And they loved it. It is a fresh approach which as far as I know, no one else has used; and a young German librarian who had decided he did not like me because I was so concerned with such things as segregation, decided he did like me after the speech and followed me around like a shepherd dog. It was all sort of fun. But heavens, how strenuous. That night, dinner at the young German's house—most informal; so I could take off my shoes and relax; and when the young people came in and saw me free of decorum, the men promptly took off their ties and loosened their collars—then to my surprise (and I suspect secret relief of the young German whose budget is probably too small for bourbon or scotch) we all asked for ice tea! And sat there drinking glass after glass of ice tea until we were called to the very nice buffet supper. I enjoyed meeting graduate students all of whom, I think, were struggling for their Ph.D.'s—they seem so young and casual and their wives all could have been my old campers. It was actually nice. But my job was not over: a TV interview next morning which went off extraordinarily well. I was cheerful and casual and mildly needling over having for the first time been accepted as a Florida author—they responded in kind, and all went well. Then I did it! The librarian asked me if his son, editor of the campus paper, could interview me. He should have known better than to do this. But I said yes because he asked me. Then he said his son wanted to know would I answer controversial questions; I being in a state of mental decomposition by this time, said yes. And boy—that interview in the paper is enough to make everybody lose his job! I answered straight his questions about intermarriage, etc; I was smiling, I was laconic, but my mood did not creep into the paper: you would have thought I had gone to Florida University to set them all straight on segregation. Oh dear. I should have had more sense; I usually do; but my host asking me is what threw me off and I am usually on northern campuses so I sort of forgot I was on a southern one. Well, I pray they won't lose their jobs—but God shouldn't listen to my prayers because I should have known better.

I am coming down to the beach soon for a rest; the old heart slowed down in Florida and now is back at its 120 per which wears me out. I'll let you know when I arrive. And thank you both again.

tlc, UGA

 Martin Luther King's involvement in the Albany [Georgia] Movement resulted in his being arrested and jailed three times. Initially arrested on December 15, 1961, he was released on bond two days later and returned on July 10, 1962, to be sentenced to forty-five days or a fine of $178. On July 13, 1962, however, he was released from jail after an unidentified man paid his fine. After violence had broken out at a July 24 mass march, King returned to lead a prayer pilgrimage to Albany's City Hall and was again arrested.[19] The following letter to Mimi Pace Newcomb, a former Laurel Falls camper and counselor, was probably written after King's July 10 sentencing. Smith wrote a similar letter about Albany to President John F. Kennedy urging him to "appeal to the conscience of white Southerners."[20] In an August 1, 1962, press conference President Kennedy commented that "the United States government was involved in sitting down at Geneva with the Soviet Union. I cannot understand why the government of Albany, City Council of Albany, cannot do the same for American citizens."[21] Thirty years later Newcomb remembers with regret her refusal to respond to this letter because at the time she did not agree with Smith and felt angry at King for leading a demonstration and thereby, in her opinion, causing trouble in her hometown. In retrospect she wishes she had tried to follow Smith's advice, for she now feels Albany's "race situation has steadily deteriorated."[22]

Temporarily in Neptune Beach [Fla.]
Undated [July 1962]

Dear Mimi:

[. . .]

Mimi dear—what I am concerned about now is Dr. Martin Luther King's being put in jail in Albany. I think I know the story in all its inconsistent and ambiguous details—as is always true, things are both good and bad; etc., but he is one of my friends and a most wonderful guy; if you only knew him you'd be sure the man is good, honest, sincere, sensitive and full of compassion and also well stocked up with brains. He should not be in jail; he felt he must not pay the fines, however, for Americans do have the right to protest, to work for their freedom and he should not have been arrested in the first place. These are symbolic doings—as is Buss Eye for that matter!—and these protests take on deep meaning. What may happen is that Albany will get into the New Orleans or Little Rock kind of mess. Now, while I would expect this sort of thing of Americus (my 25 years dealing with Americus people made me know they are historically behind the times etc.) but NOT ALBANY! I said at the time this happened: "Albany will do the right thing; I am sure of it." And I think if you younger people could speak out and explain to the others how the whole world looks at this sort of thing. Gandhi in India won over the mighty British Empire; and those of us who had kept up with what he was doing knew he would win. For nonviolence and a quiet working for one's own rights are always appealing to Western man's conscience. We Americans are made uneasy in our souls by this sort of thing: we know segregation must go; we know integration of a public kind must come; and when a town gives in quietly it is so much better for everybody concerned. What the Negroes are asking for is their God-given and Constitutional right.

It is hard for some people to understand nonviolent protest; but these people (many of whom I know well) are full of gentleness, compassion, love; they strongly oppose all verbal and physical violence; and they are our defense against the Black Muslims who want black supremacy and will use violence when the time comes. These are the people for us to fear—not the nonviolent students and their leaders like Martin Luther King. The time he was arrested in his car for some minor technical oversight (his car wouldn't start and he took the church car without seeing that a new license had not been put on it) I WAS IN THE CAR WITH HIM. He was really arrested because the cop saw my white face, followed the car out to Emory where I was staying (taking my usual X-ray treatments) and arrested him for that, using the license as an excuse. I think Dr. King should be more astute and shrewd about seeing that he never technically breaks the law. But the real reason was me. It appeared in one issue of *Atlanta Constitution* (about me) and was pulled out before nine A. M. I didn't see it; Frank did. Couldn't you and Bob and your friends do something to make officials in Albany see that this can be worked up into a world scandal and poor old Albany will pay for it for years. The right thing to do is to accept integration in the bus station etc. and quietly let Dr. King and Rev. Ralph Abernathy go back to Atlanta. [. . .]

Thank you for anything you or Bob or your friends can do to ease this situation. Atlanta has eased its hot spots by a few upperclass people like you, quietly talking to the right officials.

tlc, UGA

 The following letter to SNCC staff in Atlanta demonstrates the dual aspects of Smith's sense of herself as interpreter and clarifier for the movement, not only to white southerners but also to civil rights activists.

Undated [Late December 1962 or January 1963]

Dear All of You at SNCC:

[. . .]

I read your Newsletter with a sinking heart. It sounds so terribly bad. But things are breaking and thawing: we must hold on to that. A frozen river is a quiet thing; in thaw it is a roaring monster. We are in thaw in the South: there is bound to be much noise, much individual cruelty, much collective madness. But underneath, change is taking place—not only in streets and places but in human hearts. And this we must every one remember. I remember when I first began writing my magazine *South Today* things were so frozen that people actually thought I was mad. (And not only the Ralph McGills—but truly wise and good people thought so). I remember the stunned faces in Raleigh N.C. at a meeting of the Southern Churchmen (their faces were all right—the audience's collective face is what I remember) when I quietly said segregation is morally wrong, psychologically wrong, culturally wrong: all of us, white and Negro are harmed by it. The whites' souls are harmed, the Negroes' bodies and minds. That gasp from the audience. This was in 1943. I kept on writing, speaking out, and more important, thinking, thinking, letting this dilemma, this sickness relate, as it must, to all the other sicknesses of our soul and confusions of our mind. And people thought I was half out of my mind! Of course. That was the frozen period. If you think this thaw is bad, I wish you could have experienced the hard frozen sterile quality of those times. I say this not to minimize the horror of today but to give perspective, to help us see that sometimes noise and blood and screams and blows are not a sign of things worsening but of things getting better. If only you, as you hurt and work and are wounded and stunned by the sight of so much cruelty can absorb it and still keep your compassion, your sense of humor! (Remember what I said in the revised edition of *Killers of the Dream* about that?) I love your wonderful capacity to laugh the brutalities out of your soul, leaving it cleansed and free of hate and resentment. I wish Jim Baldwin could go through personally one of these times with you; it would relieve him of a terrible sense of guilt that is making him grow too raging, thus losing the art of looking at things in the concrete, the specific, instead of as generalization. Artists must take care not to generalize. You have something he doesn't have simply because you have *suffered while trying to change things*. This suffering, not passively but actively as you try to change the world, relieves you of hate and fear. I am sure of this. Always the Harlem Negroes have hated more acutely than have the southern members of the race because the southern members were tangling with life itself, with the concrete problems every day brought into their lives. What you remember is a certain day, a certain minute in say, a Mississippi town when you were kicked in the teeth maybe; but why were you kicked? Not because you just happened to be passing by but because you dared to try to change a specific situation. This is what the white southerner has got to learn, too. Camus worked in the underground in France; he risked his physical safety a thousand times—and he did not hate: he learned to be more acutely aware, to think more clearly, to feel more deeply.

This is why I have a special regard for you and your work. I do hope I can be of more specific help to you during this next year. I hope I get over this lung cancer to the extent that I can be of more help than I've been for a year or so. But I can always write; and was glad I could do the *Life* piece and "A Strange Kind of Love" (which was about you all really) in the *Saturday Review* of Oct. 20th, and the piece called "The Mob and the Ghost" in the *Progressive Magazine* for December. At least, I did this much this fall to show the depths of the problem: it is both horizontal and perpendicular—perpendicular to the horizontal: there is relationship between them. I feel my big contribution is probing more philosophically into the heart of the matter. But practical help I must do, too. So—if I can write a little something for you, fine; I'd like to. Or if you want to quote some of this in one of your Newsletters you are certainly free to do so.

Bless you; take care; be wary, shrewd, alert as well as bold and outthrusting; and hold on to this "strange kind of love" which is so mighty in its effect that it is often criticised more than violence itself. Some of these people want you to break down to their level and be violent; but you won't— of this I am sure. But nonviolence is not enough: the compassion that melts the cruelty not in others but in your own minds and hearts is the big thing, the real thing.

Please give my greetings to those who know me.

tlc, UGA

Jacksonville, Florida
January 20, 1963

Dear George:

It may interest you to hear that I am reviewing the *Feminine Mystique* book for *Saturday Review*. It is a very important theme Betty Friedan is concerned with, of enormous significance to our entire country as well as to women, and she has handled it well. I have enjoyed reading it, too; and was left perturbed by the picture of the state of affairs of women in America. I feel a justice in what she says, and although we can all find exceptions to alleviate the darkness of the picture, still they are exceptions—that is, there is only a minority of women who are not deeply injured by what is going on.

[. . .] I have only a few small criticisms to make, almost picky ones, but I'll make them quietly and with decent respect for the truly stupendous job she did on this book. So—I think you may count on one strong good review. Sorry you didn't or couldn't get a man to praise the book, too. And George, you may think it helps to have Pearl Buck praise books and I suppose it does with the common run of women she used to write for in the ladies journals but it would sort of prejudice any hard-thinking, intellectual reader. Because Mrs. Buck is not good on this subject of women, nor on race relations. She is sentimental. Once she was too "feministic" in the old way; now she tends to try to placate the men—after all, she writes for those journals edited by the men who have set up just this feminine mystique which she, with her descriptions of child-bearing etc., fell right into the rhythm of. Without catching on—or wanting to—I truly think she has always aimed for the popular lower-middle-class woman reader.

[. . .]

tls, UGA 2126

[Jacksonville, Fla.]
March 9, 1963

Dearest Paulie:

I miss you. That is the main reason I am writing. I get so empty, sometimes; just one long evening would make a difference, it seems, when I am so far away. I know how busy you are; and I know you don't have the energy Edie and Kay* seem to have after a day's teaching and work; I think maybe

*Friends in Jacksonville.

it is because you still feel a strain from it all. And I understand why you can't write often. But nevertheless, I miss our easy, sometimes noncommittal talk—but often it was far more. I need your "presence" which is, after all, the real Paula and what I love best about you. But I'd like to try some of my ideas and plans out on you to see how you'd react to them. Oh well, we can't get together so I won't grouch but I think seeing Maud and Frank this week made me want to see you more than ever.

Everyone is so nice to me; as Mary Lou Fagg said last night, "You've taken Jacksonville by storm." It really seems as though I have: from the old Guard to the ordinary little liberal in the Human Relations Council people seem to like me and are so gentle and kind to me.

The luncheon was a big success. I sat next to Bill or Bob Feagin (from Macon and you taught some of the Feagins I think and maybe one came to camp) who is vice-president of the Florida Publishing Co. (both news-papers). The luncheon was given by them to the Women's Press Club of Florida. I spoke off the cuff but I wowed them, apparently—even the men. Walters, the executive editor whose word is IT on the paper, sat three or four seats from me at the speakers' table, eyeing me now and then. When I spoke I saw him begin to watch me carefully; when I got close to the end I glanced at his face and it was warm, open, amused, delighted, almost affectionate as he listened to me. Everybody felt the whole room change after I began to speak. It may be worth a lot to race relations in Florida—just this one little act, for if the paper would change, things could be OK here—and editorials *are* better, lately. Anyway, the whole city was impressed that I was let speak, that it was reported so well; and this, added to the big piece in January, has made quite a hit with everybody. [. . .]

[. . .] The Dekle Taylors (ear specialist) gave me a dinner party at Ashley Montague's suggestion; had six doctors and their wives. [. . .] She, Mrs. Taylor, has invited me next week to a luncheon of her Book Club; she was to review Steinbeck's books, but changed and decided to review Lillian Smith's; she wants me to hear her do it. So I am going. This book club of 20 women is an honorable thing of ancient vintage: their mothers started it 30 years ago. So—things are stirring for L.S. and will help the book store.* "Sam" (Dr. Sam Day) came into the store before it opened and bought $9.75 of books; he then phoned me and said, "You're quite a writer." He bought the *Christmas Memory* for his mother; read it before sending it to Alabama; then bought a paperbook *Killers of the Dream*; and a new book

*Smith was in Jacksonville to help her brother Wallace start a bookstore.

called *Occupation: Angel* (nice book for a gift if you want to entertain somebody.) Then he asked me if I'd speak for his sister's Music Teachers of Florida meeting; said she'd call me. I feel, since he is well known and already interested enough to hunt up the bookstore I should do it; so next Friday I'll speak on A Writer and the Music She Hears. I am doing too much; but in a sense, I am also filling up on all sorts of human experiences which I have not had too much of for several years. Maybe it will pay off in the end. I hope so. Am trying awfully hard now to get back on the book of my pieces for Norton; and am thinking of the little book on cancer which I want to do for World. I'll do the collection pieces first so I can get that advance of $2500.00 sometime this summer. Then, maybe, I can sell to *Redbook* or somebody, excerpts from the little cancer book. How do you like the title, My Semi-Private Enemy. I don't want anything about ordeal or victory or anything slushy. I hope to make the book amusing in spots and as helpful as possible.

[. . .]

I have more to do about social affairs than I can possibly do; Edie will run any errand anytime for me; so don't worry about that; but I haven't been writing: and I am worried about making some money. And I don't have YOU to talk to; and I miss that. [. . .]

tls, UGA

TO LESLIE W. DUNBAR, DIRECTOR,
SOUTHERN REGIONAL COUNCIL

October 27, 1963

Dear Leslie:

[. . .] It would be good for me to see and talk with you. My strength, unfortunately, after this past virulent attack which has lasted so long, is not what it used to be; but I find I do better not nursing myself, and while visits tire me, certainly, they give me much to think about for days afterward. If I am living, I want to live; no half dying state for me! I do rest; I do "take care" but I need also to keep in the swim of things. Am not yet back to good writing but have caught up on much business that had been unattended to; and soon, I hope, can go back to a good writing schedule. So don't hesitate to come: you are doing me a favor when you help keep me au courant with all that is happening, especially those important matters on the deeper levels of experience. I am troubled about much; I was troubled by that recent speech of Martin Luther King's in Birmingham when he was telling his audience what God had just told him. Now hell, I say! Martin: you and

God are not that intimate. Of course the audience became almost frenzied; it was the first time I thought MLK had become really demagogic. His dream speech barely escaped it, but it was beautiful and genuinely touching for the occasion made it so; and too, it was true. But it is not true that God speaks to Martin and tells him what to do about race relations; this makes me frown and laugh and then feel queasy for a long time. I realize the temptation is great. I'd better hurry and finish my piece called The Demagogue and the Poet. Martin needs it right now, I fear. Charisma . . . a wonderful thing to have; but it crawls out of the mythic mind and when the conscious mind whistles it out, then we'd better watch for the lie is close behind. [. . .]

tlc, UGA

CHAPTER   ❧   SEVEN

Reweaving the Web,

1 9 6 4 – 1 9 6 6

In one of her last works in progress, a fragment later published in *The Winner Names the Age* as "Call Me Ishmael," Lillian Smith wrote:

> Without that knowledge of the last chapter of one's story, we can never quite know who we are—for that last chapter changes everything. Yes, everything: just a little. However sure we may be of "what we believe" [. . .] those beliefs turn to ashes on our death—and out of the ashes rises the Phoenix, the real Self we never really found. [p. 200]

The "self" that emerges from the last chapter of this text seems remarkably similar to the selves of preceding chapters. Smith's correspondence from the last two years of her life reveals thoughts about the publication of *Our Faces, Our Words* in the fall of 1964, her ideas for works to be done, and her political writing and speaking. What dominates, however, is her preoccupation with the writing of that "last chapter" and the degree to which she can re-create her life—or at least influence the interpretation of it that will emerge after her death.

 Phyllis L. Meras, correspondent for the *Providence* (R.I.) *Journal*, interviewed Smith in the fall of 1963 for a series on leading authors published in the *Journal*'s Sunday book page.[1] A year later Meras wrote requesting additional information so that the piece could appear with a review of the forthcoming *Our Faces, Our Words*.[2] Smith's response shows the conscious effort she made to provide information about her life and work that would, in turn, produce the public image she desired. Meras's article, along with a review of *Our Faces, Our Words* by Robert Taylor, appeared in the *Providence Sunday Journal* on December 13, 1964.

October 2, 1964

Dear Miss Meras:

It is nice to hear from you after so long a silence. Both Paula Snelling and I enjoyed our day with you and we hoped you, too, had found it of interest. Then, when we did not hear we feared either something had happened to you, or to your project. In the meantime, I have been struggling not with pneumonia (I had gone through that just before you came down) but my sixth siege with cancer. I have just completed six weeks of cobalt treatments—which means I have had in all 52 blasts of that powerful radiation and more than 50 during the past years of X-ray. I must be made out of lead!

Now, about the new book. No, it is a totally new idea: one born while I was lying in bed last winter ill. I decided I wanted to do some dramatic monologues which might reveal some of the complexity, conflict, ambivalence, courage, suffering, and satisfaction these young civil rights workers are experiencing. So many of them have come to see me; we have had such intimate talks far into the night; I feel I have a deep sense of what they have gone through this summer in Mississippi. So I did nine monologues. Some are the thoughts of young Negroes, northern and southern. I tried by using *not* the method of the journalist or that of the case worker *but that of the artist* to probe deep into the heart of the young of our times at this troubling moment of our history. I ended the little book by doing an epilogue in which I spoke my own thoughts on the civil rights movement. This epilogue will appear in *McCall's* Magazine around October 22 in the November issue. The editor-in-chief wrote me that he liked it very much, especially the quiet, probing, philosophical tone of it. The little book will have photographs, too. That is why I called it *Our Faces, Our Words.* But it is, remember, a creative thing [. . .] shaped by my imagination and intuition. Recordings are to be made of most of these monologues; I did some of them and the Negro actor Ossie Davis did others.

[. . .] It is entirely different from the collection of essays I was telling you about last autumn. That book will be published later by Norton—perhaps in 1965.* They are also reissuing my book, *The Journey,* in both hard covers and paperback. Since, in many ways, this is the book I feel closest to, I am very happy. It will have a new preface and a few slight changes, here and there. My novel is still unfinished; and my book for Harpers called "The Mysteries of Autobiography" is still unfinished. Cancer has a way of eating up one's days as well as one's energy; but I think I have whipped it again.

The things you said about my feelings about the dehumanizing effects of segregation and of racism are approximately right. As I told you, I have never worked to "give the Negro his civil rights" except as any right-thinking, decent citizen would work. My literary aim, my purpose has been to search and probe for the meaning of racism as a symptom of men's fear of the future, a symptom, too, of their fear of evolving into a more complex thinking human being. Many people fear the human race's further growth; they fear the new tensions of this strange and utterly wonderful age we are entering. They, in panic, prefer to cling to not just the 19th century but even a far simpler past—as if they could! It explains the Birchites and KKK and others who cling so raucously to Goldwater. If you will read the last chapter of the revised (1962) edition of *Killers of the Dream* you will see what I mean by man evolving into something far more complex, intense, *thinking* than he has been before. He is in a very real sense, and utterly unlike the rest of the material world, participating in his own evolution by the tensions set up by his own discoveries and thoughts.

In my "Credo" which I am doing for Pocket Books (for their series called the Credo series edited by Dr. Ruth Anshen) I am writing about what I believe the human being is, what I think his purpose on this earth is, etc. etc. I felt a bit overwhelmed when I was invited, along with Heisenberg and many philosophers and scientists to take part in this series. But especially as I go through this ordeal of long illness knowing death is now my intimate friend who casts his shadow on me, I find myself hungering to put down

---

*Although Smith did not complete the collection of essays, in 1978 W. W. Norton published *The Winner Names the Age,* a collection of Smith's essays and speeches edited by Michelle Cliff with a preface by Paula Snelling.

what my own experience has taught me about life and this earth man has evolved on.

And yet, with all these philosophic thoughts I am still more novelist than anything else. I am an essayist, too, yes; and perhaps in some ways I have proved myself more in this field than in that of the novel but I use my fiction technics, my intuitive awareness of individuals, of one person here and another person there even as I write essays. The book that has perhaps influenced me most in recent years is *The Phenomenon of Man* by Pierre Teilhard de Chardin. The myth that is my favorite of all myths is the Orphic myth. Put those two facts together and see what you make of it: I am not sure what *I* make of it!—And some of my favorite music is Bach and Poulenc and Bartok and yes, Mozart. So. I leave it all now with you.

tlc, UGA

TO MARTIN LUTHER KING, JR.

October 25, 1964

Dear Dr. King:

I wish I felt that I knew you well enough to call you Martin and for you to call me Lillian: because I am so fond of you and admire you so much— and am so fond of your wife. Maybe we should just begin to do it, even though we haven't had the opportunity to spend a great deal of time in personal converse.

But I am feeling an extraordinary amount of respect and awe and admiration this morning as I think of the Nobel prize which you have just won and which you so completely deserve, that maybe for me to keep a little distance is the appropriate gesture!

Let me say it plainly: I am so proud of you, so warmly happy over this distinguished award given you, so certain that you deserve it more than anyone else I know, so glad glad glad that it happened this year. In a sense, perhaps it would have been better three years from now as you continue this beautiful maturing which is so definitely a part of your personality; but we couldn't wait that long: "we" needed for you to be recognized NOW for it has not only given you courage (I know it must have helped) but it has given the rest of us courage. So many thousands of white southerners are happy and proud of you. Around this little town, people have spoken with such generous praise and genuine pleasure about this award. The award has in a subtle and profound way lifted the cause of human rights to a higher level than it had reached before; and it has also helped the cause of civil rights. (You note I make a difference between the two. Rights and relationships are intertwined but forever separate in cause and effect: rights are worthless without creative human relationships and creative human relationships cannot exist without human beings having their rights, yet they are distinct strands of the human experience.)

I want also to thank you for sending me your last two books with the beautiful inscriptions. I know you have heard that the last two and a half years have been a heavy ordeal for me: I have had cancer for twelve years but when it crept into my lungs then my real trouble began, not only a difficulty in breathing but so much pain; I have spent much of my time in hospitals gasping for breath while you were spending much of your time in jails breathing quietly and confidently, I am sure. I have seen the hurt in your eyes on television but I have never heard it in that strangely beautiful voice of yours. That voice is the most reassuring voice in the whole world, did you know that? You have perhaps no conscious control over it but deep inside you there is a faith, a certainty, a compassion, a love, a willingness to suffer and a reluctance for others to suffer that turns your voice into a work of art. White people respond strongly to it; it dissipates their anxiety, it arouses their desire to do better, be better. It is a great voice, in its way as great as Caruso: a speaking voice that reveals the human soul at its best.

I am sending you a copy of my little book called *Our Faces, Our Words* which I wrote last spring between my two long hospital bouts. My blood pressure hovered around 50 and 60 during the weeks I wrote these nine monologues and the essay which closes the book; it has some faults, it has a few omissions that should not have been but I now wonder as I look at it how I ever did it at all, as I was in bed all the time—and had no secretary. I am too poor to afford one, so I'd write a monologue in a rough draft in bed, get up and go to my typewriter across the room, type off the first draft and usually by then was so weak that I'd have to lie very still for several hours before I did anything more. But somehow it was done; and my old typist in town (who now works for the government) did the final copies for me. Because of this difficulty I omitted somehow (I don't know how) a mention of the SCLC. I mentioned you a number of times but your organization I somehow failed to mention. The little book is my creative approach to the young workers and their problems, therefore I tended to keep Core and Snick [SNCC] in mind. The monologues are of course fictitious; they are characters that I might have put in a novel but more true than any literal transcription from the mouths of civil rights workers could have been, I think, since (as is true of all art) they search for and (I hope) find the essence of the young people's struggle. I have kept in close touch, often talked to groups of them elsewhere, and I have felt that this experience tied in with my thirty-five years of intimacy with what was happening among Negroes and whites gave me the understanding to do the dramatic monologues.

[. . .]

I hope you will find the little book interesting and that you will not feel that I should have included all the various groups in my essay—the last piece in the book. Always, as I said, I was seeing the "young and the brave" and I often mentioned you for without you they could not have accomplished what they have. Oh, I know they think they could have but it required your charisma to pull them out of the sometimes dead-ends they through their immaturity got themselves into. I know you realize there will be jealousies aroused by this award, but try not to mind: the kids will grow up and learn finally to acknowledge what you have done for them and what your symbolic presence in America has done for the white Americans.

Bless you and thank you for being your wonderful self. And give my love to your wife. I've enjoyed looking at the King family calendar Mrs. King so thoughtfully sent me.

tlc, UGA

 Following is one of several versions of a letter Smith composed to George Brockway describing her response to a threatening phone call after "The Day It Happened to Each of Us," her final essay in *Our Faces, Our Words*, appeared in the November 1964 *McCall's*. Other versions of the letter were dated November 2, 1964.

Undated

Dear George:

Well—the first reaction to the *McCall's* piece was an anonymous phone call threatening to dynamite my house. The call may have been from Atlanta or Gainesville—maybe from here. It is not easy to be sure. [. . .] But this phone call (a rather nice man's voice, at 11:30 AM) gave me chills. My heart got very slow and heavy and my hands and arms went icy; I don't know why it scared me so, I've had all kinds of threats before, ever since *Strange Fruit*—and many after *Killers of the Dream*, and more after the 1954 Supreme Court decision. But things had been quiet for a long time, the people of Clayton are so wonderful to me, I guess I had sort of relaxed. I sat here alone on the mountain—or just with M. who has worked for me for many years as you know. Then I decided to tell her. After all, she is a very shrewd and often wise woman. She had listened in on the kitchen phone and already knew but she was waiting for me to make the first move.

I told her I thought I'd be rather simple and direct about this and ask some of the men in town who are my genuine friends to help me in my dilemma. Before, when the fires came, I had said nothing; I phoned for fire help but said nothing more about things being "set." This time, I decided I'd be a bit more humble and ask to be helped. And I did exactly that. I first asked a strong segregationist to help me; he used to misunderstand me and he still hates Dr. Martin Luther King. This man, with very different views from mine, is warmhearted, tender in many ways, and during my long illness he has shown a wondrous kindness. [. . .] Yet he'd like to see something evil happen to King, I think; he would not do it himself but he would be glad it happened.

This man was genuinely shocked when I told him about the threat. He said he couldn't understand it. This is something we have not probed deeply, this living on two levels; this man does not realize that hate talk causes physical violence. He is very kind, yet he can talk about "niggers"— and he doesn't seem to know that it is this kind of talk that fires up a community. Anyway, he said he'd do everything in the world to help me; he had heard nothing, he'd keep his ears open. And I relaxed. You see, I trust him: I knew he would do all he could to keep any harm from coming to me. [. . .]

Well—I then called the sheriff. I've known him since he was two. He simply "couldn't imagine why anybody would want to hurt you, Miss Lil." All my books, my acts, the tremendous controversial reputation I have—all this, brushed out of sight, partly to be nice to me, partly because he likes me therefore does not remember what he doesn't want to remember. He said he'd listen out and keep an eye on the mountain—little good it would do me with maybe sticks of dynamite already about to go off in my basement! But do you know? His words actually comforted me. Aren't we ridiculous people! Here we live in the South, in the middle of incredible melodrama, fury, violence, obscenity yet we say nice things to each other and believe somehow it will help. Our sheriff has always been a friend to Negroes; he is decent, kind, not remotely like some of the Mississippi and Alabama sheriffs we read about. We have been fortunate to have him. He has always maintained law and order up here. And make no mistake about it, my county is a decent place; the people are kind, intelligent in their attitudes toward Negroes, tolerant toward people who differ from them. My relationships with people here would make a very moving, warm story; there have been mean things, of course; some people have gossiped, others have made nasty comments to visitors from the North, but most have been courteous always, and kind, and very concerned with my illness. And they read my books and honor them by giving them serious attention. [. . .] Little towns are not always bigoted, not always stupid, not always cruel [. . .].

Back to my story of being dynamited: I called two young friends. They were direct, realistic; they said at once they knew there were fools and nuts who'd do it; "But we'll keep our ears peeled; we'll watch for signs and we'll get the GBI and FBI on it, too." Which they did. The young ones are not so devious as the older ones; they know how to add, they can get the message. And these are the ones to count on in every town.

[. . .] [A]nyone living down here and speaking out as plainly as I do, even though blessed with many friends, is in a curious kind of danger, I suppose. We just disregard it—what else can you do! And then, too, you don't want to make a martyr of yourself; and get so melodramatic over little risks. After all, everybody who does anything real and useful in this upsidedown world is running a risk.

Funny—the things that scare you. A call one night at two o'clock in which the man just said dozens of four-letter words left me trembling. Why? I don't quite know. The voice so nasty, low and nasty, and well—the human spirit in the mud is not nice to confront. I think I was trembling not from fear but from a straight look at the foulness of man when he sinks low.

Racism can pull a man so deepdown into the mire: it opens bad-smelling corridors that lead deep into one's nature. It is a psychosis, yes; but we don't explain it by labeling it. Racism is so different from prejudice; it would be helpful if people could begin to use words precisely, giving them their actual meaning. A racist will not only kill—he wants even more to give pain, to hurt terribly as he kills. It is this *giving pain* that we have to look at. And with this is always sex, sex, sex. We have scarcely begun to probe this illness. Let's call it what it is: evil. I'm not sure it is an illness, it may be simply evil. We can't understand the human condition without that word.

tlu, UGA

 Smith wrote the following letter to Marvin Rich after he was attacked and beaten by a white gang in Madison County, Mississippi, where CORE had sent him to observe elections. Black candidates were running for positions on the county's previously all-white Agricultural Stabilization and Conservation Committee, which historically discriminated against black farmers by allowing them disproportionately small acreages to cultivate.[3] Smith's analysis of the white racist brutality pointedly connects racism and homophobia and challenges those who worked for economic solutions to racial segregation to look also to the spiritual and emotional needs of its victims, especially the white males.

December 11, 1964

My very dear Marv:

This is a letter addressed to a very brave man; so brave and so damned modest about it that it shakes me. I had not heard until the last few days anything about your fearsome trouble in Mississippi recently; a bit of news drifted to me through a clipping; then Jimmy Wechsler's fine column was sent to me, today, by Joan Titus who tries to keep me au courant with all the affairs she knows are close to my heart—and which I miss cooped up here on the mountain.

When I think I complained to you about a bomb threat! I am afraid having cancer so long has made me a little sissy! (Although I think it was the dreadful fires, years ago!) Well, anyway a bomb threat is nothing compared to a twice broken nose; but worse than the brokenness was the look on those faces [. . .] the cold, nasty, evil deliberateness of this violence shown you, and the Negroes for whom you have become a protecting symbol! Do they hate Negroes so much? Can you hate anybody on earth this much? I don't believe you can; I believe it is something beyond "the Negro[,]" beyond civil rights, beyond all the apparent things. I have often thought—I *do* think that it is never a particular Negro that a white man hates but the symbol the Negro has become for Something Else. What is this Something Else? this is what we need to know. I touched on a few things in *Killers of the Dream*—but there is more, more than I have as yet thought through, or said. I know one thing is that white men are deeply attracted to Negro boys and men, sexually; I know it is not Negro women but Negro men who have seduced white man's feelings, not knowingly, but this has happened down here; and I know the sense of tabu has aroused deep anxiety in the white man (I speak of the South now) and he loathes himself for wanting something that he believes is unpardonably wrong for him to want, something that only the primitive sense of tabu can describe; not guilt as a rational man feels it, but the ancient guilt, the archaic sense of uncleanness: all this wells up in these white men, they are pulled too close, then jerked away by this primitive fear, and they hate themselves with a viciousness that is almost indescribable. Poverty? ignorance? lack of recreation? lack of a way to be creative? these are but rational answers to a profoundly deep problem of the mythic mind. A mythic mind, half drawn to the surface by Christianity is a terrifying thing—for the Cross, the suffering on it, redemption, all this only serve[s] to deepen the temptation and heighten the desire not just to kill but to mutilate. To *mutilate* is what the problem is: why do they want to mutilate? what great master form are they trying to destroy? what vision are they trying to dirty up so completely that it can never be cleaned, become visible again to the minds of men? Don't tell me that "better schools" and good jobs for everybody will take care of the white man's trouble! It won't. It will help the Negro with his but not the white man down here. Our so called best "leaders" down here feel this intuitively and they are frightened; that is why they want everybody now to concentrate on education, on getting rid of "poverty" (economic not spiritual), on "better housing." But some of the mutilators own their cars, live in fairly decent housing, have fairly good jobs. There is much more. And we must probe until we find it.

[...]

tlc, UGA

TO HOKE NORRIS*

January 18, 1965

Dear Mr. Norris:

I want to thank you for the warm, friendly mention of my little book, *Our Faces, Our Words* in your recent column. And I want to say, too, that I liked the entire column very much; you are so right: the Movement is full of ambiguities and dissidences; it has arrived at a point of no return; and although the leaders feel this, they don't quite know where they are or where to go next. I keep my fingers crossed all the time about a few of them; and others I admire tremendously. As far as I am concerned personally, all organizations are things I suspect; this has always been true of me; my temperament rejects organizations and yet I know we must have them; and as the masses push up and crowd the few thinkers and artists, the organizations will be even more urgently needed (as much as I fear them and dread them) to keep the thinkers, the critics, the artists, the scientists from being overwhelmed by the giant waves of Those From Beneath Coming Up.

[...]

*Book critic for the Chicago *Sun Times*.

A postscript to my letter.

Mr. Norris:

[. . .] I was thinking of the irony of the fact at their most successful moment the Civil Rights Movement's leaders are now at the point of no return as I said and troubled about where to go next or how to get there. [. . .]

[As you said], we as "an age" or maybe Nation or "country" do not really know our name; we have not found our spiritual identity. I implied this in all the monologues but I especially meant to show the young civil rights workers' own feeling of loss of spiritual direction. I am so glad you wrote about the "poor white" and his role in our bewilderment and our sin. Poor not in income (often he has a decent home and one or two cars) but culturally poor, morally deprived, creatively stunted. This is the "poor white" who is turning our South upsidedown. And this too fits into your feeling of irony: this "poor white" is now in control of the old quality South; this "poor white" makes decisions that only the learned, the scientifically wise should make—and we, the upper-class whites of the South are caught in a mutism. We, too, have lost our identity, we, too, do not know our name. I am glad you wrote about that in your column.

I would like to do a collection of monologues in the voices of the "poor whites." I'd like to go deep into the souls of the men who coldly (and bloodheatedly) crushed the bones of that young Negro when the three were killed;* I'd like to let them tell (through me) their thoughts, their bewilderments, their angers and resentments, the dark welling-up of their hate. Whom do they really hate? Not that poor unknown Negro boy. No, I think they hate us: they hate the upperclass whites of the South who fed them the drug of "whiteness" until they have destroyed themselves spiritually. They hate us because they, too, are segregated: segregated as rigidly socially from the Big Wheels and their families as are Negroes. This never-talked-about segregation which must be like a white fog around the poor whites is the thing that makes them hate Negroes with a psychotic violence; it isn't their competition for jobs—that is a rational fear; this other thing is deep, sick,

---

*James Chaney, Andrew Goodman, and Michael Schwerner, civil rights workers killed by Klansmen in Neshoba County, Miss., on June 21, 1964. An autopsy revealed that Chaney suffered extensive skull and bone fractures in addition to the gunshot wounds inflicted on his white companions.[4]

psychotic. In "Distance and Darkness" (*Killers of the Dream*) I tried to show some of it. I now understand more of it. I live among the poor whites of the mountains where we have here only a handful of Negroes. [. . .] Most are relatively free of resentment; but in every small town and county there are two or three hundred who have this psychotic feeling; what restrains them up here is the good climate of 90 percent of the people [. . .], this implied, silent and thick assumption of certain ethical values, certain things people don't do, don't say. And it is also respect for law. The irony is that down South the Law is in the hands of the poor whites; how far and deep do the chains of evil drag people! What would our grandfathers think, were they to come back today! Oh, they sinned, they were confused, some of them precipitated the Civil War (my family happened to be the cool-headed ones who tried to restrain the hot heads—my grandfather Simpson was an erudite, scholarly, wise, judicious man and he influenced three generations of us!) but never did they dream that their acts and words would inch by inch force their children on a twisting journey that led finally into the power of the poor whites. Irony. . . . You are so right. But it goes beyond irony, doesn't it, into tragedy.

You may or may not like President Johnson. He is a pragmatist who has a genius for accomplishing things; a pragmatist turned idealist (in recent years). Somehow, I feel he will cut enough ideological strings (and feelings) to help us work our way out of this labyrinth we got ourselves into. Maybe he will prove to be Ariadne's thread. God knows, I hope so.

[. . .]

tlc, UGA

TO LAWRENCE KUBIE

April 5, 1965

Dear Larry:

[. . .]

I was given the first Queen Esther Scroll awarded by the National Women's Division of American Jewish Congress. It pleased me to be chosen as the first recipient of this award which they hope to make into a thing of distinction. I was given it for my "creative genius," which pleased me; but the press[,] determined to diminish me, changed it to an award for her "courage and commitment." They have stereotyped me as a propagandist and friend of the Negro Cause and they are determined that I not be looked at as an important writer. This stereotyping started in *Strange Fruit* days by the enemies but since then my old friends have fallen for it, too. It seems impossible for them to admit either my intelligence or my creative ability. It hurts. Isn't it strange? One is always punished at the place in one's personality where it hurts the most. How can "the enemy" so instinctively find the most vulnerable spot! Somehow, the hostile male group has seemed to know I did not mind being called "obscene and nasty" for I knew I wasn't; they seemed to know I didn't really mind being shot or killed or burned out; they seemed to know the truth of my being which is that I want above all else to be genuinely creative and discerning and sensitive; I want to be considered as a writer—and as a woman; but not as "woman with a cause." As a writer I have a cause but it is bigger than "the Negro" or civil rights—as you well know. They know it and they have seen to it that I am not considered as a writer. This has been the unhealing wound of my life; I think it had something to do with my succumbing to cancer; my despair, my deep hurt about this; but the other side of my nature, my creativity and life-wanting qualities have fought the cancer so I've managed a cold war with a few very hot episodes for 13 long years!

[. . .] I know this shrewd, clever diminishing of me was to be expected considering I was that unforgivable thing: a "first." And a woman, too; who is not supposed to think but only feel. I know I can let a sense of persecution absolutely destroy me; not only my health but my quality as person and writer; I am fighting it, Larry; I won't succumb; just now and then it sweeps over me rather heavily.

I am trying to get going on another book: this is my way of forgetting myself, and of discovering depths in myself and in others that fascinate me; this is my way also of making something decent and real out of my life; so when I get going hard on the book I shall be for the time being, "saved" from self pity.

tls, Kubie/LC

 Arthur L. Klein, president of Spoken Arts, Inc., wrote Smith that of the three hundred records he had produced, none meant more to him than her reading from *Our Faces, Our Words*. He then compared her greatness to that of the dancers, Margot Fonteyn and Rudolf Nureyev.[5] As her reply indicates, nothing could have pleased Smith more. Basking in the warmth of his appreciation, she reflected on her involvement with the arts at Laurel Falls Camp, its importance in her life, and the degree to which her illness left her feeling isolated from so much that fed her own creative spirit.

Dear ALK:

What a wonderful letter—and it came on a day when it pulled me up, shook me a little, and well—it was wonderful, that's all. [. . .]

[. . .] You are doing a beautiful work—it is so damned much fun, isn't it, to do something you really love. Of all my projects—the three biggest being my children's camp, an absolutely incredible place it was for 25 years—my little magazine (10 years) and my book writing, I think I had more fun from the little mag which took every cent I could scrape up to put in it—and maybe more deep something, what? serenity (maybe?) from the work with the children. Martha Graham's girls came down to me for ten or fifteen years, Bennington kids (after they graduated from B.) and others—some first-class southern gals, too, and we did things with modern dance, sculpture, painting, my children's theater where we (I with their help) grew plays, each play taking three or four summers to grow out of our group talks, our constant examination of the unanswerable questions and our own personal experiences. We created a life on this mountain, an around the clock life that was deeply exciting and interesting. Now, my old girls say they cannot bear to send their kids to a summer camp for there isn't one like the old Laurel Falls. And there isn't; there never has been anything quite like it. I remember people came down from NYC to study my "methods" (they had sent me difficult children to work on) and as the secretary whipped out her pencil and the famous educator leaned toward me, I just smiled and said, "Love—I'd think; and yes, mutual respect; we like each other, you see, and we know freedom is just a word, it is really chaos, one takes it and creates out of it pattern—things you do, things you never do." She was outraged. No jargon. How could you do anything without jargon! And she said, after catching her breath, "Yes, S. does love you." "I love her, too," I said quite honestly, and "somehow together we are pushing out the messes and cleaning a little place were S. can start creating all sorts of things, sculpture and dancing but herself, too. And me," I added, "she is creating parts of me, too." Well, that was that; the lady had no theories; it really must not be an important place, after all. I often think of her; it does me good to remember. My writing brought in that awful thing, the public image; I can't grapple with it well; I hide and don't show much of myself, sometimes even to people I'd like to be close to. Fame and infamy go hand in hand; I did better when I stopped reading clippings. I still never know when I am being liked and when I am being used; but nothing matters really except: am I using others? As long as I don't, it's OK.

Oh, those two beautiful dancers; and to think I haven't yet seen Nureyev; I'm going to come up next year, now that I'm breathing better, even if I get out only once a week or once in two weeks. I can't stay away from so much that counts; this is the hardship of the illness.

You don't know how much I appreciate your generous advance and everything else—but especially your warm letters. I pray the record will sell for your sake, not just CORE's; maybe we can do another one, sometime. I am sending you a copy of *The Journey*. It is one of my books I especially like.

tlc, UGA

TO GEORGE BROCKWAY

July 3, 1965

Dear George:

[. . .]

Three biographies are being written on me. They are sort of racing with each other for material from me. It is arduous for me and funny; but my life has been kept so secretive, actually almost nobody knows of my years in China—and what they really were—or my years as the camp director—or my two years as executive secretary for a city manager—or my years with music in Baltimore—or those funny wonderful ten years with the magazine, and all those wacky house parties I had, etc. etc. Running the camp, I had to keep my right hand from knowing what my left was doing; after the "scandal" of *SF* I still was directing that camp; I could certainly not at that time let people know about my bi-racial house parties and all the rest of them, highly entertaining as they were. So, as the minister of All Souls (Washington D.C.) said in a sermon after you brought out the revised ed. of *Killers*, "I have talked with her several times for an hour or two, had dinner with her once, read her books; but I have the strange feeling I know absolutely nothing about the personal, the 'real' Lillian Smith." He sent me a reprint of that sermon but I still didn't tell him anything about the "real" LS.

The only biography with a contract is the Twayne Publisher's one: two women, Louise Blackwell and Frances Clay are doing it. They may call on you for information; [. . .]. The other two women are more concerned with the critical analysis of my work; one is going about it in a very scholarly annotated sort of way. The other wants to do a biography with critical analysis of my work. Most of these people have their Ph.D.'s; one did hers on Carson McCullers; one did hers on Flannery O'Connor; another working with the Flannery O'Connor woman did hers on rehabilitation with her emphasis on the blind. They all are cultivated, brilliant women and all like my work; they all feel I have been smothered and all are determined to excavate the corpse and hope it will still be breathing. So.

Joseph Morrison who is doing W.J. Cash's (*Mind of the South*) biography has been here, too, getting information from Paula and me. Apparently, to the Southern literary crowd's surprise we (Paula and I) know more about him, had more contacts with him than anybody else. Morrison is a nice guy; was here last Sunday; he says *Mind of the South* has sold more than 100,000 copies since I persuaded Knopf to push it again. He didn't know I had until I told him. After *Killers*, I had this decent, if quixotic notion, that I should push Cash's book; it hadn't been noticed for years; I wrote Knopf about giving it another big chance; he wrote back pretending he didn't know it hadn't been given one (good old face-saver) but he did bring it out again and sold paper rights to Anchor. So, George, I was the one who set up our biggest competitor; for they grabbed that book and hung on to keep from having to confront *Killers*. It appeals to the moderates and still does; but I think *Killers* is beginning now to make its comeback. After all, things are changing. Cash's book was not in any sense a "mind of the South"; it was actually a social history of the old South and its values and communal attitudes. But there was no in-depth probing in that book; the man wasn't capable of such, too sick himself, too involved with his own taboos to dare handle it the way I did. But we each admired and respected the other. He had read chapters from *SF* and admired them immensely. (Much to the surprise of his biographer who low rates that book, I think; Cash's opinion impressed him mightily when he came across a letter of Cash's talking about the book (*SF*).)

All this is interesting to me—and fatiguing, of course; but I feel I must feed these people information or they won't have any for a book. [. . .]

[. . .] I hear Freshman English at Uv. of Fla. is using *Memory of a Large Christmas* for this next year. Funny book to use to introduce me but "non-controversial" I suppose.

tlc, UGA

July 20, 1965

Dear Harry Golden:

[. . .] I am better; it may not last but while it is I am going to have a lovely time, doing things, writing hard, seeing the people I want to see; then if the prednesone loses its effect or stirs up too many side effects, all right, I can take that too. I've grown quite used to death; almost fond of the old fool at times when in great pain, but no longer dreading his advent as I once did; somehow that fear has gone; I really want to live and write four or five more books; but I can take it quite all right when the Moment comes—if everybody will just be gay and natural and not spoil things by being mournful around me.

I have just had twenty-four African students visit me. This is a State Dept. project and when I was asked if they could come up I of course said yes; then I went mile #2 and invited them all to have lunch with me up here on the mountain; then after a day or so thinking about it I went mile #3 and decided to make it really worth something by asking my Clayton citizens, prominent businessmen to show these students a little town that had come out of poverty into almost a state of affluence (affluence for quite a few, anyway); then I went mile #4 and asked all the politicos up here (including our State Representative) and a number of citizens and people in health work etc., to come up and have lunch with the students and me. They all accepted! So we had 48 for luncheon yesterday and it was quite an occasion: gay, gracious, friendly people all of them. The six citizens I had chosen met the students when their bus came in (they had a chartered bus) and I met them; then the men (prominent businessmen and the Mayor) took the students in their cars and showed them the town: the bank, the hospital (already completely integrated)[,] the health center (integrated)[,] several different kinds of stores, a small aluminum plant which had been developed by a local citizen (summa cum laude at Georgia Tech.), some of the residential streets, up Black Rock our beautiful state park, then they all gathered at the fire department to show how a volunteer fire department works. Everybody had fun with the red engines et cetra—then they came out to my mountain for luncheon. In the meantime the county superintendent of schools had arrived (schools to be completely integrated in September—Negro school abandoned); the State Representative had arrived; the County Agent, the Administrator of the hospital, the head of the Health

*Editor of the *Carolina Israelite*, Charlotte, N.C.

Center, an artist, a very fine pianist whose former husband was a famous musicologist in Europe (she teaches piano at University of Ga.)[,] the banker, one of his young assistants (whose mother is active in everything), the leading pharmacist of the town (top of the heap socially) and others had arrived for luncheon. Then the students and their Clayton guides arrived [. . .]. Everyone was so relaxed, so easy, so talkative (Africans and Clayton-ians) so gracious and really charming; it was quite a party. I moved around the group and finally sat down on the hillside—we were all outdoors by this time—and suddenly the students gathered around me and began asking probing but friendly questions. As I began to answer, I noticed the Clayton visitors had hushed their talk and were listening. It was quite a feat—I felt I was swimming across a deep gorge—to be completely truthful with the Africans and to be tactful with my Clayton friends who had just done so much for me—and as they said "our President." But I think I managed it all right. The Clayton people just wouldn't go home; they seemed enchanted by the whole affair (and I hear, today, that they've talked that way about it throughout the town). But the Georgia Power Co. had heard about my little project and invited the students to go through one of their big hydro-electric plants fifteen miles from here; they sent a representative to escort them so the day ended with a fascinating visit to a beautiful locale, plus a ride in the little swinging car across the deep Gorge. It was quite a good ending for some of these young men were going to be engineers, etc.

I was so proud of Clayton; so proud and touched by the way my friends took over and handled everything so well; they were impressed by the intelligence of the students and felt they got as much as they gave. [. . .]

tlc, UGA

TO EUGENE MOORE[*]

September 8, 1965

Dear Gene:

[. . .]

School opened beautifully and quietly. The two principals (each with more than 600 whites) made careful and quiet preparations; the county supt. of schools did likewise about traffic, police, no parents coming first day, nice reassuring comments on local radio and good comment in local paper [. . .]. There are thirteen Negro pupils—all we have. The little school is closed forever. The children were scared to death—especially after Watts

*Reporter, *Atlanta Journal.*

episode in L.A. I had them all over here Sunday afternoon before school opened; fed them ice cream and reassuring talk; five mothers came; (and the babies, of course). They left feeling better—especially the high school kids. There are five in high school. The one most reluctant to go to white school got promptly invited to play football and is high with happiness; the senior who is none too bright and has had fiercely bad preparation is being so well accepted as a human being and friend that he seems ecstatic. The young eighth grader is still too nervous to eat at lunch; first day, he and a sixth grader lost their lunches in the schoolroom; of course the upchucking embarrassed them fearfully; but teachers took care of it smoothly. The teachers as far as I know have been warm, human, thoughtful, strict about having absolutely no foolishness or ugliness shown. So—blessings on Clayton. The Tallulah Falls School opened with 13 Negroes, too; and Mr. Scott (Georgia Power and on the School Board) seemed—after entertaining my African students at the hydroelectric plant—now convinced that Negroes can learn and can equal whites. He had never believed it, quite, until he met the Africans who stunned him with their charm and polish and erudition. It helped him make the transition, I think.

[...]

tlc, UGA 1283A

 Smith wrote almost all her friends about the incident with the National Institute of Arts and Letters described in the following letter to Felicia Geffen, assistant secretary of the institute. Correspondence throughout the fall of 1965 reflects her continuing struggle with anger and deep depression triggered by this act she felt symbolized her lack of stature in the eyes of the literary establishment.

October 16, 1965

Dear Miss Geffen:

I want to thank you for your most courteous letter enclosing a check for $500 from the literary committee of the Artists and Writers Revolving Fund in "appreciation of my accomplishments."

I am grateful for the concern which prompted this gesture but I cannot accept the check. It is not going to be easy to explain why without going into too much detail but I think I owe it to the committee to try.

The check is obviously not an award; it is essentially "charity." A charity given to me by a group whose members have never accorded me recognition for my literary achievements. No one of my seven books—*Strange Fruit, Killers of the Dream, The Journey, One Hour*, etc.—has been given award or citation by the National Institute nor have I been invited to become a member because of my general level of writing achievement. I do not, therefore, "belong." How could I then accept aid, an aid I have not asked for, from a group who has in no way acknowledged my worth as a writer? I just couldn't. It would humiliate me on levels where I could not find the strength to deal with the hurt.

I apologize for my candor—and yet how can I write you in any other way? You see, what hurts is not having had cancer for thirteen years nor is it the struggle to meet heavy hospital bills etc.; what hurts is that my fellow writers have not read me and have made no serious attempt since *Strange Fruit* to see what I am trying to say. A stereotype was formed by both enemies and friends that walled off the view of me as a serious or talented writer. "Oh, of course, she's brave," (actually, I'm a scary cat); they said, "it is fine of her to do so much to help Negroes to get their rights." They said more—and then came the inevitable: "So we do not need ever to read her because we know what she is saying." It has been a Kafkan experience, all right; I've wandered around in a curious labyrinth, and I was condemned without trial. And so, although I don't write about "the Negro problem" and rarely about civil rights, critics and writers don't bother to try to find out what it is that is concerning me. They have failed to see that I am involved—all my creative abilities are involved—in the dehumanization of our times; I am involved with segregation that is symbol and symptom of this dehumanization; but this "segregation" is bigger than race, (conformity is also a form of segregation); it has to do with numberless relationships that are necessary not only to bind men into one world but necessary for their increasing complexity of mind and spirit as they continue to evolve themselves into human beings. I am talking about the things Teilhard de Chardin talked about, not the things Walter White talked about in his day or James Baldwin and Le Roi Jones are talking about now.

Of course, I may be wrong. It is possible that *One Hour* is not the important book many in Europe and here at home think it is; it is possible that *Strange Fruit* is the problem novel it was called in 1944 "about whites and blacks" when I think it is a book about dreamers compelled to kill their own dreams; it may be that *Killers of the Dream* is not the powerful documentary Maritain thinks it is; that *The Journey* is not the good writing and imagining and thinking that readers feel, etc. All this may be true; and yet, I cannot believe it. If I did, I could not keep on. And I must keep on; for I believe I am saying important things in a memorable way, and I'd like to live long enough to explore more deeply the paths I am now heading toward.

(Of course, as citizen and woman, as person, I also work to rid our land—and our world—of this narcistic worship of our white image; I try to help bring about creative change. This is the "Martha" part of me; but the "Mary" part is the stronger.)

Let me say, too, that I do not desperately need the Institute's money. I can manage; my publishers have been good and generous to me; a number of editors of magazines have insisted that I take advances for pieces neither they nor I have been sure I'd live to write. I can accept this beautiful generosity because they believe in me *as writer*. And two or three friends have helped; and I can accept their gifts because I love them; and of course members of my big family step in when the going gets too too rough. I confess things have not been easy. What I need, and yet how can one ask it?—is that this literary committee read my books; read them and let themselves see what I am trying to do. This understanding I do need desperately, this I would cherish more than a million dollars.

But thank you; I mean it; I am grateful for the sincerity of the committee's concern for me as a human being. I am sorry that it is a gift which I must return—as my Chinese friends in Chekiang long ago taught me to do when the situation required it.

tlc, UGA

 Alice Shoemaker, of Fallbrook, California, wrote Smith after reading her article, "Poets among the Demagogues," in the October 2, 1965, *Saturday Review* and enclosed a poem that she said the article had inspired her to complete. The poem, titled "October 1965," described her son who had returned from Vietnam, still a youth and a student but now also a trained killer, and questioned whether "fractured minds" so torn by conflicting experiences of war could build a peaceful society. By contrast, hearing the thousands of students protesting the war, the poet also wondered whether youth might yet save the people of the world.[6] Smith's response reflects much of her thinking about the antiwar protest movements of the mid-1960s.

October 30, 1965

Dear Alice Shoemaker:

Your poem touched me deeply. Much more than have the students' demonstrations, much more than the angry and often foolish "teach-ins."

You see, this is the power of a genuine seeking after deep truth. We need find only a small fragment of it, but this fragment, real, sinks deep into the heart and imagination—and these are the movers of men.

I have always defended the CO's; I have always defended the pacifists; I have never been one, myself; I am wholly against nuclear war; and 99½ percent against any form of war whatever; but that one-half percent is what haunts me. Sometimes we human beings sin so deeply that we are compelled to sin even more; this is a dreadful thing, a heart-chilling thing but I believe it is true. I am by nature the "perfectionist" type; I've had to fight to see the world as it really is; I want so urgently for it to be good, to be pure, to be creative. But I know that dualism is wrong: there is no clear evil and no clear good, no clear black and no clear white: it is wrapped together in a terrible tangle; and it is our duty—I think it is God's purpose!—for us to have to unwrap it, learning more about the good because of the evil meshed with it.

I lived in China in the 1920's—from 1922 through most of 1925. I saw all this building then; I wrote my father (I was only 24!) that communism was going to take over China because we, the strong democracy of the world, were blind, deaf, paralyzed—unwilling or unable to move forward and help these people building a firm foundation for their democracy. They did so long for the democratic way of life, the way of freedom and responsibility, of equality and differences, of creative compromise; but the USA did not listen to their cries nor the few voices raised. I was a teacher of piano in a Methodist School for rich Chinese girls: some of the general's daughters were in our camp; I knew the Soong family; Mei Ling Soong (Mrs. Chiang Kai Shek now), and I once ate supper together and since we are the same age, we talked "like two girls" together about America and China; she was very cynical then, I think secretly she still is; and her family are greedy people smoothed over with a sweet Christianity that falsifies everything real in Christianity. Well, this is the way it was then—in 1924–25: when Sun Yat Sen was begging the USA for real help; when Russia had already sent communist agents into China, many of whom were close to Sun Yat Sen; it was these years that caused Madame Sun Yat Sen (Madame Chiang's sister) to give up her hope in (and maybe her faith) in democracy.

Now, today: forty years later, your son is paying the price; the slowness with which democracy works! the sins we commit in the meantime! All this cripples us; bludgeons us; makes us go to the extreme of hating our own government as some of these college students do. They are hating something else: I know that; I have worked with the young all my life; I started off with the young sit-inners down here, encouraged them; urged them to hold on to nonviolence. Now, some of them are turning into nihilists, into anarchists of a kind of pseudo kind. Why? Because the white people of this country, in South and North, have been too slow. It is like the situation in China in the early 1920's: we whites have had our chance now for five years to do something wonderful and what have we done? We've made the young civil rights workers force us into every step we've taken! And they are hurt, they are resentful, they are angry kids now: they are saying What the hell is nonviolence, anyway? just a state of comfort for the whites? And inconsistently, of course—but we are all inconsistent—they become violent here at home and insist that we not be violent at all in Viet Nam!

It is not easy for President Johnson; I trust this man more than many of my northern friends do; because I know how all white southerners are brainwashed from infancy; I know that not one politician from the South could have gotten to Congress without taking a public stand for segregation. They all have, they all still do—except now four or five in the upper states. I knew from things Johnson said in his southern speeches when running for vice-president that he put the state of being human above the state of being white; no white southerner can deceive me; we speak down here a cryptic language at times; we speak a form of lie that every white southerner immediately translates into the truth it is intended to convey. Of course our white northern friends are confused by this secret language—a language we had to create because for 100 years we have been under an authoritarian, an almost completely totalitarian government of our states; and the national government did not reach down and pull us free from our captors—who were our state governors, and all our other officials, including the police force. We developed this cryptic language; when Johnson spoke it I knew he was OK: I knew and I got—and millions of southerners got— the message he was sending across to us. From this time on, he was saying, I am for the human being first, the American second, the southerner third; but "whiteness" doesn't count any more. So—what has happened? he has done more than any President in a hundred years to see that Negroes get their rights and their privileges.

But it has been too slow; and white southerners have sinned to almost an unpardonable degree by that terrible slowness which now is forcing the young Negroes into a mood they prayed to avoid in the early days.

I approve of the protests; I just wish they could be decent, sane, reasonable protests; but once again, too much pressure, too much delay brings the animal, the crazy-fool out in us!

Thank you for sending me your thoughts.

I hope you will read my *Killers of the Dream*; in paperback and hard. Don't let a Calif. bookstore tell you it is out of print.

tlc, UGA

 Earlier in 1965 Wilma Dykeman Stokeley had written a review of *Our Faces, Our Words* for the *Chattanooga Times* that pleased Smith. She and her husband James Stokeley, coauthors of *Neither Black nor White* (1958) and *Seeds of Southern Change: The Life of Will Alexander* (1962), had known Smith and Snelling since 1941 and shared an interest in writing about and working for social change in the South. Significantly, even while encouraging the three younger women—Louise Blackwell, Frances Clay, and Joan Titus—who were then interested in writing critical studies of her life and work, Smith turned to one who not only appreciated her work but also shared her experience of gender, race, class, time, and place and asked that she write of her "as writer and woman."

October 30, 1965

Dear Wilma:

It is late, close to midnight; I have been listening to that amazing pianist Richter play old familiar things such as Schumann's *Papillons*, and his Second Sonata. He plays divinely, except sometimes—on this recording at least—his left hand bangs when it should be strong, bold, loud and resonant. It sounds as though his left shoulder has stiffened but it may be all the fault of the recording or the piano he used. Anyway, I have been lying in my livingroom looking out on a mountain that was blazing in color at sunset and now is a dark blob with a very bright star just above it—a planet I should know, I suspect; or the big star of a constellation. I've always loved to stare at the stars and have never wanted to know their names; name stuck on a star somehow seems a silly, strictly human and not very nice-human thing to me.

Lately, I have thought of you often; ever since that beautifully tender, understanding—understanding from the point of view not of racial ideology or even human goodness, but of quality of writing—review you did of my last little book, the monologues. Four of them have been done for a recording by Spoken Arts; I'd like to send you one from me, if you'd care for it. [. . .]

I wish so much that sometime—while I am living or afterward—that you'd do at least a magazine study of me as writer and woman; of course my interest and longtime concern about segregation (both for the sake of Negro and white) would have to be part of anything written about me but I feel that you see more; and that you understand the southern situation so well and have known me over such a long span of time that your orientation would be accurate and your approach sensitive. Paula thinks so too. Whether you do it before the old cancer finally gets me doesn't really matter; but you should get your material from me or much of it before I get beyond the place of being able to help you. That is, if such a thing appeals. It may not; and that is all right, too; for temperamentally, we have to feel something deep and if we don't, we don't. I once had to refuse a famous Negro woman who begged me to do her biography; I just couldn't feel rapport, her mind was not interesting to me, her personality was, but I could not have dealt with that without being so frank that the book couldn't have been published during her lifetime. She was hurt; we continued to be friends but she did not understand that writers have to feel the other person on many levels of existence. In the case of a writer, one has to be both critical and appreciative, I think; and the life has to somehow make a pattern that in itself says the individual, unique thing about this one person and at the same time becomes almost a symbol of a way of life. I know writing about people raises all kinds of complex problems; and a hesitancy on your part will not hurt me in the least; I simply want you to know I'd like for you to do it if the idea ever appeals to you.

As I look at my life I see it as such a mixture of good and evil, shall we say? The words "noble" and "prophet" and "saint" that are used by some writers who do little pieces on me somehow seem false to me. I am so full of dreams and ideals, yes; I have felt a deep commitment to be a writer who will mirror her time and place; but I have never had a "calling" just to "help the Negro" or "to better race relations." [. . .]

I am sinner as well as saint, a grubby craftsman who cares terribly how her sentences are put together and her paragraphs as well as "prophet." I want people to have better lives but I am fascinated by the lives they do live and as artist I look at those lives as they are, not as they ought to be. I am also quick-tempered, full of wild humor, I shock my close friends sometimes by my uninhibited speech (Dr. Embree of the Rosenwald Fund used to call it "Lillian's vivacity," while Dr. Will [Alexander] would wink at me and chuckle. He had enough of old Satan in him to recognize old Satan in me.) So—when I read about this woman so well-mannered, so quietly calm and serene, so courageous I sometimes wonder who she is. I know I have taken 13 years of cancer quietly and I have fought like a tiger to live at times; I am crushed by anybody's misery. I am warm and I ache for strangers almost as much as for my own family when they are in distress; but I can be irascible, too; and impatient. I hate hypocrisy but I also adore watching an old hypocrite go through his tricks. To tell you the truth I have so many selves that I wonder sometimes how I'd do an autobiography. I have touched the fringes of hell again and again and almost once or twice barely touch[ed] the edge of heaven. I think I am more novelist than anything else; from age five and six—according to my mother and others who knew me—I seemed to feel it was my "vocation" to watch their words, their acts, and to "put it all together." Mother used to say to me, "The whole world is one big novel to you, isn't it? People are not people, they are characters to you; you mustn't try to see all around them, the way you do; you can do that only in books." And I didn't answer her (I was fourteen then) but I said to myself, "I can see all around them and it scares me to death to know I can do it." But I didn't want to worry Mother so I didn't say anything else. But now and then (she read a great deal but did not have nearly as good a mind as did my father) she said softly, "There you go again; you just can't understand everybody." But I thought I could; and when I couldn't I loved to see how far I could go and when I reached that place where everything was dark and seemed simply to "end" about that person, I kept thinking If only I were wiser I'd see more and more and more—

If there is anything valid in me talent-wise it is this ability to feel not only compassion but empathy, not only empathy but a deep sense of identity so that when I thought about a murderer I knew just why and how he could kill; when I thought of a traitor I knew just how and why he could betray; and so on. So it has been hard for me to be flattened out and cut around and misshaped into the stereotype I have strangely enough become. Three fires nearly ruined me; all were set; the one that burned all my manuscripts, 13,000 letters etc. nearly broke my heart. I have been threatened by dynamiters. I have had hundreds of mean calls but none of this could really hurt (yes, I got scared at times); what hurt was the fact that "nice people" took away from me my talent as though I didn't possess it; they stole my creativity from me; that is, they say I am not creative, not talented, not "a writer" just a nice woman helping Negroes find for themselves a better life. They somehow found exactly the way to crush me. (Of course the loss of my manuscripts, ready for publication but here and no copies elsewhere and the letters hurt but in a different way from this other hurt.)

So, as time goes by and I have another and another attack of cancer (or a new one appears—there have been six up to now) I think "Am I really going down in history as just the 'brave little woman who spent her life helping

Negroes' or am I ever going to be acknowledged as the writer I think I am—and many Europeans think I am." What tricks life plays on us! I am called brave when I am actually scary; I do what seems to me must be done and I don't think of the consequences; but I have my shivering days, too. Now—I must stop because fatigue is creeping on me; I have talked casually, in a way; desultorily, even carelessly perhaps; just as though we two were sitting here in the dim room looking out on the mountain. The music must have shaken me up inside. I have wanted to write you for a long time. I did not intend to be so candid, so deepdown as a confession. But never mind; you are sensitive, you will know what I feel and am thinking. And I am glad I've said it to you. [. . .]

tlc, UGA

TO GEORGE BROCKWAY

November 30, 1965

Dear George:

Thank you for your good, most thoughtful—and comforting—letter telling me about your valiant efforts to get *Memory* moving. I hope it all works; it should—but God knows if it will, our moods North and South being what they are these days. But it cheers me to know that you are pushing it and I do appreciate it.

I have been a bit shocked at myself for getting so hurt by that National Institute mess. At first, it made me mad; and I reacted freely but I hope courteously to the prick it gave my glands. Then, after writing the letters, it began to seem funny; so for a day or two I could laugh it off. Then suddenly, a heavy depression settled on me. I was paralyzed and could not write; somehow I felt almost for the first time in my life that I really could not write, that it had been a dream-nightmare, an illusion and a damned silly one to think I could. It all seemed so Kafkan—it still does; for they chose the only way they could truly hurt me and hurt bad, by diminishing me to exactly nothing as a writer. And everything they wrote made it worse. I sent Lewis Mumford a copy of the correspondence for we have been friends and he has written me (oh privately, not publicly has he said it) about *Journey* being such an extraordinary book. I had heard he was president or something of the Institute. Well, the letter back was full of sweetness and gentle patronage: he said he was so sorry that I did not feel I could accept the money for had I done so it would have made it easier for this Revolving Fund committee to offer it to other writers who might need it more than I do. Did you ever hear of such? What does he think I am, Mother Mary? always ready to help all the others. He also told me it was more blessed to receive than to give. Well—it is no need to put down here the profane words I screamed at him (silently). Of all the asinine virtuousness. Then he admitted (he did have the grace to do that) that he probably would have rejected it, too, just as I did. Then he jumped on me because I do not share his rabid hatred of President Johnson nor do I think saying "Negotiate!" and come home solves the Viet Nam thing. He said he was shocked at my attitude—"even Lillian Smith." I wanted to say, "Even Lillian Smith—what?" I wanted to say, "Lewis, you are a coward; you've never actually been on the firing line risking your life for any of your principles and I've spent my life risking my actual life, career, friends, happiness, serenity, everything for what I believe in, and you DARE tell me "even Lillian Smith has become reactionary." His public statement was so rude, so crudely worded that I simply could not sign it; I said nothing and did not sign. But in my letter I told him quietly, gently that I couldn't agree that telling the President to negotiate would accomplish anything. I answered his letter [he asked me not to, so that (he said) we wouldn't "argue" with each other]. I answered it and reminded him that since 1922 while in China I had been trying to get us all to see China's situation, to help Sun Yat Sen when we could have; I had tried always to get us to recognize China, to admit China to the UN: I had spoken out for coexistence while in India (1955) and had been banned by the embassy out there from speaking at any official American project. And here he is, telling me off. But I didn't stay mad; I just got more depressed; and more unable to write—anything. And then the old body reacted; the Prednesone is not helping me as it did for five months; depression kills cancer patients and I know it; I know I must fight this out. But along with this Institute thing have come several more instances of mean "backdoor" treatment. One: a telegram from a prominent Negro (who refused to blurb *Our Faces, Our Words*) saying how grateful she felt for me, for all I had done. How can a person do this sort of thing, George? Absolutely silent about my book; she was in a position to push it; I had read hers in ms. or galleys and spent a day or two helping her with it; I had also blurbed it for her publishers. But dead silence when mine came out. No help from her—then this telegram. Then a reporter in Atlanta who started off pushing me last summer: he began to backtrack in August; by late August he was able to write a piece scolding northern critics for not including southern writers in their list of "really important writers" and then

naming Carson McCullers and one or two more but leaving me out completely. He had sent me a book; he had sent me candy. I didn't say a word
when I was publicly snubbed like that. Then the Governor had a Ga.
Writers Week and the *Atlanta Journal* (*Constitution* never mentions me so I
don't even look) listed about 50 living Ga. writers (most of them I had never
heard of) but did not mention me. They listed Ralph McGill as the writer
who had done the big race job; absolute silence about me. The piece was
unsigned but in a prominent place in the paper. Then this reporter had the
nerve to send me another big box of candy. Backdoor giving of presents
instead of prestige—just as we whites used to do our servants, our mam-
mies. Well—what could I do? Send the candy back? Refuse to acknowledge
it and maintain my silence? Both treatments seemed wrong. So I wrote him
a courteous, kind, almost warm letter in which I laid it on the line. No
backdoor relationship with me; after all, why a relationship in the first place
unless it concerned me as a writer? We have no other common interest. I
hated to send it. I loathe making a scene, a crisis out of something. [. . .]
These little humiliations are the killing ones; being burned out, dynamited
or threatened with dynamiting (as I was last winter)—those things make
you feel you've accomplished something; to be hated by the right people
can seem honorable. But this kind of treatment—people being sweet to you
and then denigrating your life's work? Well, it is hard for me to take.

Thank you for the *Reappraisals*; I've read several, they are good. Am
reading Monique Nathan's *Virginia Woolf*—a beautiful book, really beautiful; photographs wonderful, excerpts from Woolf's writings just right; just
enough about her. All very good.

[. . .]

tlc, UGA

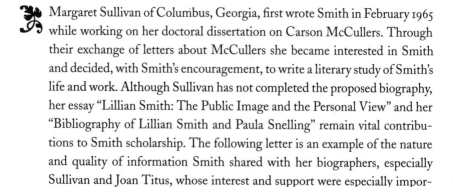 Margaret Sullivan of Columbus, Georgia, first wrote Smith in February 1965
while working on her doctoral dissertation on Carson McCullers. Through
their exchange of letters about McCullers she became interested in Smith
and decided, with Smith's encouragement, to write a literary study of Smith's
life and work. Although Sullivan has not completed the proposed biography,
her essay "Lillian Smith: The Public Image and the Personal View" and her
"Bibliography of Lillian Smith and Paula Snelling" remain vital contributions to Smith scholarship. The following letter is an example of the nature
and quality of information Smith shared with her biographers, especially
Sullivan and Joan Titus, whose interest and support were especially important to Smith in the final months of her life.

Dear dear Margaret:

Like David, with Saul, you soothed me and blessed me with your words. Thank you. It was the kind of thing I like best in you—when you are very serious and grown-up and oh so sensitively aware—and I needed it. Thank you again. I am fighting the depression—fighting it rationally, first—which seldom helps much; and fighting it by putting my mind on other people and their needs (something my old conscience, the Martha in me, responds to) and fighting it by telling my creativity to get to work and work day and night.

[. . .]

Today, I had six visitors from Italy. They are making a TV show on Martin Luther King and wanted me in it; so they drove up this morning from Atlanta, rigged up their machines and stayed with me for two hours. I enjoyed them. At first, I felt I was talking into a vacuum—as the leader of the group had to confess he had never heard of me until he reached Atlanta, so I gave him an Italian copy of *Killers of the Dream* and one of *Strange Fruit*. At first, it was hard; they were not used to my finer nuances, and the subtleties of my view of "our problem" and he simply was not prepared even to listen to it, at first. Then he began to get fascinated—and I felt the professional head of the group (the younger man was the public relations man, although he was more than that for it was really his pet project) caught on quickly to what I was trying to say. Another thing that interested me, was this: he quoted several southerners and commented on their beautiful words, their phrases—and everyone of the phrases were from some of my books. This pleased me; after all, that is what I am doing: enriching our vocabulary of human relationships; but since he had never read me he did not realize that the ideas were first put down by me. I liked this, however; and I felt maybe this is the way I will do my creative job: enlarging the psychological and philosophical awareness of the others by my words. Anyway, the day was nice; they[,] as I have always found Italians, were warm, quick to respond to every social nuance; when they arrived we gave them strong hot coffee with hot milk (they applauded me for that) and warm brownies which Mozelle had just pulled out of the oven. So: that started things off well—and while I am fatigued now that it is all over, still, it was good for me; and I hope I said a little that will help their TV show. It will be in Italy and in Italian, of course, with only a few English words now and then to give the sound of voices etc. Did I tell you I did—when Joan Titus came down—two hours of excerpts from *The Journey*. She persuaded Time-

Life Broadcast to let her borrow their elegant machine; we made the readings in my bedroom—acoustically very good place—and while my voice was a bit weak, I had that mean throat and viral malaise at that time, I believe all in all they won't be bad. I hope the next time she comes [. . .] I can do some excerpts from *Strange Fruit*: the one where Laura's mother destroys the piece of sculpture in her angered jealousy of Laura's friend, Jane; the little scene in the garden when Tillie kills the snake as her children watch (a kind of metaphor of the whole book, or at least the Negroes' part of the book); and the scene where Tracy denigrates Nonnie and turns her from the girl he loves to the "nigger" he sleeps with.* Then Esther and I want to do the Miss Susie scene from *The Journey*; Es is coming home for Christmas; [. . .]. I love her very much and shall be so happy to have her here. While she is here, maybe we'll make on my machine (not really a bad one) the Miss Susie scene, Esther doing the wacky, mad Miss Susie while I do myself, the commentator.

[. . .]

tlc, UGA

In notes for her biographers Smith listed Marjorie White of Jasper, Florida, as her oldest childhood friend. White and Paula Snelling had also known each other as students together at Wesleyan College in Macon, Georgia.

December 17, 1965

My very dear Marjorie:

It is always so good to hear from you at Christmas. And now, instead of sending a card I am going to try a letter. To catch you up on things. And perhaps, you will sometimes do the same for me. For as the years pass my old childhood friendship with you becomes sweeter and more cherished by me. How I adored you when I was a little girl! We began going with each other at age six, I think. I don't remember a time when I did not know you. [. . .] [T]he constant running back and forth to your house and to mine; your big family (Blackwell-White) fascinated me; your family had a sophistication my family did not at that time have. Your grandmother liked my father and in a way helped "bring him up" in that she discussed books with him, ideas, scolded him for foolish ideas and for too much puritanism and too much "evangelism" etc. She was good for him. A marvelous lady,

---

*This recording of Smith reading from *Strange Fruit* was made by Joan Titus in 1966 and brought out by Spoken Arts, Inc.

your grandmother. I have often wanted to write about her—changing her of course, but getting the essence of her strength and vitality, etc. And always I was adoring Marjorie; we had a very real friendship, a collaboration of the dream as two children often have; we had books but the books in your home were more appropriate for a child to read than most of those in mine; it was your Alcott books I first read; then later, I had my own; but even so, most were yours. I remember sitting under the banana shrub and reading there; why I wanted to crouch under there I don't know but I did; I remember the cucumber pickles your grandmother made that were better than any in the whole world; how you and I could do away with an entire "jar" we called it then in one day as we read. We could spend the day and read read read; hardly speak; but there was a community of the dream between us; we'd look up at each other, know what the other was feeling, go back to our books. We'd kneel down and pray sometimes asking God to persuade Mother (or your mother) to let us spend the night with each other. The prayers were not usually answered; although our parents were quite amenable about these spend the night parties. I often think of these small things for this past year has been a lonely one for me—I was not strong enough to leave the mountain ridge often—and I find myself going back to the old memories. [. . .]

It is strange how the two of us—so separated by space and surface interests—have moved along much the same paths; this has interested me and pleased me no end and Paula has often commented on it, too. Paula is just FINE; I write it, in caps; because she had 20 years when I felt she was lost, lost to herself, to the world—I can't go into it; but she was too close to me; I overshadowed her and somehow, well, she could not get a feeling about her own Self; when she finally felt she could take a job again—she had a long period of being unable to take a job, she feared it so—she became Paula again; it has been marvelous for her; this is her fifth year as librarian at Tallulah Falls School—a semi-private school but a tie-up with the state. Beautiful buildings; small student group (integrated now) and with a fairly good faculty—at least they all have to have their M.A.'s. Paula is doing something on her own; I never go down there; it is her job, her group, her project, her everything; and being on her own, out of my shadow, being Paula—a wonderful person who wins her own friends and forms her own interests—well, it has saved her. And I am made so happy by this; partly because I feared what would happen were I to die; I have had to use my savings helping Wallace and his family and for 13 years of hospitals and treatments for cancer etc. Now she has her own money; she is able to save; of course I've done what I could—

given her her little house and some land etc.—and I can die (if that is my fate) knowing that (a) she has enough to live on and (b) something to do that keeps her busy and interested. This is somewhat confidential, please; few of her friends know what a terrific time she had emotionally and psychically for so long; she was sheltered here with me; she helped me when she could; she is always such a lovely person to live with; our minds love each other; our temperaments sometimes clash but we both can forgive, we both understand and have patience with each other. She has been tender and good to me while I was ill. I keep a maid to be with me on this lonely mountain and to do the work; so Paula is not burdened that way; she lives in her own little rock house; we have dinner together every night; I am usually able to fix it or at least do my share—and Mozelle prepares things before she leaves in the afternoon. So we manage without Paula having to wait on me or do for me; but knowing she is on the ridge—we have a communication system that works—is the comforting thing for me. I often go four or five months without calling her at night; but now and then when the lung was so bad (it is better now) and my breathing would get pretty difficult, I could call her, she would come to my little house, crawl in the other bed and at least be with me and help me with my oxygen tank etc. And we talk about books, ideas, people, the world, the future, God—just as we always have done. Paula does not communicate much with her old friends but she still loves you and values her friendship with you. She has grown very pretty in her old age; and often looks ten years younger than she is.

[. . .]

tlc, UGA

 According to SNCC historian Clayborne Carson, SNCC staff members debated the merits and dangers of taking a public stand against the U.S. policies in Vietnam throughout the fall of 1965 before authorizing their executive council to draft an antiwar statement. The preparation of such a statement moved slowly, however, until January 3, 1966, when Sammy Younge, a twenty-one-year-old navy veteran and Tuskegee student who had worked with SNCC during the Montgomery demonstrations in March 1965, was shot to death for attempting to use a "white" restroom in Tuskegee. Three days later SNCC's executive committee issued a statement comparing the murder of Younge with the murder of Vietnamese and denouncing the hypocrisy of the U.S. government's claiming to preserve freedom in the world while violating international law in Vietnam and failing to enforce U.S. laws at home. Announcing their sympathy for draft resisters, the statement urged Americans to work in the civil rights movement as a valid alternative to the draft. A rash of public criticism was unleashed against SNCC, and on January 10 Julian Bond, formerly communications director for SNCC, was denied his newly won seat in the Georgia Assembly because he supported SNCC's antiwar stand.[7]

Disagreeing with both SNCC's statement and the Georgia legislators' refusal to seat Bond, Lillian Smith wrote a letter to the editor of the *Atlanta Constitution*, Eugene Patterson, in which she said that although the SNCC statement had hurt the movement, SNCC had the right to say what it did and that the Georgia Assembly did not have the right to oust Bond. In keeping with her support of Lyndon Johnson, she concluded: "Neither SNCC nor the Georgia legislature is helping Johnson bring us closer to peace." The *Constitution* published Smith's letter on the editorial page Friday, January 14, 1966, under the title "Old Dream, New Killers," and complemented it with a supportive editorial, "Lillian Smith Qualifies," which said in part:

> On this page today one of the distinguished women of American letters presents the most eloquent, and we believe the most accurate and profound, analysis of the Julian Bond incident that will be written.
>
> Her literary works, from *Strange Fruit* to *Killers of the Dream*, speak for her integrity. Her wise letter today merits honest reflection among every Southern white and every Southern Negro, for she has served and suffered for all, and seeks now to call us back from the edge of folly.

Smith's further discussion of her views of SNCC and the Bond affair in the following letter to Karl Menninger reveal in more detail her analysis of the situation. Her stand against the antiwar movement was strongly colored by her loyalty to President Johnson and by her view that U.S. policies concerning Vietnam were tied to earlier U.S. failures to constructively foster democracy in China. Her criticism of Dr. King's lack of toughmindedness indicates that Smith was not prepared to support those in the civil rights movement who no longer believed that the power structure itself could be reasoned with and made to change. While quite accurately criticizing the legislators and warning that they were reverting to dangerous old patterns by refusing to seat Bond, she still believed that the white legislators might listen to her and change their minds. In fact, it took two years of lawsuits and a U.S. Supreme Court order to seat Julian Bond in the Georgia Assembly, and the forces that led to radical changes in the movement and the dissolution of SNCC were more complex than Smith's assumptions that the innocents were being exploited by "intruders."

February 7, 1966

Dear Karl:

[. . .] How good of you, when you are so busy, to remember me! That letter in *Atlanta Constitution* (perhaps the Kisers sent it to you—Larry Kubie and they came up to see me a few weeks ago) was actually a private letter I wrote Eugene Patterson the young editor who in many ways is much more sincere, more brave and more deeply and humbly "liberal" than is Ralph McGill. For 20 years the *Constitution* has never said a good word about me, nor let me have a letter even in its public letter column. But young Patterson and I are friends; and for years I've written him letters to orient him or brief him about matters that I felt he was either mistaken about or else had had no real experience of. [. . .] Well—I wrote him when the Julian Bond thing came up—simply to give him my view and hoping as I mentioned to him that he might use any of the material or whatever in it that would help him. Next day he phoned me to say "they" wanted to run it as a letter from me. Somehow I had fitted right into their mood and point of view. I said yes, hesitantly; but I think it was all right to do it for it seems that white Georgia was slipping into a hysteria which has been avoided for years now and they hoped my letter would ease things and quiet people into a more thoughtful mood. It seemed to do just that; many people ready to jump on the Negro Movement held off; phone calls came to me, many many of them; letters from conservatives and half-liberals saying I had helped them understand the whole mess and that they, the decent people of Ga. must do something more positive.

The Mayor of Atlanta, Ivan Allen, wrote me a cozy little note "Dear Lillian" and signed "Ivan" thanking me for doing the letter. Old liberal friends called me to say, Thank God the *Constitution* has now given in and stopped treating me like a pariah. Etc. But when so many letters came I grew restive and began to think I had been too conservatively "reasonable"—but maybe not; maybe I put the wiggly little ducks in rows that somehow made sense to people.

Actually, the young Negroes are being led at present by three or four really foolish and hence dangerous revolutionaries; they are part of the New Leftist group; they are tinged with Maoist propaganda, lean toward Castro, have read Nietzsche and Marx a hundred years late; and are reading Spengler as if he wrote his stuff (lots of it good, as I know and you do, too) yesterday. But they don't see purpose in our living in this world; they can't discuss God without extreme embarrassment, they don't see a human future evolving; they think, as do most people, in spans of five years, ten, twenty, fifty instead of a hundred, five hundred, a thousand. They don't realize how terribly young the human race is; how we've just begun to grow and evolve ourselves; they can't get the feel of where we're going or how we're to get there. God knows, all of us act like fools and idiots but these kids feel sealed in Sartre's room with no exit. Now, the SNCC kids as a whole are OK—I mothered them through their first three years and I know; but this Jim Foreman came down from Chicago (a Negro school teacher who had plenty to do up there if he had looked around) and once in Atlanta took over the movement completely. He is The Boss. They have no democratic organization; they have no sponsors made of older citizens; a handful of them run the whole show, using the money that comes in just as they want to. But I want to say they've spent little of it on themselves; they are spartan in their needs and habits; except for round-the-world trips which they can't resist taking. They also have worked out some excellent projects within the last three years. But there are really two groups: Bob Moses in Miss., a Negro from Harvard, is the good one, the real saint of the movement; he is genuinely interested in helping the Negro people help themselves; he is the one who started the idea of community schools, the Freedom schools, the classes for adults, the educating of the masses etc. But in Atlanta this Jim Foreman with three or four white men from the North (one of them this mentally sick Staughton Lynd) are the dangerous ones. This "statement" was a deliberate attempt on their part to stir up the Legislature against Julian Bond so they'd have a new cause. Nobody had asked Bond or any other Negro legislator or white about his views on Viet Nam or foreign policy; they were not even thinking of such a thing; for the first time the urban legislators had enough representatives to get something done for the cities (especially for Atlanta) in housing, education, jobs, etc. This Julian Bond should have been helping with; but no, suddenly everybody was distracted by this "statement." Nobody knows who wrote it and certainly only a handful ever saw it or "passed" on it; it was a verbal bomb thrown at the legislature. [. . .] "We've been had," several of them said. But several were reported by my young friends on *Constitution* to have said out loud and before groups that though they knew they had been tricked, they dared not ignore it and let Bond in for they were getting hundreds of phone calls from their rural constituents. Of course, they should have had the sense and the guts to have done what was right, for their rural people would have simmered down in a few days. But they are so used to reacting with their reflexes (after all, they and their fathers before them were brainwashed for a century, you know) and they couldn't use their brains. The clever manipulators in SNCC knew this, of course, counted on just this and threw their bomb which promptly blew things to pieces.

The manipulators undoubtedly thought hard about what kind of statement would really upset the legislators. There were two that could do the job: (1) this one about treason and patriotism etc. etc. for the legislators themselves have said some pretty treasonous things in their fight to hold segregation; also Georgia has lost more boys in Viet Nam than any other state—so I've been told. And because SNCC used to be nonviolent—it isn't any more—Georgia legislators don't feel too good about nonviolence. The other statement could have been one saying that they believed a law should be passed in Georgia giving all citizens the right to intermarry. Well, SNCC didn't dare tackle that one. When they wrote their statement they decorated it with many insulting words, nasty adjectives that would make anybody mad were used about our government's dishonesty, it is cynical manipulating of the situation in South Viet Nam and North Viet Nam areas; there were Castro-style adjectives. It is a thoroughly nasty, insulting and dishonest statement calculated to make even me—and I've worried about Viet Nam and what we are doing out there—angry. It should be printed for people to read; everything in it could have been stated with courtesy and accuracy and would not have offended anybody. But the point—and everybody seems to overlook it—is that nobody had queried Julian Bond about his beliefs and had no intention of doing so; SNCC deliberately called a press conference four days before the legislature opened and read this statement. Then Julian Bond (who is a sincere C.O.) was asked about it and gave some tactless and foolish answers, just as did Prince Myshkin in Dostoevski's *The Idiot*. I've thought of *The Idiot* and Melville's *Billy Budd*; for Julian Bond, a poet and a very sincere, sweet lad with one kind of intelligence but not any shrewdness in his nature, reminds me of both Billy Budd and Prince Myshkin.

I've written a piece about this but so far no northern paper will touch it; they're afraid to look at the complexities of the civil rights movement; I saw this building two years ago while writing *Our Faces, Our Words*; and spoke of it in the last piece. I called these revolutionaries "the intruders"—I hoped SNCC would listen to that book; they didn't. CORE is different; so are NAACP and Urban League and of course Dr. King's group, SCLC; but King isn't too bright as a politician, he doesn't see things too clearly (he is fine, his integrity is real and I admire him)—but Karl, he needs some toughness of mind that he doesn't have. His father has more but I don't think young King listens to Papa much.

Well, this is to tell you how complicated these matters are; these intruders are ruining what once was a great youth movement.

[. . .]

tlc, UGA

James Reeb was one of three white ministers attacked by local whites in Selma, Alabama, on March 10, 1965, after a massive voting rights demonstration led by Martin Luther King was temporarily halted by police. Reeb's death a few days later brought nationwide support for the Selma project, including President Johnson's nationally televised speech calling for new voting rights legislation. At the time of his death Smith joined others in the movement, especially SNCC workers, in pointing out the discrepancy in the president's response to the death of Reeb, a white man, as compared to the lack of response to that of Jimmy Lee Jackson, a young black man whose death at the hands of police in Marion, Alabama, prompted the original plans for the Selma-to-Montgomery march.[8]

Smith's comments in the following letter, however, reflect her growing concern that the civil rights movement as she knew it was getting out of control, in part because she felt that northerners were having more influence than their knowledge and experience merited. Her discussion of these feelings with a publisher was typical of her use of correspondence to air views for which she might not otherwise find an audience.

TO HARPER & ROW PUBLISHERS, INC.

February 8, 1966

Gentlemen:

I have just finished reading Duncan Howlett's *No Greater Love*. It is a moving book and of extraordinary fairness. There is nothing sentimental about it, there is no anger against the poor whites of the south, the account of James Reeb's visit to Alabama is told with a factual precision unmuddled by hate or outrage, hence the reader is given the chance to see the problems that beset both Negro and white in Alabama with unusual clarity and justness.

I knew Jim Reeb personally—of course not in the intimate way Duncan Howlett knew him but well enough that I felt the man on these pages. I am also impressed by Duncan Howlett's writing skill: the material is handled skillfully, he has a nice narrative sense, we get Jim Reeb in all his subtle ambiguities—for there are ambiguities in this man's personality; we feel the pulls on him against which his reason sometimes rebels: the conscience that won't let go of him even when his mind tells him perhaps his usefulness might be more to the point if he stayed in the north. (Of course, I think it would have been; this is what is so sad; deeply sincere, courageous people who come South "to help" but are so ignorant of real conditions down there, so unaware of the lurking dangers down every side street.) It is a battleground down there and only veterans who know can do the job that needs to be done; I am torn by gratitude that so many northern whites want to help and frightened by their lack of know-how, by their complete unawareness not only of the dangers but the desperate psychology of the poor whites; and also, I keep wondering—will you forgive me for saying so?—why the Alabama problems upset northerners more than Harlem, more than South Side, more than Boston's ghetto and the rest of it; yet at the same time, had these 25,000 not come down to help (there were quite a few white southerners among them which the newspapers and TV did not stress) "the miracles" would not have happened; and there has been a miracle in both Alabama and Mississippi; not that things are good down there, as yet; they're very bad, still; but a definite change has taken place and those 25,000 from the rest of the country helped bring this change about. We need both: concern for Negroes in the South and concern for them in the North; being foreign missionaries (my family is full of them!) is alluring; and yet it is dangerous and seductive; what it has bred in the North is an awesome complacency, a rather unpleasant hubris. I've stayed down here on the firing line most of my life, knowing those of us who know it in our bloodstream and bones can be useful and sometimes not lose our lives; oh, I've been burned out twice, my home, my study and all my letters, manuscripts, all the data of my life destroyed. I have been shunned for years at a time—things are much better now for me—this kind of thing will happen to all who work against segregation and the poor whites' fears and resentments; but usually we know just enough not to get killed! We don't know enough to keep from losing jobs, being socially shunned and having our houses burned. But as I read Jim Reeb's story I kept thinking, Oh, if only someone had warned him not to take that different street he took! A white southerner would have known not to do it; also, Jim should have been alert as he would have been in battle and kept aware of what was creeping up on him. I am not criticising, I am mourning what still seems to me a heroic, a selfless but an unnecessary death. Of course, I don't know; each of us must do what our conscience requires of us; I have done some pretty asinine things in my life believing I "should"—but we can't be sure; and the old conscience says we must; the heart whispers we must and though our shrewd intelligence warns that a conscience and a heart are not always reliable, still—well, what can you do, if you are that kind of person, but obey?

I review books regularly for *Chicago Tribune*; I hope they'll let me do this one; I'll ask for it; for I'd like to raise some questions which may, in their turn, arouse a desire in people to read about Jim Reeb again. [. . .] I have known Dr. Howlett too and admire him very much, both his acute intelligence (which is superior to Jim Reeb's) and his grasp of American and world affairs.

Use any thing you want to of this for a blurb if it will help; a review will help more and I'll ask for the book. [. . .]

tlc, UGA

 Smith's last published essay was the introduction to *Ely* (Seabury Press, 1966), the autobiography of Ely Green, the son of a black woman and a white man reared in Sewanee, Tennessee.

TO ARTHUR R. BUCKLEY, EDITOR, SEABURY PRESS

February 8, 1966

Dear Mr. Buckley:

The book of Ely Green's is remarkable—and of extraordinary interest to me. I was fascinated by it; I felt somebody had taken me back even beyond my early childhood into those two decades before I began to remember things. It is so right; so true, as I know the twisting, ambivalent, ambiguous, good-evil-sweet-gracious-boorish South. And to hear from an almost illiterate (but highly intelligent) Negro man is a wrenching experience, even though all he said is familiar to me. Wrenching because my intuition, my child memory, my anguished (and often delighted) heart told me it was true; but here it comes from the other end of the arc, not even from a Negro woman but from a Negro man.

When I read the LeRoi Jones, the James Baldwins, and the other urban Negro haters who don't know the South at all but try to pretend they do (nothing is more absurd than Baldwin's writing of the South) I find myself getting angry; God knows we are evil enough, but it is another kind of evil, an evil so mixed with good, a sweetness so mixed with bitterness that it can drive whites and blacks utterly mad. It is so different from what the northern Negroes say it is. Maybe any educated Negro, truly educated, would need to bury these old memories in order even to become educated, even to gain new knowledge; for this kind of life we used to live was half disease, half gracious living. What could be harder to disentangle? what harder to grow out of! I think that is why so many decent, "good" people in the South are silent: they are so torn by the old memories of good and bad they are pulled equally in two opposite directions; they know they were never grossly brutal as are Klan etc., today, yet they know the love they felt for Negroes and the love Negroes felt for them was real, authentic; and yet somehow terribly terribly destructive.

Well, some of this had better go into my introduction; I am beginning to work on it today and I'll get it to you around Feb. 21. [. . .]

tlc, UGA

TO NORMAN COUSINS, EDITOR, *Saturday Review*

March 3, 1966

Dear Norman:

As I look over these past years, thinking of the troubles and burdens, and the sweet, good things that have come my way, I find that I put you near the top of the good things. How kind you have been to me! How compassionate and understanding and generous—I shall never forget.

My dear, you don't owe me any money; I am therefore returning the check with a deep feeling of gratitude; of course I am touched by your sending it to me, but you see: *I* owe *you* a piece, you don't owe me anything. [. . .] I was hoping the Roast Pig and Orpheus* thing might do; but I also knew that there was a big chance it wouldn't; it is such a special kind of thing, suggesting subtly many things it does not really say; it might puzzle most readers, except those close to the specific situation. [. . .] What I am really trying to say in it is that the vacuum left by the old white indoctrination of both Negroes and whites is a dangerous thing and must be filled by a new belief; and this is so likely to be an ideology instead of a real philosophy. That human relations will be ignored and pushed aside while empty hearts and minds seek a new ideology. I think this explains the utterly asinine behavior of the Ga. Legislature; and it also explains the asinine behavior of the four or five leaders of SNCC who have almost ruined our young man Julian Bond (such a fine boy, he is). Much that is similar to this is happening today in Communist China; for the Chinese young were left stripped of the ancient (2000 years) filial piety and the Red Chinese have been trying to fill that vacuum—with curious results. [. . .]

I feel, Norman, that we are letting ourselves get caught in the old epi-

*The essay Smith wrote about SNCC's antiwar statement and Julian Bond's being denied his seat in the Georgia Assembly.

cyclic run-around when we all argue about Viet Nam instead of confronting our problems with China. [. . .] I have no illusions about Mao or the group around him; I know some of them have paranoid ideas that are dangerous; they have not only used the most horrifying technics ever used to brainwash students and foreigners, unfortunately these methods have brainwashed their own minds, too. Just the same, we should use our energies and words to get China into the UN—or at least let her know that the USA wants her there—we should trade with her as much as possible; we should acknowledge the Mao regime as the de facto government of the mainland; we should establish steadily more and more relationships with her. I believe this. Therefore I have found it almost impossible to go off the deep end protesting the war in Viet Nam; of course it is a mess but it started under Eisenhower and Dulles and we are now trapped.

Another thing that bothers me is Sane's strategies: I am a sponsor of Sane; you are I think on its Board. I simply cannot agree that people like us who can write articulately should be marching on the White House. I also do not believe in street demonstrations except in local and domestic matters; any international matter should be, must be handled with care, with finesse, keeping all the subtle complexities in mind; how can a street march do this? It is reported all over the world and does our government great harm; carefully thought out criticism when spoken or written does not do us much harm and is necessary in order to educate the minds of our people. But marches are not educational: they push toward action but in international affairs "the people" cannot act—except through their President. I would think Norman Thomas would see this; he has been urging me hard to support this April march; I do not intend to do so. This isn't the way; they say President Johnson is influenced by people's votes; but this threat to vote for candidates on just one issue is ridiculous; the people marching hardly know where Viet Nam is; they couldn't give us 25 important facts about Asia's history for the past 60 years; they are screaming and yelling about something they know nothing much about. This distresses me and shocks me. Another thing that shocks me is to hear so-called nonviolent people, pacifists etc., use four-letter words, stridently violent adjectives; some of them call up the widows of men killed in Viet Nam; how can they do such things. Even Lewis Mumford's statements (and letters) are so terribly angry; this rage is fascinating to me—I am a critic and novelist you know—although people seem to forget it—and I find myself more fascinated by an angry Mumford than by a "cause." Why? Why such anger? Against whom is it turned?

Well, enough of this. I hope more and more of us can write something to substitute for these dangerous slogans.

tlc, UGA

TO GEORGE BROCKWAY

June 4, 1966

George:

I was operated on at Emory Hospital this past Wednesday; exploratory surgery during which a new cancer was located on the left side, completely across from all the others. Since pathology showed the usual malignant breast cells we know it is another metastasis. My seventh go-round. Dr. Brown did not try to remove tumor; too dangerous; just closed the wound up. I go to Atlanta to begin more cobalt (I take to it like goats take to tin cans so it probably won't be too lethal for me, although I've already had more than human beings are supposed to take.) Dammit it—my luck is mean lately: all this a month before Medicare begins! I'll come home each weekend; and while there will try to study, read and write. Have plenty to do if I can find the energy to do it. [. . .] Dr. Brown let me leave Emory Hospital 24 hours after surgery; I had local anaesthesia as my heart and lungs are now protesting a general anaesthesia and personally I like the local fine; I could ask questions and the surgeons talked to me as if they were having a clinic session. It was rather fun—certainly not in the least gruesome and most interesting for they told me what they found, how they found it, and talked over their decisions where I could hear; I like to be a member of everything, operations, funerals (don't know how to manage that one) as well as other things.

I've felt wretched for months; was pretty sure a new trouble was brewing but was examined five weeks ago with none finding it. Well—here we go again! Dr. Brown said he had never known a cancer to appear in such an odd place; but then I'm different, as he said; he told some young doctors "She's always different—about everything." Then he was very nice, he smiled at me and said "and the most wonderful patient I ever knew." So—that made me feel good, I must say. I do tease and carry on and I don't mourn; how can mourning help? I'll fight, tooth and nail, scream and yell if I think some good will come from it but cancer is very deaf as I have discovered; it is best to make like you're friendly with it.

[. . .]

tlc, UGA 2126

After twenty years of service on CORE's national advisory committee, Smith sent the following telegram to Floyd McKissick, national director of the Congress of Racial Equality, upon learning that delegates to CORE's national convention had voted to delete "the technique of nonviolence in direct action" as a requirement for chapter affiliation. Furthermore, like SNCC, the CORE delegates officially embraced the rhetoric of black power, condemned U.S. involvement in Vietnam, and pledged support of draft resisters.[9] If Smith's official breaks with SNCC and CORE seem to leave her in the company of moderate voices in the movement, it is important to note that in her public statements as well as in her private correspondence she consistently criticized not only the civil rights activists and organizational leaders for decisions with which she disagreed but also the leaders of white society who by resisting change had in fact fostered the violence they claimed to abhor.

July 5, 1966

I strongly protest the dangerous and unwise position CORE has taken on the use of violence in effecting racial change. I am therefore resigning from your Advisory Committee. For many years CORE was firm in its belief in the use of nonviolence and refused tactics dictated by anger and hate. Its leaders believed that only love and compassion, reason and a vigilant search for truth could bring about creative human relations. Unfortunately the stubbornness and dishonest methods of segregationists, the violence of the Klan, the blind complacency of many white church people have made it easy for the haters to take over from the more wise and patient leadership. Now we have new killers of the dream. CORE has been infiltrated by adventurers and, by nihilists, Black Nationalists, and plain old fashioned haters who have finally taken over. But the whites must carry much of the moral burden of this having occurred. White Americans have not met the creative Negro leadership half way. They demand that Negroes show more wisdom and patience than they themselves show. CORE was pushed hard by the inertia and violence of many white Americans before its wise leadership succumbed. But I do not believe in the use of violence, however great the temptation. We are working for something bigger than civil rights; we are working for better human beings, we are working for excellence in our cultural life. How can we achieve these goals unless all of us meet this challenge with honesty and intelligence and good will and speed?

tlc, UGA

In the final weeks of her life, even while undergoing chemotherapy at Emory University Hospital, Smith continued to write letters. Still in demand as a speaker, she had received an invitation to participate in the centennial celebration of Howard University as one of four lecturers on the subject "Pathways to Peace: Today and Tomorrow." In recognition of her "lifetime obedience to the dictates of your conscience, whatever the cost," it was suggested that she speak on the topic "Conscience: Inner Motivations for Peace." In response she offered to send a tape of her thoughts on the subject, "Is it Conscience or Vision that we need for the human future—or is it perhaps both?"[10] Other correspondence involved final bequests, such as her gift of a copy of the *Ely* manuscript to the Southern Regional Council archives.[11]

Most treasured by their recipients, however, are the letters of appreciation and farewell Smith wrote to some of her closest friends and family. The last letter to her sister Esther has not been released for publication. Her friend Lou Howerton gave permission to publish only the following excerpt from her final letter from Smith, but in those few sentences Smith's relationship with Howerton and their mutual friend Kathryn Ulmer are placed at the heart of her conviction that life's ultimate meaning is revealed in relationships:

> I lay here—2 A.M.—thinking a thousand thoughts about you. You look at a life, yours or someone else's and wonder about how it all began: *Why*, years ago, was I born in Jasper, Florida, near the swamps? *Why* were you born years later in Virginia? Why was K.U. born, so to speak, between my birth and yours?
>
> What was it all for? An accident? Never could I believe that.[12]

The following letter to Joan Titus is the only one of the "final letters" available for publication in its entirety.

At Hospital
August 1966

Joan dear—

I love you.

When I say this, I have said something that is deep and meaningful to me.

It began in 1959—a slow relationship began. Hard at first for both of us. Because it had to be deep and real or *nothing*.

When I last saw you, I thought of course that I'd never see you again. It was sad and yet not terrible for I felt I would never see those I deeply loved again. In a sense a fact maybe Charles Williams could endure but hard for Lil.

What have you done for me? "Let me count the ways . . ." Never! It would be blasphemy.

But three things I want to say:

Charles Williams: a name, a book, ten books? No. A silent door swung open. There was a new horizon of human experience awaiting me. Yes, Mother too understood the Charles Williams world but only dimly, intuitively but enough that it was familiar to me. All those books . . . the talks we had—your lovely laughter—your deep fears which I so often share with you in a strange twin-like way. Your ecstasy—rare but there—I *respond* to this. Your little puritanisms which I laugh at and agree with—at least my body agrees.

But beyond Charles Williams has been something big and terrible and lovely: you gave me back my hope in the future and my faith in my ability to endure the pain of rejection without losing my creative energy.

I know I must often have seemed selfish and self-absorbed. I know this evil thing *ambition* has crept over me now and then, like the girl in *[The] Place of the Lion*. You have often helped lift me above that by your love and faith.

If I get well I want to help *you* in every way I can.

All the Smiths love you. Frank thinks you are a "grand gal." "She is real and solid," he says, "a girl of tremendous character."

I consider you one of my family. And at my funeral, there will be a brief service from the Methodist *Episcopal* service: 15 minutes perhaps. In our living room. No music. Stewart will quietly read it and close it with my father's old daily benediction. No tears. Just hope. I want you there with the family.

I am to be quietly buried by the chimney on the left hand side. I prefer that my family do not watch it as I am laid into the grave. They will close it swiftly and spread flowers over the ground.

That afternoon, there will be a memorial service to which will be invited friends from all over the world who care. All the Ivy Hill colored community will be invited. 30 special friends from Clayton but of course any may come who want to. Cars will park on Frank's hill, people will walk over. There will be Bach played while they are gathering. Very short service. Stewart will read 3 selections from *The Journey*: "But now I know: all death can do is kill a man; it cannot end his life; because of human memory, etc."

and the last paragraph in *Journey*. Frances Townsend, my music protegee, will sing *one song*—if she can get there. It will be at the close and she will wander to the edge of the trees and sing "I Know that My Redeemer Liveth." One verse of it.

At the beginning of the service, before Stewart reads, the little colored and white children (my neighbors) will meet guests with trays of flowers, give each guest a flower *with a smile*.

Nothing somber, no mourning.

This is it. Death to me is a beautiful ceremonial, an "escort into the unknown," by one's friends.

A copy of this will be attached to my will. Paula and Es each will have a copy. P. is likely to go completely to pieces. Esther will not. My family will not.

The Clayton girls who are old campers will be asked by my family to be hostesses on the hill to out of town guests and after memorial service, to see that they have a bite to eat before leaving town.

Now: forget all of these plans. Push it out of your mind. For *this* letter is a letter of love and thanks. No tears, my very dear Joan.

als, Joan Titus, Cornwall, Conn.

CODA

Lillian Smith died at Emory University Hospital on September 28, 1966, and was buried next to the big rock chimney on Old Screamer Mountain, with services exactly as she had requested. Her final letter to Paula Snelling did not materialize. Perhaps, as Snelling once said to me, when Smith had written something mentally, she saw it as completed. Or perhaps, to Paula she could not say good-bye. Either way, the significance of their relationship is clear. From her retirement as librarian at Tallulah Falls School in 1970 until a stroke in 1979 left her partially paralyzed, Snelling devoted her time primarily to the preservation of Smith's work, organizing Smith's papers and answering questions from Smith scholars. Until her death in 1985, Snelling's commitment matched that of Esther and Frank Smith in making sure that death did not end the life of Lillian Smith.

Notes

PREFACE

1. Unless otherwise noted, all biographical information comes from unpublished autobiographical materials in Box 1 of the Lillian Smith Collection, UGA (hereafter cited as autob. mats., UGA).

2. Evans and Boyte, *Free Spaces*.

CHAPTER ONE

1. The Smiths' first child, a son, died in infancy. For a more extensive discussion of Smith's childhood and familial relationships, see Miller, "Out of the Chrysalis."

2. Frank Smith, personal interview, 18 October 1980.

3. "Biographical Comments," autob. mats., UGA, 6.

4. Ibid., 4.

5. Ibid., 5.

6. "1925–48 Directing the Camp," autob. mats., UGA, 2.

7. Ibid.

8. "And Then I Heard Myself Say It," autob. mats., UGA.

9. Snelling, personal interview, 30 December 1979.

10. "And Then I Heard Myself Say It."

11. "1925–48 Directing the Camp," 3.

12. Ibid.

13. Snelling to Louise Blackwell and Frances Clay, 27 August 1966, UGA.

14. "Flashback to 1925–35," autob. mats., UGA, 1.

15. Ibid., 3.

16. Ibid.

17. Ibid., 4.

18. Ibid., 5.

19. "Travels and Education," autob. mats., UGA, 7–8.

20. "Comments for Maggie," autob. mats., UGA.

21. Robinson, "Lillian Smith," 47.

22. "Flashback, 1930–35: My Winters in Macon: My Writings," autob. mats., UGA, 8.

23. "1935–36: Transition," autob. mats., UGA, 10.

24. Snelling to Louise Blackwell and Frances Clay, 27 August 1966, UGA.

25. Snelling, personal interview, 14 December 1981.

26. Jones, "Private Steps and Public Vision."

27. Snelling, personal interview, 14 December 1981.

28. Ibid.

29. LS to Jovanovich, 24 January 1960, UGA.

30. LS to Long, 22 September 1960, UGA.

31. LS to Jerry Bick, 27 October 1961, UGA.

CHAPTER TWO

1. Annie Laurie Peeler to Rose Gladney, 21 February 1992.

2. "Notes for Maggie [Long]," UGA.

3. *International Encyclopedia of the Social Sciences*, s.v. "Chinese Society," by Franz Schumann.

4. "1922–25: China: A Brief Chronological Outline of My Various Experiences, etc.," autob. mats., UGA, 2.

5. "My Various Journeys. Travel etc." autob. mats., UGA, 4.

6. Snelling to Louise Blackwell and Frances Clay, 27 August 1966, UGA.

7. *Pseudopodia* (Spring 1936): 6.

8. Snelling to Redding Sugg, 21 February 1971, UGA 1283A.

9. Quoted in a promotional flier, "The North Georgia Review (formerly Pseudopodia) begins its third year," Rainey/EU.

10. "Dear Reader," undated, Rainey/EU.

11. Autob. mats. to Joan Titus, UGA, 6.

12. "The Magazine (Houseparties)," autob. mats., UGA, 4.

13. Krueger, *Promises to Keep*, 114.

14. Salmond, *Miss Lucy of the CIO*, 119.

15. Hall, *Revolt Against Chivalry*, 256.

16. LS to Motier Harris Fisher, 17 May 1940 and undated (May/June 1940), UF.

17. See specifically her editorial, "As We Go to War," *North Georgia Review*, Winter 1942, and "Burning Down Georgia's Back Porch."

18. See Kneebone, *Southern Liberal Journalists*, esp. chap. 11.

19. White to Eleanor Roosevelt, 20 February 1942, NAACP/LC.

20. Embree to Howard Odum, 10 February 1942, RFP.

21. Undated, handwritten note attached to LS's letter, HP.

CHAPTER THREE

1. LS to Clark Foreman, 9 May 1945, SCHW/AU.

2. O'Neill, *A Better World*, 171.

3. Kneebone, *Southern Liberal Journalists*, 28, 78.

4. Answers to Questions Asked by Joan Titus, autob. mats., UGA, 4.

5. Maddox, *Billie Holiday*, 44.

6. Holiday with Duffy, *Lady Sings the Blues*, 83–84.

7. About the novel, *Strange Fruit*, autob. mats., UGA, 1–2.

8. LS Collection, UF. For further analysis of the party, see Jones, "Private Steps and Public Vision."

9. LS to Bird and Eugene Barnett, 1 October 1943, UGA 1283A.

10. Michael Carter to LS, 26 July 1943, UF.

11. Bonita Valien to LS, 1 October 1943, UF.

12. 1925–48 Directing the Camp, autob. mats., UGA, 7.

13. About the Banning of *Strange Fruit*, autob. mats., UGA, 35.

14. Nasso, *Contemporary Authors*, s.v. "Dorothy Norman."

15. Kneebone, *Southern Liberal Journalists*, 202–8.

16. Loveland, *Lillian Smith*, 57–78.

17. Ibid., 73–74.

18. S.F. Play—August 1945–February 1946, autob. mats., UGA.

19. Krueger, *Promises to Keep*, 145.

20. Meier and Rudwick, *CORE*, 4–33.

21. Mary Keene Hightower to George M. Houser, 12 July 1945, CORE/SHSW.

22. Irene Harris to Eleanor French, 12 June 1946, Brooks Creedy, Bennington, Vt. I am grateful to Mary Fredrickson for sharing this correspondence with me.

CHAPTER FOUR

1. About *Killers of the Dream*, autob. mats., UGA.

2. Writings, UGA 1283A.

3. About *Killers of the Dream*, autob. mats., UGA.

4. Ibid.

5. Lillian Smith Chronology, autob. mats., UGA.

6. LS to Parents, February 1949, UGA.

7. O'Neill, *A Better World*, 138.

8. Stella Center to LS, 11 July 1950, Box 1, Awards Folder, UGA; LS to George Brockway, 13 July 1950, UGA 2126.

9. Adams, "The Problem of 'It's a Problem,'" sec. 2:11.

10. "Television: Figuring Things Out," 75.

11. Coleman and Gurr, *Dictionary of Georgia Biography*, s.v. "Cox, Edward Eugene," by Numen V. Bartley.

12. Pauli Murray to LS, 17 March 1942–21 June 1943, UF.

13. Murray, *Song in a Weary Throat*, 256.

14. LS to Joan Titus, 9 May 1965, and to Margaret Sullivan, 4 March 1965, UGA.

15. Konutz, *The Legacy of Horace M. Kallen*, Preface.

16. Coulter, *Georgia Through Two Centuries*, s.v. "Grace Wilkey Thomas."

17. Coleman and Gurr, *Dictionary of Georgia Biography*, s.v. "Griffin, Samuel Marvin."

18. Roosevelt to LS, 24 July 1954, UGA.

19. Williams to LS, 19 October 1954, UGA.

CHAPTER FIVE

1. LS to Madame Pandit, 5 September 1954, UGA; Writing and events from 1955 on, autob. mats., UGA, 1.

2. Faulkner, "A Letter to the North," 51–52.

3. LS to Spencer, 8 March 1956, UGA.

4. Kubie to LS, 1 June 1955, Kubie Papers, LC.

5. Johnson to LS, 17 June 1955, UGA.

6. Hinton to LS, 13 June 1955, UGA. For more on the political and economic harassment of the Durrs, see Virginia Durr, *Outside the Magic Circle*.

7. Hoffman to LS, 12 July 1955, UGA.

8. Reitman to LS, 5 April 1956, UGA.

9. Murray to LS, 13 July 1956, UGA. Reprinted by permission of Frances Collin, Literary Agent.

10. Fox to LS, 20 February 1956, UGA.

11. Morris, *The Origins of the Civil Rights Movement*, 158–59.

12. Fisher to LS, 5 March 1956, UGA. The entire correspondence between Fisher and Smith has been edited and published by Anne C. Loveland in "'But We Are Not All Distant in Sympathy.'"

13. Ballard, *Free At Last*, 40–46.

14. Durr to LS, 6 December 1956, UGA.

15. LS to Bertha and Eugene Barnett, 6 May 1957, UGA 1283A.

16. Kubie to LS, 30 August 1956, Kubie/LC.

17. Mumford to LS, 29 January 1957, UGA.

18. Hill to LS, 22 March 1957, UGA.

19. Candee, *Current Biography Yearbook*, s.v. "Pike, James A(lbert), Very Rev."

20. Kubie to LS, 24 October 1957, Kubie/LC.

21. *New York Times*, 13 October 1959, p. 1, col. 6.

22. LS to Dorothy Norman, 30 November 1959, UGA.

23. Greenberg to LS, 16 November 1959, UGA.

24. Tillich to LS, 8 October 1959, UGA.

25. Titus to Rose Gladney, 7 August 1991.

1. LS to Montagu, 23 January 1963, UGA.

2. LS to Robinson, 14 February 1960, UGA.

3. LS to Barnett, 16 February 1961, UGA 1283A.

4. LS to Brockway, 20 November 1960, UGA.

5. LS to East, 17 September 1961, UGA 1283A.

6. Sion to LS, 5 July 1960, UGA.

7. LS to Long, 22 September 1960, UGA.

8. LS to Anshen, 19 May 1957, and to Denver Lindley, 30 June 1957, UGA.

9. LS to Zerwick, 27 September 1960, UGA.

10. Meier and Rudwick, *CORE*, 114–15.

11. Carson, *In Struggle*, 25; Stembridge to LS, 20 October 1960, UGA.

12. Krueger, *Promises to Keep*, 189.

13. Carson, *In Struggle*, 52.

14. Sawyer to LS, 12 August 1960, UGA.

15. Lerner to LS, 19 January 1961, UGA 1283A.

16. See LS to Larry Kubie, June 2, 1955, in chap. 5; Annie Laurie Peeler to Rose Gladney, 11 March 1992.

17. Rich to LS, 21 August, 6 September 1961, UGA.

18. LS to Long, 26 October 1961, SRC/AU.

19. Carson, *In Struggle*, 60–61.

20. Undated, UGA 1283A.

21. Quoted in Carson, *In Struggle*, 61.

22. Newcomb to Rose Gladney, 16 July 1992.

CHAPTER SEVEN

1. Meras to LS, 29 September 1963, UGA.

2. Meras to LS, 23 September 1964, UGA.

3. Meier and Rudwick, *CORE*, 342.

4. Cagin and Dray, *We Are Not Afraid*, 490–91.

5. Klein to LS, 5 May 1965, UGA.

6. Shoemaker to LS, 22 October 1965, UGA.

7. Carson, *In Struggle*, 187–88.

8. Ibid., 160–61; LS to Mrs. Lyndon Johnson, March 1965, UGA.

9. Meier and Rudwick, *CORE*, 414–15.

10. William Stuart Nelson to LS, 9 August 1966, UGA; LS to Nelson, 5 September 1966, UGA.

11. LS to Paul Anthony, 6 September 1966, SRC/AU.

12. LS to Howerton, 7 September 1966, Clayton, Ga.

Bibliography

MANUSCRIPT COLLECTIONS

Ann Arbor, Michigan
  Lillian Smith correspondence in possession of Constance McMillan Carpenter
Athens, Georgia
  Hargrett Rare Books and Manuscript Library, University of Georgia Libraries
    Lillian Smith Collection #1283
    Lillian Smith Collection #1283A
    Lillian Smith Collection #2126
    Lillian Smith Collection #2337
Atlanta, Georgia
  Robert W. Woodruff Library, Atlanta University Center
    Southern Conference for Human Welfare Archives
    Southern Regional Council Archives
  Special Collections, Robert W. Woodruff Library, Emory University
    Frank Daniel Collection
    Glenn Rainey Collection
    Lillian Smith Collection
Austin, Texas
  Harry Ransom Humanities Research Center, The University of Texas
  at Austin
    Carson McCullers Collection
Bennington, Vermont
  Lillian Smith correspondence in possession of Brooks S. Creedy
Boston, Massachusetts
  Special Collections, Mugar Memorial Library, Boston University
    Martin Luther King Collection
Cambridge, Massachusetts
  The Houghton Library, Harvard University
    Lewis Gannett Papers, bMS Am 1880 (1110)
Clayton, Georgia
  Lillian Smith correspondence in possession of Lou Howerton
  Lillian Smith correspondence in possession of Esther Smith
Cornwall, Connecticut
  Lillian Smith correspondence in possession of Joan Titus
Gainesville, Florida
  Rare Books and Manuscripts Department, University of Florida Libraries
    Lillian Smith Collection

Hyde Park, New York
  Franklin D. Roosevelt Library
    Eleanor Roosevelt Papers
Madison, Wisconsin
  The State Historical Society of Wisconsin
    Records of the Americans for Democratic Action
    Records of the Congress of Racial Equality
New Haven, Connecticut
  Beinecke Rare Book and Manuscript Library, Yale University Library
    Richard Wright Papers
New Orleans, Louisiana
  Amistead Research Center, Tulane University
    Julius Rosenwald Fund Papers
New York, New York
  Rare Book and Manuscript Library, Columbia University Libraries
    Annie Laurie Williams Collection
  Lillian Smith correspondence in possession of Harcourt Brace Jovanovich,
  Publishers
Tuskegee, Alabama
  Hollis Burke Frissell Library, Tuskegee University
    Southern Conference for Human Welfare Papers
Washington, D.C.
  Manuscript Division, Library of Congress
    Lawrence Kubie Papers
    Records of the National Association for the Advancement of Colored People,
    Correspondence of Walter White

BOOKS BY LILLIAN SMITH

Strange Fruit. New York: Reynal and Hitchcock, 1944. Reprint. New York:
  Harcourt Brace Jovanovich, 1992.
Killers of the Dream. New York: W. W. Norton, 1949. Rev. ed., 1961.
The Journey. Cleveland: World Publishing Co., 1954.
Now Is the Time. New York: Viking, 1955.
One Hour. New York: Harcourt, Brace and Co., 1959.
Memory of a Large Christmas. New York: W. W. Norton, 1962.
Our Faces, Our Words. New York: W. W. Norton, 1964.
From the Mountain: An Anthology of the Magazine Successively Titled Pseudopodia,
  the North Georgia Review, *and* South Today. Edited with an Introduction by
  Helen White and Redding S. Sugg, Jr. Memphis: Memphis State University
  Press, 1972.

The Winner Names the Age: A Collection of Writings by Lillian Smith. Edited by Michelle Cliff with a Preface by Paula Snelling. New York: W. W. Norton, 1978.

BOOKS AND ARTICLES

Adams, Val. "The Problem of 'It's a Problem.'" *New York Times*, 22 June 1952.

Ballard, Sara, ed. *Free at Last: A History of the Civil Rights Movement and Those Who Died in the Struggle.* Montgomery, Ala.: Southern Poverty Law Center Civil Rights Education Project, 1989.

Cagin, Seth, and Philip Dray. *We Are Not Afraid.* New York: Bantam, 1990.

Candee, Marjorie Dent, ed. *Current Biography Yearbook.* New York: H. W. Wilson Co., 1957.

Carson, Clayborne. *In Struggle: SNCC and the Black Awakening of the 1960s.* Cambridge: Harvard University Press, 1981.

Coleman, Kenneth, and Stephen Gurr, eds. *Dictionary of Georgia Biography.* Athens: University of Georgia Press, 1983.

Coulter, E. Merton, ed. *Georgia Through Two Centuries.* New York: Lewis Historical Publishing Co., 1965.

Durr, Virginia. *Outside the Magic Circle.* Edited by Hollinger F. Barnard. Tuscaloosa: University of Alabama Press, 1985.

Evans, Sara, and Harry Boyte. *Free Spaces: The Sources of Democratic Change in America.* New York: Harper and Row, 1986.

Faulkner, William. "A Letter to the North." *Life*, 5 March 1956.

Hall, Jacquelyn Dowd. *Revolt Against Chivalry: Jessie Daniel Ames and the Women's Campaign Against Lynching.* New York: Columbia University Press, 1979.

Holiday, Billie, with William Duffy. *Lady Sings the Blues.* New York: Lancer Books, Inc., 1956.

International Encyclopedia of the Social Sciences, 1968.

Jones, Lillian. "Private Steps and Public Vision." Paper presented at the Southeastern Women's Studies Association Conference, March 1985, University of Alabama, Tuscaloosa.

Kneebone, John T. *Southern Liberal Journalists and the Issue of Race, 1920–1944.* Chapel Hill: University of North Carolina Press, 1985.

Konutz, Milton R., ed. *The Legacy of Horace M. Kallen.* Rutherford, N.J.: Farleigh Dickinson University Press, 1987.

Krueger, Thomas. *And Promises to Keep: The Southern Conference for Human Welfare, 1938–1948.* Nashville: Vanderbilt University Press, 1967.

Loveland, Anne C. "'But We Are Not All Distant in Sympathy'—Letters of Dorothy Canfield Fisher and Lillian Smith." *Vermont History* 52, no. 1 (1984): 17–32.

———. *Lillian Smith: A Southerner Confronting the South*. Baton Rouge: Louisiana State University Press, 1986.

Maddox, Melvin. *Billie Holiday: Biography and Notes on the Music*. Alexandria, Va.: Time-Life Records, 1979.

Meier, August, and Elliott Rudwick. *CORE: A Study in the Civil Rights Movement, 1942–1968*. New York: Oxford University Press, 1973.

Miller, Kathleen Atkinson. "Out of the Chrysalis: Lillian Smith and the Transformation of the South." Ph.D. dissertation, Emory University, 1984.

Morris, Aldon D. *The Origins of the Civil Rights Movement*. New York: The Free Press, 1984.

Murray, Pauli. *Song in a Weary Throat*. New York: Harper and Row, 1987.

Nasso, Christine, ed. *Contemporary Authors*. Detroit: Gale Research Co., 1977.

O'Neill, William L. *A Better World*. New York: Simon and Schuster, 1982.

Robinson, Jo Ann. "Lillian Smith: Reflections on Race and Sex." *Southern Exposure* 4, no. 4 (1977): 43–48.

Salmond, John A. *Miss Lucy of the CIO*. Athens: University of Georgia Press, 1988.

Smith, Lillian. "Burning Down Georgia's Back Porch." *Common Ground* 2 (Winter 1942): 69–72.

Smith, Lillian, and Paula Snelling. "Editors' Note." *Pseudopodia* 1, no. 1 (1936):6.

———. "As We Go to War." *North Georgia Review* 5, no. 3–4 (1941): 26.

Sullivan, Margaret. "Lillian Smith: The Public Image and the Personal Vision." *Mad River Review* 2 (Summer–Fall 1967): 3–21.

———, with a Foreword by Paula Snelling. "A Bibliography of Lillian Smith & Paula Snelling." *Bulletin of the Mississippi Valley Collection* 4 (Spring 1971): 1–82.

"Television: Figuring Things Out." *New Yorker*, 28 June 1952.

Index

Smith, Esther (LS's sister), 2, 30, 338, 352, 354; and Laurel Falls Camp, 4, 47; and theatrical production of *Strange Fruit*, 94, 98, 99

Smith, Esther (Mrs. John R.), 75n

Smith, Frank (LS's brother), 2, 4, 7, 295, 297, 301, 305, 353, 354; as public official, 64, 69, 117–18, 168; as director of Mental Health Association, 226

Smith, Howard, 241

Smith, Lillian: as writer, xiii–xv, 8–10, 14–15, 63, 113, 115, 200–201, 211–14, 287–89, 319–20, 326–28, 333–36; background and career of, xiii–xvii, 1, 2–7; fires at home of, xv, 17, 116, 164, 178–81, 188–89, 194, 204, 224, 314, 316, 336; papers of, xv, 136; battle with cancer, xvi, 14, 113, 116, 138–39, 144, 164, 175, 181, 189, 202–4, 223, 224, 235, 239, 240, 241, 245, 263, 275, 277, 295–97, 306, 309–10, 312, 316, 320, 332, 333, 350; love affairs of, xvi–xvii, 3, 5, 7; musical training of, 3–5, 6; as camp director, 6, 7–8, 11–15, 21–23, 33, 36, 46–47, 50–51, 58, 62, 68, 74, 79–80, 322; family responsibilities of, 6–7, 11, 63, 76, 127, 240–41, 267, 305n; "Martha" vs. "Mary" conflict in, 11, 285, 295, 328, 337; as magazine editor, 12–13, 14–15, 36; as public speaker, 13, 50, 51, 70, 78–79, 97–98, 110–11, 113, 115, 119, 165, 176–78, 181, 200–201, 211n, 242, 273–74, 275, 290–91, 297–300, 306; as a *woman* writer, 14–15, 28–29, 63, 127–32, 238, 247–49, 319–20; financial concerns of, 14–15, 31, 57, 79–80, 99, 145, 168, 173, 193–94, 236, 240, 275–77, 306; lack of literary acclaim for, 15, 326–28; constraints on, 44–45, 63, 76, 79, 127; threats against, 51,

63, 128, 313–15, 316, 333, 336; awards and honors for, 115, 132–33, 181–82, 203n, 240, 296–97, 319; "smothering" of, 120–22, 134, 165, 168, 173, 174–75, 183, 184–87, 199–200, 214, 216–20, 234, 287–89, 323; as anti-communist, 144, 145, 146, 163, 165, 244, 254, 260–61; possible biographers of, 322–23, 331–34, 336–38; death and funeral of, 353–54. *See also* Clayton, Ga.; Laurel Falls Camp; Magazines; Rosenwald Fund; Snelling, Paula; Southern white women; titles of works by LS

Smith, Maud (Mrs. Frank), 7, 118, 297, 305

Smith, Wallace (LS's brother), 2, 130, 285, 291, 305n, 339

Smith College, 115

SNCC (Student Nonviolent Coordinating Committee), 251, 257, 259n, 302–3, 312, 340–41, 343, 344, 345, 348n, 351

Snelling, Paula, 28, 34, 44, 65, 77, 94, 132, 143, 169, 257, 261, 294, 309, 323; as coeditor of magazine, xiv, 12–13, 18, 23–24, 25, 45, 47–48, 59, 69; relationship with LS, xvi–xvii, 5, 8, 9, 11, 14, 30, 96–98, 117, 135–38, 180–81, 182, 185, 189, 203, 214, 224–25, 258–59, 272, 275–77, 286, 304–6, 338, 339–40; and Laurel Falls Camp, 5, 6; and LS's posthumous literary reputation, 10, 310n, 332, 354; accident of, 11–12, 24, 277; becomes librarian, 14, 275, 339–40; as book reviewer, 26–27; international travel with LS, 30, 31, 116, 164; family of, 30, 45; and Rosenwald Fund, 35, 36, 38, 49–50, 52, 57; research of, 38, 51, 54, 115, 146; health of, 48–49, 223, 224, 277; letters to, 96–101, 133–35, 136–38, 275–

77, 304–6, 354; LS's legacy to, 138n,
339–40
Socialists, 90–91
Soong Mei Ling, 329
Sousa, John Philip, 18
South: as focus of LS and Snelling's
magazine, 23–24, 51–52; LS's proposed Rosenwald book on, 32, 38–
39, 53; LS's desire for change in, 35,
201, 263, 288; LS and Snelling as
experts on, 54; ambivalence of, 133,
177, 182, 225–26, 292–93, 347–48;
persuasiveness of King's tactics in,
193–95; reaction to LS's books in,
235, 289. *See also* Censorship; Civil
rights movement; Lynchings;
Negroes; Race; Segregation; Southern whites; States' rights; Totalitarianism; White supremacy
Southbound (proposed title), 38. *See
also* Southern literature
Southern Author's Award, 132–33
Southern Churchmen, 302
Southern Conference Education Fund
(SCEF), 259n
Southern Conference for Human
Welfare (SCHW), xv, 187, 259n;
LS supports, 37, 41–42, 172, 203;
description of, 41; LS resigns from,
62, 89–93. *See also* Georgia Com-
mittee (Southern Conference for
Human Welfare)
Southern literature: projected book
on, 32, 38–39, 53
Southern myths. *See* Myth(s): south-
ern
Southern Regional Council, xv, 43, 62,
85–87, 209n, 283, 306–7, 352; auto-
graph party for LS at, 296–97
Southern Tenant Farmers Union, 36
Southern whites: liberals among, xiv,
54, 57–58, 119–22, 129, 148–49, 165,

191, 209, 221n, 250, 282, 290, 291;
motivations for segregation, 56; LS
as spokesperson for, 241–42, 281–82;
pride in King, 311; cryptic language
of, 330. *See also* "Poor whites";
Southern white women
Southern white women: LS as, 8, 65,
68–69, 76, 119–22, 149–50, 236; LS
on, 10, 15, 63, 76, 79, 83–84, 87–88,
200, 289; components of reputa-
tions of, 63; LS's work with, 170–71,
175, 177–78, 275; punishments for
uppity, 175. *See also* Association of
Southern Women for the Prevention of Lynching; "Julia"
Southern Women's Democratic Orga-
nization (N.Y.), 132
South Today, 64, 70, 203, 236, 302;
demise of, 13; LS's prestige as editor
of, 14–15; name changed to, 59;
attempted banning of, 59–60, 63,
66–70
Spelman College (Atlanta), 210
Spencer, Frank, 165, 177
Spoken Arts, Inc., 320, 331, 338n
SRC. *See* Southern Regional Council
Stalin, Joseph, 120
States' rights, 330
Stein, Gertrude, 214
Steinbeck, John, 49, 50, 96, 134
Stembridge, Jane, 256–57; letters to,
257–61
Stevenson, Adlai, 190–93, 249, 250–51
Stokeley, James, 331
Stokeley, Wilma Dykeman: letter to,
331–34
Strange Fruit (Smith), 53, 91, 110, 116,
117, 123, 128, 183, 211, 223, 243, 245,
284, 286, 298, 319–20, 322, 323, 337,
338; banning of, xiv, 13, 66, 81–82,
289; as best-seller, xiv, 62, 63, 219;
same-sex relationships in, 10; writ-

ing of, 13, 26, 29, 33, 37, 50, 54, 72–
73, 167; theatrical production of,
13, 61, 73, 94–96, 99–100, 101; lack
of literary acclaim for, 15, 327;
responses to, 48, 49, 74, 79–82, 133,
185, 231, 313, 341; themes of, 49, 55,
71, 72, 83, 269; publication history
of, 53–55, 61, 70; title of, 70, 71–72;
movie possibilities for, 73, 240,
278–81, 287–89; scrapbooks of, 180;
significance of, 278, 287–89
"Strange Fruit" (song), 71
"Strange Kind of Love, A" (Smith),
303
Student Nonviolent Coordinating
Committee. *See* SNCC
Student Nursing Corps, 3
Student Voice (SNCC newspaper), 257,
261
Studies in Human Time (Poulet), 285
Suffering: LS's views on, 201, 223, 235,
303
Sullivan, Margaret: letter to, 336–38
Sulzberger, Arthur Hays, 219
Sun Yat-sen, 19, 329, 335
Supreme Court. *See* U.S. Supreme
Court
Susanna and Her Sons (proposed movie
script), 132
Sweet Briar College, 75n
Symbol(s): in Stevenson's election,
191–92; King's use of, 193; LS on,
212, 225; King as, 255, 257, 301, 313

Talladega College, 37
Tallulah Falls School, Ga., 14, 275, 326,
339, 354
Talmadge, Eugene ("Gene"), 82, 102;
LS on, 60, 92, 103–5, 112, 128
Talmadge, Herman, 147, 148, 168, 186,
241
Tarver, Jack, 128–29

Taylor, Mr. and Mrs. Dekle, 305
Taylor, Frank, 183, 185, 186; letters to,
70–74, 80, 82–84
Teilhard de Chardin, Pierre, 260, 285,
311, 327
Temple of the Reform Jewish Con-
gregation (Atlanta): bombing of,
227, 253
Tenant farmers, 32, 33, 36
Tennesee Valley Authority (TVA), 37
Terrell, Mary Church, 75n
Theology of Culture (Tillich), 232
There Are Things to Do (Smith), 106
Thomas, Grace Wilkey, 147–49
Thomas, Norman, 349
Thompson, Miss (E. Roosevelt's sec-
retary), 58
Thompson, Melvin E., 148
Threats: to LS, 51, 63, 128, 313–15, 316,
333, 336
Thurman, Howard, 194
Tiger, Ga., 3
Till, Emmett Louis, 197–98
Tillich, Paul, 213, 247; letters to,
232–34, 261–64
Tilly, Dorothy, 74n
Time (magazine), 173, 199, 234, 290
Time-Life Broadcast, 240, 337–38
Tipton, Betty, 67–70
Tipton, James ("Jimmie"), 67, 68, 70
Titus, Joan, 316, 331, 336, 337, 338n; let-
ters to, 234–37, 352–54
To Kill a Mockingbird (Lee), 284
"Tom Harris and Family" (Smith), 10
Totalitarianism: in the South, 120–21,
330
Townsend, Frances, 354
Transcendent Unity of Religions
(Schuon), 213
Transformations of Man, The (Mum-
ford), 207–8
Truman, Harry S., 125, 250